Growth Theory and Growth Policy

The theory of economic growth has been one of the most important issues in economic study since the days of Adam Smith. This collection examines the phenomenon of economic growth with an admirable academic vigour.

With contributions from such leading academic figures as Richard Arena and Philip Arestis, this book covers a wide variety of important topics such as:

- endogenous growth: the impact of unemployment, financial factors
- neo-Schumpeterian and neo-Kaldorian approaches to growth
- monetary policy and economic growth
- health, labour productivity and growth

A theoretical approach, underpinned by some original empirical work, makes *Growth Theory and Growth Policy* a book that will be welcomed by both students and academics of macroeconomics and growth theory. The policy implications that come from the book will also make it an extremely useful read for all those involved in policy formulation.

Harald Hagemann is Professor of Economic Theory at the University of Hohenheim, Stuttgart, Germany.

Stephan Seiter is Assistant Professor of Economics at the University of Hohenheim, Stuttgart, Germany.

Routledge Studies in International Business and the World Economy

Growth Theory and Growth Policy

Edited by
Harald Hagemann and Stephan Seiter

Routledge
Taylor & Francis Group

LONDON AND NEW YORK

First published 2003
by Routledge
11 New Fetter Lane, London EC4P 4EE

Simultaneously published in the USA and Canada
by Routledge
29 West 35th Street, New York, NY 10001

Routledge is an imprint of the Taylor & Francis Group

Typeset in Times New Roman by
Newgen Imaging Systems (P) Ltd, Chennai, India
Printed and bound in Great Britain by
Biddles Ltd, Guildford and King's Lynn

British Library Cataloguing in Publication Data
A catalogue record for this book is available from the British Library

Library of Congress Cataloging in Publication Data
Growth theory and growth policy / [edited by] Harald Hagemann & Stephan Seiter.
p. cm. – (Routledge studies in international business and the world economy; 30)
Includes bibliographical references and index.
1. Economic development. 2. Endogenous growth (Economics). 3. Economic
policy. 4. Economics. 5. Hagemann, Harald. I. Seiter, Stephan. II. Series.

HD75 G773 2003
338.9′001–dc21   2002031945

ISBN 0–415–26000–0

Contents

Figures

Tables

Contributors

Richard Arena is Professor of Economics at the University of Nice and Director of the LATAPSES (CNRS), Sophia Antipolis, France. He is a member of the Executive Committee of the European Society for the History of Economic Thought. His research interests cover Economic Growth, Business Cycle Theory, Evolutionary Economics, the Economics of Knowledge and Information and History of Economic Thought.

Philip Arestis is Professor of Economics at the Levy Economics Institute of Bard College, New York, USA. He formerly taught at the Universities of Surrey and Cambridge (Department of Extra-Mural Studies), Greenwich University, University of East London, and South Bank University London. His research interests are in the areas of Macroeconomics, Monetary Economics, Applied Econometrics, Political Economy and Applied Political Economy.

Flora Bellone is Professor of Economics at the University of Corsica and at the LATAPSES (CNRS), Sophia Antipolis, France. Her main research interests are Innovation and Growth, Development and Regional Economics and Firm-Level Productivity Analysis.

Iris Biefang-Frisancho Mariscal is Senior Lecturer in the School of Economics at the University of the West of England in Bristol. She had studied economics at the Westfaelische Wilhelms-Universitaet in Muenster, Germany. Her research interests are in Applied Econometrics and Applied Macroeconomics, particularly in Monetary Economics, Wage and Unemployment Determination and EMU Developments.

Olivier Bruno is Assistant Professor at the University of Nice, France and at the LATAPSES (CNRS), Sophia Antipolis, France. His research covers Growth Theory, Monetary Theory and Finance.

Christiane Clemens is Assistant Professor at the University of Hannover. She studied economics and mathematics at the University of Hannover. Her research interests are Dynamic Macroeconomics, Distribution Theory, Growth Theory and Public Sector Economics.

Muriel Dal-Pont is Assistant Professor at the University of Nice, France and at the LATAPSES (CNRS), Sophia Antipolis, France. Her research interests include Business Cycles and Growth, Financial System Architecture and Growth, Financing of IT, Monetary Rules and Central Bank Credibility.

Georg Erber is Researcher in the Department Information Society and Competition at the German Institute for Economic Research, DIW, Berlin. He had studied economics and received a PhD from the Free University of Berlin. His main research interests include Industrial Economics, Network Economics, Economics of E-commerce, Growth and Productivity analysis.

Harald Hagemann is Professor of Economics at the University of Hohenheim, Stuttgart, Germany. In the academic year 1999/2000 he was Theodor Heuss Professor at the Graduate Faculty of Political and Social Sciences at the New School University, New York, USA. He formerly taught at the Universities of Bremen and Kiel, the Free University of Berlin, and as Visiting Professor at the Universities of Bologna, Italy, Linz, Austria, Nice, France, and at the University of Cambridge, UK where he is a Life Member of Clare Hall. His main research covers Growth and Structural Change, Technological Change and Employment, Business Cycle Theory and the History of Economic Thought.

Hugo Hollanders is Researcher at the Maastricht Economic Research Institute on Innovation and Technology (MERIT), Maastricht University, the Netherlands. He studied economics at Maastricht University. His research interests include Growth Theory and Economics of (Skill-biased) Technical Change.

Patrick Musso is Researcher at the LATAPSES (CNRS), Sophia Antipolis, France. He had studied economics at the University of Nice, France. His research covers Technological Change, Productivity and Economic Growth as well as Monetary Policy and Economic Growth.

Joan Muysken is Professor of Economics at the Faculty of Economics and Business Administration, University of Maastricht, the Netherlands. He had studied quantitative economics at the University of Groningen. He was as a Visiting Researcher at the University of Oslo and a Visiting Professor at the Catholic University of Louvain, Belgium. He also taught as an Assistant Professor at the SUNY Buffalo, New York, USA. His research interests are: wage formation, labour demand, matching problems, analysis of unemployment and endogenous growth and diffusion of technologies.

Ingrid Ott is Junior Professor of Economics at the University of Lüneburg, Germany. She studied economics and business administration at the University of Hannover. Her research interests are Growth Theory and Growth Policy, Innovation Theory and Policy.

Alain Raybaut is Assistant Professor at the University of Nice and at the LATAPSES (CNRS), Sophia Antipolis, France. His research covers Growth Theory, Business Cycle Theory and the History of Economic Thought.

Christiane Schäper works in a Research group at the University of Hannover, Germany. She had studied economics at the University of Hamburg and received a PhD in economics from the University of Hannover. Her main research interests are Regional Sciences, Growth Theory and Distribution Theory.

Stephan Seiter is Assistant Professor of economics at the University of Hohenheim, Stuttgart, Germany. In the Spring semester 2000 he was Theodor Heuss Lecturer at the Graduate Faculty of Political and Social Sciences at the New School University, New York, USA. His main research interests are Economic Growth, Technological Progress, Business Cycle Theory and Labour Market Theory.

Susanne Soretz is Assistant Professor at the University of Hannover where she studied economics and made her PhD. Her research covers Growth Theory, Public Sector Economics and Distribution Theory.

Bas ter Weel is Researcher at the Maastricht Economic Research Institute on Innovation and Technology (MERIT), Maastricht University, the Netherlands. He studied economics and received a PhD from Maastricht University. His research covers the broad range of theoretical and empirical studies of the impact of technical change on labour market outcomes and economic growth, mainly focussing on skill-biased technical change and human capital development and investment.

İ. Hakan Yetkiner is Researcher at the University of Groningen, the Netherlands. He studied economics at the Middle East Technical University (METU), Ankara, Turkey, and at the London School of Economics. His main specialization is in Growth Theory.

Martin Zagler is Associate Professor of Economics at the Vienna University of Economics and Business Administration and Visiting Professor at the Free University of Bozen/Bolzano, Italy. He had studied in Linz, Aix-en-Provence, Vienna and Florence, and was a Visiting Researcher at the European University Institute in Florence and at the University College London. His research interests include Economic Growth and Unemployment, Growth Policy, the New Economy, and Public Finance.

Thomas Ziesemer is Associate Professor of Economics at the Department of Economics at Maastricht University, the Netherlands. He had studied economics at the Universities of Kiel and Regensburg. Fields of interest: International Development and Environmental Economics; Economics of Growth and Technical Change.

1 Introduction

Harald Hagemann and Stephan Seiter

Since Adam Smith the analysis of economic growth was one of the main fields of interest in economic theory. Particularly from the late 1940s to the 1960s, many papers dealing with the explanation of growth were published. The controversy between Postkeynesian authors such as Harrod, Domar, Kaldor and Robinson and members of the neoclassical school such as Solow, Swan, Meade, Arrow or Phelps gave inspiring insights into the process of economic growth. The discussion focused on the question whether the long-run economic growth process would converge to a stable equilibrium or not. Besides many differences between these two schools of thought, most economists agreed, and still do, that technical progress is the main source of per capita income growth. For example, Solow (1957) gave evidence to this statement by applying the concept of growth accounting on the development in the USA in the period of 1909–49, and Kaldor (1957, 1961) stressed the key role of technological innovations for economic growth.

However, the overwhelming interest in growth theory declined from the early 1970s. The economic slowdown after the first oil price shock drew economists' interest to the explanation of business cycles, which had been the dominant theme in the interwar period but, after a short boom of multiplier–accelerator models after the war, had almost fallen into oblivion when the historically unprecedented growth process of the 1950s and 1960s had shifted economists' main research areas. The phenomenon of stagflation raised again the question whether monetary and fiscal policy should follow Keynesian theory or not. The period after 1973 differed from the post-war years not only with regard to the characteristics of the business cycle, but also with respect to the long-run development. The average growth rates of Gross Domestic Product as well as of productivity were significantly smaller after 1973 than before. The so-called *productivity slowdown* gave new impulses to growth theory, although first studies applied well-known approaches to explain this phenomenon (see, e.g. Bombach 1985).

In the 1980s, Paul Romer's seminal paper (1986) could be seen as the starting point of a renaissance of growth theory that has received greater attention in economic science since then. The so-called New Growth Theory challenged the traditional neoclassical approaches because of the latter's theoretical and empirical shortcomings. The Solovian-type models cannot explain endogenously steady-state per capita growth. Exogenous technical progress is the only source of productivity growth in the long-run equilibrium, i.e. per capita income will be constant, if technical progress does not accrue. Savings and investment decisions determine only the level of long-run productivity, but not its growth rate. Growth is independent of economic decisions. At least, the models do not cover the relations between economic activities and technical progress as well as productivity growth. The dominant source of growth comes from outside the model and is like 'Manna from Heaven'. The main reason for this shortcoming is the assumption of diminishing marginal returns to capital. The incentive to invest and thereby income growth per capita will peter out as the capital–labour ratio increases. New Growth Theory in contrast offers endogenous explanations of economic growth by focusing on constant returns to capital caused by externalities.

Furthermore, the standard neoclassical growth models predicted convergence between economies when its assumptions are met. In general, economies with a low capital–labour ratio should be able to realise higher growth rates of per capita income than economies with a high capital–labour ratio do. If economies show identical parameters with regard to infrastructure, time preference, supply of labour, etc. they will reach the same per capita income in the long-run as long as technical progress is a public good that is internationally available. Under these circumstances, even the steady-state growth rate will be identical in all economies that have access to technological knowledge. Empirical studies gave evidence that convergence is only found in groups of countries that are closely linked via trade in goods, services and knowledge such as the Organisation for Economic Growth and Development (OECD) members do (see, e.g. Sala-I-Martin 1996). Divergence between different convergence clubs of countries seems to be more realistic than convergence.

The finding that growth theory did not cover the empirics of growth led for example Romer (1994) to discuss a list of stylised facts that characterise current economic growth. Competition between companies is seen as a decisive precondition for technical progress. In general, research and development (R&D) lead to new products and therefore to competitive advantages for firms. Successful innovators will gain market power that enables them to gain extra profits. This is the key incentive to invest in R&D and to bear the risk of failure. Furthermore, innovators have to accept that there is no rivalry in the use of knowledge. Competitors can make use of the newly gained knowledge at zero marginal cost. This externality enables them to challenge the position of the former innovator and/or to become innovators themselves. The fact that knowledge is a public good allows the reproduction of physical processes without increasing non-rival inputs. Consequently, neoclassical economists can still assume constant returns to the application of labour and capital that guarantees a consistent explanation of the income distribution. These stylised facts go beyond the ones Kaldor (1957) referred to in his early work on growth theory. With regard to the recent developments in growth theory, particularly three items on his list are of interest. He proclaimed that (1) productivity growth does not fall in the long-run, (2) the capital–labour ratio steadily increases and (3) differences in productivity growth are caused by variations in the investment ratio.

The chapters in Part I present different contributions explaining endogenous growth. Diagnosing a great separation of the modern literature on the theory of endogenous growth on the one hand and labour economics on the other hand, *Martin Zagler* deplores the lack of models which comprise mutual causalities of growth and employment. These, however, are very important to explain long-run economic development of modern capitalist economies. He therefore aims to close this theoretical gap by developing a two-sectoral model with a manufacturing sector characterised by monopolistic competition and the payment of efficiency wages thereby creating unemployment, and an R&D sector where all profits of the manufacturing sector are reinvested. Zagler also takes up Arthur Okun's empirical observation for the US economy that there exists a rather stable macroeconomic relation between the decline in unemployment and the growth rate of real output. However, Zagler criticises the shortcomings of Okun's analysis, namely a lack of causality in either direction and the static nature of Okun's argument. Both deficiencies are overcome in his model, which develops a revised version of Okun's law, which is dynamic in nature and implies a clear causality, which runs from unemployment to economic growth. Whereas Okun's law is widely understood as a cyclical phenomenon (see Hagemann and Seiter 1999), Zagler's reinterpretation clearly expresses a long-run relationship between the level (not the change) of unemployment and the rate of economic growth. His NAWRU, i.e. the non-accelerating wage rate of unemployment, on the other hand remains unaffected by changes in the growth rate. In other words, causality in Zagler's model is not mutual but runs unidirectional from unemployment to economic growth. That measures to enhance economic growth will not exhibit any impact on the level of unemployment probably is that aspect of Zagler's contribution which is most difficult to swallow for many growth economists.

In his chapter, *Stephan Seiter* analyses the key elements of new growth theory and the Kaldorian approach to explain endogenous growth. His contribution reveals that besides all differences between the new models of growth, the assumption of constant returns to any sort of capital is crucial with regard to the factors of production that are assumed to be the driving force of economic growth. Thus, the models of new growth theory can be interpreted as variations of the AK-model. Furthermore, it is shown that Kaldor's contributions to growth theory are based on the same ideas as new growth theory is. Investment is characterised by externalities that improve the productivity of other inputs and future investment. Hence, investment is the engine of endogenous growth. However, new growth theory only focuses on the supply-side variables of growth. Any output that is produced will be sold, since entrepreneurs know the households' preferences. Here, Seiter gives evidence that Kaldorian models offer more insights by including both the demand side of endogenous growth and the determinants of investment. The interplay of demand and supply may lead to a cumulative growth process with positive or negative growth rates. Finally, the author concludes that with regard to growth policy a one-eyed focus on the supply side is not sufficient to explain endogenous growth consistently.

Flora Bellone and *Muriel Dal-Pont* examine the important relationship between finance and growth in the modern literature on endogenous growth and contrast it with the empirics of the East Asian growth experience. In the literature on the latter monetary and financial factors were hardly placed in the centre of the analysis until the financial crisis of 1997. The authors state that in contrast to the impressive relationship between high saving and investment rates, i.e. the process of capital accumulation, and the strong economic growth found out for this region, the question whether and how finance does matter for growth is still a missing link. The authors investigate two distinct lines of the endogenous growth literature, the AK or linear approach and the neo-Schumpeterian approach, for their appropriateness to deal with the finance–growth relationship. Both types of models differ in their causal structure and highlight another transmission channel why finance matters for growth. Whereas the AK approach attaches the leading role to capital accumulation, the neo-Schumpeterian approach attaches this role to technological innovations. Bellone and Dal-Pont investigate the advantages and drawbacks of the two approaches in relation to the explanation of the long-run growth process in East Asia. One important observation is that the causality from finance to growth of total factor productivity is much stronger in later stages of development when innovations become an important source for growth than in earlier stages for which neo-Schumpeterian models therefore did perform rather badly until the Soft Budget Constraint approach has offered a much better understanding of the East Asian productivity puzzle. One important result of the authors' survey of the literature is that different financial systems do better in promoting different economic activities and perform differently over time. Bellone and Dal-Pont therefore clearly express their preference for time-series analysis rather than for cross-country analysis and advocate a stages of growth theory, however not a simple one. The issue of the role of financial factors in the transition process from one stage of growth to the other is still a rather unresolved question. Moreover, even for the same stage(s) of growth great differences concerning the impact of financial structures need to be explained, which refers to the significant element of diversity in growth regimes.

Summing up Romer's and Kaldor's lists of stylised facts and the results of the chapters of Part I, it becomes evident that on the one hand investment, and most of all investment in knowledge, is an important pre-condition for growth. On the other hand, an appropriate mixture of competition and market power promotes investment and risk-bearing. The importance of investment for economic growth offers a link between short-run and long-run development. In the models of the new growth theory investment in different kinds of capital leads to external effects on the productivity of other companies. We must also take into consideration that investment does increase the production capacities and creates income in the capital goods-producing sector. Thus, changes in investment influence both potential growth due to externalities and economic fluctuations due to income effects. For this reason, growth of the potential output is path-dependent in the sense that the investment pattern of the past determines the current level of productivity as, e.g. in Arrow's paper of 1962. A strict disintegration of cycle and trend is therefore too much a simplification.

Part II connects therefore two important streams in modern macroeconomic literature: the interaction between cyclical fluctuations and long-run economic growth. Equilibrium and Real Business-Cycle models, which flourished in the late 1970s and in the 1980s, normally abstracted from the long-run trend. Modern endogenous growth theory, which started to flourish in the mid-1980s, on the other hand, in most cases abstracted from cyclical fluctuations, as it had been the case in the earlier growth literature *after* Harrod from the mid-1950s to the early 1970s. However, with regard to reality an important link between the cycle and the trend, i.e. an element of path dependency, cannot be denied. No wonder that against the background of a complete separation of these two phenomena in most theoretical models Bob Solow in the early 1990s rightly stated: 'A more urgent matter is the problem of medium-term macroeconomics and the interaction of growth and fluctuations' (Solow 1991: 16). In the spirit of Solow's statement *Richard Arena* and *Alain Raybaut* analyse two different views on learning, knowledge and cyclical growth: neo-Schumpeterian versus neo-Kaldorian approaches. Thus, as in Seiter's article, the importance of Kaldor's contributions, which is often neglected in the modern endogenous growth literature, is highlighted, here with a stronger emphasis on Kaldor's analysis of cyclical fluctuations. Although there is a basic agreement with the leading neo-Schumpeterian proponents of new growth theory 'that growth and cycles are related phenomena, with causation going in both directions' (Aghion and Howitt 1998: 4), and with Kaldor who had complained quite often about the traditional dichotomy between these two phenomena, the authors nevertheless make clear some significant differences between neo-Schumpeterian and neo-Kaldorian approaches, for which growth equilibria are only benchmarks and the prevailing state is that of economic instability or cyclical growth. Furthermore, the authors reveal also some important differences between the neo-Schumpeterian approach and Schumpeter's own view, who in assuming that learning is closely related to firms' investment activities was closer to Kaldor than to some neo-Schumpeterians, from whom he also differed in his emphasis on the creation of bank credit as a necessary condition for economic development. However, Arena and Raybaut cannot deny that Aghion and Howitt successfully introduced important Schumpeterian ideas into the modern framework of endogenous growth theory, above all the decisive role of technological innovations for cyclical fluctuations as well as for long-run growth. Thus, the neo-Schumpeterian approach made a decisive contribution to overcome the traditional dichotomy between business-cycle theory and growth theory. However, rational expectations suggest that the authors' showing that the mere introduction of a learning-by investing mechanism renders possible the coexistence of growth and cycles is based on a simple AK model with adjustment costs will not taste well for the great majority of both neo-Schumpeterian as well as neo-Kaldorian economists.

Christiane Clemens and *Susanne Soretz* focus in their chapter on the effects of individual-specific and economy-wide productivity shocks on intertemporal decision-making of risk-averse agents. This analysis is mainly based on the real business-cycle theory where technical progress leads to an increase in productivity.

Consequently, the rate of return to investment increases, too. Agents will thereby change their savings behaviour as well as their labour supply. Uncertainty rises due to technical progress. Thus, households will save more to cope with the higher risk. However, different types of income are characterised by varying risks. Clemens and Soretz base their research on two standard models of new growth theory: the AK model and Romer's pathbreaking model of 1986. In the former, capital is the only factor of production. Hence, profits are the only source of income, and agents have to bear the risk of uncertain capital income. In the latter model, labour is also an input in the production of final output. Thus, the income risk is additionally included in the model. In this setting income distribution influences economic growth, since (precautionary) savings depend on the individuals' risk aversion. The authors show that low risk aversion may be harmful to economic growth, since individuals will save less than highly risk-averse agents do.

Olivier Bruno and *Patrick Musso* also deal with the integration of short-run and long-run phenomena. Again, households' savings behaviour is the link between cycle and growth. While Clemens and Soretz refer to real business-cycle theory, Bruno and Musso stress the relevance of monetary policy and inflation for long-run economic development. The integration of monetary policy in an endogenous growth model is important because both phenomena are interrelated. On the one hand, in the second half of the 1990s, US monetary policy could be less restrictive since the high growth rates of productivity reduced the inflationary pressure due to tight labour markets. On the other hand, an increase in the interest rate caused by monetary policy can lead to a decline in investment and growth. To cover the relations between inflationary processes and households' savings Bruno and Musso develop an overlapping generations model with endogenous growth. If, for example, the level of inflation or the volatility of inflation influence savings, then any monetary policy to stabilise the price level will affect the long-run growth rate. One can also expect that an increase in the supply of money raises inflation. Thereby individuals will expect a lower return to savings. Depending on the risk aversion of households, savings might increase. In an endogenous growth model, the long-run growth rate will increase, too. The authors' analysis makes clear under which conditions the model will generate these results. Therefore, monetary policies that try to reach an inflation rate of zero could lower the growth potential of an economy. In this sense, money matters in the long-run. Furthermore, the volatility of inflation can also reduce economic growth if the return to savings depends negatively on the volatility of inflation. Again, it is the level of risk aversion that determines the final outcome.

The analysis of endogenous growth gives some interesting insights into the growth consequences of economic policies. A general conclusion that can be derived from the results in new growth theory is to stimulate investment, especially in knowledge and education. Since investment is characterised by positive externalities, a system of subsidies to internalise the externalities could make sense at first sight. The higher the externality of an investment is, the more it should be supported. Nevertheless, not all welfare effects are positive. Models based on Schumpeter's analysis of the process of creative destruction make clear that the success of innovator B could destroy the market power of the former innovator A. Unfortunately, the actual scope of an externality is difficult to measure. Furthermore, welfare economics proved that the internalisation of externalities only makes sense when technological and not pecuniary external effects exist. Thus, policymakers face the well-known information problem.

The chapters in Part III deal with relations between government intervention and economic growth. Besides the difficulties linked with the concept of externalities we further have to keep in mind that the models of New Growth Theory abstract from many important variables. Normally, standard welfare theory does not focus on the behaviour and utility function of the social planner who as a benevolent dictator is expected to maximise social welfare. However, modern public choice theory has revealed that this person might have own goals she wants to reach. *Ingrid Ott* discusses how different assumptions about the social planner's behaviour affect endogenous growth. She could be either altruistic or egoistic. The latter means that she will maximise her utility by maximising the budget relative to total output in each period or by realising the maximum budget over her infinite planning period. Ott proves that these objectives are contrary, so the social planner has to decide which goal she wants to reach or how she should weight them in her utility function. Furthermore, the consequences of her behaviour also depend on the type of input she provides and the way she finances the budget. The model shows that not only a benevolent dictator will choose the Pareto-optimum, but also an egoistic planner might realise the Pareto-optimal provision of public input. Therefore, the type of input, the social planner's behaviour, and the way to finance determines whether social welfare is maximised or not.

In many growth models, human capital plays a crucial role for endogenous growth (e.g. Lucas 1988; Romer 1990). The efficiency of the education system is relevant for the rate of growth, since human capital formation has also internal and external effects: internal because education and training increase human capital and thereby productivity of the individual, external because the increase of human capital of individuals does also increase the average human capital of society as a whole. Thus, one possibility to foster growth is via education policy. Besides its effects on growth, such a policy is justified by its implications for income distribution. A better education increases the probability of achieving higher labour incomes. Education policy would then lead to a more even personal income distribution, as it had been the case in most advanced economies in the last century. *Christiane Schäper* develops an overlapping generations model based on the approach of Galor and Tsiddon (e.g. 1996) to reveal the effects of education policy on growth and distribution. The key elements are a threshold externality of technological progress and the diminishing complementarity between investment in capital and the influence of parents' human capital on the children's human capital accumulation. Simulations run by Schäper show that education policy can affect both income distribution and economic growth positively. As in Ott's model, financing is decisive because of the incentives on investment in human capital. For example, an income tax has a twofold effect. It gives a negative incentive to save that exceeds the positive effect of governmental education policy on human capital accumulation. Furthermore, the model clarifies that the benefits of education policy only occur in the long-run, since it takes time until a better-educated generation enters the labour market and improves overall productivity. Thus, the outcome of the model enriches the debate on the Programme for International Student Assessment (PISA) study of the OECD and the steps politicians are willing to take.

Due to the technological change that is caused by the introduction of information and communication technologies (ICTs) economists are more and more interested in the effects of this technological change for the distribution of incomes. In the US which is the leading economy in the application of ICTs, the personal income distribution shows an increasing disparity over the years. *Hugo Hollanders* and *Bas ter Weel* discuss the relation between skill-biased technical change and the dispersion of wages in a general equilibrium model in which heterogeneous individuals are characterised by different abilities to acquire new skills. Thus their approach transcends the framework of the representative agent. It is assumed that heterogeneity exists upon birth. Differences in the ability to acquire new skills are not only caused by gifts or talent, but also socio-economic factors might determine whether an individual can easily acquire knowledge or not. Consequently, the income distribution is not even. In addition, any investment in knowledge on the firm level will increase the dispersion of wages, since agents who have a better ability to attain skills, are favoured by such changes in the production process. Firms are interested in hiring better-skilled workers, since they can apply more sophisticated production processes better than low-qualified workers do. Hollanders and ter Weel show that agents with a higher ability can realise a higher growth rate of human capital accumulation in the steady state. Hence, inequality increases because of a cumulative process in the sense of 'success breeds success'. If the government dislikes this development and wants to improve the position of low-skilled workers, it has to intervene in a skill-biased way. Because of the assumed initial differences between agents any measure to distribute skills more equally among individuals is neutral in the long-run. However, the government can improve the position of the low-skilled by providing public knowledge (e.g. public schools and universities) at least in the short run.

Productivity growth not only raises per capita income, but has also consequences for employment. At least in the short run, increasing efficiency might lead to a lay-off of labour, if output growth lacks behind productivity growth. Thus, fluctuations in unemployment are symptoms of the growth process. Old jobs get lost and new ones are created. Many models in New Growth Theory do not cover the problem of unemployment, labour markets are assumed to be flexible enough to reach full employment. However, if growth is based on the development of new products, the introduction of new products and the disappearing of old ones require a reallocation of labour and capital. Only if the factors of production could be shifted from one sector to another, structural unemployment could be avoided. Obviously, qualified, labour is more flexible than unqualified labour. In an economy where workers are highly qualified structural change is easier to implement and sustain than in an economy with a low-qualified labour force. However, effective labour productivity does also depend on the utilisation of factor inputs that can vary either due to cyclical fluctuations or due to the actual availability of labour. The latter can be reduced because of bad health conditions.

The chapters in Part IV stress these relations. *Georg Erber* covers the empirical testing of Okun's law that was also discussed by Zagler in Part I. Okun's law has attracted some attention over the last decades since it was first stated as an empirical regularity for the US economy in the early 1960s. Erber's chapter studies the validity of this relation for the US and the German economy in the 1990s. One result is that the US economy always showed a much more stable empirical relation between the change of the unemployment rate and the rate of GDP growth than most European economies did, in particular Germany. Because of these differences, the efficiency of a pure demand management policy by creating additional demand through deficit spending by the federal government in times of recession worked much better for the US economy. One reason for this might be attributable to the fact that testing for asymmetric adjustments with regard to acceleration and deceleration of economic growth indicates that many European economies are much less flexible to reabsorb the unemployed workers in a recovery period than the US economy is. Furthermore, the chapter offers some empirical evidence that Okun's law has become a less stable relation in the second half of the 1990s. In this period, some structural factors seem to have contributed to the instability of Okun's law both in the US as well as in Germany.

Many models in growth theory focus on human capital as the key engine of growth. However, labour productivity does not only depend on skills, but also health is important. A highly qualified engineer who is sick is not able to make use of his expertise. On an aggregate level, diseases might reduce labour supply dramatically. *Joan Muysken, I. Hakan Yetkiner* and *Thomas Ziesemer* stress the importance of health as an important determinant of growth. They proclaim a positive correlation between health and economic growth, since growing economies can use more resources to improve health conditions, and health contributes to labour productivity and output growth via its effects on human capital. The authors extend a Cass–Koopmans growth model by introducing a health accumulation function. One of their most interesting findings is that poor countries with bad health conditions should allocate resources to overcome this deficiency. A healthy population may contribute more to growth than a fast-growing capital stock. Thus, the model fits well into the experience made in the nineteenth century when many European countries started to industrialise. Physical capital and labour are complements rather than substitutes. Hence, economies will only develop successfully if both inputs meet high standards. The quality of labour also depends on the workers' health.

Obviously, many approaches in modern growth theory are based on very sophisticated models. Thus, hypotheses have to be tested. The contributions in Part V deal with some key issues in the empirical investigation of growth processes in advanced economies. *Philip Arestis* and *Iris Biefang-Frisancho Mariscal* compare and test empirically the relevance of the capital stock in wage and unemployment determination for the UK and Germany. Whereas the cointegration method is applied for long-run analysis, the authors use impulse–response analysis for studying the effects of the capital stock on wages and unemployment in the short-run. Due to the limited substitutability between capital and labour the capital stock turns out to be an important variable in both countries. The authors also come to the conclusion that in the determination of the NAIRU, i.e. the non-accelerating inflation rate of unemployment, not only supply-side factors but also demand elements matter. Capital shortage unemployment can be the medium-run consequence of a real wage level which is too high – with a negative impact on profits and indirectly on investment – or of a too low level of effective demand which is reflected in a low degree of capacity utilisation thereby negatively affecting investment activities, i.e. potentially it can be either (neo-) classical or Keynesian unemployment of the second degree. In the specific case of unified Germany the obsolete capital stock in East Germany is due to socialist heritage, i.e. it reflects the technological backwardness of the former socialist economy. After monetary and economic unification with a sudden full internal and external liberalisation of the East German economy became effective on 1 July 1990, the inherited capital stock did not offer enough profitable activities. However, the strong element of capital shortage unemployment which has existed in East Germany in the 1990s is not reflected in Arestis and Biefang's data for the whole German economy (of which the eastern countries only constitute a smaller part).

The Netherlands experienced a remarkable long boom period in the second half of the 1990s which transformed the 'Dutch disease' of the 1970s and the early 1980s into a 'Dutch miracle' or 'Polder model' (see also Schettkat and Reijnders 1999). *Joan Muysken* analyses in his contribution the long-run causes for the polder model which has at its basis a consensus-oriented tradition which is deeply rooted in the Dutch culture. Although in retrospect, 1982, with the contract of Wassenaar, is regarded as the year the Dutch model was born, it has to be pointed out that it is not based on a blueprint institutional design but instead on an evolutionary development of Dutch institutions. Muysken identifies two important features of the polder model, the wage formation process and a strong social security system which, together with the fixing of the Dutch guilder to the German mark in 1983 and the consequential low inflation record, led to a decrease in unit wage costs and thereby to remarkable gains in the competitiveness of the Dutch economy. However, despite the strength of the Dutch growth experience and particularly the good performance of the labour market in relation to other European welfare states, Muysken rightly warns to export the polder model to other countries. Economists, in contrast to some theologians, know that 'miracles' don't exist. Although the Netherlands after 1982 managed to achieve a more labour-intensive growth path, one cannot overlook that job growth in the Netherlands for a substantial part is attributed to a significant growth of part-time jobs, which is also strongly correlated to an international catching-up process in the participation rate, particularly of women. Furthermore, a large part of the growth in GDP per capita had to be used to finance the growing inactivity which in the age group between 15 and 65 is one of the highest among OECD countries. In the wake of the high unemployment after the second oil price shock there was a great shift from unemployment to disability which reduced the Dutch workforce considerably. So despite the fact that Dutch firms have been doing well since the mid-1980s and GDP has grown persistently, the net income for the average wage-earner has hardly increased in the last three decades. This has led to a growing inequality and some tensions, which may undermine the consensus model in future years, as is already indicated in the 2002 parliamentary elections.

Hugo Hollanders and *Thomas Ziesemer* also make an international comparison of the growth process in the Netherlands. Investigating the last three decades, they particularly contrast the Dutch wage, employment and productivity performance with that in (West) Germany. They deny that the relatively better development in the Netherlands after the wage moderation agreement of Wassenaar in 1982 (with the exceptional years of the 'German Sonderkonjunktur' in 1990–92 after unification) can be attributed to a country-size effect, i.e. the fact that a small open economy, such as the Netherlands, benefits more from a world-wide recovery process after the recession in the wake of the second oil price shock. An important cause for the different development has been the significant reduction of the wage wedge, i.e. the difference between the gross wage paid by the employer and the net wage earned by the worker. This has increased the number of jobs for low-paid workers and thereby contributed to a much lower productivity growth per employee, although not per hour, compared to other EU countries. In Germany, on the other hand, the costs for German unification for a substantial part were shifted over to the social security system thereby increasing the wage wedge significantly from an already relatively high level. This had a strong negative impact on the job opportunities for less qualified workers, whose wage increases from the 1960s to the 1980s had exceeded their productivity increases. The reintegration possibilities into the production process for the unemployed thus were reduced. In contrast to simple views widely held in the public, the authors make clear that the 'Dutch model' cannot be easily transferred to Germany for a couple of reasons. Germany still has a much stronger industrial sector with high export surpluses based on relatively high skills of workers and a strong trade union in the key metal industry. It will be difficult to implement a Dutch-type wage moderation policy in the manufacturing sector when a great part of the new jobs would be created for low-skilled employees in the service sector. Furthermore, the wage moderation policy irrespective of skills has created a shortage of high skills as the other side of the coin in the Netherlands. One consequence, however, is clear: Germany has to find her own way of reducing the wage wedge to substantially improve the labour market situation in the medium and long-run, with a stronger emphasis on the job potential of the service sector than it has been recognised in 'employment pact' efforts in the past.

References

Aghion, P. and Howitt, P. (1998) *Endogenous Growth Theory*, Cambridge, Mass.: MIT Press.

Arrow, K.J. (1962) 'The Economic Implications of Learning by Doing', *Review of Economic Studies*, 29: 155–73.

Bombach, G. (1985) *Post-War Growth Revisited*, Amsterdam: North Holland.

Galor, O. and Tsiddon, D. (1996) 'Income Distribution and Growth: The Kuznets Hypothesis Revisited', *Economica*, 63: S103–17.

Hagemann, H. and Seiter, S. (1999) 'Okun's Law', in P.A. O'Hara (ed.), *Encyclopedia of Political Economy*, Vol. II: L-Z, London/New York: Routledge: 819–21.

Kaldor, N. (1957) 'A Model of Economic Growth', *Economic Journal*, 67: 591–624.

—— (1961) 'Capital Accumulation and Economic Growth' in F.A. Lutz and D.C. Hague (eds), *The Theory of Capital*, London, New York, reprinted in: E. Targetti and A.P. Thirlwall (eds), *The Essential Kaldor*: 229–81.

Lucas, R.E. Jr (1988) 'On the Mechanics of Economic Development', *Journal of Monetary Economics*, 22: 3–42.

Romer, P.M. (1986) 'Increasing Returns and Long-Run Growth', *Journal of Political Economy*, 94: 1012–37.

—— (1990) 'Endogenous Technical Change', *Journal of Political Economy*, 98: S71–102.

—— (1994) 'The Origins of Endogenous Growth', *Journal of Economic Perspectives*, 8: 3–22.

Sala-i-Martin, X. (1996) 'The Classical Approach to Convergence Analysis', *Economic Journal*, 106: 1019–36.

Schettkat, R. and Reijnders, J. (1999) *The Disease that Became a Model. The Economics Behind the Employment Trends in the Netherlands*. Report prepared for the Economic Policy Institute, Washington, DC.

Solow, R.M. (1957) 'Technical Change and the Aggregate Production Function', *Review of Economics and Statistics*, 39: 312–20.

—— (1991) 'New Directions in Growth Theory' in B. Gahlen, H. Hesse and H.J. Ramser (eds), *Wachstumstheorie und Wachstumspolitik: ein neuer Anlauf*, Schriftenreihe des Wirtschaftswissenschaftlichen Seminars Ottobeuren, Vol. 20, Tübingen: Mohr.

Part I

Explaining endogenous growth

2 Efficiency, innovation and productivity

On the impact of unemployment on endogenous growth

Martin Zagler

> Then the economy may be away from any full-equilibrium path for a long time. [...] The economy may eventually return to an equilibrium path [...]: If and when it does, it will not return to the continuation of the equilibrium path it was on before it slipped of. The new equilibrium path will depend on the amount of capital accumulation that has taken place during the period of disequilibrium, and probably also on the amount of unemployment, especially long-term unemployment, that has been experienced. Even the level of technology may be different, if technological change is endogenous rather than arbitrary.
>
> (Robert M. Solow 1988: 312)

Theoretical motivation

Whilst Endogenous Growth Theory and Labour Economics have been heavily exploited in past and recent years, very little has been published on common correlations, not to mention joint causalities of growth and employment. However, one cannot deny the importance of the topic, and whilst economists appear to lack an answer, the public debate frequently asks for measures to foster both.

The first to propose a correlation between unemployment and growth was Arthur Okun (1970). In his seminal paper, first published in 1962, he basically stated that a one percentage point decline in unemployment was associated with a 3 per cent increase in real output, beyond a long-run average annual growth rate of output of 2–3 per cent. For the research proposed here, his analysis has two major shortcomings. First, whilst he empirically describes a correlation between growth and unemployment, he fails to describe a causality in one or the other direction. Second, and more important, the statement that a change in unemployment leads to growth of output is equivalent to the statement that high employment is associated with a high level of output and vice versa. Hence, Okun's argument is static in nature, whilst the following research addresses a dynamic relation, whether high levels of unemployment are related with high growth rates of output or vice versa.

Endogenous growth theory and labour markets

Before 1986, mainstream economists considered economic growth to originate outside the economic system, resulting from research and major developments that happen in laboratories or scientific institutions. Paul Romer's seminal article challenged this view. Romer found that given non-decreasing returns to scale with respect to reproducible factors of production, the capital accumulation process need not cease; hence an economy may grow without bounds (Romer 1986).

Several authors have contributed specific examples for technologies that enable a growth process as described by Romer. The simplest version is due to Sergio Rebelo (1991), who postulated a production function linear in capital. Evidently, as more capital enters the production process, the marginal product of capital does not decline, and given a real rate of interest below the marginal product of capital, the economy will pursue a constant long-run growth path. The model exhibits a major shortcoming, however. In a competitive economy, the owner of the capital stock can extract all revenues from the firm (else she would rent out her capital somewhere else), hence even if labour were necessary for production purposes, workers would receive a zero wage. Hence, the model is inappropriate to discuss employment questions.

Robert Lucas (1988) then proposed a production function with three arguments, human capital, labour and the economies (or at least the industries) average stock of human capital, which exhibits constant returns to scale with respect to private (or firm-specific) factors of production, namely human capital and labour, and with respect to reproducible factors of production, namely human capital and the average stock of human capital. As firms have an incentive to invest in human capital, they also augment the economy-wide stock of human capital, thus they induce a non-declining marginal product of human capital for any level of economic activity. Analogous to Rebelo, given an interest rate below the marginal product of human capital, the economy may grow without bounds. Whilst the firm will pay both capital and labour its private marginal product, this solution is inefficient. Economy-wide, the technology as proposed by Robert Lucas reduces to the Rebelo Ak-type, where labour is socially unproductive, and hence workers should receive a zero wage. Once again, these models are inadequate to analyse employment issues.

This evidently unpleasant characteristic of the above-mentioned growth models triggered a second wave of endogenous growth models, due to Romer (1990), Grossman and Helpman (1991), and Aghion and Howitt (1992). Basically, all three variants operate through the same channel. Splitting the labour force into two groups, labelled workers and innovators for convenience, one group can produce an ever-improved consumption good, whilst the other can permanently innovate new or better products or production processes, thus triggering a long-run permanent growth process.

These models differ in several ways from the first class of models. First, instead of human capital, they focus on research and development as the engine of growth. Second, instead of perfect competition, they are based on monopolistic competition, which enables providers of innovations and inventions with the possibility of receiving a rent for their research and development efforts. Third, they no longer build upon non-decreasing returns with respect to reproducible factors of production. Therefore, long-run growth is no longer a knife's-edge property, as argued by Robert Solow (1994).

In the second class of endogenous growth models discussed above, innovators are referred to as Schumpeterian entrepreneurs, as they derive their role through a process of creative invention or innovation. The labour market is therefore populated by simple main-d'ouvre, which leaves very limited scope for the analysis of the relation between growth and employment. Indeed, additional employment would be bad for growth, as it reduces the share of innovators, and hence the rate at which additional innovations hit the economy. In a variant to these models, Zagler (1999a: 27–9) proposes a model of innovative labour, capturing the fact that many innovations in the production process are driven by the workforce. In that respect, employment can play a positive role for the innovative capacity within the economy, as it may affect the share of time a worker will devote to innovative activities.

The common feature for both classes of models is the necessity of externalities. Whilst human capital externalities positively influence the production and accumulation process, the negative monopolistic competition externality allows innovators to accrue rents and thus enables the growth process. Externalities, however, create a gap between private market demand and supply, and the socially optimal demand or supply. In these models, there is either social excess demand for innovation, or social excess demand for human capital. Given a Walrasian economy, the social excess demand in one market must be matched with social excess supply in yet another. In endogenous growth models, this market is typically the capital market (due to the fact that the demand for credit is derived from the decision to invest) that socially provides too little capital, in other words, private saving is too low.

Under certain circumstances, the excess supply may appear in other markets as well. In the case of the labour market, of course, the term excess supply is conventionally addressed as unemployment. Given plausible frictions in the labour market, which will be discussed in the following, a causal relation between unemployment and growth can be established.

Labour market theory and economic growth

The quantity of labour exchanged, and the price of labour, the real wage rate, are determined on the labour market. A stylised version of the labour market contains a demand schedule for labour, where the quantity of labour demanded by firms and others depends (in general) inversely on its price, and a supply schedule for labour, where workers offer their labour services according to their marginal utility from leisure. Whenever there is excess supply of labour, or unemployment, as introduced above, market forces drive the wage down until demand exactly offsets supply. An equilibrium theory of persistent unemployment must therefore explain what prevents wages from falling.[1] As Layard *et al.* (1991) state, 'Either firms are not free to choose the wage, and wage bargaining forces them to pay more than they wish; or, if firms are free to choose and still pay more than the supply price of labour, it must be in their interest to do so.'

Austrian evidence has shown that neither the minimum wage approach, nor the insider–outsider approach (McDonald and Solow 1985), can explain why firms are to a large degree willing to pay beyond the negotiated wage (Zagler and Mühlberger 1998). Voluntary overpayment of workers by firms can be motivated, however, by efficiency wage models.

Given that working provides disutility at the margin (i.e. workers may wish to work, but *ceteris paribus* prefer to work marginally less), firms may use high real wages to motivate workers to contribute effort, and to prevent them from shirking. The efficiency inducing channel of high real wages may operate either through fairness considerations (Akerlof and Yellen 1990), i.e. if workers are paid at least what similar workers are paid, they will be more willing not to shirk, or through monitoring costs on behalf of the firm (Shapiro and Stiglitz 1984), i.e. instead of incurring high monitoring costs to induce effort, firms may simply prefer to pay workers more.

In both cases, wages would increase without bounds, creating unemployment. An increase in the unemployment rate raises the risk for the individual worker to get laid off, thus potentially increasing his effort for a given wage. This second effect may get large enough to induce full effort on behalf of the workers without raising wages any more (Bowles 1985).

Related literature of endogenous growth and labour market theories

Bean and Pissarides (1993) were the first to introduce frictional unemployment into a very stylised endogenous growth model. They proposed a generational model with a simple Rebelo-type production function, where new members of the labour force had to be matched to a job vacancy, according to the matching approach (Pissarides 1985). Evidently, an increase in the exogenous rate of total factor productivity fosters economic growth, but also increases the rate of job creation, thus driving the unemployment rate down along the Beveridge curve (Beveridge 1942). Whilst Bean and Pissarides can explain long-run youth unemployment, they fail to give theoretical foundations for intragenerational lay-offs, which do account for most of the current level of unemployment, at least in Austria (Gächter and Stagl 1997).

Ramon Marimon and Filippe Zilibotti (1998) recently suggested that structural change is indeed the driving force behind frictional unemployment. As some industries decline, they lay off workers, not trained or qualified to be engaged in the emerging sectors. Aghion and Howitt (1998) realised that the second type of endogenous growth models mentioned earlier are indeed models of structural change as well. In that respect endogenous growth will affect unemployment in three distinct ways. First there is the job creation effect, with new industries opening and hiring new workers. Then, there is the job destruction effect, as old firms leave the labour market. Then there is an effect, which Aghion and Howitt loosely label the indirect effect, which is indeed due to the fact that as the number of industries increases, firms can benefit less from scale effects, and production gets more labour intense, a phenomenon well known from the service sector.

Whilst all of the above models explain causality and correlation of frictional unemployment and growth, they fail to provide a rigorous framework for persistent long-term unemployment. First attempts along those lines can be found in the literature. For instance, Cahuc and Michel (1996) recently introduced minimum wages into an endogenous growth model, showing that the economy may benefit from minimum wages as it forces individuals to invest more into training, thereby internalising part of the human capital accumulation externality typical for the first wave of growth models. However, their model remains unsound, as agents fail to realise their intended work effort and consumption plans, but are not rational enough to realise this.

The paper that comes closest to the model presented below is Schaik and de Groot (1998). They construct a two-sector efficiency wage model, where unemployed voluntarily line up to obtain a job in the efficiency wage sector, which exhibits constant returns with respect to reproducible factors of production.

None of these attempts, however, adopts the empirically more sound imperfect competition models, so that we are at present far from a consensus model of equilibrium unemployment, as the initial quote of this paper by Robert Solow (1988) requests. In the following, a first attempt to fill this theoretical gap, an efficiency wage growth model that builds upon the most recent variant of endogenous growth theory, is presented.

A simple model of labour efficiency and economic growth

The model economy presented below consists of three agents, workers, manufacturers and innovators, where the latter two are separated for mere convenience. Assume that workers wish to offer one unit of labour inelastically for a given wage w_t, and spend their entire income on consumption for all relevant values of income,[2] which implies that aggregate demand c_t for a given level of unemployment u_t and a population size of unity equals $(1 - u_t)w_t$. By contrast, it is assumed for mere convenience that both manufacturers and innovators refrain from consumption. Workers will offer their labour services to both manufacturers and innovators, who produce products or innovations, respectively, under constant returns to labour inputs.

Efficiency wages in manufacturing

Manufacturers exercise monopoly power for a specific product variety, facing the following demand function,

$$x_{i,t} = p_{i,t}^{-\varepsilon} c_t \tag{1}$$

where the price $p_{i,t}$ of a particular product variety $x_{i,t}$ reduces demand with elasticity ε. In accordance with monopolistic competition models, aggregate demand fosters sales of a particular product. A particular firm i is assumed to maximise profits subject to demand (1) and technology, as given by,

$$x_{i,t} = l_{i,t}e^{-(\mu/u_t)/(w_{i,t}/w_t)} \tag{2}$$

where $l_{i,t}$ is the labour force employed in a particular firm at the wage rate $w_{i,t}$, and the exponential term is the efficiency of this workforce. In accordance with Akerlof and Yellen (1990), both an increase in the relative wage vis-à-vis the economy-wide average wage, $w_{i,t}/w_t$, and an increase in the unemployment rate u_t increase efficiency. In this chapter, μ has three distinct interpretations. The first interpretation of μ is that it represents the degree at which a firm relies on firing to induce efficiency, or the degree at which workers perceive the threat of becoming unemployed. Assume for a moment that the exponent were equal to minus unity,[3] then workers will be willing to accept wages lower than average if and only if unemployment exceeds μ. As both the relative wage and the unemployment rate depend on economic conditions outside the firm, they shall be labelled 'external efficiency'.

There is ample evidence that manufacturers can induce efficiency other than with a carrot (a high relative wage) and a stick (a high unemployment rate). Then μ may be a function of the organizational structure (e.g. introducing internal controlling), or the motivation of the workforce (e.g. internal training or promotions) within a manufacturing firm. As an increase in μ reduces efficiency, $\partial x_{i,t}/\partial \mu < 0$, 'internal efficiency' may be measured by the index $1/\mu$.

In this second interpretation of μ, it may reflect the extent at which the firm needs to rely on external efficiency, and $1/\mu$ the extent of internal efficiency. Whilst one can hardly verify the degree of motivation or the quality of organization, the firing rate is easily accessible, hence firm owners (shareholders) may prefer efficiency-inducing mechanisms that operate through the unemployment rate, requesting a high external efficiency, i.e. a high μ.

Profit maximization in manufacturing implies that firms will increase their wage until the increase in effort is just offset by an alternative increase in employment, i.e. until the output elasticity of employment is equal to the output elasticity of the wage rate,

$$\frac{w_{i,t}}{w_t} = \frac{\mu}{u_t} \tag{3}$$

Any firm will increase (reduce) its wage relative to the average wage, whenever unemployment exceeds (lies below) μ. This will equiproportionally increase (reduce) the average wage, thus inducing another round of relative wage increases (declines), implying ultimately that wages will increase without bounds (decline to a zero rate). Hence a third interpretation of μ is the non-accelerating wage rate of unemployment (NAWRU). The efficiency condition (3) implies that productivity in manufacturing will equal the inverse of Euler's number, $x_{i,t}/l_{i,t} = 1/e$.

The average wage is defined as the sum of wages paid to manufacturing workers in each firm i to its workers $l_{i,t}$, and salaries s_t to workers in the research sector l_t, divided by the entire labour force, $1 - u_t$. Noting that aggregate manufacturing employment must equal $1 - u_t - l_t$ by definition, and substituting equation (3), average wages are defined as,

$$s_t l_t + (1 - u_t - l_t)w_t\mu/u_t = w_t(1 - u_t) \tag{4}$$

The price, which manufacturing firms in this monopolistic setting will charge, equals the mark-up over costs, namely the wage per efficiency unit,

$$p_{i,t} = \frac{\varepsilon}{\varepsilon - 1}ew_{i,t} \tag{5}$$

where the mark-up depends inversely on the price elasticity of demand. The mark-up equation (5) and manufacturing technology (2) together imply that profits in manufacturing equal revenues divided by the price elasticity of demand, or total costs over $\varepsilon - 1$.

The innovation sector and economic growth

As manufacturers do not consume, and households do not save, all profits of the manufacturing sector will be reinvested. Recently, Brenner (1998: 210) suggested that this is indeed the fact for most profits. In the absence of a capital good or any other store of value, profits are invested into R&D. Assuming that the only input into R&D are employees, who receive salaries s_t, the accounting equation for the R&D sector reads,

$$s_t l_t = \frac{w_t}{\varepsilon - 1}\frac{u_t}{\mu}(1 - u_t - l_t) \tag{6}$$

where aggregate profits are expressed in terms of averages wages and the non-manufacturing labour force, by substitution of the efficiency condition (3). Whilst labour demand in the research sector can be derived from the above condition (6), we note that all workers that do not supply labour in manufacturing will be seeking employment in the innovation sector. If salaries in the innovation sector were free to adjust, the labour market would clear. We shall assume, however, that salaries will equal wages. This may be supported by the following three arguments. First, fairness considerations may justify that workers in the research sector should be paid equal wages. In particular, and this brings us to the second argument, if efficiency considerations are equally important in the innovation sector, and they certainly are, research firms would voluntarily refrain from employing the entire labour force. Third, of course, as it is existing firms which invest into research, there may not be an organizational distinction between the two sectors, and unless the labour market can be segmented,[4] salaries would equal wages. Setting wages equal to salaries in the definition of the wage index (4), we find that actual unemployment will equal the NAWRU in equilibrium. Setting wages equal to salaries in equation (6), it reduces to,

$$l_t = \frac{1 - u_t}{\varepsilon} \tag{7}$$

stating that a fixed proportion of the active workforce will be employed in R&D. The R&D sector is assumed to innovate new product varieties according to the following conventional aggregate technology (Romer 1990),

$$\dot{n}_t = \phi n_t l_t \tag{8}$$

where ϕ is productivity in R&D, l_t is the labour force employed in the R&D sector and n_t is the number of existing varieties, external to the innovator, stating that it is easier to innovate when the stock of knowledge, i.e. the existing number of innovations, is large. R&D technology (8) and the efficiency condition (3) imply that the growth rate of varieties, η, must equal $\phi(1-\mu)/\varepsilon$. This implies that output growth γ in this model economy will equal,[5]

$$\gamma = \frac{\phi(1 - \mu)}{\varepsilon(\varepsilon - 1)} \tag{9}$$

An increase in R&D productivity evidently fosters economic growth. An increase in the price elasticity of manufacturing demand, ε, reduces the mark-up (5), hence reduces revenues of the R&D sector, and therefore reduces economic growth. Finally, an increase in the NAWRU reduces the labour force in R&D, and hence economic growth. A reduction of the NAWRU, represented by a decline in μ, reduces the necessity of a high outside threat in the form of unemployment, and is hence beneficial for economic growth.

Productivity versus efficiency

The economy knows two types of efficiency, and three types of productivity. External efficiency is defined as $w_t/(w_{i,t}u_t)$, which equals in μ equilibrium, whilst internal efficiency is defined as $1/\mu$, both remaining constant over time. Productivity in R&D is defined as ϕn_t, growing at rate η. Whilst productivity in a single manufacturing firm depends solely on the degree of efficiency it can extract, and equals $1/e$, sectorwide productivity in manufacturing depends upon both the degree of efficiency, and the number of available varieties, which by substitution of manufacturing technology (1) into aggregate spending, $c_t = n_t p_t x_t$, equals $c_t/(1 - u_t - l_t) = n_t^{1/(\varepsilon-1)}/e$.

First, note that a change in internal efficiency is simply offset by a change in outside flexibility, hence efficiency in aggregate does not influence productivity of a single manufacturing firm. However, an increase in internal efficiency, or equivalently a decline in external efficiency, will raise the growth rate of R&D productivity, which equals η, by $\mu/(1 - \mu)$ per cent.[6] As the growth rate of the manufacturing sector productivity is equal to the growth rate of R&D productivity, an increase in internal efficiency will foster productivity in the manufacturing sector by the same amount. Whilst there is no direct channel of efficiency on the manufacturing sector, due to the efficiency condition (3) that holds each manufacturing firm's efficiency constant, there is an indirect channel that operates through the R&D sector. The indirect channel works as follows. If efficiency increases exogenously by a decline in μ, firms can reduce the wage premia, implying that the R&D sector can reduce salaries and thus increase output for given costs, increasing the number of varieties. Finally, note that an increase in external efficiency, e.g. due to increase of shareholders' influence, reduces productivity in the manufacturing sector and ultimately reduces output growth. This captures the common perception that an increase in the strive for (external) efficiency will reduce the innovation potential of the individual worker (Buchele and Christiansen 1992).

The role of unemployment for economic growth

The rate of unemployment has two effects in this model. First, it ensures that there is an upper bound to efficiency-induced wage increases by individual manufacturing firms, and as workers will spend their entire wage income on consumption goods, one may even claim that the 'reserve army of the unemployed' holds wages on the 'subsistence level' (Bowles 1985). Indeed, assume for a moment that the unemployment rate were, for some reason, below NAWRU, then, by the efficiency condition (3), firms would increase their wages above the average wage, reducing alongside their labour demand, until actual unemployment reaches the NAWRU level.

Second, in a dynamic sense, unemployment ensures that capacities are available for the R&D sector, thus ensuring growth in product variety and output. Indeed, the 'reserve army' provides 'new industries' with the required production factor (Sweezy 1942). The channel runs as follows. First, from the definition of the NAWRU (3), note that an increase in unemployment is offset by a one-to-one decline in every manufacturing firm's wages. This translates into a less than one-to-one increase in the average wage, due to the wage index (4). For a given manufacturing labour force, the combination of the two effects induces an increase in manufacturing profits, the right-hand-side of equation (7). Until salaries in R&D have caught up with manufacturing wages, employment in R&D increases, thus inducing a higher rate of technological progress, as can be seen from R&D technology (9).

Okun's law revisited

This chapter has started out by presenting two major shortcomings of Okun's law, its static nature and its apparent lack of causality. Both issues can be addressed on the basis of the model presented. The growth equation (10) can be interpreted as a revised version of Okun's law, with two major differences. First, it is a relation between the equilibrium rate of growth, γ, and the equilibrium rate of unemployment, μ. Thus it is a long-run relationship between unemployment and economic growth, which needs not necessarily hold in the short run, as pointed out by Erber in this volume. Second, whilst Okun's law predicts a negative relation between economic growth and the change in unemployment, the revised version presented in this chapter indicates a relation between the rate of economic growth and the level of unemployment. Whereas an increase in unemployment would induce a lower level of output in the original version of Okun's law, here a permanent increase in unemployment reduces the rate of growth of output. Hence, the revised Okun's law is dynamic in nature.

Note that the two versions of Okun's law would be observationally identical for transitory changes in the equilibrium unemployment rate. In the original Okun's law, we would observe an increase in unemployment associated with a decline in the level of output. In the revised version, we should equivalently observe an increase in the unemployment rate and a reduction in the growth rate of output, followed by a decline in unemployment and an increase in the rate of growth, as the shock to the equilibrium unemployment rate is transitory. This may explain both the early empirical success of Okun's law and its recent failure. Whilst shocks to the equilibrium unemployment rate used to be purely transitory, recent evidence suggests a large persistence of shocks to the equilibrium unemployment rate, known as hysteresis (Bean 1994).

The revised Okun's law also suggests a clear direction of causality. Whereas the equilibrium rate of unemployment (3) is independent of the rate of growth, the equilibrium growth rate (10) depends crucially on the rate of unemployment. Therefore, the model suggests that there is a clear direction of causality between unemployment and economic growth, which runs from unemployment to economic growth. The issue is not altogether irrelevant, as it has a clear indication for economic policy. Whereas measures to promote economic growth will not exhibit any impact on the level of unemployment, measures to reduce unemployment may promote economic growth.

Summary

Whilst the public debate calls for measures to foster economic growth and reduce unemployment, economists have failed to provide an analytical framework. This chapter aims to fill this theoretical gap by developing a two-sector model, where the monopolistically competitive manufacturing sector pays efficiency wages, thereby creating unemployment. Economic profits from manufacturing are reinvested in R&D. Whilst the non-accelerating wage rate of unemployment (NAWRU) remains unaffected by changes in the economic rate of growth, e.g. induced by R&D productivity gains, economic growth depends negatively on the NAWRU. This implies that measures to reduce the NAWRU, in particular by increasing internal efficiency relative to the outside threat of high unemployment, will also be beneficial for economic growth, whilst the inverse does not apply.

Notes

1 Unemployment is therefore entirely determined by non-market clearing wages, and the theoretical model presented in this chapter will pursue this track. It should be pointed

out, however, that there may not exist a non-negative level of real wages and employment at which the labour market clears. Suppose there is unemployment at the current level of real wages. A reduction of the real wage may reduce labour income if the wage elasticity of labour demand is less than unity. As labour income is a major source of aggregate income, spending may decline. This will reduce demand for consumption products, thus reducing labour demand for every given wage. If the shift in labour demand is large enough, unemployment may even increase. But even if unemployment declines, the effect may not be large enough to ensure market clearing for non-negative levels of the real wage.

2 Microfoundations for this assumption can be found in a parallel paper (Zagler 1999b).

3 This will be proven in equation (3).

4 In practice, firms should have ample opportunity to segregate the labour force on the grounds of their educational background, and thus pay different wages to employees and workers. If we assume that agents exhibit different abilities, as assumed by Weel and Hollanders in this volume, they may indeed pursue different levels of education. If they exhibit identical abilities, as will be assumed here for the sake of simplicity, workers and employees cannot be segmented on the basis of education, thus retaining the assumption of identical wages and salaries.

5 Note that the model is completely symmetric in the manufacturing sector, since (3) implies identical wages, (5) identical prices, $p_{i,t} = p_t$, (1) identical quantities, $x_{i,t} = x_t$, and (2) identical employment, $l_{i,t} = (\varepsilon - 1)(1 - \mu)/\varepsilon n_t$. There are n_t manufacturers that sell a quantity x_t of their variety at price p_t, hence $c_t = n_t p_t x_t$. As the growth rate of x_t is identical to the growth rate of a manufacturers employment $l_{i,t}$, and equal to $-\eta$, the growth rate of consumption (or output) equals the growth rate of the price p_t. By the demand function (1), we find that the growth rate of consumption and output γ equals $\eta/(\varepsilon - 1)$.

6 Define internal efficiency as $1/\mu$, then the elasticity of R&D growth with respect to internal efficiency equals, $[\partial \eta/\partial(1/\mu)]/\eta\mu = \phi\mu/\varepsilon\eta = \mu/(1 - \mu)$. To give a numerical example of the size of the effect, assume quite realistically that the NAWRU equals 5 per cent, and the average annual growth rate 2 per cent. Then a decline in the NAWRU by 10 per cent from 5 per cent to 4.5 per cent yields a 10.5 per cent increase in economic growth, from 2 per cent to 2.2 per cent. This is, by the way full in line with recent estimates of Okun's law, which states that a one per cent increase in growth reduces unemployment by 0.5 per cent.

References

Aghion, Ph. and Howitt, P. (1992) 'A Model of Growth Through Creative Destruction', *Econometrica*, 60: 323–51.

——(1998) *Endogenous Growth Theory*, Cambridge, Mass.: MIT Press.

Akerlof, G. and Yellen, J. (1990) 'The Fair Wage-Effort Hypothesis and Unemployment', *Quarterly Journal of Economics*, 105(2): 255–83.

Bean, C. (1994) 'European Unemployment', *Journal of Economic Literature*, 33: 573–619.

——and Pissarides, C. (1993) 'Unemployment, Consumption and Growth', *European Economic Review*, 37: 837–59.

Beveridge, W. (1942) *Social Insurance Allied Services*, Cmd. 6404, HMSO, London.

Bowles, S. (1985) 'The Production Process and in a Competitive Economy: Walrasian, Neo-Hobbesian and Marxian Models', *American Economic Review*, 75: 16–36.

Brenner, R. (1998) 'The Economics of Global Turbulence', *New Left Review*, 229.

Buchele, R. and Christiansen, J. (1992) 'Industrial Relations and Productivity Growth', *International Contributions to Labor Studies*, 2: 77–97.

Cahuc, P. and Michel, P. (1996) 'Minimum Wage, Unemployment and Growth', *European Economic Review*, 40: 1463–82.

Erber, G. (2003) 'Okun's Law in the US and the Employment Crisis in Germany', in H. Hagemann and S. Seiter (eds), *Growth Theory and Growth Policy*, London: Routledge.

Gächter, S. and Stagl, S. (1997) 'Segmentierung des Arbeitsmarktes und alterswirksames Unternehmensverhalten – Exkurs in die ökonomische Theorie', in R. Finder (ed.): *Die Diskriminierung Älterer am Arbeitsmarkt*, Wien: Wissenschaftsverlag: 46–56.

Grossman, G. and Helpman, E. (1991) *Innovation and Growth in the Global Economy*, Cambridge, Mass.: MIT Press.

Hollanders, H. and ter Weel, B. (2002) 'Skill-biased Technological Change in an Endogenous Growth Model with Government Intervention', in H. Hagemann and S. Seiter (eds), *Growth Theory and Growth Policy*, London: Routledge.

Layard, R., Nickell, S. and Jackman, R. (1991) *Unemployment: Macroeconomic Performance and the Labour Market*, Oxford and New York: Oxford University Press.

Lucas, R. (1988) 'On the Mechanics of Economic Development', *Journal of Monetary Economics*, 22: 3–42.

McDonald, I. and Solow, R. (1985) 'Wages and Employment in a Segmented Labor Market', *Quarterly Journal of Economics*, 100: 1115–41.

Marimon, R. and Zilibotti, F. (1998) 'Actual versus Virtual Employment in Europe: Is Spain Different?', *European Economic Review*, 42: 123–53.

Okun, A. (1970) 'Potential GDP: Its Measurement and Significance', reprinted in A. Okun (ed.), *The Political Economy of Prosperity*, Washington, DC: Brookings Institution.

Pissarides, C. (1985) 'Job Search and the Functioning of Labour Markets', in D. Carline *et al.* (eds), *Labour Economics*, London: Longman: 159–85.

Rebelo, S. (1991) 'Long-Run Policy Against Long-Run Growth', *Journal of Political Economy*, 99: 500–21.

Romer, P.M. (1986) 'Increasing Returns and Long-Run Growth', *Journal of Political Economy*, 94: 1002–35.

—— (1990) 'Endogenous Technological Change', *Journal of Political Economy*, 98: 71–102.

Schaik, A. and de Groot, H. (1998) 'Unemployment and Endogenous Growth', *Labour*, 12: 189–219.

Shapiro, C. and Stiglitz, J. (1984) 'Equilibrium Unemployment as a Worker Discipline Device', *American Economic Review*, 74: 433–44.

Solow, R.M. (1988) 'Growth Theory and After', *American Economic Review*, 78: 307–17.

—— (1994) 'Perspectives on Growth Theory', *Journal of Economic Perspectives*, 8: 45–54.

Sweezy, P. (1942) *The Theory of Capitalist Development*, New York: Oxford University Press.

Zagler, M. (1999a) *Endogenous Growth, Market Imperfections, and Economic Policy*, Basingstoke: Macmillan, and New York: St Martin's Press.

—— (1999b) 'Endogenous Growth, Efficiency Wages, and Persistent Unemployment', Vienna University of Economics & B.A. Working Paper No. 66. Available online at http://www.wu–wien.ac.at/inst/vw1/zagler/abstract/1006e.htm (24 Aug. 2000).

—— and Mühlberger, U. (1998) 'The European Employment Price Index', *Austrian Journal of Statistics*, 28: 59–69.

—— and Ragacs, Ch. (1998) 'Innovation, Company Cooperation, and the East European Transition Process', *Zagreb International Review of Economics and Business*, 1: 65–75.

3 Endogenous growth

One phenomenon: two interpretations

Stephan Seiter

Introduction

The explanation of economic growth is still one of the most interesting fields in economic theory. Generations of economists analysed the determinants of economic growth. The post-war period was certainly one of the most productive periods in this research area. Neoclassical economists like Solow (1956), Swan (1956) or Meade (1962), as well as Postkeynesians like Harrod (1939) and Domar (1946), developed various models that focused on the conditions of stable growth paths, but did not include endogenous growth. Long-run per capita income could only be explained by assuming exogenous technical progress. However, Arrow (1962) and Kaldor (e.g. 1957) stressed the endogenous character of technical progress and its links to investment.

Since the mid-1980s, the so-called *New Growth Theory* offers a new alternative approach. Investment is seen as the most important variable in determining growth. Based on Arrrow's concept of learning by doing, the assumption is made that investment in different types of capital shows positive externalities on future investment. This line of reasoning reminds one very much of Kaldor's ideas about endogenous technical progress. A comprehensive survey of both approaches might help to understand the growth process better. Therefore, we deal with a comparison of the main elements of new growth theory and of Kaldorian approaches. In the next section, the central ideas of new growth theory are presented. The following section covers the ideas of Kaldor and some more recent developments. Then, the key features are compared. Finally, some implications for economic policy are sketched.

New growth theory on endogenous growth

In the 1980s, neoclassical growth theory experienced a renaissance launched by Paul Romer's (1986) seminal paper on endogenous growth. Traditional neoclassical theory could not explain endogenous growth in the steady-state equilibrium because of the assumption of diminishing marginal returns to capital. Here, the process of capital deepening ends as soon as the return on investment equalises the rate of time preference. This point will be reached sometime, since the incentive to invest decreases with the diminishing marginal productivity of capital. Thereby, the steady-state growth equilibrium is stable, but the long-run growth rate is independent of the savings rate and the investment decision.[1]

A first step to overcome these major shortcomings was the introduction of exogenous technical progress. The increase in efficiency counters the fall in marginal productivity as the capital–labour ratio grows. Thereby, investment and growth of per capita income do not peter out. Hence, exogenous technical progress maintains the incentive to capital deepening. However, the approach does not explain the true reasons for economic growth, since an exogenous variable that seems to be sent like *manna from heaven* determines the growth rate.

To allow for endogenous growth, obviously one has to assume constant returns to capital or at least a minimum below which marginal returns cannot fall (see Jones and Manuelli 1990; Rebelo 1991). Nevertheless, this trick may imply an inconsistent explanation of the functional income distribution. According to the neoclassical model, the principal of marginal return governs the distribution of income (see Pasinetti 2000: 390). With two factors of production paid their marginal product, wages and profits will only add up to the output, if the production function reveals constant returns to scale.[2] For this reason one has either to leave labour out of the production function, so that capital is the only input that has to be paid its marginal product, or one has to assume external economies of scale.

At first sight, both approaches seem to differ, but the mechanism the model is based on is identical. The so-called AK-model represents the first group of models at best. Here output (Y) depends only on the input of capital (K) and the given level of technology (A)

$$Y = AK \tag{1}$$

The marginal productivity of capital is then given by (2) and is equal to the average capital productivity

$$\frac{\partial Y}{\partial K} = \frac{Y}{K} = \frac{\Lambda}{V} = A \tag{2}$$

Due to the assumptions, marginal productivity of capital is constant and therefore independent of the capital–labour ratio. Referring to per capita values, we have

$$f(k) = Ak \tag{3}$$

and

$$f'(k) = A \tag{4}$$

Assuming that the proportional savings rate (s) and the natural rate (n) are constant, the growth rate of the capital–labour ratio is given by[3]

$$\frac{\dot{k}}{k} = sA - n \tag{5}$$

and

$$\dot{k} = sAk - nk \tag{6}$$

Since the production function is a linear-homogeneous function of K, the growth rate of per capita income is also

$$\frac{\dot{y}}{y} = sA - n \tag{7}$$

As long as $sAK > nk$, capital deepening takes place, i.e. the capital–labour ratio grows steadily. Therefore, postulating constant returns, marginal returns show the same consequences as exogenous technical progress does in the standard neoclassical model. An increasing input of capital per worker causes per capita growth in the steady-state equilibrium. Nevertheless, the true determinants of technical progress and the reasons for constant returns are not explained. The AK-model is only an endogenous growth model with regard to the influence of the savings rate on long-run growth.[4]

There is another interesting feature of the AK-model. Combining (2) with (7) brings us to

$$\frac{\dot{y}}{y} = \frac{s}{v} - n \tag{8}$$

In the Solow model as in Harrod's and Domar's Postkeynesian models (s/v) is equal to n in the steady-state equilibrium. Thus, the productivity of capital and the savings (and investment) ratio determine the accumulation of capital. Equation (8) reminds us of the problem of long-run instability discussed by Harrod. If the growth rate of capital equalises the natural growth rate,[5] the economy will reach its steady state. As soon as the accumulation of capital differs from the natural growth rate, the capital–labour ratio will change. In Harrod's analysis, the difference in the growth rate leads to a shortage of labour when $(s/v) > n$, so entrepreneurs will change their investment behaviour. Unemployment due to a shortage of capital will emerge, when $(s/v) < n$.[6] A difference between the rate of capital accumulation and the labour-force growth rate may influence the business cycle. For this reason the AK-model raises implicitly the same questions of instability as Harrod's approach did. These were partly answered by the traditional neoclassical growth theory. However, the AK-approach skips these problems by definition. The labour market seems to be flexible enough to avoid both unemployment and a shortage of labour.[7]

A second way to model endogenous growth is to assume constant marginal returns to capital and to include labour in the production function. In this case, the assumption that the marginal principle determines the income distribution is only feasible, if external economies of scale characterise the production process. Here, new growth theory is clearly linked to Arrow's 1962 paper on the economic implications of learning by doing. Investment does not only increase the capital stock, but also changes the production process, i.e. workers must learn how to use new machines. Their skills will improve and an increase in labour productivity will occur. Furthermore, experience gained when using new processes leads to further technical progress, since the next vintage of capital goods is supposed to include this knowledge. Therefore, a firm's investment will probably show intertemporal external effects with regard to future productivity. Future investors will benefit from the experience of their predecessors.[8]

The new knowledge arising from learning is a quasi-public good because firms are not able to completely exclude others from accessing and using it. This is even more obvious with investment in research and development. Competitors might analyse newly invented products as soon as they are available in the market. They can apply the results of successful inventors without the need to invest too much on their own. On the aggregate level increasing returns to scale might emerge, while each firm produces at constant returns to scale and the factors of production receive their marginal product. The positive externalities due to the accumulation of capital and/or knowledge can counter the diminishing marginal returns on the firm level. When we assume a production function that includes labour (L), physical capital (K), firm-specific know-how (KH), and the aggregate level of know-how (KH^a), a firm's output is given by (see Romer 1987: 170)

$$Y_i = F_i(K_i, L_i, KH_i)\Phi(KH^a) \tag{9}$$

Following Arrow's approach we assume that investment is both cause and vehicle of new technologies. This means that the capital stock can be read as a measure of the knowledge available in a firm or an economy. In this case the aggregate production function is

$$Y = F(K, L)\Phi(K) \tag{10}$$

There are different possibilities to apply this line of reasoning in an endogenous growth model. For example, Romer (1986), who based his seminal paper explicitly on Arrow's concept of learning by doing, assumed that knowledge is the driving force of economic growth, since it is characterised by an increasing marginal product when it is used as an input in the production of final output. Another way to integrate the idea of externalities is the approach of Lucas (e.g. 1988). He introduces human capital as an additional factor of production that raises the productivity of other inputs, like labour and capital. Better-qualified workers can use tools and machines more productive. As the marginal returns to human capital are diminishing, another factor must cause endogenous growth. For this purpose, Lucas stated that human capital reveals constant marginal returns in the production of human capital. The incentive to invest and therefore the driving force of economic growth are located in the human capital sector. Due to this assumption, growth of per capita income exists, and investment is maintained, as long as the return on investment exceeds the rate of time preference. As a result, thriftiness forces growth, i.e. lowering the time preference leads to higher growth rates. The efficiency in the human capital sector is therefore decisive for long-run growth. As soon as the marginal productivity of human capital would converge to zero, per capita growth would peter out. Again, investment drives growth. The deepening of human capital does not decline, but drives up per capita income steadily because of the quasi-AK-production technology in the human capital sector. However, growth depends on some arbitrary assumptions: Why should human capital show constant marginal returns?

The third important group of endogenous growth models deals with the implications of product innovations on economic growth and takes up Schumpeter's idea of creative destruction. The basics for these kinds of models were laid by Romer (1990), Grossman and Helpman (1991) and Aghion and Howitt (1992a,b, 1998). In the case of consumer goods new products increase the utility of households, as investment goods they raise productivity in the final good sector. As in Romer's model of 1986 positive externalities of research and development are assumed. Each new product enriches the know-how used in the research sector making future research efforts more efficient. Furthermore, successful innovators realise extra profits for they obtain at least a temporary monopoly. As long as these profits are higher than the costs of research and development, firms will invest to invent new products. The more goods an economy has designed in the past, the more efficient researchers will be in the future.

A good example for this line of reasoning can be found in Romer's model of 1990. New designs of capital goods, respectively, new knowledge ($\dot{A}$) is a function of the stock of knowledge already available (A) and the amount of human capital (H^A) used in the research sector[9]

$$\dot{A} = \varepsilon H^A A \tag{11}$$

In the steady-state per capita output as well as the number of capital goods (and knowledge) grow with an identical rate

$$\hat{y} = \hat{A} = \varepsilon H^A \tag{12}$$

Since know-how shows constant marginal returns in the development of new designs and implies a cost-reducing effect, the incentive to do research and development does not shrink. Again, intertemporal externalities are a necessary precondition for long-run per capita income growth caused by an increasing capital–labour ratio measured in knowledge per head.

Besides all differences between the approaches of endogenous growth theory, there is a common element. Capital deepening is a necessary condition for growth. Workers must be equipped with an increasing stock of capital. Herewith, capital is a catch-all variable for all kinds of factors of production that can be accumulated: knowledge, physical capital or human capital. Growth is investment-driven. Even so, most models lack an independent investment function. Postkeynesian economists stressed especially this shortcoming when they challenged the traditional neoclassical growth theory in the late 1950s and 1960s. Usually, investors are *auxiliary persons* of the households because they will invest as much as households are willing to save. The next section will focus on this criticism and the alternative approach of Kaldor and others to handle endogenous growth in a Postkeynesian setting.

A Kaldorian explanation of endogenous growth

Long before new growth theory challenged the neoclassical growth theory based on Solow's model of 1956, Postkeynesian authors criticised the assumptions and findings of this approach. Certainly, Nicholas Kaldor was one of the most influential opponents of neoclassical growth theory. In the late 1950s and early 1960s, he (and J. Mirrlees) developed the so-called technical progress function that relates productivity growth to investment. Since new knowledge is embodied in new capital goods, one cannot differentiate between productivity growth that is induced by technological change or by an increasing capital–labour ratio. Investment per capita is accompanied by the introduction of new techniques because in general the application of a new technology requires more input of capital per worker. Furthermore, each increase in the capital–labour ratio is a vehicle of technical progress, as new machines incorporate up-to-date knowledge and are more productive than older ones. In addition, investment normally implies the reorganization of production processes and offers the possibility and the necessity to learn. Consequently, each movement along the neoclassical production function will also shift the function itself (see Kaldor 1957: 595–6). Assuming exogenous technical progress is therefore too much a simplification.

Kaldor presented several vintages of this concept (e.g. 1957, 1961, 1962 (together with Mirrlees)). In the first vintage of the technical progress functions the growth rate of labour productivity ($\hat{\pi}_t$) depends on the growth rate of the capital–labour ratio ($\hat{K}_t - \hat{L}_t$)

$$\hat{\pi}_t = F(\hat{K}_t - \hat{L}_t) \quad \text{with } F(0) > 0 \text{ and } F'(\hat{K}_t - \hat{L}_t) > 0$$

$$\text{and } F''(\hat{K}_t - \hat{L}_t) < 0 \tag{13}$$

Despite his criticism of the concept of exogenous technical progress, Kaldor assumes that productivity grows even in the absence of investment due to organisational improvements as well as newly developed concepts and knowledge. The position of the technical progress function depends on the so-called *technical dynamism* of a society. Besides the effects discussed above, this variable is influenced by the willingness and the ability to change and to adopt new technologies. Unfortunately, Kaldor is not very precise with regard to this variable. However, it reminds very much of the idea of *social capability* as discussed later in the catching-up debate started by Abramovitz (1986). The slope of the technical progress function depends on the ability to use new technologies. Kaldor assumes this capability to decline with increasing growth rates of the capital–labour ratio. Thus, a concept of declining returns to accumulation is presumed. The existence of new ideas and technologies is only a necessary, but not a sufficient condition for productivity growth that exceeds the autonomous one.

How does growth take place? In accordance with Harrod's approach, Kaldor assumes that investors want to reach a constant capital–output ratio (v_w) and pursue the accelerator principle. Furthermore, investment depends on the entrepreneurs' expected profit rate. As long as the effective value (v_t) differs from v_w, entrepreneurs will adapt their investment decision. If v_t is smaller than v_w, investment will rise, i.e. the capital–labour ratio will grow faster. According to the technical progress function, this will result in further productivity growth and stimulate output growth. Due to the assumption that the induced growth rate of productivity is smaller than the initial growth rate of the capital–labour ratio, the system converges to an equilibrium where v_w is reached and the investors' expectations are met (see Kaldor 1961).[10] In the long run exogenous variables, i.e. parameters of the technical progress function, determine the growth rate of productivity in this equilibrium (see Kaldor 1961: 274; Kaldor and Mirrlees 1962: 178–80).

At first sight, Kaldor's contribution to growth theory seems to have added nothing significantly new to growth theory. However, the technical progress function has one important feature that makes a major difference compared to the neoclassical approach. As mentioned above, the position of the technical progress function as well as its slope reflects the technical dynamism of an economy. This variable is endogenous and depends on the previous investment activity. Especially, jumps in investment may change technical dynamism. Consequently, technical dynamism is path-dependent and history matters, while the neoclassical approach lacks history. Moreover, Kaldor focuses on the importance of investment decisions. Investors decide on their own and do not behave as slaves owned by consumers. Their expectations as well as their ideas about the warranted capital–output ratio determine investment.

In his later work, Kaldor still based his research on stylised facts. In his inaugural lecture at the University of Cambridge, he referred to Verdoorn's law that states a positive correlation between productivity growth ($\hat{\pi}$) and production growth ($\hat{Y}$) (see Kaldor 1966). Productivity growth is endogenous with regard to production growth.

$$\hat{\pi}_t = a + b\hat{Y}_t \quad \text{with } 1 > b > 0 \tag{14}$$

From Kaldor's point of view, the manufacturing sector is the engine of growth due to increasing returns to scale in this sector. One percentage point of growth in this setor contributes more to overall growth than one percentage point of growth in the primary or tertiary sector. Thus, higher growth rates in manufacturing will accelerate overall growth. If manufacturing were characterised by constant returns to scale, then output growth would not induce productivity to grow. Regression analysis gave evidence that in Verdoorn's law (b) is significantly bigger than zero.[11] The reasons for this relation are static and dynamic returns to scale. The former are the consequence of diminishing unit costs due to fixed costs, the latter accrue because of learning by doing and the introduction of new capital goods. Additionally, growth in one sector favours the genesis of new sectors. Using a conveyor belt will only make sense if a firm produces many cars. As the market for cars expands, a new industry that produces assembly lines emerges and offers new possibilities to realise economies of scale as well as further productivity growth. Economies that are able to increase the demand for manufactured goods may achieve high growth rates. Evidently, Kaldor's line of reasoning is succeeding the ones of Adam Smith, Alfred Marshall and Allyn Young (1928).[12]

The assumption of increasing returns to scale has another implication. A process of cumulative causation might set in. Increased productivity leads to higher real incomes. The reaction of demand depends on the income elasticity of demand. When the growth rate of demand rises, further productivity growth might occur. Here, Kaldor's analysis is all-Kenyesian. Multiplier and accelerator lead to a cumulative circle as in Harrod's model.[13] Yet, there is a major difference. While in Harrod's approach investment only expands the capacity to produce because of more capital goods, in Kaldor's line of reasoning investment also raises productivity because of Verdoorn's law and the technical progress function. Here, we have the link to Kaldor's earlier papers on growth. The existence of a process of cumulative causation depends therefore on the interplay between productivity and production growth.

Yet, cumulative causation requires a feedback from productivity growth on demand and production growth, respectively. Verdoorn's law only secures that production growth will lead to productivity growth. Obviously, productivity growth will also lead to further growth of demand. One can think of several channels how higher productivity can increase demand. First, productivity determines the level of real wages. When the efficiency of the input factors rises, either prices may fall or wages increase in a competitive economy. However, productivity may reduce in the short run the demand for labour, when output grows with a lower rate as productivity does.[14] Less demand for labour will reduce the income of households and therefore consumption. Technical progress is therefore double-sided. In addition, technical progress will induce structural change, since according to Engel's law households will change their behaviour. The income elasticity of demand determines how the consumption pattern will adapt to increasing incomes. Moreover, technical progress does not only lead to process innovation, but also to product innovations. New goods will influence the structure of consumption, too. Old goods will disappear, while new ones will emerge.[15] Thus, the net effect of productivity growth on consumption is rather ambiguous. Second, productivity growth can lead to higher profits that might be invested. Furthermore, if entrepreneurs expect demand to grow and face capacity constraints they will raise investment. The third important element of demand are net exports. Higher productivity levels improve the international competitiveness with regard to prices. Despite reduced costs of production caused by increased efficiency, the net effect is vague. The labour costs per unit decide on competitiveness. Hereby, any increase in wages counters the productivity effects. Hence, there is also no clear answer to the question, whether productivity growth will induce additional demand or not. Overall, it is not productivity alone that determines demand, but wages and profits. Thereby, labour market institutions, e.g. regulations and/or power of trade unions are decisive. A regression of production growth on productivity growth can be read as a reduced form of a multi-equation model that covers the relations discussed above. This could be called a demand regime. In this interpretation, Verdoorn's law is an expression of endogenous technical progress that has several causes. Besides increasing returns to scale, investment-driven technical progress as covered by the technical progress function or discussed in new growth theory, may result in Verdoorn's law. Furthermore, demand might induce technical progress, too. More demand as well as changes in preferences lead firms to invest in research and development.[16]

The combination of the demand regime with Verdoorn's law represents a simple model of cumulative causation. Here, both stable and instable growth paths are possible, depending on the feedback and spillover effects between production and productivity growth. The system can converge to a stable growth rate or to a situation of falling growth rates and rising growth rates, respectively. Thus, only empirics can give evidence to the question which system applies in reality.[17]

Comparison

As shown above, Kaldor's idea of endogenous technical progress is related to modern neoclassical growth theory. For example, the first passage of Kaldor's paper of 1957 reads like the introduction of a paper on new growth theory:

> But more recently, there has been an increasing awareness of the fact that neither the proportion of income saved nor the growth of productivity per man (...) are independent variables with respect to the rate of increase in production; and that the actual rate of progress of a capitalist economy is the outcome of the mutual interaction of forces which can adequately be represented only in the form of simple functional relationships rather than by constants.
>
> (Kaldor 1957: 591)

A first common feature is the intention to explain the growth dynamics we can observe in reality. Kaldor started his consideration of growth theory with his famous list of stylised facts which should be explained by a theoretical model: (i) constant, positive growth of output and labour productivity, (ii) constant growth of the capital–labour ratio, (iii) a constant rate of profit, (iv) a constant capital–output ratio, (v) a close correlation between the investment rate and the share of profits and (vi) greater differences between the growth rates of labour productivity in different countries which are related with the investment rate and the share of profits (see Kaldor 1961: 230–1). Romer (1994) offers a list of modern stylised facts: (i) there are many firms in a market economy, (ii) discoveries can be used by different persons at the same time, (iii) physical activities can be replicated, (iv) technological advance is the result of activity and (v) many individuals and firms have market power and earn monopoly rents on discoveries (see Romer 1994: 12–13).

In both Kaldor's papers and the papers of new growth theory, investment respectively, the increase in the capital–labour ratio is seen as the most important determinant of long-run growth. Kaldor's critique of neoclassical growth theory mentioned above seems to have influenced the thinking of some neoclassical economists even if they still stick to a lot of assumptions and tools criticised not only by Postkeynesian economists. Since investment plays a crucial role in economic growth processes it is astonishing that the new neoclassical models still lack an investment function. Following the neoclassical tradition, saving determines investment. Investors only fulfil the households' wishes and in contrast to Kaldor's view do not decide on investment by themselves. This shortcoming limits the applicability of these models to reality. In this context, Kaldor's combination of technical progress function with an independent investment function offers more insights.

In both approaches, investment induces productivity growth by installing new technologies and by positive externalities. These common characteristics imply a second important feature. The long-run growth rate is path-dependent for activities of former generations influence the productivity of present and future capital accumulation. Concerning the technical progress function, this statement manifests itself in the relation between the flow of investment and the technical dynamism of an economy. The more technical dynamism an economy has acquired in the past, the more productivity growth is induced by a given growth rate of investment. With regard to the new growth theory, we find this feature e.g. in the assumption that productivity of research and development is positively related to the number of former inventions. Because neoclassical theory focuses exclusively on the supply side of growth, another element of path-dependency is not covered. For example, if firms expect less demand, they will reduce investment or stop to invest completely. Referring to modern growth theory, this implies less technical progress, since less external effects can be realised. Consequently, potential output growth falls. Thus, cyclical and long-run developments cannot be separated. The integration of the demand side and short-run relations as modelled in Postkeynesian approaches would enrich the analysis of growth. The reconciliation of neoclassical growth theory to Kaldor's line of reasoning seems to be a first step towards an integration of approaches separated so far.

Summing up: lessons for economic policy?

The analysis of economic growth is not only of interest for theoretical aspects but also for the foundation of economic policy. Summing up our discussion, which conclusions can we draw for economic policy? First, both approaches reveal the importance of investment. Thus, fostering growth would imply supporting investment. Keeping in mind the findings of endogenous growth theory, the accumulation of human capital as well as research and development should be stimulated. This statement is backed up by the fact that all modern economies are said to change from an industry to an information society where lifelong learning and knowledge become more and more decisive determinants for the competitiveness of firms and their workers.

Obviously, Kaldor's approach offers more help than new growth theory. While the models of the latter show the consequences of investment on growth, the former analyses the determinants of investment, too. Only if we know more about the variables influencing the behaviour of investors successful economic policy is possible. Therefore, a combination of both points of views would be a solid foundation of growth policy.

Second, growth is always the result of demand and supply conditions. Therefore a one-sided concentration on demand or supply policy will not be successful. For example, if the government supports the development of new products, this may increase our knowledge but it is not sure that these innovations will create new markets. For this reason, economic policy has to assist market-oriented research projects to sustain growth and employment.

Third, growth and technical progress are always characterised by structural change and therefore by transaction costs. Especially unemployment has to be mentioned. In growth theory unemployment is considered as a short-run phenomenon of the business cycles that can be eliminated in a long-run analysis. However, reality teaches us that short-run phenomena show long-run consequences and vice versa. Thus, it seems to be meaningful to develop new models where short- and long-run problems are linked with each other. In this context, reflections on Harrod's papers as well as on Kaldor's later work on the empirics of growth would be very helpful for both economic theory and economic policy.

Notes

1 For a longer discussion of the neoclassical model see, e.g. Barro and Sala-i-Martin (1995).
2 Only in this case the Euler Theorem is met. See, e.g. Solow (2000: 367).
3 We abstract from depreciation.
4 Again a good presentation of the AK-model can be found in Barro and Sala-i-Martin (1995). For a critical discussion see, e.g. Kurz (1997).
5 Abstracting from exogenous technical progress, this is the rate of labour force growth.
6 The Solow model of 1956 was developed to avoid such disequilibria. Solow challenged the assumption made by his Postkeynesian predecessors that the capital–output ratio or better the capital productivity is constant.
7 Solow (2000: 367) refers in this context to the Lewis model of 1954. In this approach, labour supply was unlimited, so the productivity of capital was constant.
8 While it is not always easy to accept this statement with respect to machines, considering the technical progress in software gives some evidence to it. New releases of word processors or spreadsheet applications are normally based on the experience gained when working with the former releases.
9 Here ε is an efficiency parameter.
10 See also Kubota (1968) and Kaldor (1970). Later Skott (1989) discussed the necessary conditions of a stable equilibrium.
11 See for a discussion e.g. Thirlwall (1983) and Hagemann and Seiter (1999).
12 Allyn Young whose classes Kaldor attended at the LSE explained clearly the relation between the division of labour, the extent of the market and the genesis of new industries. More or less, the extent of the market determines the extent of the market.
13 Kaldor refers in this context to Myrdal (1957) who was convinced that instable growth paths were more probable than the stable equilibrium paths discussed in neoclassical growth theory.
14 If Verdoorn's law is valid, productivity growth will exceed production growth as long as the latter is smaller than $a/(1 - b)$.

15 Pasinetti (1981, 1993) dealt with these developments and showed the conditions that must be met to reach full employment when technical progress manifests itself as product innovations.
16 Here one has to refer to the contribution of Schmookler (1966). See for these relations especially Boyer and Petit (1989 and 1991) and Targetti (1992).
17 Several papers of Boyer and Petit (1989, 1991) discuss this model and give empirical results. See also Pini (1995).

References

Abramovitz, M. (1986) 'Catching up, Forging Ahead, and Falling Behind', *Journal of Economic History*, 46: 385–406.

Aghion, Ph. and Howitt, P. (1992a) 'A Model of Economic Growth Through Creative Destruction', *Econometrica*, 60: 323–51.

—— (1992b) 'The Schumpeterian Approach to Technical Change and Growth' in H. Siebert (ed.), *Economic Growth in the World Economy*, Tübingen: Mohr (Siebeck): 55–76.

—— (1998) *Endogenous Economic Growth*, Cambridge, Mass.: MIT Press.

Arrow, K.J. (1962) 'The Economic Implications of Learning by Doing', *Review of Economic Studies*, 29: 155–73.

Barro, R.J. and Sala-i-Martin, X. (1995) *Economic Growth*, New York: McGrawHill.

Boyer, R. and Petit, P. (1989) 'The Cumulative Growth Model Revisited', *Political Economy: Studies in the Surplus Approach*, 4: 23–43.

—— (1991) 'Technical Change, Cumulative Causation and Growth: Accounting for the Contemporary Productivity Puzzle with Some Post Keynesian Theories', in OECD (ed.), *Technology and Productivity: The Challenge for Economic Policy, The Technology Economy Programme*, Paris: OECD: 47–67.

Domar, E.D. (1946), 'Capital Expansion, Rate of Growth and Employment', *Econometrica*, 14: 137–47.

Grossman, G.M. and Helpman, E. (1991) *Innovation and Growth in the Global Economy*, Cambridge, Mass.: MIT Press.

Hagemann, H. and Seiter, S. (1999) 'Verdoorn's Law', in Ph.A. O'Hara (ed.), *Encyclopedia of Economic Growth*, London/New York: Routledge: 1228–31.

Harrod, R.F. (1939) 'An Essay in Dynamic Theory', *Economic Journal*, 49: 14–33.

Jones, L.E. and Manuelli, R.E. (1990) 'A Convex Model of Equilibrium Growth: Theory and Policy Implications', *Journal of Political Economy*, 98: 1008–38.

Kaldor, N. (1957) 'A Model of Economic Growth', *Economic Journal*, 67: 591–624.

—— (1961) 'Capital Accumulation and Economic Growth' in F.A. Lutz and D.C. Hague (eds), *The Theory of Capital*, London, New York, reprinted in E. Targetti and A.P. Thirlwall (eds), *The Essential Kaldor*: 229–81.

—— (1966) *Causes of the Slow Rate of Economic Growth in the United Kingdom*, Inaugural Lecture at the University of Cambridge, Cambridge: Cambridge University Press.

—— (1970) 'Some Fallacies in the Interpretation of Kaldor', *Review of Economic Studies*, 37: 1–7.

—— and Mirrlees, J.A. (1962) 'A New Model of Economic Growth', *Review of Economic Studies*, 29: 172–92.

Kubota, K. (1968) 'A Re-examination of the Existence and Stability Propositions in Kaldor's Growth Models', *Review of Economic Studies*, 35: 353–60.

Kurz, H.D. (1997) 'What Could the "New Growth Theory Teach Smith and Ricardo?" ', *Economic Issues*, 2: 1–20.

Lucas, R.E. Jr. (1988) 'On the Mechanics of Economic Development', *Journal of Monetary Economics*, 22: 3–42.

Meade, J.E. (1962) *A Neoclassical Theory of Economic Growth*, 2nd edn, London: Unwin University Books.

Myrdal, G. (1957) *Economic Theory and Underdeveloped Regions*, London: Duckworth.

Pasinetti, L.L. (1981) *Structural Change and Economic Growth – A Theoretical Essay on the Dynamics of the Wealth of Nations*, Cambridge: Cambridge University Press.

—— (1993) *Structural Economic Dynamics – A Theory of the Economic Consequences of Human Learning*, Cambridge: Cambridge University Press.

—— (2000) 'Critique of the Neoclassical Theory of Growth and Distribution', *Banca Nationale del Lavoro Quarterly Review*, 53: 383–431.

Pini, P. (1995) 'Economic Growth, Technological Change and Employment: Empirical Evidence for a Cumulative Growth Model with External Causation for Nine OECD Countries; 1960–1990', *Structural Change and Economic Dynamics*, 6: 185–213.

Rebelo, S. (1991) 'Long Run Policy Analysis and Long Run Growth', *Journal of Political Economy*, 99: 500–21.

Romer, P.M. (1986) 'Increasing Returns and Long-Run Growth', *Journal of Political Economy*, 94: 1002–37.

—— (1987) 'Crazy Explanations for the Productivity Slowdown', in St. Fisher (ed.), *National Bureau of Economic Research Annual 1987*, Cambridge, Mass.: MIT Press: 163–202.

—— (1990) 'Endogenous Technical Change', *Journal of Political Economy*, 98: S71–102.

—— (1994) 'The Origins of Endogenous Growth', *Journal of Economic Perspectives*, 8: 3–22.

Schmookler, L. (1966) *Invention and Economic Growth*, Cambridge, Mass.: Harvard University Press.

Skott, P. (1989) *Kaldor's Growth and Distribution Theory*, Frankfurt am Main: Peter Lang.

Solow, R.M. (1956) 'A Contribution to the Theory of Economic Growth', *Quarterly Journal of Economics*, 70: 65–94.

—— (2000) 'The Neoclassical Theory of Growth and Distribution', *Banca Nationale del Lavoro Quarterly Review*, 53: 349–81.

Swan, T.W. (1956) 'Economic Growth and Capital Accumulation', *Economic Record*, 32: 334–61.

Targetti, F. (1992) *Nicholas Kaldor: The Economics and Politics of Capitalism as a Dynamic System*, Oxford: Clarendon Press.

Thirlwall, A.P. (1983) 'A Plain Man's Guide to Kaldor's Growth Laws', *Journal of Post Keynesian Economics*, 5: 345–58.

4 Does finance matter for growth?

The new growth theory facing the East Asian 'productivity puzzle'

Flora Bellone and Muriel Dal-Pont

Introduction

How important are financial systems to the growth of nations? Despite intensive debates, this controversial issue has persisted over the years mainly for two reasons. First, until the last decade, there have been no successful attempts in modelling the mechanisms through which financial factors may influence growth.[1] Second, the first empirical studies documenting the positive correlation between financial development and economic growth left the interpretative problem of causality unresolved.[2]

Most recently, the finance–growth relationship has found an appropriate theoretical framework in which it can be modelled. Indeed, within the Endogenous Growth Paradigm, financial markets and intermediaries prove to be potentially significant growth-enhancing factors. Moreover, financial variables behave very well in the extensive literature on growth regressions, which has been produced in support of the New Growth Theory.[3] In this respect, King and Levine's contribution (1993a) represents a successful first attempt to use modern empirical tools in order to assert the robustness of the finance–growth relationship.

Analytically, it is common to present the New Growth Theory through its two distinct and successive generations of models: the first one, the so-called AK or *linear* approach of growth,[4] and the second one, labelled as the *neo-Schumpeterian* approach of growth.[5] Acknowledging this differentiation, it is fair to say that the finance–growth literature initially built on the first approach[6] and two reasons might explain this choice. First, the simplicity of the AK framework was considered as appropriate for the study of policy-oriented variables.[7] Second, the richness of the *neo-Schumpeterian* approach was firstly presented as a way to account for the micro-foundations of technological change without affecting much the aggregate implications revealed in the AK models. The way Levine (1997) presents his *functional*[8] survey of the finance–growth literature is quite illustrative of this view. According to the author, both these frameworks *respectively* bring to light one of the two main channels through which financial factors may affect growth, i.e. *capital accumulation* and *technological innovation*.[9]

For many economists both these engines of growth can only induce scepticism. Moreover, stating on this ground, an 'analytical bridge' between both classes of endogenous growth models proves to be misleading. Indeed, elsewhere in the literature (see, in particular Romer 1992, 1993 and Aghion and Howitt 1998), it has been supported that both categories of models should be seen as *competing* rather than complementary views of the working of growth process. Specifically, the necessity to discriminate between both approaches has been emphasised in relation to empirical evidences revealed by growth accounting works on the newly industrialised East Asian countries.[10] These evidences show that, despite some evident differentiation in magnitudes, the rapid growth of *all* these countries has proved to be correlated with high investment and saving rates *but not* with high *TFP* growth rates.

Surprisingly, this empirical productivity puzzle has scarcely been emphasised in relation to the finance–growth literature.[11] Yet, it strongly questions the models developed by such a literature. The caveats can be exposed as follows. If on one side, empirical evidences argue for capital accumulation as the key feature of East Asian growth experiences and if, on the other side, one claims that finance matters for growth, then one should identify a systematic link between financial development and both saving and investment, in these countries. As we shall see, such a link is however absent from theoretical explanations as well as from the large growth regressions analysis provided by the literature. Conversely, both of them strongly support the view that finance matters for growth mainly through its impact on *TFP* growth.

Does this mean that there has been a misidentification of transmission channels? Shall we conclude that finance did not really matter in the most successful growth experiences of the late twentieth century? The purpose of this chapter is to raise these issues. To this end, we have organised the finance–growth literature in a way which allows us to emphasise fundamental differences in the *causal structure* of the two generations of endogenous growth models: the *AK* ones which ascribe the *leading* role to capital accumulation in the growth process; alternatively, the *neo-Schumpeterian* ones which give this *leading* role to technological change. In this sense, our survey adds to the comprehensive previous ones of Pagano (1993) and Levine (1997). While it integrates the most recent models on the finance–growth issue, it also provides a 'comparative growth experiences' perspective in the light of which this literature might be evaluated meaningfully.[12] In order to keep this rather ambitious attempt into reasonable bounds, we restrict the scope of analysis on several grounds. First, we focus on models investigating the one-sided causality from finance to growth.[13] Second, we largely abstract from two important issues, namely, international finance and economic policy issues.[14] In the next section, we explain why the *AK* and the *neo-Schumpeterian* models tell different stories on 'why finance matters for growth'. Both competing frameworks are then evaluated in the light of the East-Asian productivity puzzle. In the third section, we expose a more recent literature relating the *structures* of the financial system to the *stages of growth*. These growth stages are crucially distinguished according to the relative importance of technological change and capital accumulation in *driving* the expansion of industries. We then evaluate whether or not these new contributions offer a better understanding of the productivity puzzle. Finally, we suggest that finance is likely to play a significant causal role in specific episodes of *growth regimes*[15] *shifts*. Departing from the view that conceives financial systems as strict *optimising-growth* factors, the last section underlines their *causal* role in shaping growth patterns.

Financial development and growth rates

Oversimplifying the opposition between the *AK* growth approach and the *neo-Schumpeterian* one, one can say that the first approach stresses the capacity of countries to maintain high saving and investment rates while the second one stresses learning about, risking to operate, and coming to master technologies and other practices that are new to the country, if not to the world.[16] This is not to say, however, that in an *AK* framework, technological improvements are not of concern or, alternatively, that in a *neo-Schumpeterian* one, physical capital accumulation might not have any impact on long-run growth. As it will soon appear, the important point is that these two broad classes of models differ in their *causal structure* and in the hints they give about 'how to do it'.

Two competing views of 'why finance matters for growth'

Beginning with the *AK* models, while their main focus is on the accumulation of basic production factors, efficiency gains may also be an important part of the story. Indeed, this is because technology is assumed to improve automatically in proportion to capital, that this other determinant counteracts the effects of diminishing returns.

Considering such an accumulation-driven development process, as Pagano (1993) clearly emphasises, financial factors matter a lot if one can prove that those factors can contribute to *mobilising* internal savings and to *directing* them *efficiently* towards investment. Moreover, in such a growth story, the question of whether developing countries can expect to attract large inflows of foreign capital in order to complement internal saving may also be of primary concern.[17]

In such a setting, the first meaningful insight that has been achieved by the new finance and growth literature is that financial factors are important through the channel of improving the *efficiency* of saving and investment *but not* through the channel of increasing the quantity of saving and investments. This result emerges from a large variety of models[18] and holds *whatever* the function performed by the financial system or *whatever* the nature of the institutions performing the function (banks or financial markets). Indeed, in all the *AK* style models, it is the presence of externalities *à la* Romer (1986) that allows the productivity gains to translate into higher steady-state growth rates. And, in all these models, due to the well-known income and substitution effects of higher returns, the sign of the relationship between financial development and saving is ambiguous.[19]

Looking further for empirical evidence, the proponents of this literature confirmed this first insight. Specifically, Beck *et al.* (1999),[20] focusing on the role of banking sector development, find that:

> The data do not confidently suggest that higher levels of banking sector development promote growth by boosting the long-run rate of physical capital. We found similarly conflicting results on savings. [...] In sum, the results are consistent with the Schumpeterian view of finance and development: banks affect economic development primarily by influencing *TFP* growth.
>
> (Beck *et al.* 1999: 6)

This missing, or at least ambiguous, link between finance and capital accumulation appears even strongly in the specific field of the finance–growth literature which focuses on the analysis of financial reforms.[21] And once more, this result is confirmed by recent empirical works, as the one carried out by Bandiera *et al.* (2000)[22] and reaching the conclusion that:

> For the present, our results must be taken as an indication that there is no firm evidence that financial liberalisation will increase saving. Indeed, under some circumstances, liberalisation has been associated with a fall in saving. All in all, it would be unwise to rely on an increase in private savings as the channels through which financial liberalisation can be expected to increase growth.
>
> (Bandierra *et al.* 2000: 21)

Can international finance exert a stronger influence on the rate of capital formation in these models? Surprisingly, the finance–growth literature remained silent on the matter. Today, however, it is well established that one of the most striking features of the basic *AK* framework is to make capital flow in the 'wrong' direction, i.e. from the poor to the rich countries.[23] And once more, this logical point applies to all the models surveyed above. This leads Krugman (1993: 18) to conclude that 'the New Growth Theory does not offer any comfort to those who think that international financial integration is very good for development'.

In such models, however, one possibility that could change the view of how international capital flows can contribute to the growth of developing countries, is to depart from the view according to which foreign capital is a perfect substitute for domestic capital. The reason why foreign and domestic capitals can be heterogeneous is if technology differs between countries. Making such an assumption in an *AK* framework may appear rather *ad hoc*; nonetheless, once done, it may make the role of foreign capital far more impressive. Indeed, in such a context, foreign capital will have an impact on growth that might largely exceed the previously discussed impact through the capital accumulation channel.

Building on this idea and documenting its formal modelling by a detailed case study of Mauritius, Romer (1992) shows how foreign capital inflows may in fact become the cornerstone of a development story primarily driven by accumulation.[24] However, as clearly demonstrated by Romer, the Mauritius experience is a typical example of a growth story which is *not* driven by technological change. Building on the Taiwanese experience in order to document such an alternative development story, Romer points out that, in contrast, premature openness of the capital account may inhibit rather than boost the development process. And indeed, under the crucial assumptions of the *neo-Schumpeterian* view, without an explicit mechanism through which domestic firms can *learn* by their interactions with foreign ones, no meaningful guidance concerning the likelihood of an openness policy to international capital markets can be made.[25]

This cursory entry into the international finance issue allows us to assess how important the discrepancies between the positive and normative implications of the *AK* approach to growth are compared to the *neo-Schumpeterian* one. It is now time to present more comprehensively the way finance may matter for growth in a *neo-Schumpeterian* growth approach. As already mentioned, those models have first been developed in abstracting from capital accumulation processes.[26] Labour (or human capital) is the only basic production factor, whose supply is generally supposed to be fixed exogenously. The steady-state growth rate is then a direct function of the proportion of labour *diverted from* production. In such a basic framework, *TFP* growth is thus the only source of output growth.

Moreover, as emphasised by Aghion and Howitt, 'In this framework, the relationship between finance and growth starts gaining substance once agency considerations are introduced as potential sources of capital markets imperfections', (Aghion and Howitt 1998: 71). Such kind of investigations has been pioneered by King and Levine (1993b).[27] Focusing on the microeconomic behaviours characterising the relationships between the researchers – the entrepreneurs in King and Levine's words – and the financial system, their model combines two Schumpeterian ideas. The first one is that the dynamics of innovation depends on the dynamics of profit.[28] The second one is that financial institutions play an important but also very active role since they evaluate and finance entrepreneurs in their initiation of the risky innovative activity. Thus, it is the financial system which determines – or at least, strongly influences[29] – the decisions to engage in innovation. Moreover, in abandoning the assumption that utility is linear in consumption – which, in the model of Aghion and Howitt, removed any motive to use capital markets for a risk-sharing – financial system becomes desirable to provide means for individuals and entrepreneurs to diversify the risk inherent in the activity of innovation.

Such a new focus on innovation opens meaningful new doors for understanding the causality between finance and growth. First, it leads to put the emphasis on the *informational* role of financial systems through an *ex-ante selection* function[30] and an *evaluation* of returns function.[31] Second, it produces more insights on the differentiated role that can have different financial institutions.

In this respect, the model features a *functional complementarity* between banks and financial markets. On the one side, banks help to select entrepreneurs and to mobilise funds, on the other side, financial markets to diversify the risks and reveal the expected profits from innovation. Specifically, interpreting their model as that of a developed country, King and Levine present their financial intermediary as a venture capital firm which funds starting-up innovative activity in exchange of most of the firm's stocks. When the venture capital firm learns on the capacity of the entrepreneur to produce a marketable innovation, bank sells off the shares on a stock market.[32]

With the above reference to the working of developed financial systems, such a model could be seen as being appropriate only for dealing with the dynamics of industrialised countries. However, recognising that the assimilation of foreign technology is an activity much closer to innovation than to production ones, there is no reason why finance may not matter for the growth of developing countries by the same channels emphasised here.[33] And, in fact, although the model requires that property rights are clearly defined and enforced, a formal stock exchange need not exist. For example, the venture capital firm could be part of a larger financial conglomerate providing the risk-pooling and firm-evaluation activities, which are given by the stock market in the model.

Consequently, the important point remains that, putting the emphasis on the specificity of innovative-type activities, the *neo-Schumpeterian* growth approach explicitly considers that these activities need an intentional allocation of resources. In such a context, the crucial role of finance has to be thought of in relation to the ability of the country *to divert* resources from production of goods and services towards the more risky activity of assimilation and production of technological change. This view radically breaks with the *AK* approach where technological improvements occur automatically as production activities are efficiently carried out.

The East Asian productivity puzzle

Proving that the contribution of *TFP* growth to the success of the Asian Tigers has only been minor,[34] conventional growth accounting works strongly challenge both the *AK* and the *neo-Schumpeterian* approaches of development, and consequently, both views of 'why finance matters for growth'. Considering first the *AK* models, it becomes quite obvious that the only way for financial factors to be convincingly related to this productivity puzzle is as growth-*inhibiting* (and *not* growth-*enhancing*) factors. Indeed, one way of 'reconciling' high investment and saving rates with poor efficiency performance is to find factors affecting negatively the efficiency of investment without affecting much the rate of capital accumulation. This is exactly what financial factors do in the previously surveyed *AK* models However, to support such kind of explanation requires the finding of evidence on the relative inefficiency of financial systems in the East Asian countries.[35] Moreover, it has the unwilling implication that one has to accept the idea that growth rates can maintain themselves to very high levels for many decades despite an inefficient or non-liberalised financial system.

Considering next the *neo-Schumpeterian* framework, at first sight, this approach appears even less suitable than the *AK* one to address the East Asian productivity puzzle. Indeed, abstracting from the impact of financial factors on the rate of capital formation, such models cannot explain the impact of these factors outside the *TFP* growth channel. Once more then, the only solution is to find reasons according to which financial factors did not boost *TFP* growth rates in East Asian countries, and this without affecting the saving rates which must have been maintained high for other *unexplained* reasons.

One way to deal with this puzzle is to assert that the role of the financial system as stimulating innovative activities only matters for developed countries. Such a view could be justified on the ground that, *contrary* to what the proponents of the *neo-Schumpeterian* framework advocate, their models are not appropriate for dealing with development processes. And indeed, if one accepts abandoning the idea that assimilation processes are close to innovation ones, a rationalisation of the productivity puzzle could be as follows: the causality from finance to *TFP* growth is strong in later stages of development, once innovation is becoming an important source of growth, but weak in earlier stages when innovation does not matter. Such a kind of explanation may even find indirect empirical support in recent works on the link between financial and industrial structures:[36]

> It might have been expected at the outset that it would be hard to establish relations between country [financial] structure and R&D expenditure and comparatively easy to find relations with fixed capital formation since the former are frequently intangible and the latter tangible. In fact we find just the converse: we can explain a significant amount of cross-industry and cross-country variation in R&D expenditure and very little of fixed capital formation. Why is that?
>
> (Carlin and Mayer 2000: 27)

However, it remains at odds not only with previous analysis of the causality puzzle as the comprehensive one pioneered by Patrick (1966),[37] but also with more recent attempts to directly test the idea that the causality between finance and growth could be sensitive to the financial structure and the financial policies. Indeed, in this literature (see in particular Arestis and Demetriades 1996) it is advocated that 'the causality between financial intermediation and economic growth is likely to be either from finance to growth or bi-directional in the case of "Bank-based" systems. In the case of "Capital-market-based" systems, it is expected to be from growth to finance' (Arestis and Demetriades 1996: 6). Yet, acknowledging that 'bank-based' systems prevail more importantly in developing countries compared to developed ones, such a view could reinforce Patrick (1966) according to whom the causality from finance to growth should be stronger in developing countries.

Overall, the relatively 'bad' performance of the basic *neo-Schumpeterian* framework must not be taken as the end of the story. Indeed, in opening the door to investigations of the links between *financial* and *industrial* structures, these first models have induced a new round in the modelling of the finance–growth relationship, which explicitly distinguishes different *growth stages*.[38] These new models acknowledge the three following features: first, that stages of growth differ according to the relative importance of production activities and innovative-type ones; second, that the financial functions required in each type of activities also differ in substantial ways, and third, that different financial systems perform different financial functions more of less efficiently. Then, it may be worthwhile to look for a sensitivity of the finance–growth relationship to growth stages. Such a new line of inquiry then allows progress on several fronts. First, it brings the organisational aspects of financial systems to the core of the analysis. Second, it leads to discriminate between different causal mechanisms in the finance–growth relationship depending on growth stages. The strengths and weaknesses of this new round of models are evaluated in the next section.

Financial structures and stages of development

In the course of economic development, countries need to reassert their financial institutions. Specifically, a historical sequence involving financial structure and the level of output can be presented as follows: as output grows, financial intermediaries get larger, banks grow relatively to the Central Bank in allocating credit, non-banks intermediaries grow in importance, and, finally, stock markets become larger (Levine 1997). However, some authors have pointed out that this common earlier experience of developed countries should not be considered as a benchmark for the yet-industrialising countries. Specifically, developing countries could choose to rely earlier on financial markets. Indeed, since developed countries have pioneered the structural evolution and then have paid the cost of being the 'innovators' in the financial sectors as well as in the real ones, developing countries could learn from this past experience in opting from the beginning for 'the best financial system'.

Such kind of arguments has then led to a resurgence of the banks *versus* financial markets debate. However, as already emphasised, no clear assessment of the superiority of one institution over the other has emerged from the previously surveyed literature. Conversely, the functional approach privileged in this literature clearly reveals that each of these institutions could perform efficiently each of the broad classes of financial functions.[39] Moreover, none of them can be thought of as systematically performing better one or the other of those financial functions.[40] Most recently, the idea that the *most efficient financial system* may not be the same depending on the stage of development seems to have found new empirical and theoretical supports[41] through a new round of *neo-Schumpeterian* growth models based on the Soft Budget Constraint (SBC) approach. We focus here on models underlining specifically the informational problems associated with innovative investments on the line of Allen (1993).[42]

Towards an informational view

Reassessing the traditional arguments of the comparative analysis of financial systems performances, Allen concludes that 'stock markets systems have few advantages and a number of disadvantages when compared to bank-based systems' (Allen 1993: 88). He then argues that such a conclusion emerges because in presupposing a well-known production technology and an allocation resource issue which is static by nature, the standard analytical framework cannot capture all the benefits of stock markets. In contrast, taking into account the dynamics of innovation allows distinguishing the performances of financial institutions in relation to the type of activities carried out. On the one hand, banks have better performances when they finance industrial development that resorts on mature technologies' short gestation periods of investment and perfect competition. On the other hand, stock markets perform better when industrial development is based on fast technological change, and requires long construction periods of capital goods and when it takes place in an imperfect competition environment. More precisely, new technologies are characterised by the fact that they are hard to evaluate; first, because only little information is available and second, because information itself is difficult to interpret. Allen argues then that financial markets are the most efficient organisation when evidence based on experience is sparse and that, logically, one has to face a large *diversity of opinion* concerning future returns. Indeed, markets will fund uncertain projects, sanctioning rapidly the possible failures. More precisely, 'stocks markets work relatively well when there is little consensus on how a firm should be run since they provide checks that the manager's view of the production function is a sensible one' (Allen 1993: 104).

In order to provide theoretical benchmarks to his view, Allen puts the emphasis on the specificity of multi-lenders system characterised by the diversity of investors' beliefs. In such financial systems firms have a better chance to be financed. Nevertheless, when returns of projects are lower than expected, the multiplicity of beliefs does not favour new agreements among the different lenders concerning a potential additional financing or a reorganisation strategy. Such institutional arrangements produce then a favourable context in order to stop revealed inefficient projects. This idea is further developed by Allen and Gale (1998) who conclude that financial markets have considerable advantages when a new industry starts up and that among several kinds of uncertainty, investors have to face a high degree of uncertainty concerning the best management strategies to follow.[43]

Allen's view can then be summarised by the idea that for *each* kind of activities, there exists an optimal financial system structure. This view logically leads to the conclusion that bank-based systems are the most efficient form when countries' growth is promoted by the development of production activities based on well-known technologies. Alternatively, financial markets become clearly more efficient when the growth of economies is based on innovation. The soft budget constraint (SBC) literature develops the same idea while addressing explicitly the growth–finance relationship. In doing so, it offers an original approach and a better understanding of the East Asian productivity puzzle.

Centralised versus decentralised financial systems

The SBC is a phenomenon that was first identified and studied by J. Kornai.[44] That 'syndrome' is said to arise 'when a seemingly unprofitable firm is bailed out by the government or the enterprise's creditor' (Maskin 1999: 421). Building on this concept, the SBC literature offers a new perspective for the study of financial systems which consists in differentiating centralised and decentralised systems. The centralised financial system is seen as a simple representation for one bank or for few very important banks, i.e. characterised by a large size and a collective decision-making. Alternatively, the decentralised financial system is characterised by multi-investors and refers to financial markets or small banks next to financial markets, i.e. small size and individual decision-making investors. Such a distinction allows then to compare the capacities of alternative financial systems for selecting and funding growth-enhancing activities.

The core of the idea is that a SBC situation appears when 'the enterprise is not held to a fixed budget, but finds its budget constraint "softened" by the infusion of additional credit when it is on the verge of failure' (Maskin 1999: 421). Such a bank behaviour has been identified in the case of East Asian countries when, for instance, 'the state bank is unable to make a credible commitment not to refinance bad projects once some investments costs are sunk' (Qian 1994). Then, this literature compares the efficiency of both kinds of institutional arrangements in order to explain 'if' and 'how' they may lead to different selection and incentive processes through the lenders–borrowers relationship. Within the refinements of that literature we can distinguish two lines of research.

The first one tackles the issue of the East Asian financial crisis. In doing so however, this literature indirectly highlights the East Asian productivity puzzle. For instance, Bai and Wang (1999) explicitly explore a conjuncture according to which financial systems are the cornerstone for understanding an inefficient allocation characterised by high savings, high growth and high volatility.[45] In this model, a SBC situation driven by *government guarantees for large business*, cannot but lead to over-investments and misallocation of resources. In that perspective, the East Asian financial crisis is interpreted as the result of long-term accumulated problems in fundamentals, generated by financial institutional patterns systematically leading to the SBC phenomenon.

The second line of research followed by the SBC approach develops explicitly growth models and specifically focuses on the capacity of alternative systems to finance innovative projects.[46] A key assumption is then that it is necessary to invest in order to have information on innovation project. Consequently, the only way to reduce the uncertainties associated with R&D is to decide to finance it. Within that framework, models have been developed which underline two different consequences that the SBC phenomenon may have on growth. The first type of model focuses on the idea that innovations need a long gestation period in order to be developed. The second type of model emphasises the high degree of risk associated with innovation.

First, Amable and Chatelain (1995) argue that an SBC situation may have a positive impact on growth. They focus on the size effect associated with centralised–decentralised financial systems. They argue that in the decentralised system small-size investors can finance individually short-run projects (one period) but not the long-run projects (two periods), which are supposed to generate more innovations[47] when they are efficient.[48] In this model the problem occurs when, after one period, a project needs additional financing in order to generate returns.

At that exact moment nobody, except the borrower, knows if the project will be efficient or not. However, the first lender can incur a cost in order to reorganise the project, and then to increase the probability that the project will be an efficient one. It is then supposed by Amable and Chatelain that it is not easy for a small size lender to transmit its information on the probability of success of the project to another one. If the first lender cannot convince (an)other investor(s) to participate the refinancing of the long-run project, this means that it will be stopped whether it may be efficient or not. In contrast, if the size of the lender is large enough in order to support this additional financing, long-term projects will be all refinanced and this, whether they are efficient or not.[49] Large banks (i.e. a centralised system) finance both efficient and non-efficient long-run projects while a decentralised system only finances (efficient) short-run projects. The authors supposed that the amount of innovations generated by long-run projects (despite the proportion of inefficient ones) is higher than the one generated by the sole financing of short-run projects.[50] Without denying the decentralised systems efficiency in avoiding non-efficient projects, they emphasise their short-run perspective which may have negative effects on economic development.

The second model, due to Huang and Xu (1999), also focuses on the renegotiation problem but integrates ideas that are closer to Allen's view concerning the importance of lenders' heterogeneity. Alternatively to Amable and Chatelain's paper, the SBC situation may have a negative impact on technological innovation and thus growth. The authors focus here on the capacity of centralised *versus* decentralised financial systems to engage investment in risky (i.e. innovative) activities. In the modelled economy, the agent can choose between investing capital in the production of already existing good with no risk or in the research and development sector through projects which can be either efficient or non-efficient. Once again, in order to be effective, the *ex-post* selection process must be based on the commitment to stop every bad project 'even when refinancing the bad project is ex-post profitable' (Maskin 1999: 440). It is then shown that financial institutional arrangements are not neutral as some of them facilitate this screening mechanism, and thus better promote the innovation and growth process. Within such views, problems occur when the project is 'bad'. In this model, it is also assumed that reorganising a revealed inefficient project necessitates implementing a strategy. Huang and Xu suppose then that the choice of the strategy is easier with a single-investor system than with a multi-investors' one. Indeed, given the private nature of information and the possible conflicts of interest, liquidation may be better than reorganisation in a decentralised economy.

The main conclusion of the model is that a centralised (decentralised) system would be the optimal financing structure when the economy is characterised by low (high) uncertainty of innovative projects. In other words, these models underline that the financial systems that are most efficient for carrying out production activities based on well-known mature technologies are not organised in the same way as the financial systems which are most efficient for carrying out innovation activities. Such a view has found support in recent empirical studies such as that of Carlin and Mayer (2000). In this study, it is confirmed that stock-market-based systems may be suited for high-risk investment when budget constraints are important, and that banks perform better in financing more traditional activities: 'Institutional arrangements may therefore be associated with comparative advantage in undertaking certain activities even where they do not confer absolute advantage in overall activity' (Carlin and Mayer 2000: 2).

However, two main concerns can be emphasised as regards the SBC literature. First, this literature postulates rather than demonstrates that developing countries conduct less risky activities than developed ones. This view strongly contrasts with the original claim of the pioneers of the *neo-Schumpeterian* growth approach like Grossman and Helpman who introduce their 1991 book noting that:

> The process of assimilating existing technologies in the less developed countries is not unlike that of creating entirely new technologies in the developed world. In each case, learning requires an allocation of resources and investments respond to market incentives. Nor can we say a priori that the relative magnitudes of the learning efforts (compared to say, the size of the industrial base) differ greatly in the two contexts. Understanding intentional industrial innovation may be every bit as important to a theory of economic development as it is to a theory of growth in the industrialised economies.
>
> (Grossman and Helpman 1991: 13)

Consequently, identifying growth stages only by looking at the share of purely innovative projects may be a potentially misleading view. A second concern with the SBC literature is that it pushes one step further the finance–growth causality puzzle. Indeed, it remains to be investigated whether a financial system must, or must not, be already appropriately developed in order to promote innovative activities. If on the one side production activities based on mature technologies are better financed by centralised financial systems and if on the other side risky innovation activities are better funded by decentralised systems, what has a country to do which aims to increase the proportion of innovation activities? Should it begin by reforming its financial system? If the answer is positive, this means that financial institutions not only intervene in the entrepreneurial (or project) selection process (King and Levine 1993a,b) but also determine the emergence of innovation. An empirical case study of Malaysia, by Ghani and Suri (1999), already provided worthwhile hints on this causality issue. In this study, it is argued that some of the characteristics of development strategies, if they strongly sustain growth at the first stages, can reveal weaknesses in the long-run, especially as regards the innovative potential of the economy.

Looking for the determinants of the Malaysian growth,[51] the authors confirm the leading role of physical capital accumulation with a contribution averaging nearly 50 per cent (compared to the 20 per cent contribution of *TFP* growth). The investigation of bank lending and its sectoral distribution reveals that bank loans have strongly contributed to finance new investments in capital stock over the period 1971–97. The original finding comes from the negative correlation they exhibit between rapid growth in bank-lending and growth of total factor productivity.[52] The authors argue that such a rapid growth in bank-lending and the correlated low efficiency arose not only because of the guarantee provided by government but also because of 'the relative underdeveloped nature of capital markets in Malaysia' (Ghani and Suri 1999: 8). Indeed, they conclude:[53]

> While Malaysia managed to mobilize savings (both domestic and foreign) and the rapid growth in bank lending contributed to capital accumulation, it did not help raise productivity growth. Financial restraints, introduced in the form of negative directed lending, speed limits, and ceiling on lending to risky sectors, were not effective.
>
> (Ghani and Suri 1999: 11)

Thus, Ghani and Suri propose an analysis of the growth–finance relationship which underlines three original features: first, that banks contributed to growth but essentially through the accumulation channel; second, that such financial system functioning makes compatible high saving rates and low productivity levels; and third, that the rapid banking sector development associated with the underdevelopment of capital markets had a significant negative influence on *TFP* growth. In fact, that case study gives support to the idea that the financial system may be the first sphere to be reformed in order to shape the evolution of the real sphere, specifically in order to induce shifts between input-driven and productivity-driven growth regimes.

Research agenda and conclusion

In scrutinising the extensive literature on the East Asian growth experiences financial factors are scarcely put in the front of the explanation of these growth miracles. First, confronting the observed diversity of the financial institutions prevailing in the East Asian countries to the apparent common aggregate dynamics in terms of high saving, high investment and high growth doesn't give more confidence in the idea that finance has been a key ingredient of these industrialisation successes.[54] Second, the fact that all these economies crashed in the 1997 financial crisis has revealed weak financial systems rather than the wealthy ones one might have expected to have supported so many years of high growth. Third, and as primarily advocated in this chapter, the missing empirical relationship between finance and capital accumulation documented by the finance–growth literature, badly fits with the otherwise impressive relationship between capital accumulation and growth found for these countries.

To this end, we took as a starting point a clear analysis of the specificity of the financial factors role in the competing *AK* and *neo-Schumpeterian* growth approaches. In this assessment, the main advantage of the *neo-Schumpeterian* models over the more aggregated *AK* ones, has proved to be their explicit treatment of innovation as a distinct economic activity. More specifically, it turned out to be crucial for the finance–growth causality puzzle that the technology for producing knowledge is generally riskier and more time-consuming than the one for producing goods and services. On this respect, the new insights provided by this kind of models looking further for the links between the financial and the industrial *structures* are valuable.

And indeed, if, on the one side, the relative importance of production and innovation activities varies according to different industrial structures and if, on the other side, financial systems are not all alike in promoting one or the other type of activities, then one may partly resolve the productivity puzzle in advocating a *stages of growth* story. Such a view, however, reveals important limits. Until now, it left unresolved two questions. First, it neglects the question of the shift from one stage of growth to another stage, and of the importance of financial factors in such specific transition periods. Second, this view is not able to explain why, for a same stage of growth, financial structures may differ so much. In this sense, one may argue that differentiating growth stages should not be the end of the story. Instead, recognising the diversity of growth regimes appears as a promising line of research. And indeed, 'the growth experiences of developing countries are emphatically not all alike, and not just in how rapid (or slow) their average growth has been' (Pritchett 1999: 40). Conversely, one may better look for a diversity of growth regimes.

Acknowledging such a diversity, there are at least two promising empirical approaches to yield further insights into the finance–growth relationships. Both approaches ask to abandon cross-country analysis in favour of time-series ones. The first one may consist in focusing on specific *episodes* of the growth initiation. For example, Suto and James (1999) produce such an analysis of the early economic growth in the United States and Japan. Doing so, they succeed in reasserting a strong link between financial development and savings in these specific growth episodes. The second high potential lies in the analysis of growth episodes through the evolution of the possible growth determinants. Here, the Ghani and Suri (1999) paper on the determinants of the evolution of *TFP* in Malaysia, has proved to provide one of the most valuable insights on the role that financial factors may have played in the East Asian growth experiences. As far as data are available, to generalise such type of analyses to other developing countries may be a worthwhile investigation.

On the theoretical side, the finance–growth literature, which exclusively focused on steady-state growth paths, has faced its strongest limitations when addressing the economic policies issues and, more specifically, the ones related to financial reforms. Indeed, the finance–growth literature hardly produces normative guidance for the implementation of such reforms. In this perspective, a growth regimes approach may help explain why similar economic policies do not exert the same shaping effect on all countries' development. First of all, it could be the case that the impact of financial reforms is particularly sensitive to the *leading*-growth mechanism in each of the different growth regimes. Most importantly, however, it could be the case that the role of financial reforms as a development-*shaping* policy, has to be understood in relation with growth regimes *shifts* rather than with the increase or decrease of steady-state growth rates.

Acknowledgements

The authors wish to thank Philip Arestis and Harald Hagemann for their helpful comments and suggestions on an initial draft. Financial support within the Lavoisier programme of the French Foreign Department is gratefully acknowledged.

Notes

1 The first attempts built upon the seminal contributions of Gurley and Shaw (1955), Tobin (1965) and McKinnon (1973) and were restricted to the analysis of a money-growth nexus.
2 Goldsmith (1969), McKinnon (1973) and Shaw (1973).
3 For a very well-documented survey on the 'New Growth Evidence', methodological concerns and links with the new growth theoretical models, see Temple (1999).
4 This fist category of models brings together the pioneering models of Romer (1986), Lucas (1988) and Rebelo (1991).
5 This approach has been initiated by the basic models of Romer (1990) and Aghion and Howitt (1992). It also includes the impressively tractable Grossman and Helpman (1991) model.
6 Even more specifically, it developed on those models, in the line of Romer's 1986 paper, emphasising the role of externalities in the accumulation of physical capital.
7 However, this argument is not so easily acceptable. Recall that, comparatively, the trade-growth literature (see Grossman and Helpman 1991) develops itself almost entirely within the neo-Schumpeterian paradigm. The fact is that financial variables are complex by nature. On the one hand, they include conjectural policy-oriented variables close to monetary and inflationary ones. On the other hand, they reflect different institutional arrangements whose impacts on growth are more easily comparable to the ones that might have other structural variables such as the trade regimes.
8 By this adjective, Levine wants to point out the relevance of clearly differentiating five basic financial functions that may help to explain a causality running from finance to growth: specifically, financial systems facilitate risk amelioration, allocate resources, monitor managers and exert corporate control, mobilise savings and, finally, facilitate the exchange of goods and services.
9 'On capital accumulation, one class of growth models uses either externalities or capital goods produced using constant returns to scale but without the use of non-reproducible factors to generate steady state per capita growth. In these models, the functions performed by the financial system affect steady-state growth by influencing the rate of capital formation. [. . .] on technological innovation, a second class of growth models focuses on the invention of new processes and goods. In these models, the functions performed by the financial system affect steady-state growth by altering the rate of technological innovation' (Levine 1997: 691).
10 This puzzle was first emphasised by Young (1992) who chose to put in perspective the growth experiences of Singapore and Hong Kong because 'striking dissimilarities along critical dimensions emphasised in endogenous growth theory, makes these two economies a useful case study' (Young 1992: 14). From its study, he concluded that although his results 'provide evidence in favour of models of endogenous technological change' (Young 1992: 45); they may also indicate that 'linear models are no more a useful mean of thinking about the growth process' (Young 1999: 45).
11 As we will see, this is true at least until Levine's 1997 survey.
12 Such rationalisations as Levine's or Pagano's are impressive for analytically detailing the diverse potential linkages between financial and economic activities. Separating

financial functions and channels to growth however, is not appropriate if one aims at discriminating, in a more global perspective, between *alternative* explanations of comparative growth experiences

13 See Berthelemy and Varoudakis (1996), Greenwood and Smith (1997), Cooley and Smith (1992), Bencivenga, Smith and Starr (1995), Boyd and Smith (1996, 1998), Lutz and Walz (2000), for attempts to tackle the mutual causality between finance and growth.

14 On both these grounds however, we will show that discriminating between the *AK* and the *neo-Schumpeterian* approaches is very important. First, the role of the openness of the capital account proves to have potentially very different implications in each of these frameworks. Second, it should be the case that, in the view defended here, the impact of economic policies must be strongly sensitive to the leading growth mechanisms.

15 The difference between both concepts of growth *stages* and growth *regimes* will be exposed below.

16 Such a discrimination between what can be called respectively an 'accumulationist' and an 'assimilationist' view of development has been made elsewhere in the literature, for instance, by Collins and Bosworth (1996) and by Nelson and Park (1997). However, according to the latter authors, even the *neo-Schumpeterian* framework is not suitable to produce a meaningful 'assimilationist' view of development. The following argument is that those models can only deal with 'moves along a prevailing production function' (in this sense, they do not differ from the 'old' neoclassical growth approach) and such an analytical restriction does not allow to capture a crucial dimension of innovation as well as assimilation processes, i.e. the fact that they involve Knightian uncertainties. More on this issue will be discussed in the section 'Two competing views of "Why finance matter for growth"'.

17 And indeed, as Krugman (1993) points out, 'If the social return to capital is much higher than the private rate of return, any given capital inflow to a developing nation will raise its growth rate by much more than the pessimistic calculations of the standard neo-classical function' (Krugman 1993: 18).

18 From Levine (1991) and Bencivenga and Smith (1991) investigating the risk-sharing function of financial intermediaries; from Saint Paul (1992) developing the same issue but according to the role of financial markets; from Greenwood and Jovanovic (1990) investigating the informational function of financial intermediation in a context where financial intermediaries, unlike individual investors, are able to perfectly unscramble aggregate productivity shocks (see Pagano 1993 and Levine 1997, for a detailed description of the working of each of these linkages).

19 This characteristic was already emphasised Pagano pointing out that 'those models manage to run out the ambiguity and allow for positive global effect on growth rates whether in warranting, under restrictive condition, that the positive effect through enhancement of productivity will outweigh the negative effect through the diminution of the saving rate or in putting restrictive condition on the coefficient of relative risk aversion, or more simply in letting exogenous the rate of saving' (Pagano 1993: 617).

20 According to the authors, this study improves the previous work of King and Levine (1993a) both in using better data on capital accumulation and private savings (see respectively Levine and Orlov (1998) and Loayza, Lopez and Schmidt-Hebbel (1998) for a description of the databases) and in implementing new econometric techniques explicitly to confront the causality issue.

21 While the Roubini and Sala-i-Martin (1992) model exhibits a positive impact of financial liberalisation on growth due to the decrease in the leakage of resources between savings and investment, Jappelli and Pagano (1994) show that some degree of financial repression resulting in binding liquidity constraints, might increase the saving rate and then fosters growth. By the same token, liberalisation of the consumer credit market leads to a reduction in saving and growth.

22 Using Principal Components, they construct a 25-year time-series index of financial liberalisation for each of eight developing countries: Chile, Ghana, Indonesia, Korea, Malaysia, Mexico, Turkey and Zimbabwe. This index is then employed in an econometric analysis of private saving in these countries.

23 See Lucas (1990) for the first assessment of this implication.

24 Having to tackle the issue of 'why foreign investors would invest in the developing economy', Romer clearly shows that the occurrence of such inflows explicitly *requires* government interventions which have to *create* and *preserve* foreign monopoly rents.

25 Empirical evidence on the direction of foreign capital flows and of their impact on developing economies have flourished in recent years, in particular because the high volatility of such flows has been put at the front of the explanation of the NIC financial crisis (see among others Bhagwati 1998; Rodrick 1998, 1999). These studies generally find a negative or a non-significant effect of capital account liberalisation on the financial depth and growth of non-OECD countries, while the correlation becomes significant and positive when industrialised OECD countries are included in the sample (see Klein and Olivei 1999).

26 According to Aghion and Howitt (1998), such a feature is not in itself puzzling. It may be seen as a simplification allowing to focus precisely on the microeconomic structure underlying the innovation process.

27 Building on Aghion and Howitt (1992), the authors keep the feature, which consists in abstracting from capital accumulation. The authors rather point out that 'in contrast to traditional development work, we do not require that financial institutions mainly exert influence *via* the rate of physical capital accumulation' (Aghion and Howitt 1992: 515)

28 This is the original insight provided by the neo-Schumpeterian growth models characterised by a monopolistic competition framework.

29 Fundamentally, the incentive to innovate exists because of the temporary monopoly profits which prevail in the production sector of the innovative goods. However, the financial structure affects directly the *strength* of this incentive as it affects the costs of investing in innovation processes.

30 A 'rating' activity that allows to sort potentially successful entrepreneurs.

31 In the neo-Schumpeterian framework, such returns are directly given by the stream of profits which accrue from being the producer of the higher-quality good in a given industry. The financial system is then supposed, through rational stock market evaluation, to accurately reveal the expected discounted value of these profits. Note, however, that nothing explicitly justifies the necessity of such a financial service. Such function may however become central if one allows for a 'diversity of opinion' on the way one has to optimise such profits (see *infra*, note 44).

32 This conception fits European empirical observations, which reveal that, most of the time, firms using financial markets have already been financed by the banking system, this pre-requirement acting as a first selection barrier. Such a characteristic can be even stronger in some countries where the banks are really insider creditors of the firms being members of the board management, as for instance in Japan. By contrast, this effect would be less important in countries like the United States since there is no inside knowledge for the banks concerning the firms' projects.

33 Such a view of the assimilation process is exactly the one advocated by King and Levine (1993b): 'We take a broad view of innovative activity: in addition to invention of new products, we include enhancement of existing products; costly adoption of technology from other countries; and production of an existing good using new production or business methods' (1993b: 514).

34 Let us however make two qualifications to this empirical result. First, these evidences did not appear without revealing some important differentiation in magnitude among East Asian countries (see in particular, Collins and Bosworth 1996). Second, recent attempts to relax some of the strong assumptions underlying the methodology used

in conventional *TFP* measures (see Rodrick 1997; Hulten and Srinivasan 1999), have succeeded in reasserting an important contribution of *TFP* to the high growth records of some of these countries, at least during *specific* episodes of their growth stories. For instance, the *TFP* growth records of Taiwan and Hong Kong have been specifically emphasised in these new studies. The Philippines generally stand at the other end, with very low growth and negative *TFP* growth. Indonesia and Malaysia exhibit intermediate levels of performances. One might then conclude that, while valuable and robust may be the crude message according to which capital accumulation has been a primary growth-enhancing factor in these countries, the ongoing empirical debate points to the need of rejuvenating the analysis of cross-country differences in both the level and growth rate of *TFP*.

35 Case studies have flourished recently under the challenge of understanding the East Asian financial crisis. They indeed revealed some weakness within these financial systems (see, in particular, Stiglitz and Uy 1996 and Stiglitz 1998).

36 Note also that the fact that the correlation between growth and liberalisation of the capital account is significant only for OECD countries (cf. *supra*, note 33) could also be called in support to this rationalisation.

37 Indeed, as recalled by Berthelemy and Varoudakis (1996), the distinction between *demand*-pushed and *supply*-pushed financial development, emphasised by Patrick (1966), leads to a view that finance may cause growth at earlier stages of development while it may follow growth at latter stages.

38 The necessity to differentiate growth stages in economic development has been advocated first by Rostow (1960).

39 This result is supported by empirical evidence like the Allen and Santomero (1998) paper which underlines the increasing overlap between the financial services provided by both institutions.

40 This assessment is made by Levine who points out that 'Yet, we do not have adequate theories of why different financial structures emerge or why financial structures change' (Levine 1997: 703).

41 Such a view presenting stages of development and financial structures as closely inter-related variables was already present in earlier contributions (see Gerschenkron 1962 and 1968).

42 The analysis has been further developed in Allen and Gale (1998 and 1999).

43 One must notice that, compared to King and Levine (1993b) – in which there is also a risk to fail innovative projects – the important point here is from the hypothesis of different *prior beliefs* between investors. Such a hypothesis provides a stronger legitimacy to the supposition that financial markets are able to evaluate the expected returns of risky projects.

44 Kornai (1980) discussed in great detail shortage phenomena and economic and social consequences of shortage. He mainly focused on socialist economies.

45 We must notice that they only focus on the choice between risky and non-risky assets, without modelling explicitly the underlying growth mechanism.

46 For a survey on those models see Maskin (1999).

47 In fact, the model presents an innovation mechanism which increases the variety of intermediate goods as in Grossman and Helpman (1991).

48 Indeed, there are three categories of projects: short-run ones which are always efficient, long-run projects which can be efficient or not.

49 Indeed, in this model, as in the earlier one of Dewatripont and Maskin (1995), it is shown that when there is no cost of information transmission, i.e. a case of credit centralisation, *ex ante unprofitable projects* can become *sequentially optimal* once they have begun. This is due to the existence of sunk cost. Such a refinancing is common and allows unprofitable firms to survive.

50 This rather *ad hoc* assumption is justified on the ground that a long gestation period is a primary characteristic of innovative investment.

51 In contrast to the earlier literature, the study explores time series-data for an individual country rather than cross-country data in order to assert the importance of finance for growth.
52 They mention that growth in bank lending in excess of GDP growth averaged nearly 8 per cent per annum (Ghani and Suri 1999: 8).
53 In fact, the authors point out that interpreting their result as capturing a long-run relationship should be done with caution. They insist rather on the fact that they capture short-run dynamics in the specific Malaysian setting. However, as we will emphasise below, such kind of time-series analysis may nevertheless be worthwhile to be generalised.
54 See Lucas (1993) for a rationalisation of these 'growth miracles' excluding financial factors.

References

Aghion, P. and Howitt, P. (1992) 'A Model of Growth Through Creative Destruction', *Econometrica*, 60: 323–51.
—— (1998) *Endogenous Growth Theory*, Cambridge, Mass.: MIT Press.
Allen, F. (1993) 'Stock Markets and Resource Allocation', in C. Mayer and X. Vives (eds), *Capital Markets and Financial Intermediation*, Cambridge: Cambridge University Press: 81–113.
—— and Gale, D. (1998) 'Diversity of Opinion and Financing of New Technologies', Working Paper 98–30, Financial Institution Center, Wharton School, University of Pennsylvania.
—— (1999) *Comparing Financial Systems*, Cambridge, Mass. and London: MIT Press.
—— and Santomero, A.M. (1998) 'The Theory of Financial Intermediation', *Journal of Banking and Finance*, 21: 1461–85.
Amable, B. and Chatelain, J.B. (1995) 'Systèmes financiers et croissance: les effets du court-termisme', *Revue Economique*, 46: 827–36.
Arestis, P. and Demetriades, P. (1996) 'Finance and Growth: Institutional Considerations and Causality', UEL, Department of Economics, Working Paper No. 5, May, London.
Bai, C. and Wang, Y. (1999) 'The Myth of the Asian Miracle: The Macroeconomic Implications of Soft Budgets', *American Economic Review, AEA Papers and Proceedings*, 89: 432–37.
Bandiera, O., Caprio, G., Honohan, P. and Schiantarelli, F. (2000) 'Does Financial Reform Raise or Reduce Savings?', Working Paper, World Bank.
Barth, J., Caprio, G. and Levine, R. (1998) 'Financial Regulation and Performance: Cross-Country Evidence', Working Paper, World Bank, November.
Beck, T., Levine, R. and Loayza, N. (1999) 'Finance and the Sources of Growth', *Journal of Financial Economics*, 58: 261–300.
—— (2000) 'New Firm Formation and Industry Growth: Does Having a Market- or Bank-Based System Matter?', Working Paper, World Bank, May.
Bencivenga, V.R. and Smith, B. (1991) 'Financial Intermediation and Endogenous Growth', *Review of Economic Studies*, 58: 195–209.
Bencivenga, V.R. and Starr, R.M. (1995) 'Transactions, Technological Choice, and Endogenous Growth', *Journal of Economic Theory*, 67: 153–77.
Berthelemy, J.-C. and Varoudakis, A. (1996) *Politiques de développement financier et croissance*, OECD, série 'croissance à long terme'.
Bhagwati, J. (1998) 'The Capital Myth: The Difference Between Trade in Widgets and Trade in Dollars', *Foreign Affairs*, 77: 7–12.

Boyd, J. and Smith, B. (1996) 'The Co-Evolution of the Real and Financial Sectors in the Growth Process', *World Bank Economic Review*, 10: 371–96.

—— (1998) 'The Evolution of Debt and Equity Markets in Economic Development', *Economic Theory*, 12: 519–60.

Carlin, W. and Mayer, C. (2000) 'Finance, Investment and Growth', CEPR Working Paper, June.

Collins, S. and Bosworth, B. (1996) 'Economic Growth in East Asia: Accumulation *versus* Assimilation', *Brookings Papers on Economic Activity*, Washington, DC: Brookings Institution Press: 135–91.

Cooley, T. and Smith, B. (1992) 'Financial Markets, Specialization, and Learning by Doing', Working Paper No. 276, The Rochester Center for Economic Research.

Demirguc-Kunt, A. and Levine, R. (1996) 'Stock Market Development and Financial Intermediaries: Stylized Facts', *World Bank Economic Review*, 10: 291–312.

Dewatripont, M. and Maskin, E. (1995) 'Credit and Efficiency in Centralized and Decentralized Economies', *Review of Economic Studies*, 62: 541–55.

Evenson, R.E. and Westphal, L.E. (1995). 'Technological Change and Technological Strategy', in Jere Behrman and T.N. Srinivasan (eds), *Handbook of Development Economics*, vol. 9, Amsterdam: North-Holland.

Gerschenkron, A. (1962) *Economic Backwardness in Historical Perspective – A Book of Essays*, Cambridge: Harvard University Press.

—— (1968) *Continuity in History and Other Essays*, Cambridge: Harvard University Press.

Ghani, E. and Suri, V. (1999) 'Productivity Growth, Capital Accumulation, and the Banking Sector: Some Lessons from Malaysia', Working Paper, World Bank, December.

Goldsmith, R.W. (1969) *Financial Structure and Economic Development*, New Haven, CT: Yale University Press.

Greenwood, J. and Jovanovic, B. (1990) 'Financial Development, Growth and the Distribution of Income', *Journal of Political Economy*, 98: 1076–107.

—— and Smith, B. (1997) 'Financial Markets in Development and the Development of Financial Markets', *Journal of Economic Dynamics and Control*, January, 21: 145–81.

Grossman, G.M. and Helpman, E. (1991) *Innovation and Growth in the Global Economy*, Cambridge, Mass.: MIT Press.

Gurley, J. and Shaw, E. (1955) 'Financial Aspects of Economic Development', *American Economic Review*, 45: 515–38.

Huang, H. and Xu, C. (1999) 'Financial Institutions and the Financial crisis in East Asia', *European Economic Review*, 43: 903–14.

—— (1999) 'Institutions, Innovations and Growth', *American Economic Review, AEA Papers and Proceedings*, 89: 438–43.

Hulten, C. and Srinivasan, S. (1999) 'Indian Manufacturing Industry: Elephant or Tiger? New Evidence on the Asian Miracle', NBER Working Paper No. 7441.

Jacklin, C. (1987) 'Demand Deposits, Trading Restrictions, and Risk Sharing' in Edward D. Prescott and Neil Wallace (eds), *Contractual Arrangements for Intertemporal Trade*, Minneapolis: University of Minnesota Press: 26–47.

Jappelli, T. and Pagano, M. (1994) 'Saving Growth, and Liquidity Constraints', *Quarterly Journal of Economics*, 109: 83–109.

Kim, J. and Lau, L. (1994) 'The Sources of Economic Growth in the East Asian Newly Industrialised Countries', *Journal of Japanese and International Economics*, 8: 235–71.

King, R. and Levine, R. (1992) 'Financial Indicators and Growth in a Cross Section of Countries', Working Paper No. 819, The World Bank, Washington, DC.

King, R. and Levine, R. (1993a) 'Finance and Growth: Schumpeter May Be Right.' *Quarterly Journal of Economics*, 108: 717–37.

—— (1993b) 'Finance, Entrepreneurship and Growth. Theory and Evidence', *Journal of Monetary Economics*, 32: 513–42.

—— (1993c) 'Financial Development and Long-Run Growth' in Mayer, C. and Vives, X. (eds), *Capital Markets and Financial Intermediation*, Cambridge: Cambridge University Press: 156–96.

Klein, M. and Olivei, J. (1999) 'Capital Account Liberalization, Financial Depth, and Economic Growth', NBER Working Paper No. 7384.

Kornai, J. (1980) *The Economics of Shortage*, Amsterdam: North-Holland.

Krugman, P. (1993) 'International Finance and Economic development' in Giovannini (ed.), *Finance and Development: Issues and Experience*, Cambridge: Cambridge University Press.

La Porta, R., Lopez-de-Silanes, F. and Shleifer, A. (2000) 'Government Ownership of Commercial Banks', NBER Working Paper No. 7620, March.

Levine, R. (1991) 'Stock Markets, Growth, and Tax Policy', *Journal of Finance*, 46: 1445–65.

—— (1997) 'Financial Development and Economic Growth: Views and Agenda', *Journal of Economic Literature*, 35: 688–726.

—— and Renelt, D. (1992) 'A Sensitivity Analysis of Cross-Country Growth Regressions', *American Economic Review*, 82: 942–63.

—— and Orlov, A. (1998) 'Capital Accumulation Redux', mimeo, University of Virginia.

—— and Zervos, S. (1998) 'Stock Markets, Banks and Economic Growth', *American Economic Review*, 88: 537–58.

—— Loayza, N. and Beck, T. (2000) 'Financial Intermediation and Growth: Causality and Causes', *Journal of Monetary Economics*, 46: 31–77.

Loayza, N., Lopez, H. and Schmidt-Hebbel, K. (1998) 'World Saving Database', mimeo, World Bank.

Lucas, R. (1988) 'On the Mechanics of Economic Development', *Journal of Monetary Economics*, 22: 3–42.

—— (1990) 'Why Doesn't Capital Flow from Rich to Poor Countries?', *American Economic Review*, 80: 92–6.

—— (1993) 'Making a Miracle', *Econometrica*, 61: 251–72.

Lutz, A. and Walz, U. (2000) 'Financial Regimes, Capital Structure, and Growth', *European Journal of Political Economy*, 16: 491–508.

McKinnon, R.I. (1973) *Money and Capital in Economic Development*, Brookings Institution, Washington, DC.

Mankiw, G., Romer, D. and Weill, D. (1992) 'A Contribution to the Empirics of Economic Growth', *Quarterly Journal of Economics*, 107: 407–37.

Maskin, E. (1999) 'Recent Theoretical Work on the Soft Budget Constraint', *American Economic Review, AEA Papers and Proceedings*, 89: 421–5.

Masson, P., Bayoumi, T. and Samiei, H. (1998) 'Saving Behavior in Industrial and Developing Countries', *IMF Manuscript*, Washington, DC.

Nelson, R. and Pak, H. (1997) 'The Asian Miracle and Modern Growth Theory', Working Paper.

Pagano, M. (1993) 'Financial Markets and Growth: An Overview', *European Economic Review*, 37: 613–22.

Patrick, H. (1966) 'Financial Development and Economic Growth in Underdeveloped Countries', *Economic Development and Cultural Change*, 14: 174–89.

Pritchett, L. (1999) 'Patterns of Economic Growth: Hills, Plateaus, Mountains, and Plains', World Bank Group, Working Paper.

Qian, Y. (1994) 'A Theory of Shortage in Socialist Economies Based on the "Soft Budget Constraint"', *American Economic Review*, 84: 145–56.

Rajan, R. and Zingales, L. (1998) 'Financial Dependence and Growth', *American Economic Review*, 88: 559–86.

Rebelo, S. (1991) 'Long Run Policy Analysis and Long Run Growth', *Journal of Political Economy*, 99: 81–6.

Rodrick, D. (1997) 'TFPG Controversies, Institutions, and Economic Performance in East Asia', NBER Working Paper No. 5914.

—— (1998) 'Who Needs Capital-Account Convertibility?', mimeo, Harvard University, February.

—— (1999) *Making Openness Work: The New Global Economy and the Developing Countries*. Overseas Development Council, Washington, DC.

Romer, P. (1986) 'Increasing Returns and Long-Run Growth', *Journal of Political Economy*, 94: 1002–37.

—— (1990) 'Endogenous Technological Change', *Journal of Political Economy*, 98: 71–102.

—— (1992) 'Two Strategies for Economic Development: Using Ideas and Producing Ideas', *Proceedings of the 1992 Annual World Bank Conference*, 39: 5–30.

—— (1993) 'Idea Gaps and Objects Gaps in Economic Development', *Journal of Monetary Economics*, 32: 543–73.

Rostow, W. (1960) 'The Stages of Economic Growth', *World Bank Annual Conference on Development Economics*, 1992: 63–91.

Roubini, N. and Sala-i-Martin (1992) 'Financial Repression and Economic Development', *Journal of Development Economics*, 39: 5–30.

Saint Paul, G. (1992) 'Technological Choice, Financial Markets and Economic Development', *European Economic Review*, 36: 763–81.

Shaw, E. (1973) *Financial Deepening in Economic Development*, New York: Oxford University Press.

Stiglitz, J. (1998) 'Knowledge for Development. Economic Science, Economic Policy, and Economic Advice', *Paper Presented at the Annual World Bank Conference on Development Economics*, Washington, DC, April 20–21, 1998.

—— and Uy, M. (1996) 'Financial Markets, Public Policy and the East Asian Miracle', *World Bank Research Observer*, 11: 249–76.

Suto, I. and James, A. (1999) 'Savings and Economic Growth in the United States and Japan', *Japan and the World Economy*, 11: 161–83.

Temple, J. (1999) 'New Growth Evidence', *Journal of Economic Literature*, 37: 112–56.

Tobin, J. (1965) 'Money and Economic Growth', *Econometrica*, 33: 671–84.

Young, A. (1992) 'A Tale of Two Cities: Factor Accumulation and Technical Change in Hong Kong and Singapore', *NBER Macroeconomics Annual*, 1992: 13–54.

—— (1995) 'The Tyranny of Numbers: Confronting the Statistical Realities of the East Asian Growth Experience', *Quarterly Journal of Economics*, 110: 641–80.

Part II
Growth and fluctuations

5 Neo-Schumpeterian versus neo-Kaldorian approaches*

Two different views on learning, knowledge and cyclical growth

Richard Arena and Alain Raybaut

Introduction

Traditionally, the notion of economic dynamics refers to two main phenomena: economic growth and business cycles. It is not surprising therefore that the problem of the relation between short-run and long-run macroeconomic changes has consistently preoccupied economists since the end of the nineteenth century. The history of the analysis of the problem reveals the existence of three major successive attitudes.

The early writers – such as Aftalion, Spiethoff or Tugan-Baranowsky – who analysed trade cycles stressed the essential role of investment and the accumulation of productive capacity in the genesis of both growth and fluctuations. They interpreted trade cycles as intrinsic components of the long-run process of growth.

These views contrasted however with those defended by the first modern business cycle (BC) model-builders. The common feature of the first BC models was that they considered cycles and growth as two independent forms of economic change requiring different analytical devices. Thus in 1960 Pasinetti characterized the various models combining multiplier effects and some form of the acceleration principle (Frisch, Kalecki, Kaldor, Marrama, Goodwin, Hicks and Duesenberry) noting that

> the situation is that, on the one hand, the macro-economic models which provide a cyclical interpretation of the economic activity cannot give any explanation of economic growth and, on the other hand, those theories which define, or rely on, the conditions for a dynamic equilibrium to be reached and maintained cannot give an explanation of business cycle.
>
> (Pasinetti 1960: 69)

The origin of this 'situation' is to be found in the treatment of investment and its consequences on business cycles. If the multiplier/accelerator interaction permitted to take into account the influence of an increase in capital on demand, it however ignored its supply effects, i.e. its influence on economic growth. This view implicitly implied the existence of a strict dichotomy between short-run and long-run dynamics. Business cycles had to be interpreted as a pure short-period phenomenon generated by a temporary maladjustment of the market for goods. Furthermore, this approach neglected the reverse influence of economic growth on business cycles. We know, for instance, that Hicks (1950) incorporated a linear steady-state growth trend in the multiplier/accelerator business cycle model without changing its basic characteristics. The assumption of a dichotomy between growth and fluctuations prevailed until the end of the 1960s. Lucas's monetary equilibrium BC theory favoured a completely new approach to fluctuations but maintained the idea that they were independent from economic growth. Even, the various generations of early RBC models did not improve this state of affairs. As Aghion and Howitt have reminded us,

> Existing business cycles based on exogenous productivity or monetary shocks were unsatisfactory in many respects: first, they could not account for the existence of stochastic trends evidenced in empirical studies (. . .); second, aggregate demand shocks could have no lasting consequences on technology and growth; third, money had to remain neutral in the long-run, with monetary shocks being completely dichotomised in the long-run from real technological shocks.
>
> (Aghion and Howitt 1998: 235–6)

However, the convergence between more recent general dynamic equilibrium BC models and endogenous growth theory changed the way in which the relation between growth and cycles was considered. Aghion and Howitt summed it up briefly, noting that 'one of the general implications of endogenous growth theory is that growth and cycles are related phenomena, with causation going in both directions' (Aghion and Howitt 1998: 4). Two main approaches then emerged. The first corrects the shortcomings of early RBC models, offering a more sophisticated analysis of technological innovations and of their economic effects, taking, however, for granted the pure neoclassical framework (see, for instance, the volume edited by Helpman (1998)). The second approach refers to 'Joseph Schumpeter's notion of creative destruction, the competitive process by which entrepreneurs are constantly looking for new ideas that will render their rivals' ideas obsolete' (Aghion and Howitt 1998: 1). This second approach appears to be especially well equipped to establish, in line with Schumpeter, 'causal links *from* cycles *to* growth or the *reverse* causality' (Aghion and Howitt 1998: 233).

Growth and cycles in a neo-Schumpeterian framework

It comes as no surprise that a Schumpeterian framework should be regarded as most suitable to develop a dynamic analysis which includes both growth and cycles. Thus, in his 1954 article dealing with the relation between economic growth and cyclical fluctuations, Kaldor complained about the conventional dichotomy between those phenomena; he however pointed out that the dichotomous view was not shared by 'at least one distinguished author "– Joseph Schumpeter" – [who] put forward a trade-cycle theory which makes the cycle itself simply a by-product of economic progress-booms and depressions being "the form which progress takes in a capitalist society" ' (Kaldor 1954: 214). This tribute paid by Kaldor to Schumpeter underlines the pertinence of choosing a Schumpeterian framework when the purpose of the analysis is the construction of a theory of cyclical growth. Schumpeter related the long-run economic process to the way in which innovations are financed and introduced by the creation of credit. He saw this process as consisting of an upward inflationary movement related to the introduction of innovations based on the financing of entrepreneurial credit demand; followed by a recessionary movement towards equilibrium which could only be disturbed by the emergence of a new major innovation. Schumpeter's method was based on the combination of several models of a standard cycle seen as successive approximations of a complex reality. Thus, the first approximation adopted by Schumpeter corresponded to real situations to which the model of the circular flow could be applied. In this case, economic equilibrium was assumed to be 'static' and an 'ideal cycle' was described as a two-phase process, including a boom and a recessionary phase. The second approximation already specified the transition process from circular flow to economic development. The two-phase cycle was replaced by a four-phase one, also including a depression and a recovery phase. Since long waves correspond to a sequence of business cycles in the neighbourhood of a series of higher and higher equilibria, they formed a dynamic process of cyclical growth.

Now, even if Aghion and Howitt (1998) refer to Schumpeterian analysis, their conception of economic dynamics clearly differs from the *Theory of Economic Development* on crucial issues.

First, contrasting their approach with that of the so-called AK models of endogenous growth, they constantly stress their intention to go beyond the 'point of view' which 'obliterates the distinction between technological progress and capital accumulation' (Aghion and Howitt 1998: 2). Now, this purpose of their analysis is clearly opposed to Schumpeter's conception according to which the break with the circular flow and the consideration of economic development necessarily implies *both* technological progress *and* capital accumulation. For Schumpeter, technical progress *implied* capital accumulation and is, therefore, supposed to change the distribution of initial factor endowments between firms and industries. The innovator needs to draw, to its benefit, a major part of these factor endowments. In the context of a decentralised market economy, this need entails a bet on the future success of innovation and, therefore, a temporary recourse to credit in the expectation that this temporary *financing* will be substituted for, in the end, by *funding* from profits and capital accumulation.

Second, Schumpeter's analysis required him to consider the creation of bank credit as a *necessary condition* of economic development. This view is not the same as Aghion and Howitt's rejection of money neutrality: This rejection is certainly a characteristic of their approach even though credit is not, therefore, an indispensable prerequisite for their analysis.

Third, even if Aghion and Howitt regard technological progress, education or the non-neutrality of money as essential elements of their theory, it does not follow that they therefore share Schumpeter's conception of *structural change*. Fundamentally, their analysis 'relies heavily on the notion of a steady state, in which capital, output, the wage rate and knowledge (appropriately measured) all grow at the same constant rate' (Aghion, Howitt 1998: 8) and, therefore, 'for the most part [they] deal with issues in which the transition to a steady state is not critical and for those purposes [they] confine [their] attention to the steady state' (ibid.: 9). These theoretical choices strongly contrast with Schumpeter's. There are cases in which the equilibrium towards which the economic system might converge is not walrasian or 'perfect', to use Schumpeter's own terms (Schumpeter 1939: 48). Secondly, there are also cases in which the practical conditions for the realisation of an equilibrium are not fulfilled. In those cases, some situations do not correspond to 'equilibrium points' but to 'ranges within which the system as a whole is more nearly in equilibrium than it is outside of them', i.e. to 'neighbourhoods of equilibrium' (ibid.: 71). Finally, there are also cases in which no equilibrium could exist at all: 'when, for instance, say, by a war financed by government fiat, or by a "mania" or railway building, there is little sense in speaking of an ideal equilibrium coexisting with all that disequilibrium' (ibid.: 70). The question arises as to whether this 'mania' is not the equivalent of what endogenous growth theorists usually call innovations related to 'general purpose technologies (GPT)'.

Fourth, in Aghion and Howitt's approach, consumption is taken to be the sole end of economic activity. This implies an acceptance of the optimisation objective and the use of a social utility function, and is therefore based on both the concept of a representative agent and the belief that intertemporal maximisation of the expected present value of consumption is possible. Obviously, these ideas were totally alien to Schumpeter. According to him, entrepreneurs had the possibility to control prices, technical progress and to *influence consumers' preferences* (Schumpeter 1939: 73–4). Industries grew at different rates and economic change implied discontinuities that sit uneasily with marginal analysis and differential calculus (on the creation and disappearance of firms, see Schumpeter 1934: 66; on productive and technological reorganisation, see ibid.: 71).

The essential differences between Schumpeter and 'neo-Schumpeterian' theories of economic change do not of course imply that we have to discard with the latter. One cannot deny that Aghion and Howitt succeeded in introducing some Schumpeterian ideas into the mainstream framework of endogenous growth theory.

On the one hand, in accordance with Schumpeter's line of thought, Aghion and Howitt place technological innovations at the heart of economic change:

> Economic growth involves a two-way interaction between technology and economic life: technological progress transforms the very economic system that creates it. The purpose of endogenous growth theory [in Aghion and Howitt's sense – RA] is to seek some understanding of this interplay between technological knowledge and various structural characteristics of the economy and the society, and how such an interplay results in economic growth.
>
> (Aghion and Howitt 1998: 1)

On the other hand, they also stress the role of knowledge accumulation through education and social learning. Reviving, once again, Schumpeterian themes, they show how education and human capital could affect technological change, how different forms of social learning emerge and how both affect fundamental and secondary innovations (Aghion and Howitt, 1998, chs 6 and 10).

Aghion and Howitt also emphasised the effects of market structure on economic growth, introducing their own interpretation of Schumpeter's conception of competition regarded as a mechanism of creative destruction. If the analytical conception of competition clearly differs from Schumpeter's, it nevertheless permits to capture some of the central ideas suggested in the *Theory of Economic Development* as well as in *Capitalism, Socialism and Democracy*.

Finally – and this aspect is essential for our purposes – the neo-Schumpeterian approach strongly contributes to overcome the traditional dichotomy between growth and cycle theories, by analysing 'several channels through which the introduction of a general-purpose technology can lead to a deep and prolonged decline in economic activity, even though it will ultimately put the economy on a higher growth path' (Aghion and Howitt 1998: 4). The introduction of different stages in the process of innovation and social learning implies an increased degree of the heterogeneity of firms' reactions and, therefore, of the range of possible fluctuations around the steady-state path. Even if this feature and the characterisation of temporal gaps between sequential innovations might change with 'ad hoc'ism, they can, however, also be taken to be a possible reinterpretation, within a modern framework of Schumpeter's analysis, of innovative waves. Moreover, Aghion and Howitt (1998, ch. 8) offer microeconomic foundations of innovative behaviour which make sense from the point of view of contemporary analysis of industrial organisation or technological change, in particular with regard to the diffusion of innovations: the process of social learning is described as a self-organising device that permits the diffusion of innovations through trial-and-error and mimetic behaviour, analogous, to a certain extent, to Schumpeter's distinction between 'energetic' and 'hedonistic' rational attitudes (see Arena 1992: 134).

Neo-Schumpeterian results show that macroeconomic inventions do not immediately lead to an increase of productivity and growth, but rather to cycles that are initiated by deep and prolonged slowdowns and end with the economy's transition to a higher steady-state growth path. It is interesting to note that the cyclical time-path of aggregate output strongly depends on the size, the number, the speed and the success of GPTs and on the intensity of imitative behaviour. It, however, also depends on the degree of substitutability across the intermediate inputs used in final output activities specific to the manufacturing sector (Aghion and Howitt 1998: 258–60). This degree of substitutability is based on the existence of neoclassical sector-specific substitutable production functions, a point to which we shall return below.

Growth and cycles in a neo-Kaldorian framework

If, in his 1954 article, Kaldor referred to Schumpeter as an 'exception', it is necessary to recall that this is not the only exception. Another example of a cyclical growth theory has, in fact, been provided by Kaldor himself. However, Targetti has noted:

> In spite of the tribute paid by Kaldor to Schumpeter in the end of his 54 article, the views of both authors on the relation cycle-growth are at least partially divergent. For Schumpeter, technical progress is the spring of growth which cannot be anything but a cyclical process and vice-versa the cycle only appears in a growing economy. For the Kaldor of 1940, the cycle can happen without any growth; for the Kaldor of 1954 the cycle can be over-imposed but must be independent from the trend given by technical progress; for the Kaldor of the growth models, technical progress (. . .) determines the natural rate of growth which, however, can be reached and maintained without cyclical fluctuations.
>
> (Targetti 1984: XXIII)

To add to Targetti's remarks, we might notice that Kaldor did not even refer explicitly to a process of cyclical growth in his last writings. However, all the ingredients for building such a process were present in Kaldor's approach if we consider it in retrospect. First, at the end of the 1950s, Kaldor denies the logical possibility of distinguishing between the choice of techniques (within a production function) and technical progress (i.e. a shift of the production function). Kaldor considers that every kind of investment always incorporates technical progress and, even more, that investment is the main way to technical progress. Consequently, the rate of growth of labour productivity is not exogenous but increases in step with the capital/labour ratio. Second, following the tradition of Adam Smith and Allan Young, Kaldor reformulated the Verdoorn Law in a specific way to deal with dynamic increasing returns to scale.

The absence of an explicit model in Kaldor's contributions permits the formulation of various modern interpretations of the Kaldorian message. It is not, therefore, surprising to find that two main different interpretations have emerged and coexist. The first consists in integrating some elements of Kaldor's theory into consistent models – outside endogenous growth theory – whose objective is more to emphasise its originality than to investigate its compatibility with standard modern theory. One example of this approach can be found in Arena and Raybaut (1995). The second approach takes the opposite view, that it focuses on those elements in Kaldor's theory that might help to advance mainstream dynamic analysis. In this section, we will concentrate on this second approach, in order to show how the incorporation of Kaldor's ideas in an endogenous growth model might affect the usual analytical results.

To begin with, we briefly discuss the elements of the Kaldorian approach that we will use in our model below.

First, we discard with the optimisation of a social utility function. Instead the intertemporal programme will be described here in terms of the maximisation of the net present value related to the investment decisions of a representative firm.

Second, we replace the usual neoclassical production function with perfect factor substitutability with a production function in which production factors are complementary. Kaldor's criticism of the neoclassical principle of factor substitution, referring to the *creative* rather than to the *allocative* function of economic activity, is well known. In theories of allocation,

> the principle of substitution (as Marshall called it) or the "law of variable proportions" or of "limited substitutability" is elevated to the central principle on the basis of which both the price system and the production system are explained; and it is implied that the world is one where elasticities of substitution are all important. This approach ignores the essential complementarity between different factors of production (such as capital and labour) or different types of activities (such as that between primary, secondary and tertiary sectors of economy [we might add today "as between sector-specific intermediate inputs" – AR and RA]) which is far more important for the understanding of the laws of change and development of the economy than the substitution aspect.
>
> (Kaldor 1975: 400)

This analytical choice explains why, contrary to Aghion and Howitt (1998), we shall favour an AK type of endogenous growth model. In this context, it might be noted that our approach also has a 'classical' flavour since it

> assumes implicitly that (simple) labour is a producible resource, whose cost of production is constant, that is, equal to the real wage rate: at the given wage labour is in elastic supply, and the supply is fully adjusted to the needs of capital accumulation. Second, natural resources such as land are implicitly kept in a state of abundance by a sufficiently plentiful exogenous technical change of a resource-saving nature.
>
> (Kurz 1998: 55)

In accordance with Kaldor's analysis, complementarity in production arises from the existence of indivisibilities. In addition, given endogenous factors creation and increasing returns, and excluding the very short run, the supply of one product is not necessarily at the expense of another.

The learning mechanism we will retain also differs from Aghion and Howitt's, as will be explained below in more detail. The main difference refers to the relation between capital accumulation and technical progress. Following Kaldor's as well as Schumpeter's views and in clear contrast to the neo-Schumpeterian approach, we will assume that learning is closely related to firms' investment activities. In our view, in the absence of capital accumulation there is neither learning nor knowledge accumulation or technical change. This view is obviously strongly Kaldorian and derives from Smith's and Allyn Young's famous argument:

> Finally, there are the inventions and innovations induced by experience to which Adam Smith paid the main emphasis – what we now call "learning by doing" or "dynamic economies of scale". The advance in scientific knowledge in physics or in the science of engineering in the laboratory cannot by itself

secure the innumerable design improvements that result from the repeated application of particular engineering principles. The optimum design for the steam engine or for the diesel engine or the sewing machine has only been achieved after many years or decades of experience: that for the nuclear power plant is still far away. The gain in design through experience is even more important in the making of plant and equipment; hence the *annual* gain of productivity due to "embodied technical progress" will tend to be all the greater the larger the number of plants constructed per year.

(Kaldor 1972: 381)

The origin of technological change is not, therefore, related to an exogenous probability law governing the arrival rates of innovations (Aghion and Howitt 1998: 55). Technological change is here to a large extent a by-product of production and capital accumulation processes.

Finally, our conception of dynamic equilibrium also differs from Aghion and Howitt's. We already noted that, for these authors, 'the transition to a steady state is not critical' (Aghion and Howitt 1998: 9). Again, in accordance with Kaldor's view, in our approach steady states are only benchmarks. In clear contrast to the neo-Schumpeterian approach, we will see that, in our opinion, the transition to a steady state is *highly* critical: steady states can be *unstable* and *endogenous* growth cycles can appear. These results which we discuss in the last part of this contribution are indirectly related to Kaldor's distinction between 'axiomatic' theories and those based on 'stylised facts' (Kaldor 1972). Our approach is not based on axiomatic micro-foundations derived from the standard rationality assumptions but on 'stylised micro-foundations related to the identification of "ideal-typical" entrepreneurial investment behaviour'.

A neo-Kaldorian model of endogenous cyclical growth

In this section, we develop a model of endogenous cyclical growth based on the Kaldorian ideas we just discussed. As already noted, it belongs to the family of endogenous growth models of the AK type. Time is assumed to be continuous and all variables are expressed in real terms. The economy produces a single good in quantity $Q(t)$ by means of an amount of capital $K(t)$. Knowledge $A(t)$ evolves in an endogenous way, according to a global learning mechanism specified below, but appears to be an externality for the individual firm. This usual setting is modified by the introduction of adjustment costs, induced by changes in the stock of capital which grows in step with the rate of investment. Simple models of investment (e.g. user cost models) have at least two major shortcomings. First, they do not identify the mechanism through which financial variables and expectations affect investment. Second, each invested unit does lead to an instantaneous and automatic growth of the productive stock of capital $K(t)$. The introduction of adjustment costs gives at least a remotely realistic picture of actual investment decisions. Such costs come in two forms. On the one hand, internal adjustment costs refer to the costs of installing new capital goods and training new workers to operate the new machines. On the other hand, external adjustment costs refer to financial aspects of investment, based on the q theory of investment.

From this perspective, we consider that real and financial costs of investment are encapsulated in an adjustment cost function. Let $\Psi(I(t)/K(t))K(t)$ be this cost function, where $\Psi(\cdot)$ is positive, continuous, increasing and convex in $k(t) = I(t)/K(t)$, with $K(t) > 0$. Moreover, let us suppose, in accordance with the literature (e.g. Hubbard, Kashyap and Whited 1995), that $\Psi(\cdot)$ is quadratic and specified as follows:

$$\Psi(k(t)) = \frac{(k(t) - \delta)^2}{a}$$

We obtain

$$\Psi'(k(t)) = \frac{2(k(t) - \delta)}{a}$$

$$\Psi''(k(t)) = \frac{2}{a}$$

Consequently, the net value of a representative firm is given by

$$\Pi_{\text{Net}}(K(t), I(t)) = \Pi(k(t)) - \Psi\left(\frac{I(t)}{K(t)}\right)K(t) \tag{1}$$

where $\Pi(K(t))$ is the gross level of profits. In this 'AK' framework, with exogenous wages and prices, gross profits are simply given by $\Pi(K(t)) = \eta AK(t) + B$ with $\eta > 0$, $B > 0$ (Arena and Raybaut 1998).

Investment decisions of the representative firm $I * (t)$ are the outcome of the maximisation of its net present value. Thus, we have the following intertemporal optimisation problem

$$\underset{I(t)}{\text{Max}} \int_{t=0}^{\infty} e^{-rt} \left[\Pi_{\text{Net}}(K(t), I(t))\right] dt \tag{2}$$

$$\dot{K}(t) = I(t) - \delta K(t) \tag{3}$$

$$K(t) > 0, \quad I(t) \geq 0 \tag{4}$$

where r denotes the discount rate and $0 \leq \delta \leq 1$ refers to the rate of depreciation of capital.

It can be shown, given the concavity of $\Pi_N(K(t), I(t))$, that a unique optimal investment path $I^*(t)$ exists to solve our problem.

Let us now investigate the dynamic behaviour of the economy. To do so, it is convenient to denote investment per capital as follows : $k(t) = I(t)/K(t)$. For simplicity, we disregard the time factor (t) until now. We obtain the following first-order conditions

FOC.1

$$\lambda = \Psi'(k) \tag{5}$$

FOC.2

$$\dot{\lambda} = (r+\delta)\lambda + \Psi(k) - k\Psi'(k) - \eta A \tag{6}$$

The derivative with respect to time of (5) combined with (6), gives:

$$\dot{k} = \frac{\dot{\lambda} = (r+\delta)\lambda + \Psi(k) - k\Psi'(k) - \eta A}{\Psi''(k)} \tag{7}$$

Relation (7) describes the dynamics of $k(t)$, that is investment per capital.

Note that since $Q = AK$, the rate of growth of the economy is given by $g = \dot{A}/A + \dot{K}/K$. That is, the net growth rate g is equal to $\dot{A}/A + k - \delta$. Thus, in the stationary state $\dot{A} = 0$ and $A = \bar{A} = cte$, therefore $g = k - \delta$.

We first investigate the dynamical properties of an *economy without learning*. In this case, $A = \bar{A} = cte$, and the dynamics of the growth rate is fully described by the one-dimension differential equation in $k(t)$ (7).

Substituting the respective values of, Ψ, Ψ', Ψ'' into (7), we finally obtain

$$\dot{k} = \frac{(k-\delta)(2r+\delta-k) - a\eta\bar{A}}{2} \tag{8}$$

It is obvious that equation (8) has two positive stationary values for k,

$$k_1^* = r + \delta - \sqrt{r^2 - a\eta\bar{A}} \quad \text{and} \quad k_2^* = r + \delta + \sqrt{r^2 - a\eta\bar{A}}$$

where the first is below and the second above the golden rule. Assume that $K < K_{max}$, with $K_{max} = aB/2(\Delta + r\sqrt{\Delta})$ both equilibria can be selected.

The lower equilibrium k_1^* is locally unstable, while the higher k_2^* is locally stable. Moreover, it can be shown that for all initial conditions $k_1^0 < k(0)$, the economy converges monotonously to the higher growth rate k_2^*. Thus, without learning growth is steady, stable and non-cyclical. The phase diagram is depicted in Figure 5.1.

We now introduce a *learning mechanism* into this framework. A recurring difficulty in the representation of technological change, raised in particular by Young (1993), is that an investment in new technologies does not realise all its productive potential from the moment of its implementation. Furthermore, we know that in the presence of several competing technologies, new technologies are not necessarily better than old ones. As Young has shown, new technologies are often less efficient than old ones while they are still in the process of being developed. The approach to technical change in terms of learning by doing, which we favour here allows us to overcome this difficulty. It brings the learning dimension associated with the choice of the new technology that is being implemented. Here, it is the

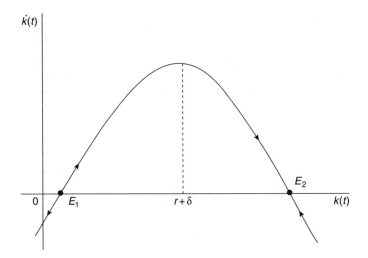

Figure 5.1 Economy without learning.

period of learning, that is, of the accumulation of experience and improvement, that develops the potential productivity of a new technology. As we know, there are at least three ways to increase efficiency: either due to incremental innovations affecting the existing stock of capital and resulting in a total efficiency of new capital goods, or due to the acquisition of skills related to the use of new capital goods, or finally due to the existence of spillover effects occurring when there are capital goods of differing ages (Gilchrist and Williams 1998) or different kinds of activities (Evans *et al.* 1998).

As is well known, a formal and complete study of this type of learning mechanism has been provided by Sato and Uzawa. More recently, Romer has shown that in the presence of large spillover and learning effects in the endogenous growth framework, the growth rate of per capita income may well be unbounded upwards. While Greiner and Semmler (1995) have focused on the role of learning by doing in the existence of endogenous cyclical growth paths. Following the approach of Greiner and Semmler, our intention is to show that the effects of learning can be bounded. Thus, in contrast to traditional models of endogenous growth, we consider that learning is closely related to firms' investment activities.

The dynamics of learning is thus described by a relation of the following kind

$$\dot{A} = \Phi\left(\frac{I}{K}\right) - \gamma A \tag{9}$$

with $A > 0$, and where γ is a parameter, and Φ is a positive, increasing function of $k = I/K$.

This formulation is founded both on the Kaldorian tradition and on the more recent empirical works devoted to the relation between per capita growth and rates of equipment investment (see e.g Delong and Summers 1991). Thus, we will assume that there exists a nonlinear relation between gross investment and the accumulation of knowledge (Feitchinger and Sorger 1988; Greiner 1996; Greiner and Semmler 1997). From this point of view, Greiner (1995) has developed a two-sector growth model in which human capital is increased through learning by doing. He shows that persistent endogenous growth cycles do exist when there is a bunching of investment at nearby dates. This clustering of investment is explained by 'adjacent complementarity with respect to the capital stock', that is, 'increasing capital at time t_3 implies a reallocation of resources from distant dates t_1 to nearby ones' (Greiner 1996: 594). This means that this property leads to a clustering of investment and an overshooting of the capital stock $K(t)$ with respect to its steady-state value. Let us now consider an economy with an initial capital stock $K(0) < K^*$ (steady-state value of K). Consequently, investment increases up to the point at which the steady state is reached. However, adjacent complementarity at nearby dates eventually leads to a capital stock greater than K^*. Now, since $K(t_n) > K^*$, investment must decrease. The same overshooting mechanism implies that a phase of under-investment should replace that of over-investment, leading to a cyclical growth path.

Equations (8) and (9) form a dynamical system in $(k(t), A(t))$. The remainder of this subsection focuses on the analysis of the local dynamic properties of this system.

We first characterise the *stationary states* of this system. The following result holds

From equation (8), we obtain the isokine $\dot{k} = 0$, $f(k) = A$, where

$$f(k) = \frac{-k^2 + 2(r + \delta)k - 2r\delta - \delta^2}{a\eta}$$

from equation (9), we obtain the isokine $\dot{A} = 0$, $h(k) = A$, where

$$h(k) = \frac{\Phi(k)}{\gamma}$$

Hence, any steady-state value of k, k^*, is a solution of the equation $f(k) - h(k) = 0$. Accordingly, the existence and multiplicity of stationary states result from the shape of the learning function.

Now, assume that $\forall k, \gamma > 0, 0 < k < 2r + \delta$. Assume further that $\Phi(k)$ satisfies the following properties

$$\Phi'(k) > 0 \tag{10}$$

$$\Phi(k) \geq 0 \tag{11}$$

$$\Phi(k) < \frac{\gamma r^2}{a\eta} \tag{12}$$

then two positive stationary values of k, k_1^* and k_2^* exist. Assume again that $K < K_{\max}$, with $K_{\max} = -aB/\left(a\eta A^* - (k_2^* - \delta)^2\right)$, then the two equilibria can be selected.

The meaning of this condition in terms of the learning mechanism is the following. First, condition (10) means that knowledge increases with investment per capita. Second, condition (11) means that apart from learning by investing and doing, knowledge increases are also partly autonomous. Finally, condition (12) simply requires that the learning process should be bounded from above. As a result, the model has two stationary states, one low (k_1^*, A_1^*), and the other, (k_2^*, A_2^*) high, with respect to the golden rule growth rate $r + \delta$.

The main findings concerning the dynamics of the model are summarised in Table 5.1.

The low stationary state (k_1^*, A_1^*) is either locally unstable (and consequently cannot satisfy the transversality conditions), or is a saddle point. The characteristics of the learning curve and of the adjustment cost function imply that the high stationary state does not exhibit the saddle-path property. In this case, the model has two negative real roots or two imaginary roots with negative or zero real parts. Therefore, indeterminacy (cf. Benhabib and Farmer 1994; Benhabib and Perli 1994) or endogenous growth cycles can exist in some neighbourhood of the high stationary states (k_2^*, A_2^*). Assume that the model has two distinct complex eigenvalues. In this case, it is possible to show that an admissible critical value of γ, $\bar{\gamma}$, exists (cf. Greiner and Semmler 1997). The model then has two pure imaginary roots. Moreover, a Hopf bifurcation arises for this value. That is, the real part of the roots crosses the imaginary axis at a non-infinite speed. Accordingly, the economy exhibits endogenous cyclical growth paths. Note that in this case the closed trajectories always satisfy the transversality conditions.

Table 5.1 Dynamics in a neighbourhood of the steady states

k^*	$0 < k_1^* < r + d - \gamma$	$k_2^* < r + \delta$
Trace	$+$	0 or $-$
Det	$+$ or $-$	$+$
Dynamics	Saddle point or locally unstable	Indeterminacy/endogenous cycles

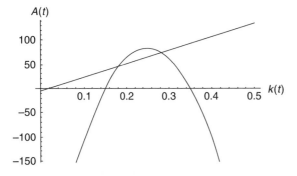

Figure 5.2 Numerical example.

(a)

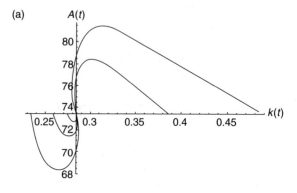

(b)

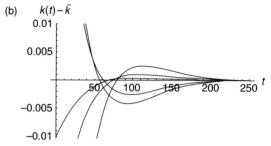

(c)

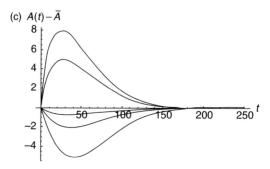

Figure 5.3 Example of local indeterminancy of the high stationary state (k_2^*, A_2^*) with cyclical growth $(\gamma = 0.02)$: (a) Phase diagram, (b) Dynamics of $k(t)$ and (c) Dynamics of $A(t)$.

Finally, we illustrate these findings with a *numerical example*. We specify the learning function as follows:

$$\Phi(k) = \mu_3 k^3 + \mu_2 k^2 + \mu_1 k + \mu_0$$

where $\mu_3 = 0.55$, $\mu_2 = -0.1$, $\mu_1 = 5.5$, and $\delta = 0.1$, $a = 0.1$, $r = 0.05$. Hence, we obtain the following diagram in (k, A) (see Figure 5.2).

Consequently, it is easy to check that the model has two positive stationary states (k_1^*, A_1^*) and (k_2^*, A_2^*).

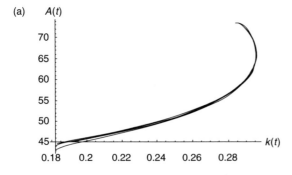

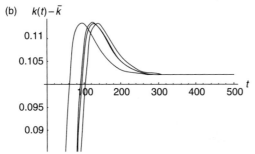

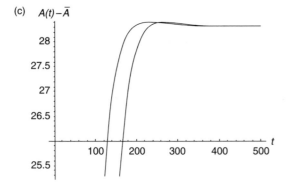

Figure 5.4 Example of global indeterminancy of the high stationary state (k_2^*, A_2^*): initial conditions in a neighbourhood of the low equilibrium (k_1^*, A_1^*) locally unstable. (a) Phase diagram, (b) Dynamics of $k(t)$ and (c) Dynamics of $A(t)$.

This example indicates that growth cycles can emerge in the AK framework with learning for admissible values of the real interest rate. Only one admissible value of γ exists, which captures the weight of decreasing returns to the learning technology, $0 < \tilde{\gamma}$, such that the model has two pure imaginary roots and generates endogenous growth-cycles paths. When γ is smaller than the critical value, the

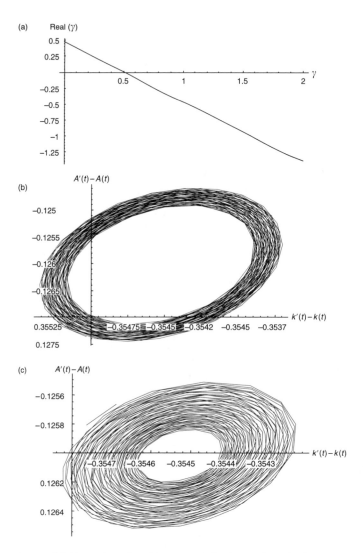

Figure 5.5 Examples of endogenous cyclical growth paths in a neighbourhood of the high equilibrium (k_2^*, A_2^*) for $\bar{\gamma} = 0.504528$. (a) Real part of the eigenvalues as function of γ, (b) and (c) Phase diagram.

higher stationary state is indeterminate. Therefore, it has been shown that the mere introduction of a learning by investing mechanism makes possible the existence of growth and cycles in the 'AK' framework with adjustment costs. Moreover, it appears that low decreasing returns to the learning technology go together with indeterminacy of the higher steady state (Figures 5.3–5.5).

In this section, our objective was to explore a neo-Kaldorian approach to cyclical growth based on microeconomic foundations. Normally, models in this tradition favour a purely macroeconomic treatment of technical change and of the effect of learning. References to behaviour of individuals or groups only provide an implicit foundation for the representation of the economy at the aggregate level. Second, this type of cyclical growth model is usually entirely expressed in real terms. However, it is well known that financial factors play a central role in the process of diffusion and development of new technology. The framework developed in this chapter attempts to address these issues. First, the treatment of technical change through learning mechanisms is examined. We demonstrate that the shape of the learning curve plays a crucial role, by showing that the long-term dynamics of the economy is not, in the general case, independent of the short-term paths it follows. Second, the modelling of investment decisions and of their financing is achieved by introducing internal and external adjustment costs.

Concluding remarks

Our contribution contrasted two ways of building a theory of cyclical growth. The neo-Schumpeterian approach incorporates some of Schumpeter's ideas into a basically neoclassical interpretation of endogenous growth theory. Our neo-Kaldorian approach includes some of Kaldor's views in a simple AK type of endogenous growth theory. This precludes some of the major axiomatic assumptions of the neoclassical analytical tradition. A comparison of both approaches highlights different results. The neo-Schumpeterian approach shows that the introduction of GPT might lead to slumps in economic activity before, however, finally reaching a higher steady-state growth path. Our neo-Kaldorian reformulation points out that steady states are only benchmarks and that the prevailing situation is that of economic instability, indeterminacy or cyclical growth. The straightforward conclusion from this comparison is twofold. First, if the neo-Schumpeterian view includes some of Schumpeter's ideas, this framework proves to be insufficient to take account of permanent out-of steady-state processes. On the contrary, the introduction of Kaldor's ideas in a simple AK type of model is sufficient to deal with economic instability and endogenous cycles. Second, this first general result confirms Keynes's famous opinion according to which, 'the ideas of economists and political philosophers, both when they are right and they are wrong, are more powerful than is commonly understood.' Adapting another sentence taken from *The General Theory*'s 'concluding remarks' to the context of the present contribution, we might perhaps add that modern economists 'who believe themselves to be quite exempt from any intellectual influences, are usually the slaves of some defunct economist' (Keynes 1936/1973: 383).

Acknowledgements

A first version of this contribution was presented to the Spring Meeting of the Arbeitskreis Politische Ökonomie 'New Developments in Growth Theory and

Growth Policy', Stuttgart, 7–9 May 1999. We would like to thank P. Arestis, H. Hagemann, S. Seiter and the participants to this meeting for their stimulating criticism and suggestions; and S. Blankenburg for her highly valuable help in the preparation of the final version of this contribution. Usual caveats apply.

References

Aghion, P. (1998) *Endogenous Growth Theory*, Cambridge, Mass.: MIT Press.

—— (1999) 'On the Macroeconomic Effects of Major Technological Change', *Les Cahiers de l'Innovation* no. 99002, CNRS, Maison des Sciences Economiques, Paris.

—— and Howitt, P (1992) 'A Model of Growth Through Creative Destruction', *Econometrica*, 60: 323–51.

Arena, R. (1992) 'Schumpeter after Walras: "Economie Pure" or "Stylised Facts"?', in S.T. Lowry (ed.), *Perspective on the History of Economic Thought*, Vol. 8, *Contribution to the History of Economics*, London: Edward Elgar.

—— (1998) 'Credit and Financial, Markets in Keynes Conception of Endogenous Business Cycles: An Interpretation', in G. Abraham-Frois (ed.), *Non Linear Dynamics and Endogenous Cycles*, Berlin: Springer-Verlag.

—— and Raybaut, A. (1995) 'Cycles et Croissance: Un Point de Vue Neo Kaldorien', *Revue Economique*, 46: 1433–44.

Benhabib, J. and Farmer, J. (1994) 'Indeterminacy and Increasing Returns', *Journal of Economic Theory*, 63: 19–41.

—— and Perli, R. (1994) 'Uniqueness and Indeterminacy on the Dynamics of Endogenous Growth', *Journal of Economic Theory*, 63: 113–46.

Chamley, C. (1993) 'Externalities and Dynamics in Models of Learning by Doing', *International Economic Review*, 34: 583–609.

Delong, B. and Summers, L. (1991) 'Equipment Investment and Economic Growth', *Quarterly Journal of Economics*, 106: 445–502.

Evans, G., Honkapohja, S. and Romer, P. (1998) 'Growth Cycles', *American Economic Review*, 88: 493–515.

Feitchinger, G. and Sorger, G. (1988) 'Periodic Research Development' in G. Feitchinger (ed.), *Optimal Control Theory and Economic Analysis*, Amsterdam: North Holland, pp. 121–41.

Gilchrist, S. and Williams J.C. (1998) 'Putty Clay and Investment: A Business Cycle Analysis', FED Washington, DC, *Finance and Economics Discussion Series* 98-30.

Greiner, A. (1996) 'Endogenous Growth Cycles – Arrow's Learning by Doing Reconsidered', *Journal of Macroeconomics*, 18: 587–605.

—— (1997) 'Saddle Path Stability, Fluctuations and Indeterminacy in Economic Growth', *Studies in Nonlinear Dynamics and Econometrics*, 1: 105–18.

—— and Semmler, W. (1995) 'Multiple Steady States, Indeterminacy and Cycles in a Basic Model of Endogenous Growth', *Journal of Economics*, 63: 79–99.

Helpman, E. (1998) *General Purpose Technology and Economic Growth*, Cambridge Mass.: MIT Press.

—— and Trajtenberg, M. (1994) 'A Time to Sow and a Time to Reap: Growth Based on General Purpose Technologies', Center for Economic Research Policy, Working Paper No. 1080-Quoted and Reported by P. Aghion, and P. Howitt (1998) op. cit.

Hicks, J. (1950) *A Contribution to the Theory of the Trade Cycle*, New York: Oxford University Press.

Hubbard, R.G., Kashyap, A.K. and Whited, T.M. (1995) 'Internal Finance and Firm Investment', *Journal of Money Credit and Banking*, 27: 683–701.

Kaldor, N. (1954/1960) 'The Relations of Economic Growth and Cyclical Fluctuations', *Economic Journal*, 64: 53–71, republished in N. Kaldor (1960), *Essays on Economic Stability and Growth*, London: Duckworth.

—— (1972) 'The Irrelevance of Equilibrium Economics', *Economic Journal*, 82: 1237–55, reprinted in F. Targetti and A. Thirwall (eds) (1989), *The Essential Kaldor*, London: Duckworth.

—— (1975) 'What is Wrong with Economic Theory', *Quarterly Journal of Economics*, 85: 891–6, reprinted in F. Targetti and A. Thirwall (eds) (1989), *The Essential Kaldor*, London: Duckworth.

Keynes, J.M. (1936) *The General Theory of Employment, Interest and Money*, London: Macmillan, reprint of 1973.

Kurz, H. (1998) 'The Path of Economic Growth: Some Recent Developments', in H. Hagemann and H. Kurz (eds), *Political Economics in Retrospect. Essays in Memory of Adolph Lowe*, London: Edward Elgar.

Pasinetti, L. (1960) 'Cyclical Fluctuations and Economic Growth', *Oxford Economic Papers*, 12: 215–42, republished in L. Pasinetti (1975), *Growth and Income Distribution-Essays in Economic Theory*, Cambridge: Cambridge University Press.

Romer, P. (1990) 'Endogenous Technical Change', *Journal of Political Economy*, 98: 71–102.

Targetti, F. (1984) 'Una biografia intellecttuale', introduction to N. Kaldor, *Equilibrio, distribuzione e crescita*, Torino: Giulio Einaudi Editore.

Young, A. (1993) 'Inventions and Bounded Learning by Doing', *Journal of Political Economy*, 101: 443–72.

6 Endogenous growth and economic fluctuations

Christiane Clemens and Susanne Soretz

Introduction

For a long time, the predominant view on growth and business cycle theory has been that the economy follows a long-run smooth evolution called *trend* that is disturbed by random events. According to this, business cycles are defined as deviations from trend. Implicitly, it is assumed that there is no interaction between long-run and cyclical components. This interpretation of overall macroeconomic performance consequently leads to a separate treatment of both phenomena within macroeconomic theory.

The real business cycle theory traces back to Kydland and Prescott (1982) and Long and Plosser (1983). Common to most contributions of this branch of research is the discussion of detrended macroeconomic models, that is 'to view long-run growth as exogenous and, hence, independent of the fundamental shocks' (Jones *et al.* 1999: 1). Attention is mainly drawn towards the impact of permanent and transitory shocks on economic performance with emphasis biased towards the effects of short-run disturbances. Contrary to this, the proponents of modern growth theory, pioneered by Romer (1986), mostly keep to a deterministic framework that matches the concept of a smooth trend.

This separation of growth and business cycle theory is challenged by Prescott (1986), who argues that there is little empirical evidence that productivity shocks do not affect long-run growth. For Germany, his argument is supported by empirical studies of Neusser (1991) and Reimers (1991). Further evidence that output variability and expected growth are related is provided by Kormendi and Meguire (1985) and by Ramey and Ramey (1995) although their conclusions regarding the sign of correlation differ.

Our aim is to integrate the analysis of long-run economic development and of economic cycles within one consistent framework. This allows for a comprehensive understanding of how growth and fluctuations interact. Our paper draws from real business cycle theory in that we assume productivity shocks as the source of economic uncertainty. This approach is motivated empirically with the Solow-residual that reflects the part of the growth rate that cannot be explained by endogenous factors. The time-series of the Solow-residual can then be viewed as realisations of a stochastic technology process. In RBC-theory the agents of the model respond to technological shocks with a change in their intertemporal savings decision and their labour supply. Yet, in general, all changes of the macroeconomic variables are considered to be of transitory nature. A permanent effect of fluctuations on economic behaviour is only achieved if the underlying stochastic process displays the characteristics of a stochastic trend – in short, if we assume fundamental shocks.

Only recently the integration of growth and business cycle theory has gained attraction, for instance with the contributions of Cazzavillan (1996), Collard (1999), Jones *et al.* (1999) or Smith (1996a). Their work is supported by one of the most striking observations of empirical macroeconomics, namely that the volatility of aggregate income exceeds the volatility of aggregate consumption. As Carroll and Samwick (1997) point out, there is a strong notion to smooth consumption by transferring irregular income flows via accumulation into regular consumption flows.[1] Hubbard *et al.* (1993), Skinner (1988) and Zeldes (1989) conclude from their empirical studies that in this context the bequest motive as well as the motive for precautionary saving form two important factors. Caballero (1990) stresses the strong empirical evidence especially in favor of precautionary savings.

The precautionary motive for saving was first discussed theoretically by Leland (1968) and Sandmo (1970). Both authors argue that the risk-averse agent responds to uncertainty within the intertemporal decision on consumption and saving. Additional savings can then be viewed as a self-insurance on capital markets against future income risk. As Sandmo (1970) points out, both, the source of income as well as the individual degree of risk aversion are important to explain the appearance of precautionary saving. He distinguishes between capital risk and income risk, the latter for instance arising from uncertain wage incomes. This interdependence between uncertainty and savings gains a broader interpretation if it is discussed within the theory of endogenous growth. In modern growth theory, the growth rate of the economy is an endogenously determined function of factors that affect aggregate savings. Hence, if risk impacts on savings there also will be an effect on long-run growth. This argument establishes the combination of growth and business cycle theory and helps to overcome the separate treatment of the two branches of macroeconomic theory.

Recent applications to stochastic growth theory, e.g. Devereux and Smith (1994) and Obstfeld (1994), focus on aspects of international risk sharing. Another field of interest has been the analysis of fiscal policy. The contributions of Turnovsky (1993, 1999a,b), Smith (1996b), Clemens and Soretz (1997), Corsetti (1997), Clemens (1999), Soretz (2000) and Clemens *et al.* (2002) are devoted to the role of tax policy and public spending in stochastically growing economies.

Up to now, the question to what extent different types of risk – capital risk and income risk – contribute to long-run growth of the economy has been of minor importance. One of our objectives will be to stress the part different sources of income take in the explanation of stochastic growth. For this reason, we contrast two classes of endogenous growth models, both of them subject to productivity shocks. On the one hand, we discuss the AK-type model *à la* Jones and Manuelli (1990). The stochastic version of this framework dates back to Eaton (1981). In this economy the agent is exposed to capital risk only. On the other hand, we examine the stochastic variant of the Romer (1986) model. The agent of this economy receives capital and wage incomes. In terms of Sandmo (1970), he is subject to a capital as well as an income risk.

Our chapter addresses the question of how the presence of technological shocks affects long-run growth of the economy. Furthermore, we ask for the consequences of alternative assumptions on factor income distribution. To answer the first question, we set up a fairly general model assuming aggregate as well as individual-specific productivity shocks. In the section on 'Elements of the model and individual optimisation', the intertemporal decision-making of a risk-averse agent is discussed. This enables us to draw conclusions regarding the consequences of risk on long-run growth. The section on 'Technology and market equilibrium', specifies the two alternative production technologies that allow for the determination of market equilibrium. In the section on 'Precautionary saving in the presence of capital and income risk', the market equilibria for both technologies are compared, the results giving new insights to the question which part different types of income play in the determination of long-run stochastic growth. The final section summarises the results. Technical details are relegated to the Appendix.

Elements of the model and individual optimisation

Our basic model is a general approach to the question of how uncertainty impacts on long-run growth. This allows for a more rigorous understanding and a comprehensive discussion of intertemporal wealth accumulation in a risky environment.[2] For this reason, all details concerning alternative production technologies are deferred to the next chapter.

We consider an economy populated by a continuum $[0,1]$ of infinitely lived individuals. The agents are homogeneous with respect to their preferences and their ex ante endowments. Each of them maximises welfare according to the von Neumann–Morgenstern expected utility function

$$V_i(0) = \mathrm{E}_0 \int_0^\infty U[C_i(t)]e^{-\beta t}\, dt \tag{1}$$

The single argument of lifetime utility (1) is the intertemporal consumption flow $C_i(t)$, which we assume to be instantaneously deterministic. E_0 is the expectations operator conditional on time 0 information. The parameter β is the discount rate, positive by assumption. Let the current period utility function be strictly concave with positive third derivative and of the constant relative risk-aversion form (CRRA):

$$U[C_i(t)] = \begin{cases} \dfrac{C_i(t)^{1-\rho}}{1-\rho} & \text{if } \rho > 0, \rho \neq 1 \\ \ln C_i(t) & \text{if } \rho = 1 \end{cases} \tag{2}$$

The coefficient ρ denotes the Arrow–Pratt measure of relative risk aversion and equals the reciprocal of the intertemporal elasticity of substitution.

The agents hold two assets in their portfolios. The first are riskless bonds $B_i(t)$ which are considered to be perpetuities, paying a sure instantaneous nominal yield of r_B. With payouts reinvested and continuously compounded $B_i(t)$ follows the differential equation

$$dB_i(t) = r_B B_i(t)\, dt \tag{3}$$

The second asset is risky physical capital. For simplicity, depreciation is neglected. At each instant of time, individual production is subject to two types of risk: Hicks-neutral aggregate and idiosyncratic productivity shocks, which are taken to be uncorrelated. The random components $dz(t), dz_i(t)$ are increments to standard Wiener processes with zero mean and variance $\sigma^2 dt$, and $\sigma_i^2 dt$ respectively. We assume aggregate and individual-specific risk to be serially (and individually) independent. In accordance with the law of large numbers, idiosyncratic uncertainty vanishes on the aggregate level. Under the additional assumption that production is linear in the accumulable factors, the individual capital stock evolves according to the stochastic differential equation

$$dK_i(t) = \psi(t)K_i(t)\, dt + K_i(t)(\sigma(t)dz(t) + \sigma_i(t)dz_i(t)) \tag{4}$$

$\psi(t)$ is the instantaneous expected rate of change. As subsequently will be shown, $\psi(t)$ equals the expected growth rate of the economy. The diffusion coefficient incorporates the instantaneous standard deviations $\sigma(t)$, $\sigma_i(t)$ of both types of risk. In case both, $\psi(t)$ and $\sigma(t)$, $\sigma_i(t)$, are time and state independent, accumulation is described by a homogeneous stochastic differential equation with constant coefficients. The individual capital stock follows a stochastic trend such that permanent effects of the productivity shocks have to be taken into account.

The other factor of production, labour $L_i(t)$, is assumed to be inelastically supplied. For analytical convenience, the labour force is normalised to unity. Given the assumption of Hicks-neutral productivity shocks, wage incomes as well as capital incomes are stochastic. In terms of Sandmo (1970), the agents are exposed to capital and income risk.

Individual wealth $W_i(t)$ is the sum of the holdings of financial wealth and real capital

$$W_i(t) = B_i(t) + K_i(t) \tag{5}$$

with the corresponding portfolio shares $K_i(t)/W_i(t) = n$ and $B_i(t)/W_i(t) = 1 - n$. The assumptions (3)–(5) immediately imply the following expression for intertemporal wealth accumulation of agent i

$$dW_i(t) = [r_B W_i(t) + (r_K - r_B)K_i(t) + \omega - C_i(t)]\, dt + dw_i(t) \tag{6}$$

Real capital has an expected return r_K, while the expected wage rate is given by ω. The stochastic process of wealth is defined as $dw_i(t) = [r_K K_i(t) + \omega](\sigma\, dz(t) + \sigma_i\, dz_i(t))$.

The objective of agent i is to select her rate of consumption as well as her portfolio of assets in order to maximise the expected value of lifetime utility (1) according to the wealth constraint (6), taking prices as given[3]

$$\max_{C_i, K_i, W_i} V_i(0) = E_0 \int_0^\infty U[C_i] e^{-\beta t}\, dt$$

$$\text{s.t.} \quad dW_i = [r_B W_i + (r_K - r_B) K_i + \omega - C_i]\, dt + dw_i \tag{7}$$

$$\text{and} \quad K_i(0) > 0,\, z(0) = z_i(0) = 0$$

Let $V[W_i(t), t]$ represent the agent's maximum feasible level of lifetime utility. The value function V is considered to be real-valued, strictly concave, continuously differentiable in W, and separable in time, that is

$$V[W_i(t), t] = e^{-\beta t} J[W_i(t)] \tag{8}$$

Utilising a value function for the solution of the model is the common approach for this class of dynamic models. This is due to the fact that, although accumulation follows a continuous-time stochastic process, it is not differentiable with respect to time. Application of Itô's Lemma allows for the derivation of the stochastic differential of the value function. Then, given the program (7), we obtain the following objective function:

$$\max_{C_i, K_i, W_i} L = e^{-\beta t} \{ U(C_i) - \beta J(W_i) + J'(W_i)[r_B W_i + (r_K - r_B) K_i + \omega - C_i]$$

$$+ \tfrac{1}{2} \sigma_W^2 J''(W_i) \} \tag{9}$$

Taking derivatives of (9) with respect to C_i, K_i, and W_i leads to the usual first-order conditions. These can then be employed to derive the optimal values for consumption and asset holdings if we additionally take into account, that the current period utility function displays constant relative risk aversion[4,5]

$$C_i^* = [J'(W_i)]^{-1/\rho} \tag{10}$$

$$K_i^* = -\frac{J'(W_i)}{J''(W_i)} \cdot \frac{r_K - r_B}{r_K^2(\sigma^2 + \sigma_i^2)} - \frac{\omega}{r_K} \tag{11}$$

The optimal values of consumption and physical capital are functions of the derivatives of the value function $J'(W_i)$ and $J''(W_i)$. Substitution of C_i^* and K_i^* into the derivative of the objective function (9) with respect to wealth, $\partial L/\partial W_i$, leads to a stochastic differential equation in $J(W_i)$:[6]

$$0 = J'(W_i)(r_B - \beta)$$

$$+ J''(W_i) \left[r_B W_i - \frac{(r_K - r_B)^2}{r_K^2(\sigma^2 + \sigma_i^2)} \cdot \frac{J'(W_i)}{J''(W_i)} + \frac{r_B \omega}{r_K} - [J'(W_i)]^{-1/\rho} \right]$$

$$+ \frac{1}{2} J'''(W_i) \frac{(r_K - r_B)^2}{r_K^2(\sigma^2 + \sigma_i^2)} \cdot \frac{[J'(W_i)]^2}{[J''(W_i)]^2} \tag{12}$$

Equation (12), when evaluated at the optimum (C_i^*, K_i^*), is an ordinary differential equation. This emanates mainly from two assumptions: time separability and infinite time-horizon. Together with the assumptions on current period utility and on production technology (next section) this allows for the determination of a closed-form solution of the model. The usual solution procedure is trial and error, finding a function $J(W_i)$ that satisfies the optimality conditions. We conjecture that the propensity to consume out of wealth μ as well as the portfolio shares $n, 1 - n$ are constant in steady-state growth, that is

$$C_i^* = \mu W_i, \quad K_i^* = n W_i, \quad B_i^* = (1 - n) W_i \quad \text{with } \mu, n = \text{const} \quad (13)$$

If this conjecture turns out to be correct, the expected equilibrium growth path can be completely described as a nonstochastic function of the underlying parameters. With (13), it is now possible to determine the derivatives of the value function with respect to wealth from the first-order conditions (see equation (A.6) below). Using this in (11) and (12) leads to the following expressions for the optimal expected propensity to consume out of wealth and optimal portfolio choice

$$\mu = \frac{\beta}{\rho} + \frac{\rho - 1}{\rho} \left[r_B + \frac{1}{2} \frac{(r_K - r_B)^2}{\rho r_K^2 (\sigma^2 + \sigma_i^2)} \right] + \frac{r_B \omega}{r_K W_i} \quad (14)$$

$$n = \frac{r_K - r_B}{\rho r_K^2 (\sigma^2 + \sigma_i^2)} - \frac{\omega}{r_K W_i} \quad (15)$$

The consumption–wealth ratio μ is a function of the real rates of return on assets, the wage rate and the preference parameters. By now, three of them are unknown. The market prices r_B, r_K and ω are to be determined in equilibrium. The solution conjecture is consistent with the macroeconomic equilibrium if, after substitution for the market prices, μ and n are invariant with respect to wealth. This is not necessarily the case at this point of the analysis, as can easily be seen from (14) and (15).

The propensity to consume is the sum of two terms. The part that is independent of the variances of the technological disturbances will be referred to as drift component. The second part, the so-called diffusion component, reflects the individual response to aggregate and idiosyncratic risk, and is crucially determined by the index of relative risk aversion ρ.

The differential on asset returns $r_K - r_B$ is the main factor in explaining the size of the portfolio share n. The more the expected return on physical capital exceeds the nominal interest rate on bonds, the larger the corresponding portfolio share will be. From equation (15) it becomes obvious that the agent is only willing to hold risky physical capital, if he is compensated by a risk premium, that is $r_K > r_B$.

The optimal values for consumption and portfolio choice can now be used to determine the expected growth rate of individual wealth. Combining (14) and (15) with the intertemporal budget constraint (6), and taking regard of $E[dw] = 0$, enables us to express the expected accumulation of wealth $\psi = E(dW)/(W\,dt)$

by the following relationship:

$$\psi = \frac{1}{\rho}(r_B - \beta) + \frac{1}{2}(\rho + 1)\frac{(r_K - r_B)^2}{\rho^2 r_K^2 (\sigma^2 + \sigma_i^2)} \tag{16}$$

The expected growth rate, is the sum of two components. The second reflects the individual response to productivity risk. Hence, within the framework considered here, it is evident that permanent or fundamental shocks affect long-run growth. The expected growth rate is determined completely by the underlying parameters of the model and by market prices. From (16), it becomes obvious that only asset returns are relevant to accumulation as ψ is independent of wage incomes. Nevertheless, we will demonstrate in the section of 'Precautionary saving in the presence of capital and income' that in competitive equilibrium the growth rate is affected by the factor income distribution.

Technology and market equilibrium

In this section, two alternative extensions to the basic approach of the previous section are discussed. In order to determine the overall macroeconomic equilibrium, it is necessary to implement a specific production technology into the existing framework. We are especially interested in the consequences of different sources of random income flows. For this reason, we consider both, a linear technology, namely the AK-model, as well as the human capital approach of Romer (1986). Common to both is the important feature of new growth theory that, with returns to reproducible factors sufficiently bounded away from zero, the requirements for ongoing growth of per-capita incomes are met.

The usage of the linear technology within models of endogenous growth traces back to Jones and Manuelli (1990) or Rebelo (1991), although a stochastic version was already discussed by Eaton (1981). In this setting, capital is viewed broadly, as to encompass physical and human capital, public infrastructure, etc. The important aspect for our analysis will be that households receive an income solely from the accumulable factor. In terms of Sandmo (1970), the agents are exposed to capital risk only.

The instantaneous output flow dY_i^{AK} is assumed to be generated from capital K_i by the stochastic process[7]

$$dY_i^{AK} = \gamma K_i (dt + dz + dz_i), \quad \gamma > 0 \tag{17}$$

Recall, that dz represents the aggregate Hicks-neutral productivity shock, whereas dz_i reflects individual-specific technological disturbances. Note that due to normalization, ex ante aggregate and individual quantities are identical.

The second technology applies the learning-by-doing setting first discussed by Arrow (1962) and further developed by Romer (1986). The key assumption of this model is that each firm's technical knowledge displays the characteristics of a pure public good, which are non-rivalry and non-excludability. The agents of the model neglect the external effect of human capital accumulation. Hence, only private capital returns enter into the determination of optimal individual investment. This private return to physical capital falls short of the socially optimal one. Consequently, a competitive equilibrium is characterised by a suboptimally high propensity to consume and suboptimally low savings when compared to the efficient path. The stochastic output flow of firm i in the Arrow–Romer economy can be written as follows

$$dY_i^{AR} = \gamma K_i^\alpha (L_i A)^{1-\alpha}(dt + dz + dz_i), \quad \alpha \in (0, 1) \tag{18}$$

The stock of knowledge A acts as a Harrod-neutral growth parameter and is enhanced by investment in privately owned capital. In macroeconomic equilibrium A equals K, the economy-wide stock of capital. Due to the knowledge spillover, aggregate production is linear in capital, thus assuring permanent growth. Note that although labour is normalised to unity, (17) and (18) are not identical. The agents receive stochastic wage incomes. In contrast to the AK-model, the agents of the Arrow–Romer economy are subject to both types of risk: capital and income risk.

The assumptions on production technology enable us to determine the macroeconomic equilibrium. The agents are ex ante homogeneous and do not differ with respect to their investment and consumption plans. We assume perfect competition in the factor markets. The factor returns can then be obtained by the usual marginal productivity conditions. The expected capital return of the AK-model can then be determined as

$$r^{AK} = \gamma \tag{19}$$

whereas expected factor returns of the Arrow–Romer model are given by

$$r^{AR} = \alpha\gamma \tag{20}$$

$$\omega = (1 - \alpha)\gamma K \tag{21}$$

Substitution of (19), (20) and (21) respectively, into the optimal values for the expected consumption wealth ratio (14) and the expected portfolio share (15) yields

$$\mu^{AK} = \frac{\beta}{\rho} + \frac{\rho - 1}{\rho}\left[r_B + \frac{1}{2}(\gamma - r_B)n^{AK}\right] \tag{22}$$

$$n^{AK} = \frac{\gamma - r_B}{\rho\gamma^2(\sigma^2 + \sigma_i^2)} \tag{23}$$

and

$$\mu^{AR} = \frac{\beta}{\rho} + \frac{\rho - 1}{\rho}r_B + (\gamma - r_B)n^{AR} - \frac{1}{2}(\rho + 1)(n^{AR})\gamma^2(\sigma^2 + \sigma_i^2) \tag{24}$$

$$n^{AR} = \frac{\alpha\gamma - r_B}{\rho\alpha\gamma^2(\sigma^2 + \sigma_i^2)} \tag{25}$$

Equations (22)–(25) verify for both technologies the solution conjecture (13) of the preceding section. The consumption–wealth ratio as well as the portfolio share of physical capital are constant in equilibrium.

This is an appropriate point to draw first conclusions. Under uncertainty, the agent's decision-making is twofold. First, he chooses the optimal allocation of consumption over time. This decision determines the total amount of wealth. Second, he develops a portfolio strategy on capital and financial markets. A further observation of (22) and (24) reveals that these decisions obviously cannot be viewed independently for both of the underlying technologies. In general, the propensity to consume out of wealth is determined by portfolio choice. The response of μ to a change in n crucially depends on the differential of asset returns and on the index of relative risk aversion. Contrary, optimal portfolio allocation is not affected by consumption choice. This result can be attributed to the assumption of constant relative risk aversion. One important feature of these preferences is that the individual degree of risk aversion is invariant with respect to wealth. Hence, the portfolio shares do not change when individual wealth grows. Another important determinant for these results is the Markov-property of the underlying stochastic processes. Due to this property, historical realisations of the stochastic process do not have an effect on future activities when the presence is known. In short, there is no path dependence. The conclusions drawn for both endogenous growth models coincide with the results of Merton (1969) and Samuelson (1969) for the intertemporal consumption-based capital asset pricing model (C–CAPM).

Up to this point, the only unknown variable left is the sure nominal interest rate r_B. This can be determined via an arbitrage argument. According to the assumptions on aggregate and individual-specific risk, the agents are ex ante homogeneous. On the aggregate level, they are subject to the *same* realization of the productivity shock which cannot be diversified on the national level. Regarding the idiosyncratic risk, the agents have identical subjective probability distributions. Under complete information, they may agree to trade state-contingent Arrow securities such that individual shocks are completely pooled. But, in the framework considered here, there simply is no institution, credit or international capital market that could offer a sure bond.[8]

Hence, in autarky, the individual capital stock equals individual wealth. The same argument applies to the aggregate level. This enables us to obtain the certainty equivalent to capital return for each technology from the equilibrium values of the portfolio share (23) and (25). Setting $n^{AK} = n^{AR} = 1$ yields

$$r_B^{AK} = \gamma - \rho\gamma^2(\sigma^2 + \sigma_i^2) \tag{26}$$

$$r_B^{AR} = \alpha\gamma - \alpha\rho\gamma^2(\sigma^2 + \sigma_i^2) \tag{27}$$

If the sure interest rate takes on the value (26), or (27) respectively, the agent is indifferent between investment in physical and financial capital. The arbitrage conditions reflect a well-known result from finance theory. A risk-averse investor is only willing to hold equity if he is compensated with a higher return. The expected marginal product of capital exceeds the interest rate by the amount of the risk premium which is given by the second term on the right-hand side of (26) and (27). The size of the risk premium is crucially affected by the variances of the productivity shocks and the degree of risk aversion. The higher the Arrow–Pratt index of relative risk aversion, the greater the risk premium will be. This theoretical result is confirmed by empirical findings of Mehra and Prescott (1985) who analyzed the average excess return of US stocks over government bonds.[9]

A further analysis of (26) and (27) reveals that both differ with respect to the factor α. At this point it becomes evident that the agents of the Arrow–Romer model neglect their individual contribution to human capital accumulation. For this reason both, the expected capital return as well as the safe interest rate, are lower than in the AK-model. If we now substitute for the arbitrage conditions and $n = 1$ in the definitions of the propensity to consume and the expected growth rate, the model reduces to the following core relationships

$$\mu^{AK} = \frac{\beta}{\rho} + \frac{\rho - 1}{\rho}\gamma + \frac{1}{2}(1 - \rho)\gamma^2(\sigma^2 + \sigma_i^2) \tag{28}$$

$$\mu^{AR} = \frac{\beta}{\rho} + \frac{\rho - \alpha}{\rho}\gamma + \gamma^2(\sigma^2 + \sigma_i^2)\left(\alpha - \frac{\rho + 1}{2}\right) \tag{29}$$

and

$$\psi^{AK} = \frac{1}{\rho}(\gamma - \beta) + \frac{1}{2}(\rho - 1)\gamma^2(\sigma^2 + \sigma_i^2) \tag{30}$$

$$\psi^{AR} = \frac{1}{\rho}(\alpha\gamma - \beta) + \gamma^2(\sigma^2 + \sigma_i^2)\left(\frac{\rho + 1}{2} - \alpha\right) \tag{31}$$

As mentioned above, the growth rates are the sum of two components. The first term is equal to the growth rate of the respective deterministic model. Yet, in contrast to the riskless environment, a marginal return to capital exceeding the rate of time preference is not a sufficient condition to assert positive growth. Furthermore, the second component has to be taken into account, which reflects the individual response to technological risk. The main determinant of this term is the measure of risk aversion ρ. Additionally, in the Arrow–Romer model the capital income share α plays an important role. From (28) to (31) follows immediately that expected growth in the Arrow–Romer economy is only lower than on the Pareto-efficient path if the certainty equivalent to capital return, r_B, is positive. Again, in a stochastic setting additional requirements regarding the feasibility of solutions have to be met.[10]

The expected growth rates (30) and (31) are time-invariant functions of the underlying parameters of both economies. A rise in the rate of time preference leads to a decline in the growth rate as current consumption becomes more attractive. The household reduces future consumption possibilities via less accumulation. The discount rate appears only in the first component and replicates the results known from the deterministic setting. A rise in the productivity parameter γ affects growth twofold. On the one hand, it increases mean capital income thus enhancing accumulation. This effect is measured by the change of the first component. On the other hand, a rise in γ increases the volatility of stochastic capital income parts. Whether this suppresses or encourages growth crucially depends on the degree of risk aversion and is the focus of attention in the following chapter.

Let us now turn to the effects of uncertainty on macroeconomic equilibrium. The most important insight from (30) and (31) is that there is a linkage between growth and business cycle theory. Economic fluctuations have long-lasting effects on macroeconomic trend. Higher risk in the economy, as measured by an increase of the variances of the technology shocks σ^2 and σ_i^2, affects the diffusion component of the expected growth rate to the extent already discussed above for the parameter γ. From (30) and (31) it can be seen that the addition of any uncorrelated, that is *independent*, risk has a size effect on the growth rate and does not change qualitative results. In the presence of complete markets the agents may eliminate idiosyncratic income risk by trading Arrow securities (Arrow 1964). In this case $\sigma_i^2 = 0$. The agents are identical and macroeconomic performance is only influenced by the aggregate productivity shock.[11] Figure 6.1(a) contrasts the two cases.[12] It is evident that in the presence of both technological shocks the evolution of the capital stock is more erratic than with perfect pooling of individual-specific risk. But furthermore, there is a change in long-run growth. The law of motion of the capital stock is described by a geometric diffusion process, that is capital is log-normally distributed in time and follows a stochastic trend. Figure 6.1(b) illustrates this result. In general, the capital stock of time t can be derived for $\psi \in \left\{\psi^{AK}, \psi^{AR}\right\}$ as a solution of (4):

$$K(t) = K(0) \cdot \exp\left\{\left(\psi - \frac{1}{2}\gamma^2\left(\sigma^2 + \sigma_i^2\right)\right)t + \gamma[\sigma z(t) + \sigma_i z_i(t)]\right\} \quad (32)$$

We can now turn to the second purpose of this chapter, namely to explain to what extent the factor income distribution affects long-run growth. Our attention is especially directed towards the distinction between capital and income risk and the specific role the individual degree of risk aversion plays for intertemporal decision-making.

Precautionary saving in the presence of capital and income risk

The Arrow–Pratt measure of relative risk aversion affects the expected growth rate of the economy twofold. On the one hand, it appears within the intertemporal elasticity of substitution in the first component of the equilibrium macroeconomic variables. The economic interpretation is as usual: the lower the intertemporal elasticity of substitution, the less the agents are willing to deviate from a smooth pattern of consumption over time. Consequently, this part of the growth rate decreases with an increase in ρ. On the other hand, the coefficient of risk aversion appears in the second component of the growth rates.[13] Here, a change in ρ leads to the opposite

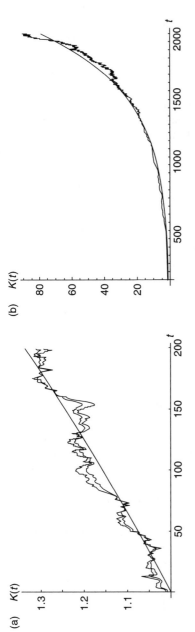

Figure 6.1 Stochastic endogenous growth: (a) Aggregate and idiosyncratic risk and (b) Long-run exponential growth.

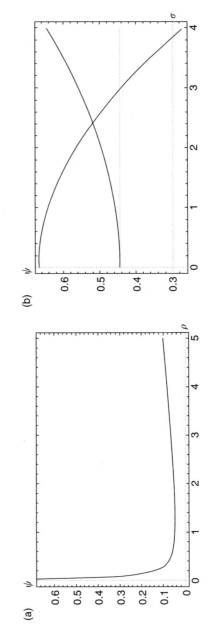

Figure 6.2 Growth effects of the diffusion component: (a) Growth and risk aversion and (b) (Non) precautionary saving and certainty equivalence.

response. Higher risk aversion corresponds to an increase in savings. These coun-terworking effects of the index of risk aversion on expected growth are illustrated in Figure 6.2(a).

As we are primarily concerned with the effects of productivity risk on long-run growth, we focus our attention on the second component of equations (30) and (31). We are able to distinguish three different cases. First, if the index of relative risk aversion is sufficiently high the second component is of positive sign, and the growth rate of the stochastic economy exceeds the deterministic one. Following Leland (1968) and Sandmo (1970), the agents have a motive for precautionary sav-ings. The risk-averse individual tries to self-insure on intertemporal capital markets with an increase in accumulation. In Figure 6.2(b) this case is represented by the increasing line. The higher individual risk, the larger the growth rate will be. As marginal utility is convex in consumption, a rise in uncertainty increases expected marginal utility. To satisfy the Euler equation, expected future consumption grows relative to current consumption thus leading to a rise in accumulation.

In the second case, if the coefficient of risk aversion is sufficiently low, the growth rate of the stochastic environment falls short of the deterministic one. This case is given by the decreasing line in Figure 6.2(b). In this situation the agent favours (safe) current consumption to (risky) future consumption. The third case, where the diffusion component of the expected growth rate vanishes, is called *certainty equiv-alence*. The growth rate of the stochastic setting equals the deterministic one. In Figure 6.2(b), the case of certainty equivalence is represented by the dotted line.[14]

Let us now turn towards the question, to what extent the source of income affects these general results. Following Sandmo (1970), in the presence of a pure capital risk, the agent's response to an increase in uncertainty is ambiguous. The intertemporal income and substitution effects are of opposite sign. Increased saving raises both the mean and the volatility of future income flows. While the rise in expected future income encourages savings via the intertemporal income effect, the increase in volatility depresses growth, due to the negative substitution effect.

These results are reflected by the expected growth rate of the AK-model (30). Given the assumption of CRRA-preferences, the net effect of positive income and negative substitution effect depends solely on the degree of individual risk aversion ρ. The case of precautionary savings corresponds to the dominance of the income effect and is given for $\rho > 1$. The intertemporal effects exactly offset for $\rho = 1$, the case of certainty equivalence. For $\rho < 1$, the expected growth rate of the stochastic environment falls below the growth rate of the deterministic one, due to the domination of the substitution effect.

If we contrast these results for a pure capital risk with the determinants of growth in the Arrow–Romer model, there is one significant difference. The sign of the diffusion component of the expected growth rate (31) is not only determined by the coefficient of relative risk aversion but additionally by the factor income dis-tribution, as measured by the capital income share α. Given the assumption of a Hicks-neutral productivity shock, all factors of production are affected by the dis-turbances to the same extent. Consequently, the agents of the Arrow–Romer model are exposed to both, income as well as capital risk.[15] Sandmo (1970) concludes for the case of a pure income risk that decreasing absolute risk aversion is a sufficient condition for saving out of precautionary motives. For the constant relative risk-aversion preferences considered here, this condition is satisfied for any $\rho > 0$. Within the Arrow–Romer model, the partial elasticity of production, α, decides on the question to what extent capital and income risk contribute to precautionary saving. Due to the impact of income risk, a motive for precautionary savings can already be observed for any $\rho > 2\alpha - 1$. A higher share of income risk on overall risk corresponds to a lower value of α. From this we conclude that the margin of certainty equivalence is shifted downwards towards values of $\rho < 1$. Note that in the presence of income risk the case of logarithmic preferences does no longer correspond to certainty equivalence but to precautionary savings.

Summary of results

This chapter was concerned with two questions. The first question was, to what extent fundamental productivity shocks – modelled by a stochastic trend – affect long-run growth. We demonstrated that risk-averse agents respond to individual and aggregate uncertainty within their intertemporal allocation of consumption and their portfolio choice. Usually, they will choose a growth rate that deviates from the one of the deterministic setting. The addition of any independent distributed risk has a size effect on the expected growth rate of the economy.

We identified the individual attitude towards risk, as measured by the Arrow–Pratt index of relative risk aversion, as an important factor for explaining long-run expected growth. Higher risk aversion corresponds to higher growth. With precautionary savings, the risk-averse agents try to self-insure on intertemporal capital markets. Contrary to this, low risk aversion may even cause the growth rate of the stochastic environment to fall below the deterministic one.

The second question was, to what extent the factor income distribution affects the results. To answer this question, we considered two alternative approaches to modern growth theory, namely the AK-model and the Arrow–Romer model. While in the first setting the agents are subject to a pure capital risk, the agents of the second model receive stochastic capital as well as labour incomes. The important result of this analysis is, that in the presence of income risk the phenomenon of precautionary savings already occurs for lower values of the measure of relative risk aversion. The higher the income share of non-accumulable factors, the lower the risk aversion needs to be to cause additional saving. This results can be ascribed to the fact that under income risk an increase in savings raises the mean of future income flows, while under capital risk savings additionally affect the variability of future returns.

Notes

1 The two most important theoretical explanations for this phenomenon are the life-cycle hypothesis and the permanent-income hypothesis.
2 The set-up draws from Merton (1969).

3 For notational convenience, the (t) part of the variables is omitted.

4 The details of optimisation are given in the Appendix.

5 The optimal amount of financial wealth can be obtained residually with $B = W - K$.

6 The respective derivative is given by equation (A.3) in the Appendix.

7 Accordingly, $Y(t)$ denotes the cumulative production of time t.

8 We implicitly assume that even the public sector does not provide an insurance in form of government bonds (see Corsetti 1997; Clemens and Soretz 1997). The macroeconomic effects of international capital market integration are discussed by Devereux and Smith (1994) and Obstfeld (1994).

9 Mehra and Prescott (1985) came to the conclusion that the differential return of 6.2 per cent points can only be explained by unrealistic high values for individual risk aversion.

10 Of course, the transversality condition has to be satisfied to assure the case of bounded utility. For details see equations (A.4) and (A.7) in the Appendix.

11 If we discuss idiosyncratic risks on incomplete markets the agents become heterogeneous with respect to their capital accumulation. Market-clearing prices then depend on the entire distribution of agent types. In our model the evolution of types would be endogenous which causes analytical intractability. For a detailed discussion see Clemens (1999).

12 The model was parametrically specified as follows: $K(0) = 1, \alpha = 0.35, \beta = 0.03$, $\gamma = 0.5, \rho = 1.5, \sigma = 0.05, \sigma_i = 0.03$. Figure 6.1(a) plots 200 periods, Figure 6.1(b) plots 2000 periods.

13 Epstein and Zin (1989) developed a preference representation that separates the IES and the coefficient of relative risk aversion. For implementation in stochastic growth models see Obstfeld (1994), Smith (1996b) or Clemens and Soretz (1999).

14 Note, that this case should not be mistaken for risk-neutral decisions, that is $\rho = 0$.

15 The importance of the factor income distribution is even stressed, if we allow for distributive disturbances, see Clemens and Soretz (1998).

References

Arrow, K.J. (1962) 'The Economic Implications of Learning by Doing', *Review of Economic Studies*, 29: 155–73.

—— (1964) 'The Role of Securities in the Optimal Allocation of Risk Bearing', *Review of Economic Studies,* 31: 91–6.

Caballero, R.J. (1990) 'Consumption Puzzles and Precautionary Savings', *Journal of Monetary Economics*, 25: 113–36.

Carroll, C.D. and Samwick, A.A. (1997) 'The Nature of Precautionary Wealth', *Journal of Monetary Economics*, 40: 41–71.

Cazzavillan, G. (1996) 'Public Spending, Endogenous Growth, and Endogenous Fluctuations', *Journal of Economic Theory*, 71: 394–415.

Clemens, C. (1999) *Endogenes Wachstum, Einkommensunsicherheit und Besteuerung*, Marburg: Metropolis.

—— and Soretz, S. (1997) 'Macroeconomic Effects of Income Taxation in a Model of Stochastic Growth', *Finanzarchiv*, N. F. 54: 471–93.

—— (1998) 'Risk Sharing and Factor Incomes in a Stochastic Growth Model', in F. Haslinger and O. Stönner-Venkatarama (eds), *Aspects of the Distribution of Income*, Marburg: Metropolis.

—— (1998), 'Konsequenzen des Zins- und Einkommensrisikos auf das wirtschaftliche Wachstums', *Zeitschrift für Wirtschafts- und Sozialwissenschaften*, 119: 593–614.

——, Levine, D.K., Zame, W., Avisubet, L., Chiappori, P.-A., Ellickson, B., Rubinstein, A. and Samuelson, L. (2002) 'Government Expenditure and Stochastic Growth: Optimal Policy and the Risk Premium', in *Proceedings of the 2002 North American Summer Meetings of the Econometric Society: Macroeconomics – Theory*, Online volume: http://levozon.dklevine.com/proceedings/index.html

Collard, F. (1999), 'Spectral and Persistence Properties of Cyclical Growth', *Journal of Economic Dynamics and Control*, 23: 463–88.

Corsetti, G. (1997) 'A Portfolio Approach to Endogenous Growth: Equilibrium and Optimal Policy', *Journal of Economic Dynamics and Control*, 21: 1627–44.

Devereux, M.B. and Smith, G.W. (1994) 'International Risk Sharing and Economic Growth', *International Economic Review*, 35: 535–50.

Eaton, J. (1981) 'Fiscal Policy, Inflation and the Accumulation of Risky Capital', *Review of Economic Studies*, 48: 435–45.

Epstein, L.G. and Zin, S.E. (1989) 'Substitution, Risk Aversion, and the Temporal Behaviour of Consumption and Asset Returns: A Theoretical Framework', *Econometrica*, 57: 937–69.

Hubbard, R.G., Skinner, J. and Zeldes, S.P. (1993), 'The Importance of Precautionary Motives in Explaining Individual and Aggregate Saving', National Bureau of Economic Research, NBER Working Paper Series No. 4516, Cambridge: Mass.

Jones, L.E. and Manuelli, R.E. (1990) 'A Convex Model of Equilibrium Growth: Theory and Political Implications', *Journal of Political Economy*, 98: 1008–38.

—— and Stacchetti, E. (1999) 'Technology (and Policy) Shocks in Models of Endogenous Growth', National Bureau of Economic Research, NBER Working Paper Series No. 7063, Cambridge: Mass.

Kormendi, R.C. and Meguire, P.G. (1985) 'Macroeconomic Determinants of Growth. Cross-Country Evidence', *Journal of Monetary Economics*, 16: 141–63.

Kydland, F.E. and Prescott, E.C. (1982) 'Time to Build and Aggregate Fluctuations', *Econometrica*, 50: 1345–70.

Leland, H.E. (1968) 'Saving and Uncertainty: The Precautionary Demand for Saving', *Quarterly Journal of Economics*, 82: 465–73.

Long, J.B. and Plosser, C.I. (1983), 'Real Business Cycles', *Journal of Political Economy*, 91: 39–69.

Mehra, R. and Prescott, E.C. (1985) 'The Equity Premium. A Puzzle', *Journal of Monetary Economics*, 15: 145–61.

Merton, R.C. (1969) 'Lifetime Portfolio Selection under Uncertainty: The Continuous Time Case', *Review of Economics and Statistics*, 51: 247–57.

Neusser, K. (1991) 'Testing the Long-Run Implications of the Neoclassical Growth Model', *Journal of Monetary Economics*, 27: 3–37.

Obstfeld, M. (1994) 'Risk-Taking, Global Diversification, and Growth', *American Economic Review*, 84: 1310–29.

Prescott, E.C. (1986) 'Theory Ahead of Business-Cycle Measurement', *Carnegie-Rochester Conference Series on Public Policy*, 25: 11–44.

Ramey, G. and Ramey, V. (1995) 'Cross-Country Evidence on the Link Between Volatility and Growth', *American Economic Review*, 85: 1138–51.

Rebelo, S. (1991) 'Long-Run Policy Analysis and Long-Run Growth', *Journal of Political Economy*, 99: 500–21.

Reimers, H.E. (1991) *Analyse kointegrierter Variablen mittels vektorautoregressiver Modelle*, Heidelberg: Physica-Verlag.

Romer, P.M. (1986) 'Increasing Returns and Long-Run Growth', *Journal of Political Economy*, 94: 1002–37.

Samuelson, P.A. (1969) 'Lifetime Portfolio Selection by Dynamic Stochastic Programming', *The Review of Economics and Statistics*, 51: 239–46.

Sandmo, A. (1970) 'The Effect of Uncertainty on Savings Decisions', *Review of Economic Studies*, 37: 353–60.

Skinner, J. (1988) 'Risky Income, Life Cycle Consumption and Precautionary Savings', *Journal of Monetary Economics*, 22: 237–55.

Smith, T.R. (1996a), 'Cyclical Uncertainty, Precautionary Saving and Economic Growth', *Economica*, 63: 477–94.

——(1996b) 'Taxes, Uncertainty, and Long-term Growth', *European Economic Review*, 40: 1647–64.

Soretz, S. (2000) 'Steuerpolitik und Wirtschaftliches Wachstum', Marburg: Metropolis.

Turnovsky, S. (1993) 'Macroeconomic Policies, Growth, and Welfare in a Stochastic Economy', *International Economic Review*, 34: 953–81.

——(1999a) 'On the Role of Government in a Stochastically Growing Economy', *Journal of Economic Dynamics and Control*, 23: 873–908.

——(1999b) 'Productive Government Expenditure in a Stochastically Growing Economy', *Macroeconomic Dynamics*, 3: 544–70.

Zeldes, S.P. (1989) 'Optimal Consumption with Stochastic Income: Deviations from Certainty Equivalence', *Quarterly Journal of Economics*, 104: 275–98.

Appendix

The first-order conditions of the programme (9) are:

$$0 = U'(C_i) - J'(W_i) \tag{A.1}$$

$$0 = J'(W_i)(r_K - r_B) + \frac{1}{2}\frac{\partial \sigma_W^2}{\partial K_i} J''(W_i) \tag{A.2}$$

$$0 = J'(W_i)(r_B - \beta) + J''(W_i)\big[r_B W_i + (r_K - r_B)K_i + \omega - C_i\big]$$
$$+ \frac{1}{2}\sigma_W^2 J'''(W_i) \tag{A.3}$$

The condition (A.1) together with (A.3) determines the optimal allocation of consumption over time and requires equalised marginal utility. Equation (A.3) is a substitute for the Bellman equation, which is generally used in continuous-time stochastic optimisation. As we consider economies of scale within the Arrow–Romer framework, Bellman's principle of optimality cannot be applied here (see Clemens, 1999). Equation (A.2) is the arbitrage condition for portfolio choice in equilibrium.

In addition, for a feasible consumption programme, the transversality condition has to be satisfied to assert convergence of (1) and to exclude the case of unbounded utility. The TVC is given by:

$$\lim_{t \to \infty} E_t\big[e^{-\beta t} J(W_i)\big] = 0 \tag{A.4}$$

Equation (10) is obtained from (A.1) by taking account of $U'(C_i) = C_i^{-\rho}$. The optimal value of K_i can be determined by recalling the assumption of independently distributed shocks. According to this, the overall technological variance is the sum of the variances of the aggregate and individual-specific productivity shocks

$$\frac{E(dz + dz_i)^2}{dt} = \frac{E(dz)^2}{dt} + \frac{E(dz_i)^2}{dt} = \sigma^2 + \sigma_i^2 \tag{A.5}$$

The derivative of the variance of wealth σ_W^2 with respect to K_i is then given by: $\partial \sigma_W^2 / \partial K_i = 2r_K (r_K K_i + \omega) \cdot (\sigma^2 + \sigma_i^2)$. Solving for K_i leads to equation (11) of the text.

From the necessary condition (A.1) and the functional form of current period utility (2) follows immediately:

$$
\begin{aligned}
J'(W_i) &= U'(C_i) = C_i^{-\rho} > 0 \\
J''(W_i) &= U''(C_i) \cdot C_i'(W_i) = -\rho \mu C_i^{-(\rho+1)} < 0 \\
J'''(W_i) &= U'''(C_i) \cdot C_i'(W_i)^2 = -\rho(\rho+1)\mu^2 C_i^{-(\rho+2)} < 0
\end{aligned}
\tag{A.6}
$$

Equation (A.6) implies that the value function satisfies the conditions claimed above. $J(W_i)$ is strictly concave and three times differentiable in W. Substitution for the respective derivatives in (11) and (12) yields equations (14) and (15) of the text.

The intertemporal welfare of agent i can now be expressed as a function of initial capital stock $K_i(0)$, the consumption–wealth ratio μ and the expected growth rate. Substitution of the steady-state values, taking regard of (32) and integration leads to

$$V_i[K_i(0), 0] = \frac{K_i(0)^{1-\rho}}{1-\rho} \cdot \frac{\mu^{1-\rho}}{\beta - (1-\rho) \cdot (\psi - (1/2)\rho\gamma^2(\sigma^2 + \sigma_i^2))} \tag{A.7}$$

Individual welfare is bounded, if the transversality condition is satisfied, or to be more specific, if $(1-\rho) \cdot (\psi - (1/2)\rho\gamma^2(\sigma^2 + \sigma_i^2)) - \beta < 0$.

7 Monetary policy, inflation volatility and economic growth

Olivier Bruno and Patrick Musso

Introduction

Monetary policy design issues are often analysed through monetary policy rules aimed at stabilising the economy around its long-run equilibrium.[1] This equilibrium is usually assumed to be fully determined by structural variables (as, for instance, the natural rate of unemployment) and consequently it is supposed to remain unaffected by monetary policy. Inflation generates only welfare cost for economic agents (inflation tax) and inflation volatility is a source of destabilising mistakes. Then, according to these approaches, price stability must be the main objective of central banks. In a world of nominal and/or real rigidities, preventing the economic system from adjusting instantaneously, monetary policy rules are implemented in order to control the evolution of money supply or the interest rate maintaining the economy around its natural level.

This theoretical point of view is rooted in empirical works using vectorial autoregressive (VAR)[2] methodology in order to specify short run real dynamics generated by non-expected monetary shocks.[3] The impact of the systematic part of monetary policy (which is assumed to be perfectly forecasted) is never studied in VAR models, even if its value is about 95 per cent of the total variation of monetary instruments (McCallum 1999).

The aim of this chapter is to show that expected monetary policy could have a real impact on long-run equilibrium, by influencing households' saving behaviour. In the first part of the chapter we briefly survey the literature related to long-run effects of monetary policy. In the second part, we develop an overlapping generations model (with two agents and one homogeneous good) in which money is introduced *via* a traditional cash-in-advance constraint. We show that expected monetary policy has a non-linear positive impact on saving and on long-run economic growth. In the last part of the chapter, the non-linear relationship between inflation, money and economic growth is extended in order to stress the impact of inflation's volatility on growth. We propose a version of our model where money growth rate is stochastic. We show that inflation volatility and economic growth are negatively linked. As a direct consequence, optimal monetary policy lies more on inflation stability than on zero inflation targeting.

The long-run effects of monetary policy

On the theoretical ground, the long-run effects of monetary policy were first studied in Solow's (1956) neoclassical growth framework. For instance, Tobin (1965) and Sidrauski (1967) analysed the link between the evolution of money supply, expected inflation and long-run equilibrium stock of physical capital. Recently, the link between inflation and growth has been dealt with in the framework of endogenous growth models (Jones and Manuelli 1995; Judson and Orphanides 1996). However, this theoretical literature is not able to provide a clear statement of the relationships between inflation and growth. As Stein (1970) wrote it 'my main conclusion is that equally plausible models yield fundamentally different results' (Stein 1970 in Orphanides and Solow 1990: 224).

Whereas it is commonly accepted that an increase in money growth rate necessarily induces an inflationary process, the real effect of monetary policy depends on the presumed link between money and the stock of physical capital. Whatever the way money is introduced in a general equilibrium model, an expansionary monetary policy will have a positive impact on capital accumulation and economic growth if money and physical capital are substitute goods (Tobin 1965; Ireland 1994). On the contrary, when money and capital are pure complementary goods, expected inflation and economic growth are negatively correlated (Gomme 1993; Jones and Manuelli 1995; Marquis and Reffert 1995). Finally, if money is a pure means of exchange and if other means of payment are available, monetary policy and expected inflation are neutral on real equilibrium (Sidrauski 1967). Nevertheless, despite the diversity of these results, some important insights were made in this research area by the use of endogenous growth models. Indeed, these models offer an analytical framework that can explain the mechanisms by which money supply and expected inflation may act on long-run economic growth. Many endogenous growth models underline the fundamental role played by households' saving rate in the growth process (Romer 1986; Rebelo 1991). Consequently, a monetary policy that positively affects this variable could have a real effect on long-run economic growth. Moreover, empirical analyses concerning the link between money and saving are less ambiguous than empirical works on money and growth. In the majority of OECD countries, periods of inflation slowdown and periods of low inflation are strongly correlated with a low level of households' saving propensity (see for instance Koskela and Viren 1994; Callen and Thimann 1997). Indeed, Allard (1992) draws clear conclusions concerning the recent period of inflation's slowdown in France: 'The contribution of decreasing inflation to the decrease of households' saving rate seems to be of primordial importance. Its total impact is more or less the same from one equation to another and it will explain between 3.6 and 4.5 points of the fall of the saving rate between 1984 and 1988' (Allard 1992: 761).[4]

The empirical analysis of inflation and growth relationship is quite tricky, so that it is a commonplace to assert that long-run effects of monetary policy are hardly quantifiable. Numerous studies have been realised on the subject and their conclusions are often ambiguous and weak.[5] The few significant results can be summed up by the following features:

- Inflation is strongly positively correlated with the evolution of monetary growth (McCandless and Weber 1995).
- Inflation volatility is positively related with its medium level (Barro 1996; Temple 1998).
- Long-run economic growth is inversely linked with inflation volatility (Judson and Orphanides 1996; Andrés *et al.* 1996).
- There is a positive correlation between monetary growth and long-run economic growth for low and medium inflation countries (OECD countries). This relation is no more significant if we take other countries into account (McCandeless and Weber 1995).

Whereas the first two points are common results of standard endogenous growth models, the last two features are hardly taken into account by these models. On the one hand, concerning the inverse link between growth and inflation volatility, it is generally acknowledged that, in a stochastic framework, a rise in inflation volatility induces precautionary saving that in turns fosters capital accumulation and by the way long-run economic growth. On the other hand, a positive relationship between money growth rate and economic growth rate for low and medium level of inflation, while this relation is non-existent or negative[6] for high level of inflation is hard to explain in traditional endogenous growth models. This kind of result suggests that monetary policy is non-neutral and that the impact of inflation on growth rate is strongly non-linear.

In the following sections, we develop an overlapping generations model with endogenous growth that takes into account the effect of the level of inflation and inflation volatility on households' saving rate. This model allows us to reproduce the four main stylised facts we mentioned.

The model

We develop an overlapping generations model with endogenous growth within a pure competitive framework. In each period of time (indexed by t) two kinds of agents coexist in the economy: the young and the old (each agent lives two periods). We assume that the size of each generation (young and old) is normalised to one and remains constant through time. Money is introduced into the model by the way of a cash-in-advance constraint applied to young people's income. Prices are assumed to be perfectly flexible and agents are supposed to make rational expectations.

The households

Each generation is composed of identical households endowed with one unit of labour when they are young. We assume that young people have an inelastic labour supply and receive a real wages w_t (which is paid at the end of the period). We suppose that wages are perfectly flexible and that full employment is always achieved. Young people can use wages either to purchase the homogeneous consumption good in period t, or to get cash or to buy real private bonds (saving). The level of physical capital used by firms at period $t + 1$ is equal to period t level of saving. Saving and cash balances constitute the income of old people (money demand embodies store-of-value motives). We exclude bequests, which means that old people spend all their available income in the consumption of the homogeneous good in $t + 1$. The budget constraints of households, in real terms, are the following[7]

$$c_t^t + s_t + m_t = w_t \tag{1}$$

$$c_{t+1}^t = R_{t+1}^e s_t + m_t \frac{P_t}{P_{t+1}^e} \tag{2}$$

where P_t denotes the price of the homogeneous consumption good in period t and P_{t+1}^e its expectation for $t + 1$. c_t^t represents the real amount of consumption of the young generation in t whereas c_{t+1}^t is the real amount of consumption of old people in $t + 1$. Here, s_t stands for the amount of real saving in t and m_t is the amount of real cash balance of young people in t. R_{t+1}^e is the expected factor of return on saving and P_t/P_{t+1}^e is the expected return factor on money balances. Households' intertemporal budget constraint can be written

$$\frac{c_{t+1}^t}{R_{t+1}^e} + c_t^t + \frac{m_t}{R_{t+1}^e}\left[R_{t+1}^e - \frac{P_t}{P_{t+1}^e}\right] = w_t \tag{3}$$

According to relation (3) a positive amount of real saving in t requires that $R_{t+1}^e > P_t/P_{t+1}^e$. We assume that this condition is always realised which means that holding money balances is expensive. Consequently, households hold money only if it provides them a liquidity service or if a holding constraint is imposed on money balances. Actually, there is a wide diversity of liquidity constraints in the literature. The usual way to introduce money in overlapping generations models is to link the amount of cash balance held by agents in t to the level of consumption expected in $t + 1$ (Hahn and Solow 1995) or directly to the amount of consumption in t (Artus 1995). It is also possible to associate the amount of cash balances held by agents in t to the level of saving at the same period (Tirole 1985; Guillard 1998). This last form is closer to a cash constraint than to a real liquidity constraint.[8] In this chapter we adopt this last perspective and we retain the following holding constraint

$$m_t = \mu w_t \quad \text{with } 0 < \mu < 1. \tag{4}$$

It means that the amount of money young people must hold in t is equal to a fraction μ of their total real income in the same period.[9] This holding constraint can also be interpreted as a demand function for money (see Villieu 1993). Otherwise, this relation is not incompatible with the idea that money brings also liquidity service, as μ can be compared to the inverse of the velocity of money.

Finally, we assume that agents' preferences in each generation are strictly increasing, strictly converging and homothetic. They could be described by a life-cycle utility function $U\left(c_t^t, c_{t+1}^t\right)$, since households only care about present and future levels of consumption. In the following, we retain a CES utility function

$$
U\left(c_t^t, c_{t+1}^t\right) = \frac{c_t^{t^{1-\theta}}}{1-\theta} + \beta \frac{c_{t+1}^{t^{1-\theta}}}{1-\theta}
\tag{5}
$$

where $0 < \beta < 1$ is a discount factor and θ a measure of agent's risk-aversion; in CES utility function it is also the inverse of intertemporal elasticity of substitution.

The firms

We assume that n firms evolve in a competitive framework and produce the homogeneous good (that can be used either for consumption or for capital accumulation in the following period) with physical capital and young people labour force. We will use a convex technology

$$
y_{it} = A_t k_{it}^{\alpha} l_{it}^{1-\alpha} \quad \text{with } 0 < \alpha < 1, i = 1, \ldots, n \quad \text{and} \quad K_t = \sum_{i=1}^{n} k_{it}
\tag{6}
$$

with y_{it}, l_{it}, k_{it} respectively denoting the production of firm i and the quantity of labour and capital used by this firm at period t. Otherwise, following Romer (1986) we assume a learning-by-doing externality, $A_t = a K_t^{1-\alpha}$, with K_t being the total amount of capital available in the economy at time t. Taking this externality into account, the individual production function turns to be

$$
y_{it} = a K_t^{1-\alpha} k_{it}^{\alpha} l_{it}^{1-\alpha}
\tag{7}
$$

and the aggregate production function is $Y_t = a K_t$.

This class of production functions allows us to generate endogenous growth while keeping a competitive framework. Indeed, the production function (7) exhibits constant return to scale in K_t and k_t taken together, whereas decreasing return characterises each factor taken separately. This special formulation allows us to obtain easily endogenous growth without loss of generality in our main results. Indeed, we will therefore be able to find these results using a more sophisticated model that explicitly embraces the innovative process, as soon as the model preserves the positive relationship between households' saving, capital accumulation and economic growth.

Profit maximisation of a representative firm i allows to determine the equilibrium real wage rate. Profit of firm i at period t is equal to

$$
\Pi_{it} = y_{it} - w_t l_{it}
$$

Profit-maximising is done ignoring the learning externality, and we obtain the first condition concerning labour

$$
\frac{\partial \Pi_i}{\partial l_{it}} = 0 \quad \text{and} \quad l_{it} = \left[w_t (1-\alpha)^{-1} a^{-1} K_t^{\alpha-1} k_{it}^{-\alpha} \right]^{-1/\alpha}
$$

Under the assumption of clearing market, that is $\sum_{i=1}^{n} l_{it} = L_t^D = L_t^O = 1$ (the supply of labour is equal to one in each period) and $\sum_{i=1}^{n} k_{it} = K_t^D = K_t$, the equilibrium real wage rate is given by

$$w_t = (1 - \alpha) a K_t = \overline{w} K_t \quad \text{with } \overline{w} = (1 - \alpha)a \tag{8}$$

Moreover, the real return on capital and saving is given by

$$R_t = \frac{\Pi_t}{K_t} = \frac{a K_t - (1 - \alpha)a K_t}{K_t} = \alpha a = \overline{R} \quad \text{with } \Pi_t = \sum_{i=1}^{n} \Pi_{it} \tag{9}$$

Money supply

Let us assume that money supply $\overline{M}_t$ is exogenous and grows at the rate ε_{t+1} from one period to another, so

$$\overline{M}_{t+1} = \varepsilon_{t+1} \overline{M}_t \tag{10}$$

Moreover, under the assumption of a normalised population size, the equilibrium on money market is given by $\overline{M}_t = P_t m_t$. Using the cash liquidity constraint (4) and these two relations, it is possible to calculate the factor of inflation

$$\pi_t = \frac{P_{t+1}}{P_t} = \frac{\varepsilon_{t+1} w_t}{w_{t+1}}$$

Finally, using the equilibrium value of the real wage rate (equation (8)), we have

$$\pi_t = \frac{\varepsilon_{t+1}}{\gamma_t} \tag{11}$$

with $\gamma_t = Y_{t+1}/Y_t = K_{t+1}/K_t$ being the real growth factor of the economy. Equation (11) is similar to the Chicago Rule, stating that inflation rate is equal to zero as soon as the factor of monetary growth (ε_{t+1}) is equal to the real growth factor (γ_t) of the economy.

Money, saving and steady growth

The relationship between expected inflation and saving

The level of saving available at each period is given by the intertemporal optimal choice of households. Indeed, when they are young, people maximise their utility under their intertemporal budget constraint (3). Using (4), (8), (9), (11) and knowing that $K_{t+1} = s_t$ the budget constraint can be written as

$$\frac{c_{t+1}^t}{\psi} + c_t^t = (1 - \mu)w_t \tag{12}$$

With $\psi = \overline{R} + \overline{w}\mu/\varepsilon_{t+1}$ the global effective return on total saving. The optimal amount of saving in period t is equal to[10]

$$s_t = \frac{(1 - \mu)\varepsilon_{t+1}\beta^{1/\theta}\psi^{1/\theta}}{\varepsilon_{t+1}\left[\overline{R} + \beta^{1/\theta}\psi^{1/\theta}\right] + \overline{w}\mu}w_t \tag{13}$$

where $((1-\mu)\varepsilon_{t+1}\beta^{1/\theta}\psi^{1/\theta})/(\varepsilon_{t+1}\left[\overline{R}+\beta^{1/\theta}\psi^{1/\theta}\right]+\overline{w}\mu)$ stands for households' propensity to save income at period t. This value is always between zero and one if we assume a positive value for the factor of actualisation ($\beta > 0$). It is easy to compute the impact of monetary policy on households saving behaviour

$$\frac{\partial s_t}{\partial \varepsilon_{t+1}} = \frac{\overline{w}^2\mu(1 - \mu)\beta^{1/\theta}\psi^{1/\theta}(\theta - 1)}{\left[\varepsilon_{t+1}(\overline{R} + \beta^{1/\theta}\psi^{1/\theta}) + \overline{w}\mu\right]^2\theta}K_t > 0 \quad \text{if } \theta > 1 \tag{14}$$

If households' risk aversion (θ) is larger than one,[11] there is a positive link between money growth factor ε_{t+1} and saving. It should be stressed that this relation is not linear, but concave

$$\frac{\partial^2 s_t}{\partial \varepsilon_{t+1}^2} = -\frac{\overline{w}^2\mu(1 - \mu)\beta^{1/\theta}\psi^{1/\theta}(\theta - 1)Z}{\varepsilon_{t+1}\left(\overline{R}\varepsilon_{t+1} + \overline{w}\mu\right)\left[\varepsilon_{t+1}(\overline{R} + \beta^{1/\theta}\psi^{1/\theta}) + \overline{w}\mu\right]^3\theta^2}K_t < 0$$

with

$$Z = \left(\overline{R}\varepsilon_{t+1} + \overline{w}\mu\right)\left(2\overline{R}\varepsilon_{t+1}\theta + \overline{w}\mu\right)$$
$$+ \varepsilon_{t+1}\beta^{1/\theta}\psi^{1/\theta}\left(2\overline{R}\varepsilon_{t+1}\theta + \overline{w}\mu(2\theta - 1)\right) > 0$$

According to the fact that any increase in the rate of money growth has an inflationary effect (see equation (16) *infra*), relation (14) means that there exists a positive correlation between expected inflation and households' saving rate for low level of inflation. The function being concave and bounded,[12] the positive effect of an increase in the inflation rate on saving vanishes if inflation is already high.

Evidence of OECD countries confirm the positive link between expected inflation and households' saving and we retain from here to onwards the assumption of a low intertemporal elasticity of substitution ($\theta > 1$).[13]

As endogenous growth mainly depends on capital accumulation, the positive link between expected inflation and households' saving rate will have a direct impact on real growth rate.

Steady growth and inflation

Because $K_{t+1} = s_t$, we can easily determine the real growth rate of the economy

$$\gamma_t = \frac{K_{t+1}}{K_t} = \frac{s_t}{K_t} = \frac{\overline{w}(1 - \mu)\varepsilon_{t+1}\beta^{1/\theta}\psi^{1/\theta}}{\varepsilon_{t+1}\left[R + \beta^{1/\theta}\psi^{1/\theta}\right] + \overline{w}\mu} \tag{15}$$

Dynamic equilibrium stemming from equation (15) is always unique and perfectly determined under the assumptions we made about production technology (AK model) and household's preferences. There is no transitory dynamics, as agents immediately choose the level of saving that drive them to the steady growth path.

The positive correlation we have stressed between money growth rate, expected inflation and saving rate can be directly transposed to the real growth factor as

$$\frac{\partial \gamma_t}{\partial \varepsilon_{t+1}} = \frac{1}{K_t}\frac{\partial s_t}{\partial \varepsilon_{t+1}} > 0 \quad \text{and} \quad \frac{\partial^2 \gamma_t}{\partial \varepsilon_{t+1}^2} = \frac{1}{K_t}\frac{\partial^2 s_t}{\partial \varepsilon_{t+1}^2} < 0$$

It is also possible to value precisely the inflation factor

$$\pi_{t+1} = \frac{\varepsilon_{t+1}}{\gamma_t} = \frac{\varepsilon_{t+1}\left(R + \beta^{1/\theta}\psi^{1/\theta}\right) + \overline{w}\mu}{\overline{w}(1 - \mu)\beta^{1/\theta}\psi^{1/\theta}} \tag{16}$$

Any increase in the money growth rate induces a rise in inflation. The positive correlation between the factor of money growth, expected inflation and steady growth rate of the economy can be explained as follow. An increase in the rate of money growth leads to a rise in inflation, which in turn depreciates agents' monetary balances: as a consequence, the total expected return of saving decreases. If the intertemporal elasticity of substitution of economic agents is low (agents' risk-aversion is higher than one), young people offset this partial loss of forthcoming revenue by rising their saving rate. This behaviour has a positive influence on capital accumulation and long-run economic growth.

Nevertheless, the positive link between expected monetary growth, inflation and real economic growth is non-linear, as monetary balances depreciation is lower the higher the inflation rate. The expected component of monetary policy will have a positive impact on economic growth only for low-inflation rates. This result allows us to formulate an original theoretical interpretation of empirical results obtained by McCandeless and Weber (1995) or Barro (1996). According to these studies, there is a positive correlation between money growth and long-run economic growth only for low-inflation economies. In a situation of high inflation, an increase in monetary growth will accelerate inflation only. Thus, the relation between expected inflation and economic growth is bounded since the maximal rate of economic growth is reached when ε_{t+1} tends towards infinity

$$\gamma_{max} = \lim_{\varepsilon_{t+1} \to \infty} \gamma_t = \frac{\overline{w}(1 - \mu)(\overline{R}\beta)^{1/\theta}}{R + (\overline{R}\beta)^{1/\theta}} > 0$$

In high inflation regimes (or hyperinflation) it is always possible to reduce inflation without constraining real economic growth rate. On the contrary, in low-inflation states, a zero-inflation target policy will be at the origin of a high and durable cost in terms of economic growth. This result is in accordance with many empirical works underlining the asymmetric impact of inflation-cut policy. It becomes therefore possible to explain that in some particular cases monetary policy is likely to have a sizeable impact on income and growth, whereas in other cases these effects are low or negligible. Until now, this paradox was explained in the framework of the new classical economic models of monetary policy (Lucas 1972, 1973) opposing the real effect of non-expected monetary shocks to the neutral impact of expected monetary shocks on income and growth. What appeared to be a consensus has been called into question by econometric works. Then, the non-linear correlation between inflation and growth we assert brings an answer to this paradox allowing real impact of expected monetary shocks. Our relation between the factor of inflation, the factor of real growth rate and the factor of money growth rate can be sketched (Figure 7.1).

The real growth factor is strongly, directly influenced by a permanent change in expected inflation. Neither propagation mechanisms nor nominal or real rigidities are necessary to explain this persistent impact of expected inflation on real growth. On the contrary, it comes from the fact that households' optimal saving rate depends on the expected level of inflation. Capital accumulation is positively related to expected inflation.

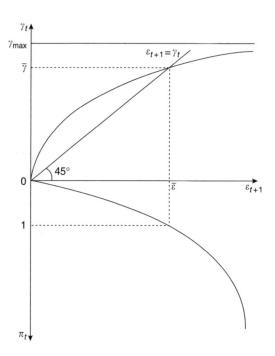

Figure 7.1 Relationship between steady growth factor, inflation and money growth factor.

Nevertheless, because of the concavity of the relation between money and growth, our results hold only in steady state. Thus, a non-regular monetary policy would produce non-symmetrical economic fluctuations. An increase in the expected factor of inflation generates a smaller rise of the economic growth factor compared to the slowdown induced by a similar decrease in the expected factor of inflation. It is obvious that out of steady state, perfectly expected inflation's volatility has a direct impact on the average growth rate of the economy. In order to extend these results to the case of non-expected monetary policy and inflation's volatility, we develop in the last part of the chapter a version of our model in which the monetary growth factor becomes stochastic. Then, we analyse the impact of the volatility of monetary policy, and consequently the volatility of inflation, on economic growth.

Inflation volatility and economic growth

The aim of this section is to analyse the impact of inflation volatility on long-run economic growth.

Introducing uncertainty

Let us assume that the money supply process can be described by the following lottery

$$\Pr(\varepsilon_{t+1} = \bar{\varepsilon} + \sigma) = \Pr(\varepsilon_{t+1} = \bar{\varepsilon} - \sigma) = \tfrac{1}{2} \quad \text{with } 0 < \sigma < \bar{\varepsilon} \tag{17}$$

with $\bar{\varepsilon}$ and σ respectively denoting the mean and standard deviation of the stochastic process driving money supply.

In this framework, the global return on saving is now stochastic. Let $\Psi(\sigma) = (\overline{R} + \mu \overline{w})/(\bar{\varepsilon} + \sigma)$ be the global return on saving when the monetary shock is positive and $\Psi(-\sigma) = \overline{R} + \mu \overline{w}(\bar{\varepsilon} - \sigma)$ is the global return on saving when the monetary shock is negative. The expected global return on saving is, then

$$E[\psi] = \bar{\psi} = \frac{1}{2}(\psi(\sigma) + \psi(-\sigma)) = \overline{R} + \frac{\mu \overline{w} \bar{\varepsilon}}{\bar{\varepsilon}^2 - \sigma^2} \tag{18}$$

It is noticeable that an increase in the volatility of money supply raises the expected global return on saving. This result is due to the fact that monetary policy effects are non-linear. A positive shock on money supply has a smaller effect on the return on saving than a negative shock of the same magnitude.

Households maximise their expected utility, choosing an amount of saving so that

$$\underset{s_t}{\text{Max}} \frac{[(1 - \mu)\overline{w} - s_t]^{1-\theta}}{1 - \theta} + \frac{\beta}{2} \frac{1}{1 - \theta} \left[(s_t \psi(\sigma))^{1-\theta} + (s_t \psi(-\sigma))^{1-\theta} \right] \tag{19}$$

The solution of this problem is given by

$$s_t = \frac{(1-\mu)w_t}{1 + 2^{1/\theta}\beta^{-1/\theta}\left[(\psi(\sigma)^{1-\theta} + \psi(-\sigma)^{1-\theta})\right]^{-1/\theta}} \qquad (20)$$

Here, again, saving is positively linked to the money growth rate.

Inflation volatility and growth

The calculation of the economic growth factor from equation (20) is straightforward

$$\gamma_t = \frac{(1-\mu)\overline{w}}{1 + 2^{1/\theta}\beta^{-1/\theta}\left[(\psi(\sigma)^{1-\theta} + \psi(-\sigma)^{1-\theta})\right]^{-1/\theta}} \qquad (21)$$

An increase in the standard deviation of money supply (σ) raises the volatility of inflation. We can now compute the effect of inflation volatility on economic growth

$$\frac{\partial\gamma_t}{\partial\sigma} = -\frac{2^{1/\theta}\beta^{-1/\theta}\overline{w}^2(\theta-1)(1-\mu)\mu\left[\psi(\sigma)^{1-\theta} + \psi(-\sigma)^{1-\theta}\right]^{-(1+\theta)/\theta}\Omega}{\theta\left[1 + 2^{1/\theta}\beta^{-1/\theta}\left[\psi(\sigma)^{1-\theta} + \psi(-\sigma)^{1-\theta}\right]^{-1/\theta}\right]^2} \qquad (22)$$

with

$$\Omega = \left[\frac{\psi(-\sigma)^{-\theta}}{(\bar{\varepsilon}-\sigma)^2} - \frac{\psi(\sigma)^{-\theta}}{(\bar{\varepsilon}+\sigma)^2}\right]$$

One can easily verify that the sign of equation (22) only depends on Ω. This sign is negative when $\Omega > 0$, that is when the value of the parameter θ is such that

$$\theta < \frac{\log[(\bar{\varepsilon}-\sigma/\bar{\varepsilon}+\sigma)^2]}{\log\left[(\bar{\varepsilon}+\sigma)[(1-\alpha)\mu + \alpha(\bar{\varepsilon}-\sigma)]/(\bar{\varepsilon}-\sigma)[(1-\alpha)\mu + \alpha(\bar{\varepsilon}+\sigma)]\right]} = \bar{\theta} \qquad (23)$$

This condition is always verified for plausible values of the parameters. If we consider, for instance, that $\alpha = 0.35$ (the capital share), $\bar{\varepsilon} = 2.5$ (which corresponds to an average growth rate of roughly 2 per cent per year), $\mu = 0.5$ (the holding constraint) and $\sigma = 0.25$ (the standard deviation of the money supply ε), we find $\bar{\theta} = 7.35$. This value is far higher than the one usually found in empirical measures of risk aversion (empirical studies generally report a value of θ lower than 3).[14]

Hence, the rate of economic growth is negatively linked to the volatility of money supply and inflation. This result is due to the fact that the volatility of inflation induces a rise of the global return on saving. If the household's risk-aversion is reasonably low, this will induce a lower rate of saving. However, if the risk-aversion parameter is greater than $\bar{\theta}$, the precautionary premium (Kimball 1990) is so high that households increase their saving rate despite the rise of the global return on saving.

Conclusion

In this chapter, we propose a simple model of endogenous growth that puts forward the non-linear impact of monetary policy on long-run economic growth. A zero-inflation policy is, hence, susceptible to induce a persistent and perceptible decrease in the household's rate of saving that might, in turn, be harmful to the long-run rate of economic growth.

Moreover, we show that, out of steady state, the volatility of inflation (expected and non-expected) decreases the rate of growth. In a stochastic framework, the precautionary saving induced by inflation volatility is indeed always overcome by an income effect due to the rise of the global expected return of saving. These results are supported by several empirical studies concerning the relationship between inflation and saving as well as those devoted to the influence of inflation volatility on economic growth.

Notes

1 See for instance Artus *et al.* (1999).
2 Sims (1992) proposes a comparative study of the impact of monetary shocks for various OECD countries. See also Romer and Romer (1989, 1994) for an alternative approach.
3 Cochrane (1998) gives an evaluation of the real effects of expected monetary shocks.
4 Translation from French is ours.
5 The results of these models strongly rely on the choice of the sample and on the length of the periods that are used. Moreover, the relation often depends on one or two observations whose have extreme values (Levine and Renelt 1992; Levine and Zervos 1993; Bruno and Easterly 1998).
6 See Barro (1996).
7 Superior index is linked to the birth date of the considered generation.
8 See Cretez *et al.* (1999) for a review of the impact of these different cash-in-advance constraints on the level of capital accumulation in exogenous growth models.
9 This assumption implies that a part of consumption in $t + 1$ will be financed thanks to real money balance holds in period t.
10 Under the assumption concerning households' preferences the maximising programme has a positive solution when the first-order conditions are realised.
11 This means that the intertemporal elasticity of substitution is lower than one.
12 The right term of equation (14) tends towards zero when ε_{t+1} tends towards infinity.
13 This assumption is in accordance with numerous attempts to estimate the value of the intertemporal elasticity of substitution (see Hall 1988).
14 See Dotsey and Sarte (1997) and Walsh (1998).

References

Allard, P. (1992) 'La modélisation de la consommation des ménages en France', *Revue d'Economie Politique*, 102: 727–68.
Andres, J., Domenech, R. and Molinas, C. (1996) 'Macroeconomic Performance and Convergence in OECD Countries', *European Economic Review*, 40: 1683–704.
Artus, P. (1995), *Macro Economie*, Economica.
Artus, P., Penot, A. and Pollin, J.-P. (1999) 'Quelle règle monétaire pour la Banque Centrale Européenne ?', *Revue d'Economie Politique*, 109: 309–74.

Barro, R. (1996) 'Inflation and Growth', *Federal Reserve Bank of St. Loius Review*, 78: 155–68.

Bruno, M. and Easterly, W. (1998) 'Inflation Crises and Long-Run Growth', *Journal of Monetary Economics*, 41: 3–26.

Bullard, J. and Keating, J. (1995) 'The Long-Run Relationship between Inflation and Output in Postwar Economies', *Journal of Monetary Economics*, 36: 477–96.

Callen, T. and Thimann, C. (1997) 'Empirical Determinants of Households Saving: Evidence from OECD Countries', IMF Working Papers, WP/97/181.

Christiano, L., Eichenbaum, M. and Evans, C. (1998) 'Monetary Policy Shocks: What Have We Learned and to What End?', NBER Working Paper No. 6400.

Cochrane, J. (1998) 'What do the VARs Mean? Measuring the Output Effects of Monetary Policy', *Journal of Monetary Economics*, 41: 277–300.

Cretez, B., Philippe, M. and Wigniolle, B. (1999a) *Monaie, dette et capital*, Paris: Economica.

Cretez, B., Michel, P. and Wigniolle, B. (1999b) 'Cash-in-Advance Constraints in the Diamond Overlapping Generations Model: Neutrality and Optimality of Monetary Policies', *Oxford Economic Paper*, 51: 451–2.

Dotsey, M. and Sarte, P.D. (1997) 'Inflation Uncertainty and Growth in a Simple Monetary Model', *Federal Reserve Bank of Richmond*, mimeo.

Feenstra, R. (1986) 'Functional Equivalence Between Liquidity Costs and the Utility of Money', *Journal of Monetary Economics*, 17: 271–91.

Gomme, P. (1993) 'Money and Growth Revisited', *Journal of Monetary Economics*, 32: 51–77.

Guillard, M. (1998) 'Croissance, inflation et bulles', *Document de travail*, EPEE, 98 01.

Hahn, F. and Solow, R.M. (1995) *A Critical Essay on Modern Macroeconomic Theory*, Cambridge, Mass.: MIT Press.

Hahn, F. and Solow, R. (1997) A Critical Essay on Modern Macroeconomic Theory, MIT Press.

Hall, R. (1988) 'Intertemporal Substitution in Consumption', *Journal of Political Economy*, 96: 339–57.

Haslag, J. (1997) 'Output, Growth, Welfare, and Inflation: A Survey', *Federal Reserve Bank of Dallas Economic Review*, 2nd quarter: 11–21.

Ireland, P. (1994) 'Money and Growth: An Alternative Approach', *American Economic Review*, 84: 47–65.

Jones, L. and Manuelli, R. (1995) 'Growth and the Effects of Inflation', *Journal of Economic Dynamics and Control*, 19: 1405–28.

Judson, R. and Orphanides, A. (1996) 'Inflation, Volatility and Growth', Board of Governors of the Federal Reserve System, mimeo.

Kimball, M.S. (1990) 'Precautionary Saving in the Small and in the Large', *Econometrica*, 58: 53–73.

Koskela, E. and Viren, M. (1994) 'Taxation and Households Saving in Open Economies. Evidence from the Nordic Countries', *Scandinavian Journal of Economics*, 96: 425–41.

Langlais, E. (1995) 'Aversion au risque et prudence : le cas d'un risque de taux d'intérêt', *Revue Economique*, 46: 1099–119.

Levine, R. and Renelt, D. (1992) 'A Sensitivity Analysis of Cross-Country Growth Regressions', *American Economic Review*, 82: 942–63.

Levine, R. and Zervos, S. (1993) 'What We have Learned About Policy and Growth from Cross-Country Regressions?', *American Economic Review*, 83: 426–30.

Lucas, R. (1972) 'Expectations and the Neutrality of Money', *Journal of Economic Theory*, 4: 103–24.

—— (1973) 'Some International Evidence on Output-Inflation Trade-offs', *American Economic Review*, 63: 326–34.

McCallum, B. (1999) 'Analysis of the Monetary Transmission Mechanism: Methodological Issues', NBER Working Paper No. 7395.

McCandless, G. and Weber, W. (1995) 'Some Monetary Facts', *Federal Reserve Bank of Mineapolis Quarterly Review*, 19: 2–11.

Marquis, M. and Reffert, K. (1995) 'The Inflation Tax in a Convex Model of Equilibrium Growth', *Economica*, 62: 109–21.

Orphanides, A. and Solow, R. (1990) 'Money, Inflation and Growth', in Benjamin Friedman and Frank Hahn (eds), *Handbook of Monetary Economics*, Oxford: North-Holland.

Rebelo, S. (1991) 'Long-Run Policy Analysis and Long-Run Growth', *Journal of Political Economy*, 99: 500–21.

Romer, P. (1986) 'Increasing Returns and Long-run Growth', *Journal of Political Economy*, 94: 1002–37.

Romer, C. and Romer, D. (1989) 'Does Monetary Policy Matter? A New Test in the Spirit of Friedman and Schwartz', *NBER Macroeconomics Annual*, Cambridge, Mass.: MIT Press: 121–70.

—— (1994) 'What Ends Recessions?', *NBER Macroeconomics Annual*, Cambridge, Mass.: MIT Press: 13–57.

Rotemberg, J.J. (1994) 'Prices and Output: An Empirical Analysis Based on a Sticky Price Model, NBER Working Paper No. 4948.

Sandmo, A. (1970) 'The Effect of Uncertainty on Saving Decision', *Review of Economic Studies*, 37: 353–60.

Sidrauski, M. (1967) 'Rational Choice and Patterns of Growth in a Monetary Economy', *American Economic Review, Papers and Proceedings*, 57: 534–44.

Sims, C. (1992) 'Interpreting the Macroeconomic Time Series Facts: The Effects of Monetary Policy', *European Economic Review*, 36: 975–1000.

Solow, R. (1956) 'A Contribution to the Theory of Economic Growth', *Quarterly Journal of Economics*, 70: 65–94.

Stein, J. (1970) 'Monetary Growth theory in Perspective', *American Economic Review*, 60: 85–106.

Temple, J. (1998) 'Inflation and Growth : Stories Short and Tall', Hertford College, Oxford, Working Paper.

Tirole, J. (1985) 'Asset Bubbles and Overlapping Generations', *Econometrica*, 53: 1499–528.

Tobin, J. (1965) 'Money and Economic Growth', *Econometrica*, 33: 671–84.

Villieu, P. (1993) 'Les modèlesà encaisses préalables : un renouveau des fondements microéconomiques de la macroéconomie monétaire', *Revue d'Economie Politique*, 103: 613–94.

Walsh, C. (1998) *Monetary Theory and Policy*, Cambridge, Mass.: MIT Press.

Part III

Growth and government intervention

8 Altruism and egoism of the social planner in a dynamic context

Ingrid Ott

Introduction

The models of endogenous growth theory investigate different determinants of ongoing growth. Externalities in the accumulation of the private inputs, but also productive public inputs are analysed. Because of market failure the decentrally obtained results are not efficient, and a social planner may cause welfare gains through intervention. This planner usually is equipped with perfect information and internalises the external effects arising from the accumulation of private capital (Romer 1986), technological knowledge (Grossman and Helpman 1991), (Aghion and Howitt 1992), human capital (Lucas 1988) or from the financing of a productive governmental input (see e.g. Barro 1990; Barro, Sala-i-Martin 1992, 1995; Turnovsky 2000).

Within the latter models, the task of the public agent is not only to internalise externalities arising from the sources mentioned above. Instead, the public agent also has to provide the governmental input. It is financed by taxing revenues of the government if the public input has the characteristics of a pure public good. At the same time, the government also provides services that have the characteristic of excludability (see e.g. Aschauer 1989; Bös 1991; Seitz 1994 or Kapur 1995). For these so-called club goods, the government may levy duties from the users or exclude those who will not pay. The optimal financing instrument then is a user fee covering the arising costs (see e.g. Musgrave 1959; Atkinson and Stiglitz 1980; Cornes and Sandler 1996 or Ott 2000).

The social planner within endogenous growth models with productive governmental expenditure could be interpreted as an agent of the government who has no electoral constraints. Mostly he is assumed to act altruistically and hence seeks to maximise utility attained by the representative agent. Such behaviour of the public agent is doubted within public choice literature (see e.g. Bernholz and Breyer 1994 or Mueller 1989). An introduction to self-interested government in endogenous growth theory takes place, for example, in the article of Barro (1990). He analyses apart from the typical altruistic behaviour a public agent who seeks to maximise personal utility attained from consumption of a private good. The planner uses the total amount of his taxing revenue for the provision of the public input *and* his personnel consumption. As his personnel utility depends on private consumption, he tends to maximise the net revenue that remains after the provision of the public input.

In this chapter, first, two kinds of a productive governmental input are analysed: the provision of a pure public good and a club good. It is shown that only in the case of a club good there exists no external effect as the individuals pay for the use of the public input and the decentral optimisation leads to a Pareto-optimal provision of the input, if the user fee is set correctly. Second, it is investigated what happens if a public agent interferes with altruistic respectively egoistic intention in the market process. In contrast to Barro (1990), egoistic behaviour consists in maximising the available budget. Therefore, besides the usual benevolent behaviour of the social planner, selfishness of a public agent in a dynamic context is analysed.

The formal frame is an endogenous growth model in which the inputs are private capital and a productive governmental input. The planner determines the way of financing the public input. After the derivation of the market equilibrium and the social optimum, it is analysed how a budget-maximising planner determines the way of financing. Selfishness in this context may be interpreted in two different ways. On the one hand, he may maximise his budget in each period in relation to total output. This results in a maximisation of the expenditure ratio. On the other hand, the planner may prefer to maximise his budget over his infinite planning horizon. It is shown that both goals are contrary, so that the planner may not maximise expenditure ratio and long-run budget in the same instance. Then both goals are linked together and weighted through a planner's utility function. As a result – independent of the characteristics of the public input – the planner chooses an efficient amount and financing of the public input only, if he maximises his budget in the long-run. In the case of maximising the expenditure ratio, he departs from an efficient provision and increases the part of distortionary tax financing. In the case of the public input as club good a transition from fee financing to a mixed financing consisting of fees and taxes results. If the public input is a pure public good, the planner increases the tax rate on income. The consequences in both cases are a welfare loss because of the distortionary effect that arises from an income tax.

The structure of the chapter is as follows. After describing the assumptions of the model in the next section, market equilibrium and social optimum for the two types of the public input are derived (See section on 'Market equilibrium and social optimum'). The section on 'The egoistic public agent' analyses selfish behaviour of the public agent in a dynamic context and the resulting consequences for welfare. The chapter ends with a short summary.

Set-up of the model

Starting point of the analysis is a model of endogenous growth with constant returns to scale in the accumulated inputs. The infinitely long-lived representative individual maximises his overall utility, U, as given by

$$U = \int_0^\infty u(c)e^{-\rho t}dt \tag{1}$$

The function $u(c)$ relates the weighted flow of utility to the quantity of instantaneous consumption, c. It is increasing in c, concave and satisfies the Inadaconditions. The multiplier, $e^{-\rho t}$, involves the constant rate of time preference, $\rho > 0$. The utility of the representative household in each period is given by

$$u(c) = \begin{cases} \dfrac{c^{1-\sigma}}{1-\sigma} & \text{if } \sigma > 0, \sigma \neq 1 \\ \ln c & \text{if } \sigma = 1 \end{cases} \qquad (2)$$

Hence, the elasticity of marginal utility equals the constant $-\sigma$. The households supply their working force inelastically, so that labour–leisure choice is not considered. Besides, population growth is not considered as well, and the number of people is normalised to unity.

There is one homogeneous good y produced by the firms that have access to the production function

$$y = f(k, G) = kf\left(\frac{G}{k}\right) \equiv kf(\cdot) \qquad (3)$$

Here, y denotes the production per capita; k represents the amount of capital available to the representative firm and equals the sum of capital per capita. The second input, G, is provided by the government and equals total quantity of the publicly provided good. Rivalry in the use of the public input G, as analysed by e.g. Barro and Sala-i-Martin (1995), Turnovsky and Fisher (1998), as well as Turnovsky (2000), does not arise. The numbers of individuals is normalised to one, hence individual and aggregate variables coincide. With the assumption of constant returns to scale in the private inputs, the production function may be rewritten to be linear in private capital k thus allowing for ongoing growth. Both inputs are essential. The marginal product of each input is positive, but decreasing $(f_G, f_k > 0, f_{GG}, f_{kk} < 0)$, and the function satisfies the Inada-conditions. The partial productivity of the public input G is given by

$$\eta_{y,G} \equiv \eta = \frac{f'(\cdot)G/k}{f(\cdot)} \qquad (4)$$

The following analysis does not presuppose altruistic behaviour of the public agent but the consequences of altruistic behaviour on welfare are analysed as reference. Then, the consequences of selfish behaviour of the social planner on welfare are explored.

Market equilibrium and social optimum

Public good with excludability

The government provides the input G that has the characteristics of non-diminishability but excludability. Therefore, any individual's use of G has no effect on the amount available to other firms and the government may exclude non-payers from the use of G. It is supposed that there exists no governmental production, as the public sector buys a part of private production, y, and makes it available as the public input.[1] G and y may be exchanged as to $1:1$.

The provision of the public input G is financed by duties of the firms. The government, represented by a social planner, may levy a proportional income tax τ or charge a user fee q from the producers. The budget is balanced in each period, debt or credits do not exist. Therefore, the public budget constraint, which is composed of the aggregate expenditures G and aggregate revenues as sum of fees and taxes, has the form:

$$G = \tau y + qG, \quad 0 \le q, \tau \le 1 \tag{5}$$

Setting $q = 0$ ($\tau = 0$) indicates financing solely by taxes (fees), and $\tau \ne 0, q \ne 0$ represents a mixed financing. The model does not allow for negative fees or tax rates. In providing the public input, the social planner not only determines the amount of G but also the financing. He decides if the enterprises have to pay only fees, respectively, taxes or a mixture of both.

Market equilibrium: The representative agent uses his income for private consumption c, extinction of taxes τy and fees qG as well as for the accumulation of private capital that is depreciated at the rate δ. This leads to the intertemporal constraint the private household has to consider while optimising:

$$\dot{k} = (1 - \tau)y - qG - c - \delta k \tag{6}$$

The optimisation problem may be formalised by a Hamiltonian comprising equations (1), (2), (3) and (6). Because of the excludability of the public input, the individuals not only decide on the amount of consumption and capital, but also on the use of the public input G. It results the steady state growth rate of consumption per capita γ that depends on the endogenous fiscal instruments of the social planner τ and q:

$$\gamma(\tau, q) = \frac{1}{\sigma} \left[(1 - \tau) \left(f(\cdot) - \frac{q}{1 - \tau} \frac{G}{k} \right) - \delta - \rho \right] \tag{7}$$

The growth rate determines the optimal consumption path and displays the characteristic that a reallocation of consumption may not increase lifetime utility respectively total welfare. It satisfies the Keynes–Ramsey-rule, and consumption per capita grows at a positive rate, if the net marginal product of capital $(1 - \tau)(\partial y/\partial k) - \delta$ exceeds the rate of time preference. The economy initially jumps onto the steady state, i.e. there are no transitional dynamics in the model. In the steady state, private consumption as well as the governmental expenditure and output grow at the same constant rate.

To realise the steady state growth rate, the optimal fees and tax rates have to be determined. A clear connection between rates of taxes and fees can be derived from the public budget constraint (5) and the decisions of the individuals on the use of the public input G

$$q(\tau) = \frac{\eta(1-\tau)}{\tau + \eta(1-\tau)}, \quad \frac{\partial q}{\partial \tau} < 0 \tag{8}$$

Because of this interdependence, the growth rate of consumption per capita in equation (7) may be rewritten to depend exclusively on the tax rate. Together with the relation $G/k = (G/y)f(\cdot)$ the following growth rate results:

$$\gamma(\tau) = \frac{1}{\sigma}\left[(1-\tau)f(\cdot)\left(1 - \frac{\eta}{\tau + (1-\tau)\eta}\frac{G}{y}\right) - \delta - \rho\right] \tag{9}$$

Thus, the growth rate of consumption not only depends on the exogenous para-meters σ, δ, ρ and η but also on the level of the tax rate and the endogenously determined expenditure ratio G/y. An increase in the rate of taxes sets off two contrary effects. On the one hand, an increase in the tax rate is followed c.p. by a negative substitution effect, because it lowers the marginal product of capital, and private capital accumulation becomes more expensive. Capital accumulation is substituted by consumption. This is the negative effect of taxation on growth. On the other hand, there is the effect of a higher productivity, because of the higher tax rate c.p. total amount of the public input increases. Because both inputs, private capital k as well as public input G in the production function (3), are complemen-tary, an increase in the amount of one input improves productivity of the other input: a higher G as a consequence of the higher tax rate implies an increase in the marginal productivity of k. The incentive to accumulate capital rises as well as γ. The total effect of a higher tax rate on γ therefore depends upon which effect dominates.

In analogy to Barro (1990) it can be shown that the level of total welfare, represented by lifetime utility of the representative agent in equation (1), is concave in γ. For that reason, a maximisation of γ is identical with maximising total welfare. Maximisation of the growth rate in equation (9) results in a minimum tax rate $\tau^* = 0$ and together with equation (8) the optimal rate of fees $q^* = 1$ follows. A lower rate of fees for $q \in [0, 1]$ implies a decrease in the growth rate and a loss of welfare. Hence, the decentral choice would lead to a provision of the publicly provided input that is solely financed by fee revenues. Non-payers are excluded from the use of the public input and the realised level of the growth rate γ^* in equation (9) becomes:

$$\gamma^* = \frac{1}{\sigma}[f(\cdot)(1-\eta) - \delta - \rho] \tag{10}$$

The social optimum: It is also possible to contemplate the production conditions through the eyes of an altruistic planner that in case of any market failure can improve the decentrally obtained result. In providing the public input G, the social planner does not only determine the amount of G but also the financing. He decides whether the enterprises have to pay only fees or taxes respectively or a mixture of both. The planner faces the following accumulation constraint

$$\dot{k} = y - c - G - \delta k \tag{11}$$

and decides on the determination of the private consumption, capital as well as the public input.

This restriction together with equations (1), (2) and (3) leads to the planned growth rate

$$\gamma_p = \frac{1}{\sigma} \left[f(\cdot) \left(1 - \frac{G}{y} \right) - \delta - \rho \right] \tag{12}$$

It becomes optimal if production efficiency is reached, i.e. if marginal costs and marginal product of the public input coincide. G and y are modelled as the same good in different application. Hence, the marginal costs of G in units of y are one. The marginal product of the public input may be derived from equation (3) as $\partial y / \partial G = f'(\cdot)$. That is, production efficiency is realised if the expenditure ratio equals partial productivity of the public input η (see equation (4)). Together with equations (5) and (8) it becomes clear that this requires a pure financing by fees. Therefore, the determination of $\tau^* = 0$ leads to an adjustment of marginal product and marginal costs.

It has been proven that already in the case of the decentral optimisation the households would prefer a Pareto-optimal provision of the public input, and the growth rates in equations (10) and (12) coincide. Hence, to realise the Pareto-optimum the planner has to fix the expenditure ratio at the optimal level η by charging fees only. This goes along with the principle of equivalence in a dynamic context. Because of $\tau^* = 0$, private and social marginal product of capital are identical, and the possibility to exclude non-payers from the use of G gives rise to a consideration about the use of G not only for the planner but also for the private agent.

A pure public good

In the case of the public input as pure public good, decentral and central solutions do not coincide. This part presents how the results of the previous section are changed if the public input is a pure public good so that the provision has to be financed exclusively by taxes (see Barro 1990). In addition, the economic reasons for the differences in the two models are analysed.

The assumptions about behaviour and total welfare, represented by equation (1) or (2) respectively, production in equation (3), supply of labour as well as about population growth are the same as in section on 'Public good with excludability'. The fundamental difference consists in the characteristic of the public input as a pure public input, so that the possibility to exclude non-payers from the use of the public input G does not exist. This has consequences for the public budget constraint, private capital accumulation and the behaviour of the private individuals while optimising. The result is that in case of a positive income tax private and social marginal product of capital fall apart and total welfare may be increased through altruistic public intervention (for the distortionary effects of taxes in a dynamic context compare e.g. Lucas (1990), Ballard and Fullerton (1992), Chamley (1985), Chamley (1986) and Turnovsky (2000)).

Market equilibrium: The public input is solely financed by taxes on income (τ) and the budget constraint in equation (5) is replaced by:

$$G = \tau y \tag{13}$$

Thus, the private capital accumulation in comparison to equation (6) is also changed to:

$$\dot{k} = (1 - \tau)y - c - \delta k \tag{14}$$

In contrast to the previous section the private individuals do not decide on the use of the public input, so that formally G as state variable is dropped. The individuals only decide about the amount of c and k. As result of the decentral optimisation, the following growth rate of consumption per capita ϕ may be derived:

$$\phi(\tau) = \frac{1}{\sigma}[(1 - \tau)f(\cdot)(1 - \eta) - \delta - \rho] \tag{15}$$

Here, ϕ depends on the familiar exogenous parameters and on the endogenously determined tax rate τ. It satisfies the Keynes–Ramsey rule and has an interior maximum because there are – analogously to the previous section – two contrary effects from an increase in the tax rate on growth. However, the optimal tax rate does not coincide with the one established in section on 'Public good with excludability'. Because the income tax is the only revenue of the government, it has to be positive in order to ensure a positive amount of the necessary production input. Maximisation of the growth rate in equation (15) leads to a tax rate $\tau^* = \eta$. At the same time the choice of the income tax determines the expenditure ratio (see equation (13)).

The social optimum: In contrast to the previous section, the decentral result is not Pareto-optimal. This can be proven through the result obtained by an altruistic social planner. While maximising total welfare, he has to consider the condition in equation (11) which leads, together with the restrictions in equations (1), (2) and (3), to the welfare-maximising Hamiltonian. The planner chooses the time paths of c, G and k and realises the growth rate ϕ^*. The latter is identical with γ^* and γ_p respectively in equations (10) and (12). It exceeds the decentrally determined growth rate in equation (15) because the planner takes into account the social marginal product of capital that exceeds the private marginal product. Hence, the decentrally determined growth rate falls apart from the planned growth rate γ_p in equation (12).

Now it has to be clarified how the social planner may realise the Pareto-optimal growth rate in the economy: first, the planner determines the optimal amount of the public input $(G/y)^* = \eta$, because optimal provision requires that the condition for efficiency $\partial y/\partial G = 1$ has to be fulfilled. Second, the planner finances

Table 8.1 Comparison of fees and taxes

	Financing by income taxes	Financing by fees
Public input	Non-rival, non-excludable	Non-rival, excludable
Budget constraint	$G = \tau y$	$G = \tau y + qG$
		$q(\tau) = \dfrac{\eta(1 - \tau)}{\eta + (1 - \eta)\tau}$
Accumulation of capital	$\dot{k} = (1 - \tau)y - c - \delta k$	$\dot{k} = (1 - \tau)y - c - qG - \delta k$
Expenditure ratio	$\dfrac{G}{y}(\tau) = \tau$	$\dfrac{G}{y}(\tau, q) = \dfrac{(1 - \tau)\eta}{q}$
Decentral and optimal growth rate	$\phi < \phi^*$	$\gamma = \gamma^*$
Optimal growth rate	$\dfrac{1}{\sigma}[f(\cdot)(1 - \eta) - \rho - \delta]$	$\dfrac{1}{\sigma}[f(\cdot)(1 - \eta) - \rho - \delta]$
Optimal expenditure ratio	$\dfrac{G}{y}(\tau^*) = \eta$	$\dfrac{G}{y}(\tau^*, q^*) = \eta$

his expenditure by a tax on consumption or a lump-sum tax that in contrast to the proportional income tax have no distortionary effects on the private accumulation decisions.[2] However, under the assumptions of an income tax as the only revenue, the first-best optimum may not be derived. Thus, the planner at least determines the optimal amount of the expenditure ratio and sets the income tax rate to finance the provision of the public input. As decentral and planned growth rate are similar, maximisation in both cases leads to the optimal expenditure ratio and the income tax ensures a second-best optimum. Table 8.1 gives a summary of the central differences between the models discussed in section on 'Market equilibrium and social optimum'.

The egoistic public agent

Alternative specifications of egoism

Within endogenous growth models, the social planner may be interpreted as a person who is underlying no electoral constraints and seeks to maximise utility attained of the representative individual. This altruistic behaviour of the public agents is generally doubted within public choice theory. Various reasons are analysed why public agents do not always act in a socially optimal, but in a selfish manner (see e.g. Bernholz and Breyer 1994 or Mueller 1989). Considering an endogenous growth model with productive governmental input, egoism of the social planner could consist in maximising personnel consumption, as analysed e.g. by Barro (1990). The planner uses his net revenue that remains after the provision of the public good to purchase a certain quantity of consumer goods. He receives utility from consumption in the same manner as private households. It results in the optimal expenditure ratio because this allows for a maximal tax base.

Aside from this interpretation of a self-interested government, the planner may also be interpreted as a budget-maximising bureaucrat. Following the arguments of Niskanen (1971), bureaucrats tend to maximise their personal utility instead of the utility of their agents and end up in the provision of an inefficient high amount of public goods. This argument is supported e.g. by Tullock (1965), Migué and Bélanger (1974), Orzechowsky (1977) as well as Romer and Rosenthal (1978). Because both inputs are essential for production, the firms cannot renounce on the use of the public input and have to accept any financing chosen by the planner.

This section analyses how a planner acts if he wants to maximise his personal utility attained from a maximal budget. As the formal frame is a dynamic model, the budget may be interpreted as the available budget in each period or as the sum of the budget over the considered time-horizon. To formalise these two concepts of the budget one may look at a planner who maximises his budget in relation to total income in each period or the budget over time independent of the amount of the income in each period. In what follows, the first case will be called relative budget, the second case will be called absolute budget.

The result is that a self-interested government provides the public input efficiently if its object is to maximise total budget. On the other hand, if the planner tends to maximise his relative budget, he selects an inefficient high level of the income tax rate that ends up in a suboptimal low level of the growth rate and welfare losses. The welfare loss is bigger, the higher the income tax rate is. Corresponding to the public input as pure public good, egoism of the planner means that the income tax rate will increase. In the case of the fee-financed public input the planner will require a suboptimal low amount of fees and close the financing gap through tax revenues. Hence, in this case the income tax will increase as well. Moreover, it can be shown that a planner may not maximise his absolute and relative budget at the same time. Therefore, the importance of each object for the planner is essential for the obtained results. The following sections analyse each goal on its own and then combine them with a Cobb–Douglas utility function of the planner.

Budget maximisation in case of club goods

Maximising the relative budget: The relative budget of the planner refers to total expenditure in relation to total production, i.e. the expenditure ratio (G/y). It may be received from the individual optimisation with respect to the public input G together with equation (5) as:

$$\frac{G}{y}(\tau, q) = \frac{(1 - \tau)\eta}{q} \tag{16}$$

The expenditure ratio is automatically determined by fixing the rates of taxes and fees. In case of the optimal fiscal instruments $\tau^* = 0$ and $q^* = 1$, the expenditure ratio becomes $(G/y)^* = \eta$. However, the planner may enforce every expenditure ratio he wishes to realise, and is not obliged to set rates of taxes and fees optimally. Hence, he may choose any level of taxes and fees to maximise the expenditure ratio. Transformation of equations (8) and (16) eliminates the dependence on the rate of fees q and leads to:

$$\frac{G}{y}(\tau) = \eta + (1 - \eta)\tau, \qquad \frac{\partial(G/y)}{\partial\tau} > 0 \tag{17}$$

The expenditure ratio increases with the tax rate. Because τ is in the interval [0,1], the expenditure ratio has a minimum in case of $\tau^* = 0$, for $\tau = 1$ the expenditure ratio becomes $(G/y) = 1$. Total production is used to provide the public input. At the same time, the corresponding user fee is $q = 0$, as can be seen from (8). Thus, if the planner maximised his relative budget, he would select pure financing by taxes. At the same time, the levels of the growth rate and welfare decrease. This results from the distortionary effects already mentioned of the income tax: in the case of financing solely by fees, private individuals decide consciously about the use of the public input. This does not apply for tax financing, in which case the decision about the obligatory tax and the use of the public input are separated.

Although a tax rate at the level $\tau = 1$ maximises the expenditure ratio, this solution is not feasible because the resulting growth rate becomes negative (see equation (7)). As consumption and output per capita in the steady state grow at the same rate, a negative growth rate of consumption implies a shrinking economy. To avoid this, a maximum tax rate $\tau_m < 1$ that at least allows for zero growth has to be determined. This goes along with a maximum expenditure ratio $(G/y)_m < 1$ and at the same time a minimum rate of fees $q_m > 0$. These fiscal instruments may be derived by equalising (9) to zero together with equation (8). Hence, in the case of maximising the relative budget the planner will go on to an inefficient financing mix consisting of fees and taxes. At the same time, he puts up with a welfare loss as the suboptimal choice of the fiscal instruments goes along with a suboptimal low level of the growth rate.

Maximising the absolute budget: Because the budget in steady state grows at the same rate as consumption per capita, the absolute budget becomes maximal when the optimal level of the growth rate γ^* in equation (10) is realised. Therefore, the self-interested planner will set the Pareto-optimal rate of fees to $q^* = 1$ and renounce on any taxing income. At the same time, he maximises his personnel utility as well as welfare of the representative agent, but the latter fact is not of interest for the planner's decision.

From equation (12) it is obvious that the expenditure ratio influences the growth rate and therefore it is possible to analyse the effects of a changing relative budget on the absolute budget:

$$\frac{\partial\gamma}{\partial(G/y)} = \frac{f(\cdot)}{\sigma(1-\eta)}(f'(\cdot) - 1) > 0 \Longleftrightarrow \frac{G}{y} < \eta \tag{18a}$$

$$\frac{\partial\gamma}{\partial(G/y)} = \frac{f(\cdot)}{\sigma(1-\eta)}(f'(\cdot) - 1) < 0 \Longleftrightarrow \frac{G}{y} > \eta \tag{18b}$$

The growth rate has a maximum if $f'(\cdot) = 1$ and with this, the Pareto-optimal expenditure ratio $(G/y)^* = \eta$ applies. If the expenditure ratio is suboptimally low, an increase of (G/y) goes along with a rising growth rate; in case of a suboptimally high expenditure ratio, any further expansion of the expenditure ratio ends up in a decreasing growth rate. Hence, the planner may only maximise growth rate *and* expenditure ratio simultaneously if the latter is suboptimally low. From equation (17) follows

$$\tau \left(\frac{G}{y} \right) = \frac{1}{1 - \eta} \left[\frac{G}{y} - \frac{\eta}{1 - \eta} \right] \Rightarrow \frac{G}{y} \geq \eta \Leftrightarrow \tau \geq 0 \qquad (19)$$

Thus, for all rates of taxes $\tau \in [0, 1]$, the growth rate decreases with an increase in the expenditure ratio with the consequence that maximisation of the relative and the absolute budget at the same time may not be realised.

The egoistic planner's aspiration to maximise his own utility may be concluded in two different ways: First, as the realisation of a maximum expenditure ratio $(G/y)_m$ that allows at least for zero growth and second, as a budget growing at the rate γ^*. From the derivative of equation (12) it becomes clear that both goals cannot be reached at the same time.

Maximising absolute and relative budget: If the planner pursues a mixture of both goals and is ready to accept a higher growing budget as compensation for a lower expenditure ratio, one could portray his preferences within a Cobb–Douglas utility function with the relative importance of each goal expressed by the exponents φ:

$$U_e \left(\gamma, \frac{G}{y} \right) \equiv \gamma^\varphi \cdot \left(\frac{G}{y} \right)^{1 - \varphi}, \quad 0 \leq \varphi \leq 1 \qquad (20)$$

where γ represents the growth rate in equation (12) and (G/y) is the expenditure ratio as shown in (17). To get an explicit solution for the maximisation of (20), γ will be changed by a linear transformation through addition of $(\rho + \delta)/\sigma$. The resulting growth rate will be called γ_0 in the following presentation. It is positive for all expenditure ratios in the interval $[\eta, 1]$ and has the same formal qualities as γ in (12), especially a maximum at the optimal level of the expenditure ratio. φ_m is that weight ratio that corresponds to γ_0 and restricts the feasible interval $\varphi \in [\varphi_m, 1]$.

Both goals, maximisation of the expenditure ratio with a minimum growth rate at zero and pure maximisation of the growth rate of the budget, are contained in the utility function: $\varphi = 1$ means that the planner prefers a maximisation of γ, whereas $\varphi = \varphi_m$ implies a level of the expenditure ratio that allows for zero growth. If φ is within $\varphi_m < \varphi < 1$, the planner wants to realise a mixture of both goals. In this case, he chooses the lower expenditure ratio, the more important a growing budget is for him (see equation (21)). Maximisation of the utility function in (20) leads to the selfish planner's expenditure ratio:

$$\left(\frac{G}{y} \right)_e = \frac{\varphi \eta + (1 - \eta)(1 - \varphi)}{(1 - \eta)(1 - \varphi) + \varphi}, \quad \forall \varphi_m \leq \varphi \leq 1 \qquad (21)$$

where the index e indicates the solution that corresponds to the maximisation of (20). The resulting expenditure ratio lies within the interval $[\eta, (G/y)_m]$ and the restriction of φ in (21) corresponds to a retransformation of γ_0 to γ.

The expenditure ratio is the result of definite rates of taxes and fees. How these instruments depend on the weight ratios of the planner may be derived by solving equation (17) for τ and using equation (21). The planner will decide to choose the following rate of fees:

$$q_e = \frac{\varphi\eta}{(1 - \eta)(1 - \varphi) + \varphi\eta}, \quad \forall \, \varphi_{\min} \leq \varphi \leq 1, \quad \frac{\partial q_e}{\partial \varphi} > 0 \qquad (22)$$

q_e is in the interval $[q_m, 1]$, and increases with φ, that is if the planner prefers a maximum budget growth. For all $\varphi < 1$, he will provide a mixed financing. In case of $\varphi = 1$, the public input is solely financed by fees, i.e. the provision is Pareto-optimal. While maximising his personnel utility, the planner also maximises the utility attained by the representative agent, but the latter fact is not the motivation for his choice of taxes and fees.

Moreover, fixing the rate of fees automatically determines the corresponding level of the tax rate. The selfish planner's tax rate τ_e results from (22) together with (17):

$$\tau_e = \frac{(1 - \eta)(1 - \varphi)}{(1 - \eta)(1 - \varphi) + \varphi}, \quad \forall \, \varphi_m \leq \varphi \leq 1, \quad \frac{\partial \tau_e}{\partial \varphi} < 0 \qquad (23)$$

The implications of (23) are familiar to those in the case of the rate of fees: the planner will fix a lower tax rate if he prefers a high growth rate of the public budget. If instead he intends to maximise the expenditure ratio, he will choose a tax rate as high as possible but is limited to the upper boundary τ_m. He then departs from the Pareto-optimal provision and maximises his own utility at the cost of individual welfare, because the proportional income tax distorts the intertemporal allocation.

The interdependencies between planner's utility, growth rate and expenditure ratio as well as rates of taxes and fees may be illustrated graphically as demonstrated in Figure 8.1. It contains the relations analytically ascertained in equations (8), (12), (17) and (20). Depending on the relative weights of each goal φ the levels of the growth rate, expenditure ratio and rate of fees are unequivocally determined. For a certain exogenous level $\varphi_b \in (\varphi_m, 1)$ the indifference curve corresponding to the planner's utility function (20) might be depicted by the graph U_b in Figure 8.1. It results in a growth rate $\gamma_b < \gamma^*$, an expenditure ratio $\eta_b \in (\eta, (G/y)_m)$ and a tax rate $\tau_b \in (\tau_m, 1)$. The Pareto-optimal solution is represented for $\varphi = 1$, in which case the indifference curve would be a parallel to the abscissa. The other polar case, that is $\varphi = \varphi_m$, corresponds to a tangent point of indifference curve and the function $\gamma(G/y)$ for a growth rate at the level γ_0, a corresponding expenditure ratio $(G/y)_m$ and the fiscal instruments τ_m and q_m.

It may be concluded that the level of φ not only determines the amount of growth rate and expenditure ratio but at the same time the levels of the fiscal instruments. In case of maximising the absolute budget, the Pareto-optimal financing-mix results,

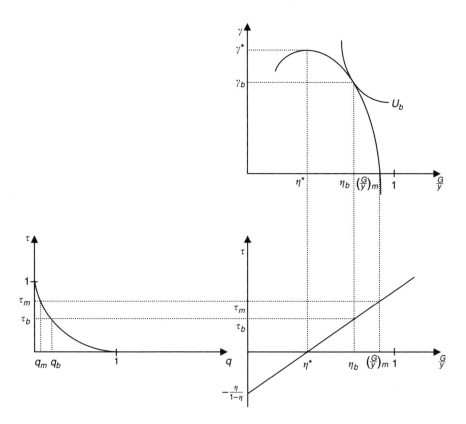

Figure 8.1 Interdependencies between planner's utility, growth rate, expenditure ratio, rates of taxes and fees.

whereas for each $\varphi \neq 1$ a mixed financing consisting of fees and taxes results. The share of taxes increases with the importance for the planner to maximise his relative budget and the part of taxes on total financing becomes maximum for the polar case $\varphi = \varphi_m$ that goes along with zero growth. The results of an egoistic behaviour of the planner are summarised in Table 8.2.

The case of a pure public good

The following part analyses how the results of selfishness of the social planner are changed if the public input is a pure public good, i.e. excludability does not arise. Again, egoism of the planner is defined as to maximise relative or absolute budget respectively a mixture of both. It results a suboptimal financing in both cases. In the case of maximising the absolute budget the planner will chose a second-best financing. As the familiar consequences of different financing instruments for

Table 8.2 Consequences of different weight ratios of the planner's goals

	$\varphi = \varphi_m$	$\varphi_m < \varphi < 1$	$\varphi = 1$
$U_e\left(\gamma, \dfrac{G}{y}\right) \equiv \gamma^\varphi \cdot \left(\dfrac{G}{y}\right)^{1-\varphi}$	$\max \dfrac{G}{y}$ s.t. $\gamma \geq 0$	$\max \dfrac{G}{y}, \gamma$	$\max \gamma$
$\left(\dfrac{G}{y}\right)_e = \dfrac{\varphi\eta + (1-\eta)(1-\varphi)}{(1-\eta)(1-\varphi) + \varphi}$	$\left(\dfrac{G}{y}\right)_m$	$\eta < \left(\dfrac{G}{y}\right) < \left(\dfrac{G}{y}\right)_m$	$\left(\dfrac{G}{y}\right)^* = \eta$
$q_e = \dfrac{\varphi\eta}{(1-\eta)(1-\varphi) + \varphi\eta}$	q_m	$q_m < q < 1$	$q^* = 1$
$\tau_e = \dfrac{(1-\eta)(1-\varphi)}{(1-\eta)(1-\varphi) + \varphi}$	τ_m	$0 < \tau < \tau_m$	$\tau^* = 0$
$\gamma = \dfrac{1}{\sigma}\left[f(\cdot)\left(1 - \dfrac{G}{y}\right) - \rho - \delta\right]$	0	$0 < \gamma < \gamma^*$	γ^*

growth and welfare from the last section arise, the following presentation of the consequences of selfish planner's behaviour are kept short.

Maximising the relative budget: In the case of G as pure public good the expenditure ratio solely is determined by the proportional income tax (see equation (13)). Because the expenditure ratio rises together with the tax rate, the selfish planner would choose a maximum tax rate to maximise his relative budget. Again, a tax rate at the level $\tau = 1$ would lead to a negative growth rate so that this solution is not feasible. Thus, to realise feasible solutions the planner would once again be restricted by an upper boundary of the income tax rate τ_m that allows at least for zero growth.

Maximising the absolute budget: If the planner tends to maximise his influence in the long-run, he will maximise the growth rate in equation (15). Therefore, he sets the optimal expenditure ratio already derived in section on 'Market equilibrium and social optimum'. It results in $(G/y)^* = \eta$ that together with equation (5) automatically determines the optimal tax rate $\tau^* = \eta$, as the planner is restricted to a pure financing by income taxes. Under these conditions the distortionary income tax rate leads to the highest possible growth rate and thus to the maximum of the absolute budget. If the possibility of a non-distortionary financing instrument existed, this would lead to a welfare gain. Because of the budget constraint in equation (5), these instruments are not analysed here.

Maximisation of the relative and absolute budget: The goal of maximising the relative and absolute budget at certain levels of weight ratios may be concluded by the same utility function as in the last section, e.g. by equation (20). Because expenditure ratio and income tax rate coincide, maximising equation (20) leads to the selfish planner's tax rate

$$\tau_e = \frac{\varphi\eta + (1-\eta)(1-\varphi)}{(1-\eta)(1-\varphi) + \varphi}, \quad \forall\, \varphi_m \leq \varphi \leq 1 \tag{24}$$

where φ_m again ends up in zero growth. The derivative $\partial \tau_e / \partial \varphi$ is negative for all $\varphi \in (\varphi_m, 1)$ and the planner chooses the lower tax rate, the more important the goal to maximise the growth rate. $\varphi = 1$ leads to the optimal tax rate $\tau^* = \eta$ that goes along with the efficient expenditure ratio and the second-best growth rate. The maximally feasible tax rate is determined by φ_m and corresponds to $\tau_m < 1$. Besides, it becomes obvious that the planner would never choose a tax rate lower than τ^* as the income tax is his own revenue. One may conclude that although the optimal level of the public input may be realised, selfish behaviour of the planner never leads to a suboptimal *low* level but may lead to a suboptimal high level of the public input. A central difference to the last section is that, although for $\varphi = 1$ the tax rate $\tau^* = \eta$ leads to a Pareto-optimal expenditure ratio, this only goes along with a second-best growth rate.

Summary

This chapter analyses how Pareto-optimal financing of a productive governmental input changes if this input has the characteristic of excludability or not. It is proven that in the first case, the decentral optimisation leads to financing consisting of fees only and hence allows for an efficient provision. A transition to a financing by proportional income tax reduces welfare, because the tax has a distortionary effect on the individual accumulation of capital. Therefore, a benevolent social planner determines the efficient rates of fees and taxes that may be already derived from the decentral decisions. In doing so, he maximises the growth rate and with this total welfare. In case of the public input as pure public good, the market equilibrium leads to a suboptimal low growth rate if the financing consists of distortionary taxes. An altruistic social planner may improve the market solution proceeding to non-distortionary fiscal instruments. The comparison of the two models shows that the optimal ways of financing in the two models differ, but efficient expenditure ratios and growth rates coincide. The differences are the consequence of the possibility to exclude non-payers from the use of the essential input that does not exist in the case of the public input as pure public good.

The second part of the chapter analyses how the efficient provision will be changed by intervention of a selfish public agent. This social planner tends to maximise his available budget. This can be interpreted in two different ways: on the one hand, he may maximise his budget in relation to total output in each period (maximising relative budget); on the other hand, he may seek for a maximally growing budget (maximising total budget). It is shown that the two goals are contrary, and that the egoistic planner determines different rates of fees and taxes depending on which goal dominates. Both goals can be linked together in a planner's utility function. It becomes clear that if the planner wants to maximise his absolute budget, he will choose the Pareto-optimal provision of the public input if excludability exists. If the public input is a pure public good and an income tax is the only financing instrument, the planner will choose a second-best solution that allows for maximum growth under those conditions. On the contrary, the planner accepts welfare losses through distortionary effects of the income tax if he wants to maximise his relative budget. It results in the corner solution with zero growth. This applies independently of the characteristics of the public input.

Notes

1 Alternatively, one could suppose that the government disposes of the same production technology as the private firms and produces G at his own. This assumption would not affect the results.
2 Because labour-leisure choice is not considered, a tax on consumption in this context acts like a lump-sum tax.

References

Aghion, P. and Howitt, P. (1992) 'A Model of Growth through Creative Destruction', *Econometrica*, 60: 323–51.

Aschauer, D.A. (1989) 'Is Public Expenditure Productive?', *Journal of Monetary Economics*, 23: 177–200.

Atkinson, A.B. and Stiglitz, J.E. (1980) *Lectures on Public Economics*, New York: McGraw-Hill.

Ballard, C.L. and Fullerton, D. (1992) 'Distortionary Taxes and the Provision of Public Goods', *Journal of Economic Perspectives*, 6: 117–31.

Barro, R.J. (1990) 'Government Spending in a Simple Model of Endogenous Growth', *Journal of Political Economy*, 98: 103–25.

—— and Sala-i-Martin, X. (1992) 'Public Finance in Models of Economic Growth', *Review of Economic Studies*, 59: 645–61.

—— (1995) *Economic Growth*, New York: McGraw-Hill.

Bernholz, P. and Breyer, F. (1994) *Grundlagen der Politischen Ökonomie, Band 2, Ökonomische Theorie der Politik*, 3rd edn, Tübingen: Mohr & v. Siebeck.

Bös, D. (1991) *Privatization – A Theoretical Treatment*, Oxford: Clarendon Press.

Chamley, C. (1985) 'Efficient Taxation in a Stylised Model of Intertemporal General Equilibrium', *International Economic Review*, 26: 451–68.

—— (1986) 'Optimal Taxation of Capital Income in General Equilibrium with Infinite Lives', *Econometrica*, 54: 607–22.

Cornes, R. and Sandler, T. (1996) *The Theory of Externalities, Public Goods and Club Goods*, 2nd edn, Cambridge, Mass.: Cambridge University Press.

Grossman, G. and Helpman, E. (1991) 'Quality Ladders in the Theory of Growth', *Review of Economic Studies*, 58: 43–61.

Kapur, A. (1995) Airport Infrastructure, the Emerging Role of the Private Sector, Technical Paper 313, Washington, DC: World Bank.

Lucas, R.E. (1988) 'On the Mechanics of Economic Development', *Journal of Monetary Economics*, 22: 3–42.

—— (1990) 'Supply-Side Economics: An Analytical Review', *Oxford Economic Papers*, 42: 293–316.

Migué, J.L. and Bélanger, G. (1974) 'Toward a General Theory of Managerial Discretion', *Public Choice*, 17: 27–43.

Mueller, D. (1989) *Public Choice II*, 2nd edn, Cambridge: Cambridge University Press.

Musgrave, R.A. (1959) *The Theory of Public Finance*, New York: McGraw-Hill.

Niskanen, W.A. (1971) *Bureaucracy and Representative Government*, Chicago: Aldline-Atherton.

Orzechowsky, W. (1977) 'Economic Models of Bureaucracy: Survey, Extensions, and Evidence', in T.E. Borcherding (ed.), *Budgets and Bureaucrats: The Sources of Government Growth*, Durham, NC: Duke University Press: 229–59.

Ott, I. (2000) 'Bureaucratic Choice and Endogenous Growth', *Finanzarchiv*, 57: 225–41.

Romer, P.M. (1986) 'Increasing Returns and Long-Run Growth', *Journal of Political Economy*, 94: 1002–37.

Romer, T. and Rosenthal, H. (1978) 'Political Resource Allocation, Controlled Agendas and Status Quo', *Public Choice*, 33: 27–43.

Seitz, H. (1994) 'Public Capital and the Demand for Private Inputs', *Journal of Public Economics*, 54: 287–307.

Tullock, G. (1965) *The Politics of Bureaucracy*, Washington, DC: Public Affairs Press.

Turnovsky, S.J. (2000) *Methods of Macroeconomic Dynamics*, 2nd edn, Cambridge, Mass.: MIT Press.

—— and Fisher, W.H. (1998) 'Public Investment, Congestion, and Private Capital Accumulation', *Economic Journal*, 108: 399–413.

9 Growth and distribution effects of education policy in an endogenous growth model with human capital accumulation

Christiane Schäper

Introduction

Endogenous growth theory suggests that government policy is able to play a fundamental role in the economic growth process through its influence on factors determining the long-term rate of growth. Major determinants of economic growth under discussion are e.g. investment or saving rate, population growth, human capital and income distribution (for an overview see Levine and Renelt 1992).

The influence of human capital on economic growth is still controversial empirically, mainly due to data problems (see e.g. Benhabib and Spiegel 1994 and Barro and Lee 1993). A positive impact of a more equal distribution on economic growth has been emphasised theoretically as well as empirically by Persson and Tabellini (1994), Alesina and Rodrik (1994), Perotti (1993, 1994, 1996) and Clarke (1995). This relationship is not a new subject: Kuznets (1955) pointed out that in the historic process of economic development of some industrialised countries income inequality first rose and then declined, leading to the famous U-curve hypothesis (UCH). Due to ambiguous empirical results, some economists favour the UCH, others doubt its existence (see e.g. Ogwang 1995 and Anand and Kanbur 1993).

The model presented here is based on Galor and Tsiddon (1996) as well as Galor and Tsiddon (1997). Both, the work of Galor and Tsiddon as well as this chapter, focus on the interdependence of human capital accumulation, personal distribution of income and economic growth. We combine their proposal of a threshold externality of technological progress with their example of diminishing complementarity between capital investment and the influence of parental human capital on human capital accumulation of the children's generation. In addition, this chapter for the first time introduces governmental education policy to this kind of analysis, discusses reasonable parameter values and presents some simulation results. The main result is that education policy is able to enhance economic growth and to lead to a more equal distribution under certain conditions.

The chapter is organised as follows: in the next section we present our basic model. Section on 'Simulation of the basic model' describes our choice of parameters as well as simulation results for this basic model. Section on 'Education Policy' introduces the education policy and presents simulation results as well. The chapter ends with a discussion.

The basic model

We consider a small open overlapping-generations economy in a perfectly competitive world with two sectors and perfect capital markets. Prices and population size are assumed to be constant throughout this study, all transactions take place at the end of the periods. Two groups of individuals differ in human capital and therefore in income. Externalities of the parents' human capital influence human capital accumulation of the children and, hence, economic growth and the evolution of income distribution.

Production

In every period, the economy produces a single homogeneous good which can be used for either consumption, investment or saving. Production follows a constant-returns-to-scale technology with endogenous technological progress. Output at time t, Y_t, is a function of the quantities of physical and human capital employed in production at time t, K_t and H_t, and the production technology at time t, A_t. Changes in A_t can be interpreted as technological change at time t, which is labour augmenting in our formulation. The parameter γ reflects the partial production elasticity of physical capital, $(1 - \gamma)$ the production elasticity of efficiency labour. Due to $k_t \equiv K_t/A_t H_t$ and $y_t \equiv Y_t/A_t H_t$, the production function $Y_t = K_t^{\gamma}(A_t H_t)^{1-\gamma}$ can be written as

$$Y_t = A_t H_t f(k_t) = A_t H_t (k_t)^{\gamma} \tag{1}$$

The production function is twice continuously differentiable with $f'(k_t) > 0$ and $f''(k_t) < 0 \quad \forall \quad k_t > 0$, $\lim_{k_t \to 0} f'(k_t) = \infty$ and $\lim_{k_t \to \infty} f'(k_t) = 0$. Hence, it satisfies standard neoclassical properties. Physical capital K_t depreciates totally after every period.

Factor prices

Under perfect competitiveness and given the wage rate and the rate of return to physical capital at time t, w_t and r_t respectively, producers choose the profit-maximising amounts of physical and human capital employed in production, K_t and H_t. Their demand functions for physical and human capital can therefore be written as

$$r_t = f'(k_t) \tag{2}$$

and

$$w_t = A_t[f(k_t) - f'(k_t)k_t] \equiv A_t w(k_t) \tag{3}$$

Since we observe a world interest rate stationary at level $\bar{r}$ and unrestricted international lending and borrowing in the small open economy, its rate of return to physical capital is also stationary at the level $\bar{r}$:

$$r_t = \bar{r} \tag{4}$$

As a result from (2) and (4), the ratio of physical capital to efficiency labour is stationary: $\bar{k} = f'^{-1}(\bar{r})$. Therefore, the wage rate has a variable and a constant part, A_t and $\bar{w}$ respectively: $w_t = A_t w(\bar{k}) = A_t \bar{w}$. Wage incomes depend on technological progress and on the amount of the individual's human capital.

Technological progress

The level of production technology in period $t + 1$ depends on the amount of average human capital of the parents in period t:

$$A_{t+1} = A(h_t) \quad \text{with } h_t \equiv H_t/N \tag{5}$$

where N is the constant number of individuals within a generation. Generally, technological progress could be a monotonically non-decreasing function of human capital. In order to distinguish two externalities of the parental human capital, technological progress follows a threshold externality in this analysis: as long as the average human capital is below some threshold level $\hat{h}$, the level of technology equals a certain level A^1, whereas it increases to a higher level A^2, as soon as the average level of human capital reaches the threshold level $\hat{h}$:

$$A_{t+1} = A(h_t) = \begin{cases} A^1 & \text{if } h_t < \hat{h} \\ A^2 & \text{if } h_t \geq \hat{h} \end{cases} \quad \text{with } A^2 > A^1 \tag{5'}$$

Hence, we only observe two levels of technology in our economy.[1]

Individuals

In every period a new generation of N individuals is born. They are identical in their preferences and their production function of human capital, but they differ in their parents' level of human capital. First, we will describe homogeneous individuals, later we will analyse heterogeneous dynasties. Every individual i lives for three periods. In the first period she borrows capital at the market interest rate $\bar{r}$, in order to finance consumption in the first period $c_t^{1,i}$ and to invest the amount x_t^i of capital in human capital accumulation. The individual's level of human capital h_{t+1}^i additionally depends on h_t^i, the human capital of her parent.[2] We assume a Cobb–Douglas technology for human capital formation with positive, but diminishing returns with respect to each input:

$$h_{t+1}^i = \mu + x_t^{i\alpha} h_t^{i\beta} \quad \text{with } \mu > 0, \alpha \in (0, 1) \tag{6}$$

Even if the individual does not invest in human capital accumulation, she is at least endowed with $\mu > 0$ units of human capital: the constant μ represents raw labour with no skills acquired. The constant parameter α measures the influence of physical capital investment on human capital accumulation, β, however, measures the influence of the parent's human capital on the individual's. We assume that the latter parameter is a function of the parental human capital and decreases with higher values. This results in diminishing complementarity between the parent's human capital h_t^i and x_t^i, the amount of invested physical capital:[3]

$$\beta = \beta(h_t^i) > 0 \quad \text{with} \quad \beta'(h_t^i) \leq 0 \quad \forall \, h_t^i > 0 \tag{7}$$

We assume that $\lim_{h_t^i \to 0} \alpha + \beta(h_t^i) > 1$ and $\lim_{h_t^i \to \infty} \alpha + \beta(h_t^i) < 1$ for

$$h_{t+1}^i = \mu + x_t^{i^\alpha} h_t^{i^{\beta(h_t^i)}} \quad \text{with} \quad \mu > 0, \alpha \in (0, 1) \tag{6'}$$

This nonlinear difference equation exhibits increasing returns to scale at lower levels and decreasing returns to scale at higher levels of the parent's human capital. Under these assumptions multiple steady states are possible, as will be shown below. The individual i of generation t generates labour income in the second period $t + 1$: it is given by the supplied quantity of human capital h_{t+1}^i times the wage rate per human capital unit w_{t+1}:[4]

$$I_{t+1}^i = w_{t+1} h_{t+1}^i = \overline{w} A_{t+1} h_{t+1}^i \tag{8}$$

The individual allocates income between consumption in this second period $c_{t+1}^{t,i}$ and savings s_{t+1}^i, after she repaid her loan of the first period $(1+\bar{r})(x_t^i + c_t^{t,i})$. Hence, saving of an individual i of generation t is

$$s_{t+1}^i = \overline{w} A_{t+1} h_{t+1}^i - (1 + \bar{r})(x_t^i + c_t^{t,i}) - c_{t+1}^{t,i} \tag{9}$$

The gross return on these savings is consumed by a member i of generation t at time $t + 2$:

$$c_{t+2}^{t,i} = (1+\bar{r})s_{t+1}^i = (1+\bar{r})\left[\overline{w} A_{t+1} h_{t+1}^i - (1+\bar{r})(x_t^i + c_t^{t,i}) - c_{t+1}^{t,i}\right] \tag{10}$$

Our individual faces the following optimisation problem: given interest rate $\bar{r}$, wage rate $\overline{w} A_{t+1}$ and the level of the parental human capital h_t^i, the individual chooses the amount of capital investment in human capital x_t^i, consumption in the first period $c_t^{t,i}$ and savings in the second period s_{t+1}^i, in order to maximise the intertemporal utility function $U^{t,i}$. We assume a standard and frequently used utility function of constant intertemporal elasticity of substitution λ (CIES) with the rate of time preference ρ:[5]

$$\max U^{t,i} = U^{t,i}\left(c_t^{t,i}, c_{t+1}^{t,i}, c_{t+2}^{t,i}\right)$$

$$= \frac{\left(c_t^{t,i}\right)^{1-\lambda} - 1}{1 - \lambda} + \left(\frac{1}{1+\rho}\right) \frac{\left(c_{t+1}^{t,i}\right)^{1-\lambda} - 1}{1 - \lambda}$$

$$+ \left(\frac{1}{1+\rho}\right)^2 \frac{\left(c_{t+2}^{t,i}\right)^{1-\lambda} - 1}{1 - \lambda} \tag{11}$$

subject to $x_t^i, c_t^{t,i}, s_{t+1}^i \geq 0$ and (6'), (8), (9) and (10).

The solution is characterised by the following necessary and sufficient conditions:

$$\frac{c_{t+1}^{t,i}}{c_t^{t,i}} = \left(\frac{1+\bar{r}}{1+\rho}\right)^{1/\lambda} \quad \text{and} \quad \frac{c_{t+2}^{t,i}}{c_{t+1}^{t,i}} = \left(\frac{1+\bar{r}}{1+\rho}\right)^{1/\lambda}$$

$$\frac{\partial h_{t+1}^i}{\partial x_t^i} = \frac{(1+\bar{r})}{\bar{w}A_{t+1}}. \tag{12}$$

Capital investment in human capital formation of the individual amounts to

$$x_t^i = \left[\frac{\alpha\bar{w}A_{t+1}(h_t^i)^{\beta(h_t^i)}}{1+\bar{r}}\right]^{1/(1-\alpha)} \tag{13}$$

and leads to the following non-linear first-order difference equation, when combined with (6′), which describes the dynamic evolution of human capital of each dynasty i:

$$h_{t+1}^i = \Omega(h_t^i, A_{t+1}) = \mu + \left[\frac{\alpha\bar{w}A_{t+1}}{1+\bar{r}}\right]^{\alpha/(1-\alpha)} (h_t^i)^{\beta(h_t^i)/(1-\alpha)} \tag{14}$$

Unfortunately, it is not possible to solve this difference equation analytically, but it is possible to consider some important features. Let us assume that $\lim_{h_t^i \to 0} \Omega'(h_t^i, A_{t+1}) = 0$, $\lim_{h_t^i \to \infty} \Omega'(h_t^i, A_{t+1}) = 0$ and $\Omega(h_t^i A_{t+1}) > h_t^i$ for some $h_t^i > 0$. Together with our assumption of variable returns to scale, these assumptions ensure that multiple steady states are possible, as shown in Figure 9.1.

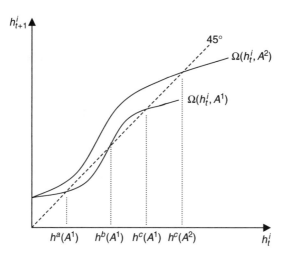

Figure 9.1 Human capital accumulation.

At very low levels of parental human capital the increases of human capital of the children are hardly observable. Due to increasing returns to scale, human capital rises up to a certain point, where decreasing returns start. For a certain level of the constant μ and the level of technology A^1, the system $h^i_{t+1} = \Omega(h^i_t, A^1)$ can be characterised by three steady-state equilibria: $h^a(A^1)$ and $h^c(A^1)$ are locally stable, $h^b(A^1)$ is unstable.

The starting value of the parents' human capital determines the dynamic evolution of the economy:[6] if an economy starts to the left of the unstable steady state $h^b(A^1)$, the process ends at the lower stable steady state $h^a(A^1)$. If it starts to the right of $h^b(A^1)$, it ends at the higher steady state $h^c(A^1)$. For a higher level of production technology A^2, the dynamic system $h^i_{t+1} = \Omega(h^i_t, A^2)$ may even be characterised by a unique stable steady state $h^c(A^2)$. In this case, the economy develops monotonically towards the higher steady state, independently of the starting value of the parents' human capital. Therefore, this dynamic system exhibits a supercritical pitchfork bifurcation:[7] a change at a certain level of technology can lead to a change in transitional dynamics.

It is necessary to notice the importance of the parents' human capital. We can distinguish two types of externalities: first, a local or family externality occurs due to the influence of the parental human capital on human capital accumulation of their children (see equation (14)). Second, there is a global or technological externality, since the parental human capital contributes to the average level of human capital, which in turn determines the prevailing level of technology (see equation (5′)). The interaction of these two externalities determines the distribution of human capital and income and, hence, economic growth in the case of heterogeneous dynasties.

Evolution of the distribution of human capital and income

We now give up the assumption that individuals are homogeneous and consider two types of dynasties, $i = H, L$. Individuals still have the same preferences and production function for human capital, but differ now in their parents' human capital, namely

$$h^H_0 > h^L_0 \quad \text{with } h^L_0 = h^a(A^1) \text{ and } h^H_0 = h^b(A^1) + \varepsilon \tag{15}$$

where $\varepsilon > 0$ is sufficiently small. We assume that at time 0 dynasty L starts at the lower steady state with low human capital, whereas dynasty H starts to the right of the unstable steady state with higher values of human capital. We define the ratio of individuals of dynasty L to the entire population as $\theta = N^L/N$ as well as the proportion of individuals of dynasty H as $(1 - \theta) = N^H/N$ with $\theta \in (0, 1)$. Furthermore, we assume that at time 0 the average level of human capital is below the threshold level $\hat{h}$:

$$\theta h^L_0 + (1 - \theta)h^H_0 = h_0 \quad \text{and} \quad h_0 < \hat{h} \tag{16}$$

As the production technology at time 1 depends on the average level of human capital at time 0, it remains at level A^1, so that dynasties H and L evolve according to $h_1^i = \Omega(h_0^i, A^1)$ for $i = H, L$. Namely, dynasty L evolves according to

$$h_1^L = \Omega(h_0^L, A^1) = \mu + \left[\frac{\alpha \overline{w} A^1}{1 + \overline{r}}\right]^{\alpha/(1-\alpha)} (h^a)^{\beta(h_t^i)/(1-\alpha)} = h^a(A^1) = h_0^L$$

(17)

There is no incentive for the children of dynasty L to invest a larger sum into human capital accumulation: their human capital remains stationary at the level of their parents, as does their income in the second period of life: $I_1^L = I_0^L = \overline{w} A^1 h^a(A^1) = $ constant for all $t \geq 1$.

For the members of dynasty H, however, it is beneficial to increase their investment in human capital. Therefore, dynasty H develops along the graph $h_{t+1}^i = \Omega(h_t^i, A^1)$ to the right of the unstable steady state $h^b(A^1)$ towards the stable equilibrium $h^c(A^1)$:

$$h_1^H = \Omega(h_0^H, A^1) = \mu + \left[\frac{\alpha \overline{w} A^1}{1 + \overline{r}}\right]^{\alpha/(1-\alpha)} (h^b + \varepsilon)^{\beta(h_t^i)/(1-\alpha)} = \Omega(h^b + \varepsilon, A^1)$$

(18)

with $h_1^H > h_0^H = h^b + \varepsilon$ and $I_1^H = \overline{w} A^1 h_1^H > I_0^H = \overline{w} A^1 h_0^H$. The children's human capital and their income at time 1 are higher than at the beginning. As dynasty L's human capital and income are stationary, whereas human capital and income rise for dynasty H, the distributions of human capital and income become more unequal during economic growth, due to the local externality of H's parental human capital. But, since human capital of dynasty H rises, the average level of human capital approaches the threshold level $\hat{h}$ and the global externality of parental human capital occurs. At some time $t*$ the level of technology changes from A^1 to A^2:

$$\theta h_{t*}^L + (1 - \theta)h_{t*}^H = h_{t*} \geq \hat{h} \quad \text{with } h_{t*+1}^i = \Omega(h_{t*}^i, A^2) \quad \text{for } i = H, L \quad (19)$$

The technological progress leads to a higher wage rate and induces a change in human capital accumulation of dynasty L: it is now beneficial for members of dynasty L to increase their investment in human capital, too. Consequently, the two dynasties evolve along the same dynamical system and converge to the unique stable steady-state equilibrium $h^c(A^2)$:

$$h_{t*+1}^i = \Omega(h_{t*}^i, A^2) = \mu + \left[\frac{\alpha \overline{w} A^2}{1 + \overline{r}}\right]^{\alpha/(1-\alpha)} (h_{t*}^i)^{\beta(h_{t*}^i)/(1-\alpha)} \quad \text{with } i = H, L$$

(20)

Due to the global externality, economic growth is accompanied by a decrease in income inequality after time t^*. The interaction of the two externalities of the parents' human capital leads to a non-linear relationship between human capital as well as income distribution and economic growth: during economic development inequality first rises because of the local externality, it then decreases due to the global externality. This equals the pattern of the UCH of Kuznets.[8] In the new equilibrium, at $h^c(A^2)$, we can observe an equal distribution of human capital and income, but economic growth stops, since the economy lacks incentive for human capital accumulation.[9] It is important to notice that the initial distribution of human capital determines the observed pattern in the evolution of distribution and growth. Other initial distributions may lead to a monotonic decline in income inequality associated with economic growth (e.g. both dynasties start to the right of $h^b(A^1)$), or with development towards the low equilibrium $h^a(A^1)$ (e.g. both dynasties start to the left of $h^b(A^1)$). Here, we focus on the more interesting case of a nonlinear development of the distributions of human capital and income.

Simulation of the basic model

As the dynamic difference equation (14) cannot be solved analytically, we use simulation experiments to confirm the results of the preceding section.

Choice of parameters

For the partial production elasticity of physical capital γ we choose 0.3: this parameter is well discussed in the literature.[10] Furthermore, we select 0.9 as the real interest rate per period $\bar{r}$, reflecting that one period lasts about 25 years and given a life expectancy of 75 years.[11] The interest rate has a large impact on the simulation results, because it determines other parameters as well: the ratio of physical capital to efficiency labour units $\bar{k}$ amounts to 0.208, the constant part of the wage rate $\bar{w}$ is 0.437, given the selected value of $\bar{r}$.

For the rate of time preference of the individuals ρ we select 0.95: hence, we assume that the individuals have strong time preference, compared to the real interest rate $\bar{r}$ of 0.9. According to the literature, the value 1.75 is employed as the intertemporal elasticity of substitution of utility λ.[12] After sensitivity analyses, we choose 3.0 as the constant μ for the difference equation of human capital accumulation, as well as 1.0 and 1.25 for the two levels of production technology A^1 and A^2, respectively. In our model, the parameter β, the elasticity of the children's human capital due to changes of the parental human capital, varies in order to reflect a decreasing influence of the parental human capital h_t^i on human capital formation. We consider the following expression to reflect this tendency: $\beta = (h_t^i)^{-\kappa}$. Furthermore, we assume κ to be 0.1, resulting in a slowly decreasing β. For several combinations of different values of $\bar{r}$, A^1, A^2, γ, κ and μ, a value from 0.6 to 0.7 for the parameter α leads to a stable dynamic system and we choose 0.64 as a medium value. Sensitivity analyses show that small parameter variations still lead to a dynamic system with multiple steady-state equilibria and bifurcation. In order to facilitate the simulations, the number of individuals per generation is set to 100 and the threshold level of technological progress $\hat{h}$ equals

90 units of human capital. The model is simulated over 100 time-periods, which seems to be quite long. It is necessary, however, to keep in mind that the major purpose of this simulation is to have a baseline for the analysis of education policy in the next section of this chapter. Changes in income quintiles of the bottom 20 per cent of population will be considered as changes in income distribution. Economic growth will be measured by changes in production per capita.

Simulation results

First, we analyse the model for homogeneous individuals. The steady-state values of the process of human capital accumulation described in (14) and their characterisations are presented in Table 9.1.

For the analysis of heterogeneous individuals we choose $3.9 = h^a(A^1)$ and 30 as initial values for human capital of dynasty L and dynasty H, respectively. Our simulations illustrate the importance of the ratio of the members of dynasty L to the entire population, $\theta = N^L/N$, for the development process of the economy. As long as the ratio is between 0 and 0.5, the transitional dynamics equal our analysis of the preceding section a phase of divergence in human capital and income is followed by convergence, until both dynasties reach the steady state $h^c(A^2)$. If the ratio exceeds 0.5, only the phase of divergence occurs: dynasty L remains at the low steady state $h^a(A^1)$, whereas dynasty H reaches $h^c(A^1)$. In this case, no technological progress takes place, since the average level of human capital remains permanently below the threshold level of technological progress. This result of two types of possible transitional dynamics is different from the theoretical analysis of Galor and Tsiddon (1997) and especially Galor and Tsiddon (1996): they do not consider that transitional dynamics in their model depend on the ratio of the members of L to the entire population and the choice of parameters, especially the threshold level of technological progress.

For further analysis of our model, we, therefore, distinguish between two cases: (a) a rich economy with a ratio of dynasty L to total population $\theta = 0.2$ and (b) a poor economy with $\theta = 0.8$. Simulation results for some variables of these two cases are summarised in Table 9.2.

These results show that a lower ratio of dynasty L to the entire population θ of 0.2 leads to higher average human capital, wage income and production over the entire simulation period. The threshold level of technological progress is passed in period 21. As Figure 9.2 shows, we observe three phases of economic

Table 9.1 Steady states in the basic model

Steady states	Values	Stable/unstable
$h^a(A^1)$	3.9	Stable
$h^b(A^1)$	26.9	Unstable
$h^c(A^1)$	180.1	Stable
$h^c(A^2)$	564.9	Stable

Table 9.2 Simulation results for two examples of economies

Variables	(a) Rich economy $\theta = 0.2$	(b) Poor economy $\theta = 0.8$
Average human capital h_t in period 0	24.8	9.1
Average human capital h_t in period 100	564.9	39.1
Average wage income $I_t + 1$ in period 0	10.8	4
Average wage income $I_t + 1$ in period 100	308.7	17.1
Production per capita Y_t/N in period 0	5.1	1.9
Production per capita Y_t/N in period 100	147	8.1
Threshold level of technological progress $\hat{h}$ passed in period ...	21	—
End value of human capital of dynasty L h^L_{t+1} reached in period	564.9 / 73	3.9 / 1
End value of human capital of dynasty H h^H_{t+1} reached in period	564.9 / 41	180.1 / 47

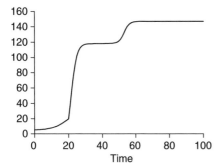

Figure 9.2 Production per capita, $\theta = 0.2$.

growth: the first one, as dynasty H accumulates human capital, the second, as the average level of human capital passes the threshold level of technological progress and the economy starts producing at the higher level of production, and the last one, as dynasty L reaches higher growth rates of human capital. As long as the local externality of parental human capital of dynasty H prevails, until period 21, the income distribution becomes more and more unequal in Figure 9.3. When the global externality dominates the local connection, inequality in our economy decreases.

The results in case (b), the poor country, are totally different: average levels of human capital, wage income and production remain permanently at lower levels than in case (a). Since the threshold level of technological progress is never passed, the local externality of the parental human capital of H leads to a moderate growth process (shown in Figure 9.4) and increasing divergence in human capital and income between H and L (see Figure 9.5). Compared to case (a), the phase of convergence is missing.

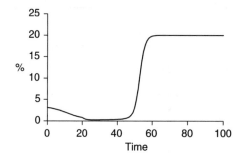

Figure 9.3 Income share of bottom 20 per cent, $\theta = 0.2$.

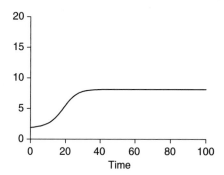

Figure 9.4 Production per capita, $\theta = 0.8$.

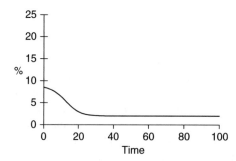

Figure 9.5 Income share of bottom 20 per cent, $\theta = 0.8$.

The above cases show two types of transitional dynamics for certain initial values of human capital and parameter values. Small variations in parameter values lead to similar results. If we vary initial values of human capital for dynasty H and L, the results are ambiguous: higher initial values for H lead to higher average levels at the beginning and faster convergence towards the new equilibrium. Higher values for L, however, lead to higher average levels at the beginning, but as long as they are located to the left of the unstable steady state $h^b(A^1)$, the development of the economy is similar to our analysis.

Some aspects of the transitional dynamics of our economy may not be desirable: for some economies, low economic growth is combined with an increasing polarisation of income distribution. For others, higher economic growth is related to a temporary widening of income disparity, until convergence starts. The next section will show whether education policy can change these aspects.

Education policy

Based on the analysis of the preceding section, economic policy could be directed towards two aims: first to enhance economic growth as a whole, second to shorten the phase of divergence and to reduce the amount of income disparity in this phase. Since, in our model, economic growth and changes in income distribution depend on accumulation of human capital, education policy serves as growth and distribution policy. We focus on two types of policy in this chapter: first, we analyse public investment financed by income taxation, and second, we consider public investment financed by lump-sum tax (school fees). Let us assume that all children in our economy benefit from education policy and that public investment does not lead to transaction costs. First, we present changes in the theoretical analysis; later, we compare some simulation experiments with those for the basic model in the preceding section.

Income taxation

The wage income of the first parental generation is taxed: these tax revenues are used to finance public investment for the first generation of children. In the second period of life, these children become the second parental generation and finance public investment for the second generation of children and so on. The tax rate τ is constant over all generations, the amount invested per child, π_t, varies: as human capital and income increase, tax revenues and public investments increase as well. The government faces a budget constraint: overall tax revenues T_t equal the sum of tax revenues per dynasty, which in turn is the tax revenue of a member of the dynasty times the number of members. This sum is equal to the total amount of investment that is per capita investment times the number of children:

$$T_t = N^L \tau w_t h_t^L + N^H \tau w_t h_t^H = N \pi_t \tag{21}$$

As $\theta = N^L/N$ and $(1 - \theta) = N^H/N$, it is easy to prove that the amount of per capita investment equals the tax payment on the average wage income ($I_t = w_t h_t$) of the parental generation, namely

$$\pi_t = \theta \tau w_t h_t^L + (1 - \theta) \tau w_t h_t^H = \tau w_t h_t \tag{22}$$

Public investment leads to an increase in human capital. We simply add the amount of investment per capita in equation (6') and get a modified version of (14) for the accumulation of human capital, after solving the children's maximisation problem:[13]

$$h_{t+1}^i = \mu + \pi_t + \left[\frac{(1-\tau)\alpha \bar{w} A_{t+1}}{1+\bar{r}} \right]^{\alpha/(1-\alpha)} (h_t^i)^{\beta(h_t^i)/1-\alpha} \quad \text{with } i = H, L$$

(23)

Equation (8) for wage income in the second period of life changes to

$$I_{t+1}^{i,\text{gross}} = w_{t+1} h_{t+1}^i$$

$$= w_{t+1}\mu + w_{t+1}\pi_t + w_{t+1} \left[\frac{(1-\tau)\alpha\bar{w} A_{t+1}}{1+\bar{r}} \right]^{\alpha/(1-\alpha)} (h_t^i)^{\beta(h_t^i)/(1-\alpha)}$$

(24)

Net of tax payments, we get the following equation for net income:

$$I_{t+1}^{i,\text{net}} = (1-\tau)w_{t+1}h_{t+1}^i = (1-\tau)w_{t+1}\mu + (1-\tau)w_{t+1}\pi_t + (1-\tau)w_{t+1}$$

$$\times \left[\frac{(1-\tau)\alpha\bar{w} A_{t+1}}{1+\bar{r}} \right]^{\alpha/(1-\alpha)} (h_t^i)^{\beta(h_t^i)/(1-\alpha)}$$

(25)

for $i = H, L$. It describes the part of wage income that can be used for consumption, saving and private loan repayment.

What are the differences to (14) and (8) of the basic model? Human capital is higher due to public investment, but lower because of the disincentive of future taxation. The net effect is decisive:

$$\text{if } \pi_t - \left(1 - (1-\tau)^{\alpha/(1-\alpha)}\right) \left[\frac{\alpha\bar{w} A_{t+1}}{1+\bar{r}} \right]^{\alpha/(1-\alpha)} (h_t^i)^{\beta(h_t^i)/(1-\alpha)} > 0 \quad (26)$$

human capital is higher compared to the basic model. As the investment effect is the same for both dynasties, but the disincentive higher for dynasty H because of higher income, it is reasonable to assume that the net effect might be positive for the children of the poor and negative for the children of the rich. In this case, education policy stimulates human capital accumulation of the poor, but in contrast hinders that of the rich: a tendency towards higher equality in human capital and income must occur, according to the redistribution effect of income taxation. Whether public investment has positive growth effects depends on the overall effect on aggregate human capital. If the losses of human capital of dynasty H can be compensated by gains of human capital of dynasty L, the economy will face higher economic growth. If the losses are not compensated, education policy leads to lower growth. The simulations will show which net effect prevails in our model for our choice of parameters.

Lump-sum tax

In our next case, public investment in education is financed by school fees, equal to a lump-sum tax in the individuals' second period of life. Every period the government invests the same amount π per capita, giving the total amount

$$B_t = N\pi \tag{27}$$

with

$$\pi = \theta \tau w_t h_t^L + (1 - \theta) \tau w_t h_t^H = \tau w_t h_t \quad \text{for } t = 1 \tag{28}$$

In order to make the two types of education policy in this chapter comparable, we assume that in the first period the government's loan equals the tax revenue of the first period in the case of general income taxation ((22) and (28) are identical for the first period): in both cases we start with the same amount of total investment. In contrast to wage-income taxation, the amount of public investment is assumed to remain constant over the entire analysis.

The first period's investment is financed through public borrowing on international capital markets. Hence, the lump-sum tax per capita in the second period of life of the children's generation includes per capita investment in the first period and interest payment on this amount: also the government has to repay its loan B in the second period plus interest payments. Therefore, repayment of the government R on international capital markets amounts to

$$R_{t+1} = (1 + \bar{r})B_t = (1 + \bar{r})N\pi \tag{29}$$

Adding public investment per capita additively in (6′) and lump-sum taxes in (8) and solving the maximisation problem of the individuals, leads to

$$h_{t+1}^i = \mu + \pi + \left[\frac{\alpha \overline{w} A_{t+1}}{1 + \bar{r}} \right]^{\alpha/(1-\alpha)} (h_t^i)^{\beta(h_t^i)/(1-\alpha)} \quad \text{with } i = H, L \tag{30}$$

Public investment promotes human capital accumulation in this case, resulting in an increase of gross income, compared to the basic model:

$$I_{t+1}^{i,\text{gross}} = w_{t+1} h_{t+1}^i = w_{t+1}(\mu + \pi) + w_{t+1} \left[\frac{\alpha \overline{w} A_{t+1}}{1 + \bar{r}} \right]^{\alpha/(1-\alpha)} (h_t^i)^{\beta(h_t^i)/(1-\alpha)} \tag{31}$$

In order to make the two types of education policy comparable, net income in this case is also equal to income disposable for consumption, saving and repayment of private loans. Net income, therefore, is lower due to school fees:

$$I_{t+1}^{i,\text{net}} = w_{t+1} h_{t+1}^i - (1 + \bar{r})\pi = w_{t+1}(\mu + \pi) - (1 + \bar{r})\pi$$

$$+ w_{t+1} \left[\frac{\alpha \overline{w} A_{t+1}}{1 + \bar{r}} \right]^{\alpha/(1-\alpha)} (h_t^i)^{\beta(h_t^i)/(1-\alpha)}, \quad i = H, L \tag{32}$$

Whether net income is higher or lower than wage income in the basic model depends on

$$w_{t+1}\pi - (1 + \bar{r})\pi \gtreqless 0 \tag{33}$$

If the wage rate w_{t+1} exceeds the interest factor $(1 + \bar{r})$, net income and utility increase (vice versa). Since both dynasties tend to have higher human capital, education policy in this case enhances economic growth: increases in human capital due to public investment are relatively higher for dynasty L, but dynasty H may get into an area of human capital accumulation with higher increases than before. This leads to higher average levels of human capital with earlier technological progress, eventually accompanied by higher income equality. These positive effects are probably paid for by losses in the individuals' utility.

Simulation results

As shown in the section above, education policy can be able to improve economic growth and income equality, but maybe at the price of utility losses: in some cases it was not clear whether net effects were positive or negative. Our simulation results will show, how transitional dynamics change due to education policy. Compared to the basic model, we add the tax rate τ. In the case of income taxation, it determines tax revenues available for public investment. We assumed international borrowing of the government to be equal to these tax revenues of the first period in the case of school fees: here, the tax rate τ additionally serves as a benchmark for public borrowing.

In our basic model, we assumed non-negative consumption. Given the choice of parameters discussed above, this restricts feasible tax rates in the education policy cases. In the case of public investment financed by wage-income taxation, the maximum feasible tax rate is 0.41, for any ratio of dynasty L to total population, θ.[14] If education investment is financed via school fees in the second period of life, the ratio θ matters: possible maximum tax rates vary from 0.07 up to 0.43. If the ratio θ is higher, tax rates can be higher, since due to lower average income, the same amount of per capita investment is only feasible with higher taxation.

In the following presentation of simulation results for the poor and the rich economy with $\theta = 0.2$ and $\theta = 0.8$, respectively, we choose 10 per cent as the tax rate τ. In cross-section data public expenditures on education in per cent of GDP vary from 2 to 8 per cent.[15] In our analysis only wage income is taxed and a 10 per cent taxation of wage income in our model equals a 7 per cent tax rate on total production or GDP. Lower tax rates show the same simulation effects, eventually less obvious. We focus on changes in production per capita and changes in the income share of the bottom 20 per cent of the population compared to the basic model over the entire simulation.

Figure 9.6 shows contrasting effects of the two types of education policy on the evolution of production per capita in the rich economy with $\theta = 0.2$: financed by lump-sum tax, public investment leads to enhanced economic growth and slightly higher values in the new equilibrium. Income-tax financing, however, results in

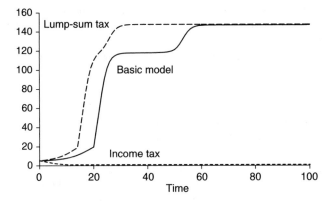

Figure 9.6 Education policy and production per capita, $\theta = 0.2$.

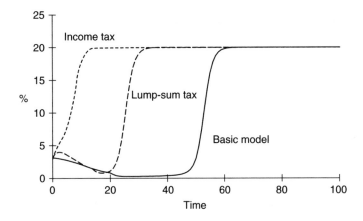

Figure 9.7 Education policy and income share of bottom 20 per cent, $\theta = 0.2$.

monotonically declining production: for the individuals of dynasty H the disincentive of future taxation is higher than the investment effect of education policy. The losses of total human capital of dynasty H are not compensated by gains of total human capital of dynasty L.[16]

But, as Figure 9.7 shows, negative growth in the case of income taxation is accompanied by a monotonic rise in income equality: less production is divided more equally. The U-shape of the income share development of the bottom 20 per cent in the basic model is reduced by public investment financed by school fees: it even shows a temporary tendency towards decreasing inequality at the beginning. The phase of divergence of income is less pronounced and equality in income reached earlier, compared to the basic model.

The next two Figures 9.8 and 9.9 show some results for the poor economy with $\theta = 0.8$. The development of the economy does not change in case of school-fee financed public investment: as in the basic model, no technological progress occurs. But production per capita as well as the income share of the bottom 20 per cent are slightly increased. We recognise the same temporary tendency towards higher equality at the beginning as in the case of $\theta = 0.2$, though it is less pronounced. Income-tax-based education policy still has a negative impact on economic growth and leads to permanent increase in income equality.

Sensitivity analyses show similar results for other tax rates and values of the ratio of dynasty L to the entire population, so that the effects of education policy presented here are quite robust. Public investment financed by lump-sum tax may serve as growth and redistribution policy, in correspondence with our theoretical analysis. The results of income-tax-financed education policy show negative effects on economic growth, since the net effect of public investment and future

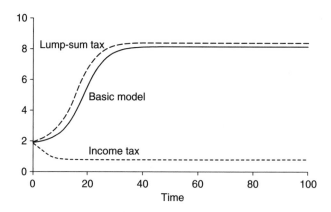

Figure 9.8 Education policy and production per capita, $\theta = 0.8$.

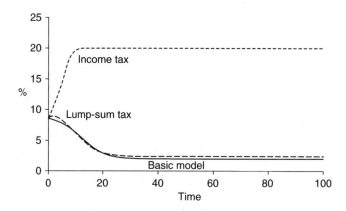

Figure 9.9 Education policy and income share of bottom 20 per cent, $\theta = 0.8$.

taxation on human capital accumulation is negative in our simulations. However, it exhibits redistribution effects.

Generally, the effects of education policy above are just observable after some periods. As we assumed that one period lasts for 25 years, long time-lags occur due to the structure of the overlapping-generations model. Nevertheless, this type of analysis can still explain general properties of public policy. If governments would intensify education policy today, the long-term effects on growth and distribution would still need 10–15 years to become observable, when former students participate in the labour force.

Discussion

Simulations of our endogenous-growth model, with interdependence of income distribution and economic growth, result in two types of transitional dynamics: they are determined by the ratio of the poor dynasty to total population size and the threshold level of technological progress. Education policy is not able to change this dichotomy. However, education investment is able to enhance economic growth and income equality, depending on the way of financing it. In the case of income-tax financing, the disincentive of future taxation dominates the investment effect of governmental education policy. Negative economic development and income redistribution occur. In the case of school-fee financing, governmental education policy is able to improve economic growth and income equality at the same time.

Therefore, at first sight education policy seems to be an ideal mean for growth and distribution policy. With the type of model used here, education policy can only make sense in the long run, which may be interpreted as a period of at least 10–20 years for today's governments. However, at second sight, education policy leads to an intergenerational redistribution of utility: from further analysis, not presented here, we notice that individuals of earlier generations pay for benefits of future generations by losses of their utility. This result is mainly based on the assumptions of perfect foresight and finite horizons in our model. Any policy disturbing the individual's decision-making in this framework must lead to inferior results for this generation. Therefore, possible extensions of our analyses could be the introduction of other types of education policy and the inclusion of political decision processes versus the analysis of a social planner.

Notes

1 A continuous technical progress could be interpreted as a process of innovations, resulting in improvements of goods or new goods. The threshold technology, however, could describe major inventions in economic development, like e.g. automobiles or information technology.

2 The human capital of the individual born in period t is accumulated in period t, but supplied on the labour market in period $t + 1$ and indexed correspondingly. The importance of the parental human capital has been stressed by e.g. Becker and Tomes (1986), Hauser and Sewell (1986).

3 See e.g. Becker and Tomes (1986: S31) and Ashenfelter and Zimmerman (1993).
4 The income in (8) is available for saving, consumption and private loan repayment. In Section 4, this is the definition for net income, whereas gross income also includes taxes and fees payable to the government. Therefore, (8) describes gross as well as net income in this section.
5 See e.g. Blanchard and Fischer (1989: 43/44).
6 Variable returns to scale are not a necessary condition for development or poverty traps, see Azariadis and Drazen (1990) and Azariadis (1996).
7 This can be proven according to Gandolfo (1996).
8 Kuznets formed his hypothesis for some industrialised countries. Though the UCH is still controversial empirically, it is considered as a stylised fact.
9 Smooth technological progress would lead to continuous economic growth in the steady state.
10 See e.g. King and Rebelo (1990).
11 E.g. Blomquist and Wijkander (1994) get values between 0.7 and 1.1 endogenously.
12 See e.g. Lucas (1990).
13 In subsequent periods, public investment stimulates private investment in human capital: parental human capital taken into account at solving the children's maximistion problem is higher than without education policy.
14 If we used higher tax rates, negative consumption would occur and violate the assumption

$$c_t^{t,i}, c_{t+1}^{t,i}, c_{t+2}^{t,i} \geq 0$$

15 See e.g. data of Barro and Lee (1993).
16 The general conclusion is that disincentives lead to lower growth rates. Negative growth rates in this case emerge mainly due to choice of parameters.

References

Alesina, A. and Rodrik, D. (1994) 'Distribution Politics and Economic Growth', *Quarterly Journal of Economics*, 109: 465–90.
Anand, S. and Kanbur, S.M.R. (1993) 'The Kuznets Process and the Inequality–Development Relationship', *Journal of Development Economics*, 40: 25–52.
Ashenfelter, O. and Zimmerman, D.J. (1993) *Estimates of the Returns to Schooling from Sibling Data: Fathers, Sons, and Brothers*, Cambridge, Mass.: NBER Working Paper No. 4491.
Azariadis, C. (1996) 'The Economics of Poverty Traps, Part I: Complete Markets', *Journal of Economic Growth*, 2: 449–86.
—— and Drazen, A. (1990) 'Threshold Externalities in Economic Development', *Quarterly Journal of Economics*, 105: 501–26.
Barro, R.J. and Lee, J.-W. (1993) 'International Comparisons of Educational Attainment', *Journal of Monetary Economics*, 32: 363–94.
Becker, G.-S. and Tomes, N. (1986) 'Human Capital and the Rise and Fall of Families', *Journal of Labor Economics*, 4: s1–39.
Benhabib, J. and Spiegel, M. (1994) 'The Role of Human Capital in Economic Development, Evidence from Aggregate Cross-Country Data', *Journal of Monetary Economics*, 34: 143–73.
Blanchard, O. and Fischer, S. (1989) *Lectures on Macroeconomics*, Cambridge, Mass.: MIT Press.
Blomquist, N. and Wijkander, H. (1994) 'Fertility Waves, Aggregate Savings and the Rate of Interest', *Journal of Population Economics*, 7: 27–48.

Clarke, G. (1995) 'More Evidence on Income Distribution and Growth', *Journal of Development Economics*, 47: 403–27.

Galor, O. and Tsiddon, D. (1996) 'Income Distribution and Growth: the Kuznets Hypothesis Revisited', *Economica*, 63: S103–17.

——(1997) 'The Distribution of Human Capital and Economic Growth', *Journal of Economic Growth*, 2: 93–124.

Gandolfo, G. (1996) *Economic Dynamics*, 3rd edn, Heidelberg: Springer.

Hauser, R.-M. and Sewell, W.H. (1986) 'Family Effects in Simple Models of Education, Occupational Status, and Earnings: Findings from the Wisconsin and Kalamazoo Studies', *Journal of Labor Economics*, 4: s83–120.

King, R. and Rebelo, S. (1990) 'Public Policy and Economic Growth: Developing Neoclassical Implications', *Journal of Political Economy*, 98: 126–50.

Kuznets, S. (1955) 'Economic Growth and Income Inequality', *American Economic Review*, 45: 1–28.

Levine, R. and Renelt, D. (1992) 'A Sensitivity Analysis of Cross-Country Growth Regressions', *American Economic Review*, 82: 942–63.

Lucas, R. (1990) 'Supply-Side Economics: An Analytical Review', *Oxford Economic Papers*, 42: 3–42.

Ogwang, T. (1995) 'The Economic Development – Income Inequality Nexus: Further Evidence on Kuznets' U-Curve Hypothesis', *American Journal of Economics and Sociology*, 54: 1–2.

Perotti, R. (1993) 'Political Equilibrium, Income Distribution, and Growth', *Review of Economic Studies*, 60: 755–76.

——(1994) 'Income Distribution and Investment', *European Economic Review*, 38: 827–35.

——(1996) 'Growth, Income Distribution, and Democracy: What the Data Say', *Journal of Economic Growth*, 1: 149–87.

Persson, T. and Tabellini, G. (1994) 'Is Inequality Harmful for Growth?', *American Economic Review*, 84: 600–21.

10 Skill-biased technological change

On endogenous growth, wage inequality and government intervention

Hugo Hollanders and Bas ter Weel

Introduction

One of the most prominent observations when analysing labour-market trends in the OECD countries over the past three decades is the fact that labour demand seems to favour more skilled workers, replaces tasks previously performed by unskilled workers, and intensifies inequality. Despite the marked increase in the supply of skilled workers, this shift has caused dramatic declines in unskilled employment rates throughout the OECD, which in some countries and periods has been accompanied by profound shifts in relative wages. The latter trend has been particularly strong in the United States and the United Kingdom and has attracted a lot of attention in the literature.

For example, Katz and Murphy (1992) find for the United States that between 1979 and 1987 the average weekly wage of college graduates with one to five years of experience has increased by some 30 per cent relative to the average weekly earnings of comparable high-school graduates. Acemoglu (2000) finds that in 1971 a worker at the 90th percentile of the wage distribution earned 266 per cent more than a worker at the 10th percentile of the wage distribution did. By 1995, this figure has increased to 366 per cent. Evidence from other countries, brought together by e.g. the OECD (1996), Berman, Bound and Machin (1998), Machin and van Reenen (1998), Berman and Machin (2000) and Hollanders and ter Weel (2000), suggests similar strong patterns for the United Kingdom, while in Australia, Austria, Belgium, Canada, Japan, Portugal and Spain wage inequality has also risen but to a lesser extent. The figures for Denmark, France, Germany, Italy, the Netherlands and Sweden are less pronounced and show no strong pattern of rising wage inequality since the 1970s.

In search of explanations for these large shifts in the composition of aggregate labour demand various lines of thought have been developed. The direction of the explanations differs widely from trade with low-wage countries (Wood 1994) and trade between the United States and the European Union countries (Davis and Reeve 1997) to arguing that recent technical change has been in favour of the skilled workers (Krugman 1995 and Acemoglu 2000).[1] According to Berman and Machin (2000) a consensus has now been formed on the technology-based hypothesis, which claims that changing technology under given market conditions is the main driving force behind the shift in labour demand towards the skilled. However, solutions to the problem are not offered very often and are mostly not considered in a thorough manner. The OECD (1998), e.g. only states that investment in human capital and upgrading of skills will offer a solution to the weak position of low-skilled workers in its member countries without specifying precise action.

This chapter considers in a theoretical fashion the consequences of this 'skill-biased technical change' (SBTC) by modelling technical change in such a manner that skilled workers profit relatively more from the technical advancement than unskilled workers do. Building a model to explain and explore SBTC does this. The way of modelling SBTC developed here has recently been applied by Acemoglu (1998) and is referred to as directed technical change. Acemoglu points out that when technical change is endogenous, an increase in the supply of skilled workers increases the market size for skill-complementary technologies and may induce SBTC. A related paper by Caselli (1999) focuses on the substitutability among new technologies. These new technologies (or technological revolutions) are either skill-biased or de-skilling. The former appear if the new skills are more costly to acquire than the skills required by the old type of technology. The latter appear in the opposite case. Kiley (1999) considers SBTC in a setting of increasing product variety. He addresses the question whether an endogenous technology bias can overturn the depressing effect of increases in skilled-labour supply on the relative wage rate. The mechanism he applies is similar to the one used by Acemoglu (1998). Lloyd-Ellis (1999) discusses a skill-biased endogenous growth channel in a model where a certain minimum level of skills is required to implement new ideas and technologies. The rate of absorption of new technologies is fundamental to his findings. When the rate of absorption declines, the rate of technical change and labour-productivity growth falls, which leads under an assumed specific skewed distribution of skills to wage inequality. Finally, Galor and Moav (2000) model SBTC under the assumption that the state of transition brought about by technical change raises the rate of return to ability. In their model, individuals are subject to two opposing effects: erosion and productivity effects. They find wage inequality in the short-run, while the economy converges to a steady-state equilibrium with a positive growth rate of output per worker by a positive endogenous rate of technical change (see also Gould *et al.* 2000).

These approaches point towards the importance of a complementarity of skill accumulation and technical change, indicating a particular direction of technical change. However, they only use two types of skills: skilled and unskilled workers. Moreover, the models are not able to give general equilibrium properties in a long-run steady-state solution, which are necessary to develop policy measures to solve the problem. Finally, they are not modelled in an endogenous growth setting, hence leaving the growth process undetermined.

The approach developed in this chapter considers a general equilibrium model with heterogeneous labour in a continuum of skills ranging from no skills to a certain maximum level of skills. The heterogeneity of the individuals populating this economy does already exist upon birth, i.e. every individual is born with some ability or talent, which can be developed during life. This framework is discussed in terms of a steady-state approach to the changing skills profile over time.

Firms in this economy divide their time between investing in knowledge creation to enhance their product and production process (it is assumed that there is only one product in this economy) to become more efficient and in that way obtain a higher level of profits. Firms employ labour and prefer relatively skilled labour to relatively unskilled labour. This provides a positive feedback loop of investment decisions, which gives individuals an incentive to invest in human capital, since process innovations go hand in hand with a higher level of lifetime utility.

The framework considered makes it relatively more complex to model the exact implications of technical change for different groups in society because it steps outside the representative agent framework. Therefore, we focus on steady-state analysis only. However, despite this complexity, the model provides a more realistic picture of the dilemmas and problems governments face to come up with a solution for this perturbing problem of inequality.

The remainder of this chapter builds an endogenous growth model to show the effects of SBTC on wages and its consequences on the wage distribution. The plan of this chapter is the following. In the next section, a model of SBTC is built and explored. The section on 'Government policies to reduce the bias in skill accumulation' discusses government policy along the lines of the framework and the conclusions developed in the next section. The chapter ends with some concluding remarks.

A model of skill-biased technical change

Consider a closed economy with competitive markets populated by a large number (N) of heterogeneous Ramsey consumers. These consumers have standard, discounted, constant elasticity preferences resulting in the following utility function:

$$U_{t,s} = \frac{C_{t,s}^{1-\sigma} - 1}{1 - \sigma} e^{-\rho t} \tag{1}$$

where the discount rate ρ and the coefficient of relative risk aversion σ are both strictly positive. $C_{t,s}$ is defined as the amount of consumption of a person with skill level s at time t. The skill level s is assumed to be uniformly distributed over a range $[0, 1]$. Moreover, every individual in this economy has a different skill level, which can be viewed as the ability this individual is born with at time $t = 0$. Hence, for each skill level there exists only one individual.[2]

Capital accumulation for each individual is defined as net income minus consumption

$$\dot{K}_{t,s} = (1 - \tau)r_t K_{t,s} + (1 - \tau)w_t(1 - u_{t,s})H_{t,s} - C_{t,s} \tag{2}$$

where τ is a capital income tax for both physical and human capital, r_t is the return on physical capital $K_{t,s}$, w_t the return on human capital $H_{t,s}$, and $u_{t,s}$ is the amount of time spent to acquire additional human capital; $(1 - u_{t,s})$ is the amount of time spent to produce output. This budget constraint implies that all wealth generated or all savings is immediately transformed into physical capital.

Accumulation of human capital is assumed to be skill-biased since individuals with a higher skill level profit more from technical progress than individuals with a lower level of skills. Acemoglu (1998) refers to this fact as 'directed technical change' in favour of skilled labour. Equation (3) defines this as follows: individuals with a higher skill level profit exponentially from an increase in technical progress A_t, i.e.

$$\dot{H}_{t,s} = A_t^s u_{t,s} H_{t,s}^\beta B_t^\gamma - \mu H_{t,s} \tag{3}$$

with $0 < \beta < 1$; μ is the exogenous rate of depreciation of human capital. Throughout this chapter, however, no depreciation of skills or human capital is assumed, i.e. $\mu = 0$. B_t is knowledge provided publicly by the government, whereas A_t is provided privately as a result of the R&D process firms are engaged in, and it is assumed that no public action is taken to directly influence the supply of private knowledge. The stock of public knowledge is enhanced at some costs collected by the government in the form of capital income taxes τ (cf. equation (2)).

Now, maximising utility, subject to the budget constraint and human capital accumulation, leads to the following Hamiltonian

$$\Omega = \frac{C_{t,s}^{1-\sigma} - 1}{1 - \sigma} e^{-\rho t} + \lambda_1 \left(A_t^s u_{t,s} H_{t,s}^\beta B_t^\gamma - \mu H_{t,s} \right)$$
$$+ \lambda_2 \left((1 - \tau) r_t K_{t,s} + (1 - \tau) w_t (1 - u_{t,s}) H_{t,s} - C_{t,s} \right)$$

Solving this problem results in a standard Euler equation for the individual with skill level s

$$\hat{C}_{t,s} = \frac{(1 - \tau) r_t - \rho}{\sigma} \tag{4}$$

where the after-tax return on capital $(1 - \tau) r_t$ is assumed to exceed the discount rate ρ and a hat over a variable indicates its growth rate. In the steady state the rental rate r has to be constant because the growth rate of the marginal product of capital equals zero by definition.[3]

Optimising with respect to $H_{t,s}$ yields the growth rate of human capital which depends both on the growth rates of private and public knowledge accumulation, A_t and B_t, respectively

$$\hat{H}_{t,s} = \frac{s\hat{A}_t + \gamma \hat{B}_t}{1 - \beta} \tag{5}$$

This equation is of central importance to our analysis because it shows that public knowledge accumulation adds an unbiased amount of human capital to the individual's existing human capital stock. The equation also indicates that private human capital accumulation is biased and it depends on the skill levels an individual incorporates.

In order to compute the overall level of human capital we must add up all individuals. Since the impact of skills is normalised, Appendix B shows that this leads to

$$H_t = N \int_0^1 H_{t,s} ds = \left(\frac{(1-\beta)N}{t\hat{A}_t}\right) \left(e^{((\hat{A}_t + \gamma \hat{B}_t)/(1-\beta))t} - e^{((\gamma \hat{B}_t)/(1-\beta))t}\right) \quad (6)$$

Equation (6) shows that the steady-state growth rate of the overall level of human capital converges to

$$\lim_{t \to \infty} \hat{H}_t = \frac{\hat{A}_t + \gamma \hat{B}_t}{1-\beta} \quad (7)$$

which equals the growth rate of human capital of the individual with the highest ability $s = 1$. This result indicates that the skill bias increases because fewer and fewer individuals embody relatively more and more human capital.[4] The recognition of the importance of the notion of knowledge accumulation is challenging not only the traditional focus on the R&D process, but the whole spectrum of scientific and technical activities from invention to diffusion, from basic research to technical mastery. Such a view of technical change rejects the definition of technical capabilities in terms of knowledge or information with the connotation that industrial technology is like a recipe; understood by particular individuals and readily articulatable and communicable from one individual to another with the requisite background training and skills. Knowing how to produce a product is as much experienced tacit skill as articulatable knowledge. Contrary to the implicit general theory, skills of a skilled worker in the art are not interchangeable: who works with the recipe makes a difference. Therefore, training new workers has become much more expensive when one takes these arguments into account and the human capital employed by firms will increasingly be embodied in less skilled individuals, thereby further increasing the gap between skilled and unskilled workers.[5]

The government collects capital income taxes (τ) on both human and physical capital to finance the accumulation of public knowledge. This can be expressed as follows

$$\dot{B}_t = \tau r_t K_t + \tau w_t \left(N \int_0^1 (1 - u_{t,s}) H_{t,s} ds\right) \quad (8)$$

Public knowledge is invested in the accumulation of human capital as can be observed from equation (3). The intention and main objective of the government is to distribute income and therefore implicitly human capital more equally. However, the collection of additional capital income taxes has both a positive and negative effect. Since the taxes are used to stimulate the level of the available public knowledge, they have a positive effect on overall productivity. On the other hand, additional capital income taxes have a negative effect on the private accumulation of physical and human capital, as shown below.

Firms allocate human capital between final goods production and technology production. Using $(1 - \varphi)$ of the human capital stock available to the firm, they produce output Y_t using a standard increasing returns-to-scale Cobb–Douglas production function with labour-saving technical change

$$Y_t = K_t^\alpha \left(A_t N \int_0^1 ((1 - \varphi_t)(1 - u_{t,s})) H_{t,s} ds \right)^{1-\alpha} \tag{9}$$

where $0 < \varphi < 1$ and $\alpha > 0$. Firms dedicate φ of their available human capital stock to enhance technical progress, i.e.

$$\dot{A}_t = \left(N \int_0^1 (\varphi_t (1 - u_{t,s})) H_{t,s} ds \right)^\delta A_t^\xi \tag{10}$$

where $0 < \delta < 1, 0 < \xi < 1$ and $\delta + \xi < 1$.[6]

Firms then maximise profits according to the following Hamiltonian:

$$\Pi = K_t^\alpha \left(A_t N \int_0^1 ((1 - \varphi_t)(1 - u_{t,s})) H_{t,s} ds \right)^{1-\alpha} - r_t K_t$$

$$- w_t N \int_0^1 (1 - u_{t,s}) H_{t,s} ds + \lambda_3 \left(N \int_0^1 (\varphi_t (1 - u_{t,s})) H_{t,s} ds \right)^\delta A_t^\xi$$

Defining $H_{t,f}$ as

$$N \int_0^1 (1 - u_s) H_{t,s} ds$$

and taking partial derivatives with respect to the control variables K_t, $H_{t,f}$ and φ, and the state variable A_t, yields the following expressions for the steady-state growth rate of the physical and human capital stock available to the firm and the stock of private knowledge, respectively:

$$\hat{K}_t = \frac{(1 + \delta - \xi)}{\delta} \hat{A}_t \tag{11}$$

$$\hat{H}_{t,f} = \frac{(1 - \xi)}{\delta} \hat{A}_t \tag{12}$$

and

$$\hat{K}_t = \hat{C}_t \tag{13}$$

The restriction $\delta + \xi < 1$ ensures that the growth rate of the physical capital stock in equation (11) is positive.[7] An increase in ξ and δ, the effectiveness of private knowledge respectively human capital in the production of private knowledge, has a positive effect on the growth rates in equations (11) and (12).

Table 10.1 Investigating equations (14)–(16)

	$\partial \hat{K}_t$	$\partial \hat{H}_t$	$\partial \hat{A}_t$
∂r_t	>0	>0	>0
$\partial \rho$	<0	<0	<0
$\partial \sigma$	<0	<0	<0
$\partial \xi$	—	<0	>0
$\partial \delta$	—	<0	>0

Using equations (11)–(13) the outcomes for the growth rates of K_t, H_t and A_t can be re-expressed in the parameters of the model. This results in equations (14)–(16):

$$\hat{C}_t = \hat{K}_t = \frac{(1 - \tau)r - \rho}{\sigma} \tag{14}$$

$$\hat{H}_t = \frac{(1 - \xi)((1 - \tau)r_t - \rho)}{(1 - \xi + \delta)\sigma} \tag{15}$$

and

$$\hat{A}_t = \frac{\delta((1 - \tau)r_t - \rho)}{(1 - \xi + \delta)\sigma} \tag{16}$$

From these three equations, and already pointing to the discussion in the next section, it can be observed that capital income taxes have a negative effect on the steady-state growth rate of all three variables. The rationale is intuitively straightforward and consistent with the fact that negative externalities have negative effects on growth rates.

Formally, equations (14)–(16) can be examined by investigating the effects of each of the exogenous parameters in the growth rates of K_t, H_t and A_t in the Table 10.1.

In the next section, we explore these results and show how the skill bias due to the bias in private human capital accumulation, as a result of dispersion in abilities, can be reduced by government intervention.

Government policies to reduce the bias in skill accumulation

Firm-specific innovations are induced and occur because of the effort of the firm's research department on the one hand, and public knowledge from the public basin on the other hand. Public knowledge is enhanced by research performed at universities and other research institutes financed by the government through variable B_t. Their output in the form of knowledge is often published in scientific journals or transmitted by channels such as conferences. This improves the overall knowledge stock in the economy in an unbiased way and induces innovative activities. As proven above, firms increase labour productivity levels in a skill-biased manner which in turn lead to higher levels of innovative activities in the research department and higher levels of production in the manufacturing division.

Equation (5) implies that in the long run or steady state individuals with a higher ability experience a higher growth rate of human capital. The dispersion in levels of human capital between high- and low-skilled individuals thus increases over time. Hence, the need for government intervention to deal with this dispersion is valid and necessary.

In this section, a partial equilibrium analysis is performed on several variables in the model. First, it can be shown that technical progress originating in the private sector leads to an increase in the efficiency of human capital production biased towards individuals with higher initial abilities. This can be shown by investigating a case in which there are two individuals with abilities s_i and s_j, where $s_i > s_j$. Using equation (5) the set-up of this problem can be shown by the following expression

$$\frac{\hat{H}_{s_i}}{\hat{H}_{s_j}} = \frac{s_i \hat{A}_t + \gamma \hat{B}_t}{s_j \hat{A}_t + \gamma \hat{B}_t}$$

From this expression for two different levels of skills it can be easily observed that an increase in the growth rate of private knowledge A_t leads to a biased increase in the growth rate of the ratio of human capital, i.e. the ratio $\hat{H}_{si}/\hat{H}_{sj}$ increases. This means that the relatively skilled individual (the individual with skill level s_i) profits more from this enhancement in the accumulation of private knowledge than the relatively unskilled individual (the individual with skill level s_j) does. More formally

$$\frac{\partial(\hat{H}_{s_i}/\hat{H}_{s_j})}{\partial \hat{A}_t} = \frac{(s_i - s_j)\gamma \hat{B}_t}{(s_j \hat{A}_t + \gamma \hat{B}_t)^2} > 0$$

With respect to government intervention, the opposite result can be obtained. As is defined above, government intervention by means of a capital income tax τ hurts relatively skilled labour more than relatively unskilled labour because the tax is on the income of both physical and human capital income. Physical capital is assumed to be distributed equally, but human capital not. Therefore, an increase in public knowledge, financed by an increase in capital income taxes has a positive effect on the individual with skill level s_j relative to the individual with skill level s_i. Hence, it can be shown in a more formal way, that an increase in the growth rate of public knowledge leads, *ceteris paribus*, to a relative increase in the growth rate of the unskilled individual's human capital

$$\frac{\partial(\hat{H}_{s_i}/\hat{H}_{s_j})}{\partial \hat{B}_t} = \frac{(s_j - s_i)\gamma \hat{A}_t}{(s_j \hat{A}_t + \gamma \hat{B}_t)^2} < 0$$

Focusing on the short run only, these effects can best be studied by investigating level effects of relative skill embodiment instead of growth rates. Again assuming two individuals with skill level s_i and s_j, where $s_i > s_j$, the relative level of human capital can be expressed in natural logarithms, using equation (5), as follows:

$$\ln\left(\frac{H_{t,s_i}}{H_{t,s_j}}\right) = \frac{(s_i - s_j)((1 - \tau)r_t - \rho)\delta t}{(1 - \xi + \delta)(1 - \beta)\sigma}$$

This expression leads to the following proposition:

Proposition 1   Relative dispersion in the relative level of skills as measured by $\ln(H_{t,si}/H_{t,sj})$ increases in the short run if:

(a) δ increases, because an increase in δ enhances and stimulates the accumulation of private knowledge A_t which in turn enhance human capital accumulation $H_{t,s}$ as can be observed from equations (10) and (12);

(b) ξ increases, because an increase in ξ enhances and stimulates the accumulation of private knowledge A_t as can be observed from equation (10);

(c) β increases, since from equation (3) it can be seen that an increase in β leads to a higher rate of human capital accumulation. This increased human capital accumulation leads in turn to a faster increase of SBTC through the effects defined in equation (10);

(d) r_t increases, because an increase in the return to physical capital stimulates investment, which enhances the accumulation of skills through the complementarity between skills and physical capital, as can be seen from equation (2);

(e) ρ and σ decrease, since present consumption is valued higher than future consumption, following the properties of equation (1). This leads to less need for skills, and hence the private investment in skills will fall. Lower private investment leads to less dispersion over time; and finally and most importantly

(f) τ decreases. This can be proven by the following expression and is a quite straightforward result, since an increase in capital income taxes decreases the amount invested in the accumulation of private knowledge leading to the skill bias, while leading to an increase in the amount invested in the accumulation of neutral public knowledge, i.e.

$$\frac{\partial \ln(H_{t,s_i}/H_{t,s_j})}{\partial \tau} = \frac{-(s_i - s_j)\delta r_t t}{(1 - \xi + \delta)(1 - \beta)\sigma} < 0$$

This completes the investigation of Proposition 1.

This result shows that there is to some extent scope for the government to reduce the short-run level effects of SBTC which are prevalent in the private sector. However, as noted above there remains a long-run bias in human capital growth rates in favour of relatively high-skilled individuals.

However, recently, as noted by e.g. Acemoglu (1998) and Muysken and ter Weel (2000), the supply of relatively high-skilled labour increased in a dramatic fashion, while the wage premium or reward for this high-skilled labour increased in an even more dramatic way. This process of so-called directed technical change in which the direction of technical change is driven by the supply and availability of a particular level of labour has led and is leading to a further process and development of (wage) dispersion resulting in (wage) inequality throughout the OECD countries. Government intervention by means of providing a public threshold level of knowledge embodied in every single individual is therefore becoming increasingly important. The shift in the accumulation of private knowledge can be modelled by dividing the labour force in so-called haves and have-nots, with regard to the level of skills needed to be part of the working labour force, as follows

$$\dot{H}_{t,s} = A_t^{\max(s-\bar{s},0)} u_{t,s} H_{t,s}^{\beta} B_t^{\gamma} - \mu H_{t,s}$$

which states that individuals have to embody a certain minimum or threshold level of skills to profit from private knowledge accumulation. If their skill level is below this threshold level, they cannot enhance their skills by means of private knowledge accumulation. Hence, there is a strong case for the government to intervene in this process and to provide education and training to guarantee that the (overall) level of skills is sufficiently high. However, another problem of this trend is that it is increasing over time, i.e.

$$\frac{\partial \bar{s}}{\partial t} > 0$$

frustrating government's efforts to enhance skills.

Government policies to enhance the position of relatively low-skilled workers should therefore be 'skill-biased' in the sense that it should aim at improving the position of relatively low-skilled workers. The way the effects of government intervention is modelled in this framework does suggest that efforts made by the government to distribute skills and therefore income more equally among individuals are neutral: every single individual profits, *ceteris paribus*, in the same manner from γB_t. This knowledge, provided through a 'public basin' of knowledge, accessible for every single individual reduces the skill-bias, but only once; over time the bias will again increase. Therefore, government policies have to be effective both in the long run and induce a skill-bias in order for relatively low-skilled individuals, like individuals s_j in the example above, to profit more from the effort made by the government.

Concluding remarks

This chapter has provided a unique framework in which SBTC is explained by means of private investments in knowledge among firms. The investment in knowledge among firms is biased towards relatively skilled individuals because their ability to acquire this knowledge is assumed to be higher. This engine of growth leads to large levels of dispersion in wage income and human capital embodiment. On the other hand, accumulation of public knowledge leads to an unbiased or neutral increase in wage income and human capital embodiment.

This framework stresses the need for continuous government intervention to reduce the ongoing dispersion in human capital formation induced by SBTC.

Moreover, the endogenous decision of individuals to school themselves proves not to be sufficient to deal with SBTC in a comprehensive manner.

Acknowledgements

We would like to thank Thomas Ziesemer and an anonymous referee for helpful comments on an earlier draft of this chapter. Furthermore, the discussions with seminar participants at the German Association of Political Economy (Universität Hohenheim, Stuttgart) and the Maastricht Economic Research Institute on Innovation and Technology (Maastricht University, Maastricht) are gratefully acknowledged.

Notes

1 See e.g. Chennells and Van Reenen (1999) and ter Weel (1999) for an overview of more than one hundred studies addressing the causes and consequences of the recent burgeon in wage inequality.
2 Most models in the literature divide the labour force in a skilled and unskilled segment, following the properties first stated in McDonald and Solow (1985). The results of these approaches are often crowding-out of unskilled labour because unskilled labour and capital are substitutes while skilled labour and capital are assumed to complement each other. The latter induces an engine of growth, which leads to a large dispersion in wages and results in inequality in society.
3 Appendix A provides the proof for these results and properties.
4 Although fewer and fewer individuals will embody relatively more and more human capital, it should be pointed out that no individual will end up holding the entire stock of human capital.
5 Moreover, this trend can also induce a sector bias in technical change, since some sectors might have more resources and scope to invest in knowledge, both codified and tacit, which can lead to large differences in the accumulation of tacit knowledge, inducing an absorbing effect on high-skilled labour from other sectors – cf. Haskel and Slaughter (1998) for one of the initial empirical assessments of the sector bias of technical change.
6 The latter restriction is in line with empirical findings that show that the growth predictions of traditional models of Uzawa (1965) and Romer (1986) with $\delta = \xi = 1$, contradict post-war growth experiences, investigated by Jones (1995b), of the major OECD countries. This is confirmed by the steady-state solution for φ which shows that the traditional specification $\delta = \xi = 1$ can be ruled out (see equation (C.10) in Appendix C). Furthermore, the restriction that the production of technology exhibits decreasing returns-to-scale is imposed. Jones (1995a) imposes the restriction $\xi < 1$ and shows that this leads to a model in which a balanced growth path is consistent with an increasing number of persons devoted to technology production.
7 See Appendices C and D for full proof.

References

Acemoglu, D. (1998) 'Why Do New Technologies Complement Skills? Directed Technical Change and Wage Inequality', *Quarterly Journal of Economics*, 113: 1055–89.
—— (2000) 'Technical Change, Inequality, and the Labor Market', NBER Working Paper No. 7800.

Berman, E., Bound, J. and Machin, S. (1998) 'Implications of Skill-Biased Technological Change: International Evidence', *Quarterly Journal of Economics*, 113: 1245–79.

—— and Machin, S. (2000) 'SBTC Happens! Evidence on the Factor Bias of Technological Change in Developing and Developed Countries', mimeo, Boston University.

Caselli, F. (1999) 'Technological Revolution', *American Economic Review*, 89: 78–102.

Chennells, L. and Van Reenen, J. (1999) 'Has Technology Hurt Less Skilled Workers? An Econometric Survey of the Effects of Technical Change and the Structure of Pay and Jobs', Working Paper 99/27, Institute for Fiscal Studies.

Davis, D.R. and Reeve, T.A. (1997) 'Human Capital, Unemployment and Relative Wages in a Global Economy', NBER Working Paper No. 6133, National Bureau of Economic Research, Cambridge, Mass.

Galor, O. and Moav, O. (2000) 'Ability Biased Technological Transition, Wage Inequality, and Economic Growth', *Quarterly Journal of Economics*, 115: 469–97.

Gould, E.D., Moav, O. and Weinberg, B.A. (2000) 'Precautionary Demand for Education, Inequality, and Technological Progress', mimeo, Hebrew University.

Haskel, J.E. and Slaughter, M.J. (1998) 'Does the Sector Bias of SkillBiased Technical Change Explain Changing Wage Inequality?', NBER Working Paper No. 6565.

Hollanders, H. and ter Weel, B. (2000) 'Technology, Knowledge Spillovers and Changes in Skill Structure', MERIT Research Memorandum 00–001.

Jones, C.I. (1995a) 'R&D-Based Models of Economic Growth', *Journal of Political Economy*, 103: 759–84.

—— (1995b) 'Time Series Tests of Growth Models', *Quarterly Journal of Economics*, 110: 495–525.

Katz, L.F. and Murphy, K.M. (1992) 'Changes in Relative Wages, 1963–1987: Supply and Demand Factors', *Quarterly Journal of Economics*, 107: 35–78.

Kiley, M.T. (1999) 'The Supply of Skilled Labour and Skill-Biased Technological Progress', *Economic Journal*, 109: 708–24.

Krugman, P. (1995) 'Technology, Trade and Factor Prices', NBER Working Paper 5355.

Lloyd-Ellis, H. (1999) 'Endogenous Technological Change and Wage Inequality', *American Economic Review*, 89: 47–77.

Machin, S. and Van Reenen, J. (1998) 'Technology and Changes in Skill Structure: Evidence from Seven OECD Countries', *Quarterly Journal of Economics*, 113: 1215–44.

McDonald, I.M. and Solow, R.M. (1985) 'Wages and Employment in a Segmented Labor Market', *Quarterly Journal of Economics*, 100: 1115–41.

Muysken, J. and ter Weel, B. (2000) 'Overeducation and Crowding Out of Low-Skilled Workers', in L. Borghans and A. de Grip (eds), *The Overeducated Worker? The Economics of Skill Utilization*, Cheltenham: Edward Elgar.

OECD (1996) *Technology, Productivity and Job Creation*, OECD: Paris.

—— (1998) *Employment Outlook*, OECD: Paris.

Romer, P.M. (1986) 'Increasing Returns and Long-Run Growth', *Journal of Political Economy*, 94:1002–37.

ter Weel, B. (1999) 'The Computerization of the Labour Market', mimeo, Maastricht Economic Research Institute on Innovation and Technology Research.

Uzawa, H. (1965) 'Optimum Technical Change in an Aggregative Model of Economic Growth', *International Economic Review*, 6: 18–31.

Wood, A. (1994) *North-South Trade, Employment and Inequality*, Clarendon Press: Oxford.

Appendix A: Consumer optimum

Consumers maximise life-time utility with respect to the budget constraint and their human capital accumulation function. This results in the Hamiltonian Ω, which is defined as:

$$\Omega = \frac{C_{t,s}^{1-\sigma} - 1}{1 - \sigma} e^{-\rho t} + \lambda_1 \left(A_t^s u_{t,s} H_{t,s}^\beta B_t^\gamma - \mu H_{t,s} \right)$$
$$+ \lambda_2 [(1 - \tau) r_t K_{t,s} + (1 - \tau) w_t (1 - u_{t,s}) H_{t,s} - C_{t,s}]$$

The control variables in the Hamiltonian are $C_{t,s}$ and $u_{t,s}$. Taking partial derivatives with respect to the control variables gives us equations (A.1) and (A.2):

$$\frac{\partial \Omega}{\partial C_{t,s}} = C_{t,s}^{-\sigma} e^{-\rho t} - \lambda_2 = 0 \tag{A.1}$$

and

$$\frac{\partial \Omega}{\partial u_s} = \lambda_1 A_t^s H_{t,s}^\beta B_t^\gamma - \lambda_2 (1 - \tau) w_t H_{t,s} = 0 \tag{A.2}$$

Taking partial derivatives with respect to the state variables $H_{t,s}$ and $K_{t,s}$ gives the following pair of differential equations:

$$\dot{\lambda}_1 = -\frac{\partial \Omega}{\partial H_{t,s}} = -\lambda_1 \left(\beta A_t^s u_{t,s} H_{t,s}^{\beta-1} B_t^\gamma - \mu \right) - \lambda_2 (1 - \tau) w_t (1 - u_{t,s}) \tag{A.3}$$

and

$$\dot{\lambda}_2 = -\frac{\partial \Omega}{\partial K_{t,s}} = -\lambda_2 (1 - \tau) r_t \tag{A.4}$$

Dividing equation (A.4) by λ_2, taking growth rates of equation (A.1) and equating the results give us the solution for the individual with skill level s. This is a standard Euler equation:

$$\hat{C}_{t,s} = \frac{(1 - \tau) r_t - \rho}{\sigma} \tag{A.5}$$

Dividing equation (A.3) by λ_1, making use of equation (A.2) and then expressing this in growth rates gives the solution for $\hat{H}_{t,s}$:

$$\hat{H}_{t,s} = \frac{s \hat{A}_t + \gamma \hat{B}_t}{1 - \beta} \tag{A.6}$$

Dividing equation (A.4) by λ_2 and expressing equation (A.2) in growth rates results in the growth rates for co-state variables which satisfy:

$$\hat{\lambda}_2 = -(1 - \tau) r_t \tag{A.7}$$

and

$$\hat{\lambda}_1 = \hat{\lambda}_2 + \hat{w}_t = -(1 - \tau)r_t + \hat{w}_t \tag{A.8}$$

Dividing equation (A.3) by λ_1, making use of equation (A.2) and solving for $u_{t,s}$, gives the following expression for the amount of time consumers spend on human capital accumulation:

$$u_{t,s} = \frac{\hat{H}_{t,s} + \mu}{(1 - \beta)(\hat{H}_{t,s} + \mu) - \hat{\lambda}_1 + \mu} \tag{A.9}$$

Making use of equations (A.6), (A.7) and (A.8), and assuming no depreciation of human capital ($\mu = 0$), this expression can be rewritten as

$$u_{t,s} = \frac{s\hat{A}_t + \gamma\hat{B}_t}{(1 - \beta)(s\hat{A}_t + \gamma\hat{B}_t + (1 - \tau)r_t - \hat{w}_t)} \tag{A.10}$$

Appendix B: Equilibrium level of human capital

From equation (A.6) follows the solution for the level of human capital $H_{t,s}$:

$$H_{t,s} = H_{0,s}e^{((s\hat{A}_t + \gamma\hat{B}_t)/(1-\beta))t} \tag{B.1}$$

Assuming that all individuals start with the same level of human capital $H_{0,s} = 1$, the overall level of human capital can be calculated – by integrating over equation (B.1) for all individuals – as:

$$H_t = N \int_0^1 H_{t,s}ds = N \int_0^1 e^{((s\hat{A}_t + \gamma\hat{B}_t)/(1-\beta))t}ds \tag{B.2}$$

Solving this integral and substituting $s = 0$ and $s = 1$ leads to the solution for H_t:

$$H_t = \left(\frac{(1 - \beta)N}{t\hat{A}_t}\right)\left(e^{((\hat{A}_t + \gamma\hat{B}_t)/(1-\beta))t} - e^{((\gamma\hat{B}_t)/(1-\beta))t}\right) \tag{B.3}$$

This expression gives us the overall level of human capital at time t.

Appendix C: Firm optimum

The Hamiltonian for the firm's profit maximization problem is defined as:

$$\Pi = K_t^\alpha \left(A_t N \int_0^1 ((1 - \varphi_t)(1 - u_{t,s}))H_{t,s}ds\right)^{1-\alpha} - r_t K_t$$

$$- w_t N \int_0^1 (1 - u_{t,s})H_{t,s}ds + \lambda_3 \left(N \int_0^1 (\varphi_t(1 - u_{t,s}))H_{t,s}ds\right)^\delta A_t^\xi$$

The amount of human capital available to the firm can be found by solving:

$$N \int_0^1 (1 - u_{t,s}) H_{t,s} ds$$

$$= N \int_0^1 \left(\frac{-((1-\beta) + \beta s)\hat{A}_t - \beta\gamma\hat{B}_t + (1-\beta)(1-\tau)r_t}{(1-\beta)(-(1-s)\hat{A}_t + \gamma\hat{B}_t) + (1-\beta)(1-\tau)r_t} \right)$$

$$\cdot e^{((s\hat{A}_t + \gamma\hat{B}_t)/(1-\beta))t} ds$$

which leads to the following solution

$$\frac{-\beta N \left(e^{((\hat{A}_t + \gamma\hat{B}_t)/(1-\beta))t} - e^{((\gamma\hat{B}_t)/(1-\beta))t} \right)}{\hat{A}_t t} + \frac{(-\hat{A}_t + (1-\tau)r_t)N}{1-\beta} \cdot$$

$$\left(\sum_{n=1}^{n=\infty} \left(\frac{(n-1)!(1-\beta)^n}{\hat{A}_t t^n \left(-(1-s)\hat{A}_t + \gamma\hat{B}_t + (1-\tau)r_t \right)^n} \right) e^{((s\hat{A}_t + \gamma\hat{B}_t)/(1-\beta))t} \right)_{s=0}^{s=1}$$

It can be shown that this expression has a finite solution (n is the index of summation). For convenience, this solution is defined as $H_{t,f}$.

The Hamiltonian can now be rewritten as

$$\Pi = K_t^\alpha (A_t(1 - \varphi_t)H_{t,f})^{1-\alpha} - r_t K_t - w_t H_{t,f} + \lambda_3 (\varphi_t H_{t,f})^\delta A_t^\xi \quad \text{(C.1)}$$

The control variables are K_t, $H_{t,f}$ and φ_t. Taking partial derivatives with respect to the control variables gives equations (C.2) to (C.4), i.e.

$$\frac{\partial \Pi}{\partial K_t} = \alpha \left(\frac{(1-\varphi_t)A_t H_{t,f}}{K_t} \right)^{1-\alpha} - r_t = 0 \quad \text{(C.2)}$$

$$\frac{\partial \Pi}{\partial H_{t,f}} = (1-\alpha)(1-\varphi_t)^{1-\alpha} K_t^\alpha A_t^{1-\alpha} H_{t,f}^{-\alpha} - w_t + \lambda_3 \delta \varphi_t^\delta A_t^\xi H_{t,f}^{\delta-1} = 0 \quad \text{(C.3)}$$

and

$$\frac{\partial \Pi}{\partial \phi_t} = -(1-\alpha)(1-\varphi_t)^{-\alpha} K_t^\alpha A_t^{1-\alpha} H_{t,f}^{1-\alpha} + \lambda_3 \delta \varphi_t^{\delta-1} A_t^\xi H_{t,f}^\delta = 0 \quad \text{(C.4)}$$

Taking partial derivatives with respect to the state variable A_t gives the following differential equation for λ_3:

$$\dot{\lambda}_3 = -\frac{\partial \Pi}{\partial A_t} = -(1-\alpha)(1-\varphi_t)^{1-\alpha} K_t^\alpha A_t^{-\alpha} H_{t,f}^{1-\alpha} - \lambda_3 \xi \varphi_t^\delta A_t^{\xi-1} H_{t,f}^\delta \quad \text{(C.5)}$$

Furthermore, the change in private knowledge is given by:

$$\dot{A}_t = (\varphi_t H_{t,f})^\delta A_t^\xi \quad \text{(C.6)}$$

Dividing equation (C.6) by A_t and taking growth rates, gives the following relation between the growth rates of human capital and private knowledge:

$$\hat{H}_{t,f} = \left(\frac{1-\xi}{\delta}\right)\hat{A}_t \tag{C.7}$$

Rewriting equation (C.2) in growth rates, and making use of equation (C.7), gives a relation between the growth rates of physical capital and private knowledge:

$$\hat{K}_t = \left(\frac{1+\delta-\xi}{\delta}\right)\hat{A}_t \tag{C.8}$$

Using (C.4) to rewrite (C.3) in growth rates, and making use of equations (C.7) and (C.8) leads to the conclusion that wages grow with the same rate as private knowledge:

$$\hat{w}_t = \hat{A}_t \tag{C.9}$$

The part of the human capital stock available to firms that is devoted to the production of new knowledge is equal to:

$$\phi_t = \frac{\delta}{((1-\xi)/\delta) - \delta + \xi} \tag{C.10}$$

It can be shown that $0 < \varphi_t < 1$.

Appendix D: Equilibrium growth rate of the physical capital stock

The accumulation of the stock of physical capital K_t equals the sum of the accumulation of the individual capital stocks:

$$\dot{K}_t = N \int_0^1 \dot{K}_{t,s} ds \tag{D.1}$$

Making use of equations (2), (4), the definition for $H_{t,f}$

$$H_{t,f} = N \int_0^1 (1 - u_{t,s}) H_{t,s} ds$$

and the fact that

$$K_t = N \int_0^1 K_{t,s} ds$$

equation (D.1) can be rewritten as

$$\dot{K}_t = (1-\tau) r_t K_t + (1-\tau) w_t H_{t,f} - e^{(((1-\tau)r_t - \rho)/\sigma)t}$$

The steady-state relations between the growth rates of K_t, H_t and A_t, as expressed in equations (C.7) and (C.8), leads to the conclusion that the growth rate of the physical capital stock equals that of consumption

$$\hat{C}_t = \hat{K}_t = \frac{(1-\tau)r_t - \rho}{\sigma} \tag{D.2}$$

Part IV

Growth and employment

11 Okun's law in the US and the employment crisis in Germany

Georg Erber

What is Okun's law?

Arthur M. Okun (1928–80), an American economist and long-time member of the US Council of Economic Advisors published in 1962 a paper which made a statement about a stable macroeconomic relation between the change of the unemployment rate and the growth rate of real output for the US economy, measured by the gross domestic product, i.e.

$$\Delta ur \sim g_{GDP}^{a} \tag{1}$$

ur denotes the unemployment rate and Δur the respective first difference between the average annual unemployment rates of the current and the previous year. The character g denotes the annual growth rates of the GDP (gross domestic product) calculated as the difference between the natural logarithms of the annual GDP data of the actual and the previous year. The superscript a denotes the actual GDP while p denotes the respective potential GDP.

Okun's law therefore states that the change in the unemployment rate should change proportionally with the growth rate of the GDP under the assumption that the source of unemployment change was due mainly to an underutilisation of the available production capacities of an economy.[1] As long as the economy runs below its long-term growth path, however, both variables should be negatively correlated, i.e. an increase of economic activity will *mutatis mutandis* proportionally reduce the unemployment rate. Okun's law therefore rested on the Keynesian view that in a recession idle capacities could be easily utilised by the economy to reduce unemployment if a sufficient demand expansion stimulates economic growth. This assumes a sufficient degree of flexibility with regard to structural adjustments necessary in this process.

Okun's law was formulated at the high tide of Keynesianism in the US when demand management by the government was a widely accepted principle for economic policy design. Through direct deficit spending of the government or tax breaks additional demand could stimulate additional growth of the economy and by this reduce the actual unemployment rate.

This relation later on became known as *Okun's law* (see e.g. the reference article by Hagemann and Seiter 1999). Since then, it proved a very useful relation, in particular for the US, to predict the potential decline of unemployment when GDP growth rates are known or targeted by economic policy-makers.

Even after Keynesianism came under attack by the Monetarist counter-revolution in the US during the 1970s, the empirical regularity between the GDP growth rate and the change in the unemployment rate still remained a valid fact.

In times when the US economy was slipping into a major recession, American governments have regularly used deficit spending or tax breaks as an instrument to stimulate the economy after the collapse of the New Economy boom in spring 2000. The current US government of George W. Bush, even though generally not considered as believing in Keynesianism, has again rapidly expanded the government deficit to more than 160 billion dollar to accomplish a rapid turnaround in the US economy during the year 2002 with a first quarter annualised growth rate of more than 5 per cent after it had become negative in the two quarters before.[2]

Other ways to state Okun's law are that the unemployment rate and the difference between actual and potential output growth rate are proportional,

$$ur \sim g_{GDP}^a - g_{GDP}^p \tag{2}$$

or that the ratio between actual and potential output is constant and equal to a long-term steady state of output growth,

$$\frac{GDP^p}{GDP^a} \sim g_{GDP}^l \tag{3}$$

We will focus here on using the first representation that is still used by present-day economists like Paul Krugman (cf. e.g. 1994: 114) for taxonomic purposes (see Figure 11.1). For a discussion of the problems related to the empirical analysis with the two other forms see e.g. Perry (1977). Figure 11.1 illustrates this relation for the US economy for the years 1961–2003.

Obviously there is a strong negative linear correlation between both variables, i.e. an increase of economic growth rates reduces unemployment and vice versa. The two parameters plus a third one accounting for a long-term increase or decline of unemployment change with regard to a historical time trend are completing the deterministic part of the model specification. The random term (u) is assumed to fulfill the standard assumption that the random variable is not autocorrelated and has an expectation value of zero and a constant variance over time.

$$\Delta ur_t = \alpha - \beta \cdot g_{GDP,t} + \gamma \cdot t + u_t \quad \text{and} \quad u_t \sim N\left(0, \sigma_u^2\right) \tag{4}$$

Of course, the direction of causality, if there exists one,[3] cannot be deduced from a scatter gram. Granger causality tests using annual data give no definite answer as well.[4]

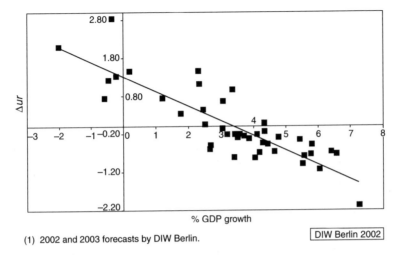

(1) 2002 and 2003 forecasts by DIW Berlin.

Figure 11.1 Okun's law for the US (1961–2003).

Sources: OECD and own calculations.

Okun's law in the US in the 1990s and early twenty-first century

In the past decade of the 1990s, the US experienced a surge in its economic growth associated with a similar recovery of its weak productivity performance since the beginning of the first oil price shock in the mid-1970s. Particularly in the second half of the 1990s a period of high economic growth driven by a surge of heavy investments in information and communication technology equipment in particular gave raise to a new term, the *New Economy*, for summarising this highly unexpected development if one considers the growth perspectives at the beginning of the decade. Figure 11.2 shows the past and prospective growth pattern of the US economy.

Associated with this development an unexpectedly high decline in the actual unemployment rate occurred (see Figure 11.3).

While in the past decades until the mid-1990s the non-accelerating inflation rate of unemployment (NAIRU) was considered to be at the 6 per cent level, the US experienced unemployment rates far below this threshold down to 4.5 per cent in 1998 and 1999 without a significant increase of inflationary pressures on its economy. The US economy experienced therefore high growth and low unemployment, which was not considered to be viable by most economists until the mid-1990s. The graphical representation of Okun's law relation in Figure 11.4 shows the shift in this development from the past pattern.

The previously observed downward-sloping linear relationship between the two variables of Okun's law has become much less pronounced or even highly blurred. As the graph takes the time sequence of the annual observations into account by

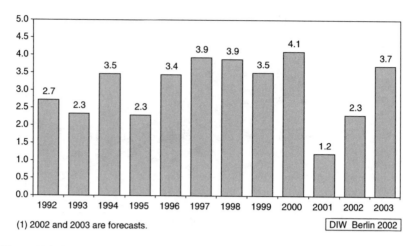

Figure 11.2 GDP for the US (annual growth rates in per cent at 1995 prices).
Sources: OECD and own calculations.

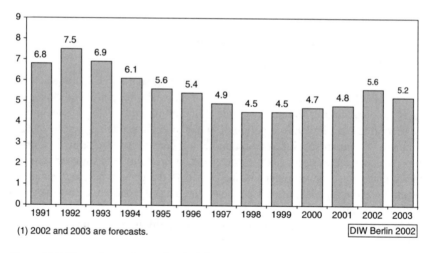

Figure 11.3 Unemployment rate for the US (annual growth rates in per cent at 1995 prices).

Sources: OECD and own calculations.

connecting the values on a year-by-year basis, their irregular movements become visible (see Figure 11.4). A shift in the NAIRU of the US economy in the second half of the 1990s seems to have contributed to a less stable relation shift.

Estimating Okun's law including a time-shift variable with a standard OLS-estimator for the US data gives the results shown in Table 11.1.

While we obtain fairly similar results if we estimate Okun's law for the overall time-period from 1961 until 2001 and the subperiod until 1995 with regard to the three parameters, the results change significantly for the second half of the 1990s.

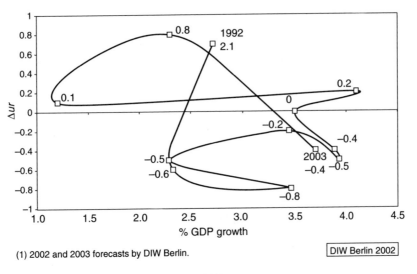

(1) 2002 and 2003 forecasts by DIW Berlin.

DIW Berlin 2002

Figure 11.4 Okun's law for the US (1992–2003).

Sources: OECD and own calculations.

Table 11.1 Estimating Okun's law for the US

Estimation period	Constant term	g_{GDP}	Time	R^2 DW
1961–2001	1.7	−0.39	−0.02	0.80
	(8.9)	(−12.0)	(−3.2)	2.21
1961–1995	1.9	−0.41	−0.03	0.82
	(8.9)	(−12.0)	(−3.9)	2.50
1996–2001	−0.56	−0.32	0.04	0.99
	(−1.0)	(−16.0)	(2.9)	1.93

Source: Own calculations.

The impact of the GDP growth rate decreases and the sign of the constant term and the time-shift variable change if we estimate the relation separately for this subperiod. Excluding the time-shift variable from the estimation would result in lower parameter values for the Okun coefficient of about −0.37. The negative value of the parameter estimate for the time-shift variable shows that there is some continuous tendency present in the US economy to lower the unemployment rate. This might be attributed to an increasing flexibility in the US labour and product markets. The strange results for the second half of the 1990s just point in the opposite direction which seems to be implausible and is probably due to the fact that the US economy started to grow above its long-term growth path. Currently it is still an unsolved puzzle whether the temporary acceleration in the US GDP growth rate observed since the mid-1990s will shift back to the previous historic levels or if the higher growth path will be maintained after the recovery of the US economy in the coming years.

Summing up the results from our exercise, we might conclude that the New Economy boom since the mid-1990s has raised some questions concerning the stability of Okun's law for the US. However, the value of the Okun coefficient implies that an increase in the GDP growth rate of 1 per cent could lower the unemployment rate of about 0.4 per cent. Therefore a growth-oriented macroeconomic policy could have a significant impact to lower unemployment quite rapidly if the economy has run out of steam.

Okun's law in Europe

In some previous work, the author tested the hypothesis that Okun's law has not necessarily to be symmetric (see Erber 1994). The reason for this conjecture was that the high unemployment rates emerging in Europe during the second half of the 1970s and the 1980s show a persistent asymmetric adjustment when a recovery occurred after a major recession. While the classical form of Okun's law assumed a symmetric reaction of the unemployment rate to changes in the real output growth rate, econometric tests of the hypothesis of an asymmetric relation showed that in many European OECD member countries (see Erber 1994) contrary to the US, labour market flexibility was significantly lower in an upswing period of a business cycle than during a recession. Labour shake-outs occurred in Europe in short dramatic recessions in the 1970s and 1980s, but a recovery, even when it lasted for a significantly longer time-period, could not completely compensate the previous loss of employment. A further observation for Western Europe was that the elasticity between a decrease/increase of the employment rate with regard to real output growth went down over time, when a time-trend variable was included in the model equation.

This poses the question whether Okun's law was or still is a valid empirical regularity similar to the US, which makes it a useful building bloc for macroeconomic policy designs for Europe and Germany in particular. Taking the past results from estimates of Okun's law for the OECD member countries for the years from 1960 until 1995 the following estimates resulted:

> The countries with the highest absolute values for output growth elasticities with respect to changes in unemployment rates are the United States and Spain with −0.43. Behind these countries follow Finland (−0.39), Canada (−0.37), the United Kingdom (−0.37), Australia (−0.32), France (−0.31) and Germany (−0.26). Japan's elasticity is much lower with −0.04.
>
> (Erber 1994: 21)

Therefore, output growth did not show the same magnitude of unemployment reduction everywhere in Europe. In particular, Germany was clearly underperforming with regard to the leading countries, like Spain, in Europe, where output growth had a large impact on unemployment reduction such as in the US economy.

In Europe structural rigidities in the economy emerged during the 1970s and 1980s, which significantly altered the usefulness of Okun's law as a policy tool especially to solve labour market problems. Similar to the Phillips curve this basic macroeconomic relation lost much of its usefulness for macroeconomic labour market policies in Europe.

Okun's law in Germany in the 1990s

This paper addresses the more recent development of this relationship in the 1990s in the US and Germany as examples for an assessment of the present situation how far Okun's law has important policy implications for tackling current labour market problems in Germany as the largest and in many respects dominant economy in Europe and in particular the euro zone.

It is important to notice that the labour market situation in Germany and the US showed completely divergent developments especially since the last major recessions in 1992 in the US and 1993 in Germany (the year when the unification boom ended). While in the US, unemployment rates came down to their lowest levels since the first oil price shock with 4.5 per cent in 1998 and 1999, in Germany unemployment rates stayed fairly high at about 9 per cent if one uses the standardised rates of the OECD statistics. Since the OECD does not report unemployment rates for East and West Germany separately we use here the national rates instead.

Germany suffered and still is suffering from the uncompleted transition process of the East German economy to catchup with the Western part which resulted from the unification shock, when the former GDR economy had to meet international standards of competitiveness from one day to another with the beginning of the German monetary union in July 1990. Because most of the economic structure, physical capital and to a substantial degree also the human capital of the former GDR economy became obsolete, unemployment boomed when companies in East Germany now part of the Federal Republic of Germany struggled to meet quality and cost efficiency standards of the West. If one looks at the Okun relation for the East German economy during the transition process of the 1990s, one notices that it is completely obsolete as an analytical instrument for policy analysis to deal with the labour market problems (Figure 11.5).

Even higher real output growth than in the US economy after 1992 could not stop the necessary structural adjustment and associated labour shake-out to narrow the productivity gap to the West German economy.

To catch up with West German productivity, wage and income levels, the economy in East Germany dismissed more and more parts of its previously employed labour force. The integration of the East German economy into the Western market system even took place during a period where relocations of traditional production, especially in the manufacturing industries, in the developed OECD countries to other locations of the world economy put additional stress on the national production system, a phenomenon described as globalisation.

Looking at Okun's relation for West Germany reveals that the former West German economy lost much of its attractive properties, such as comparatively

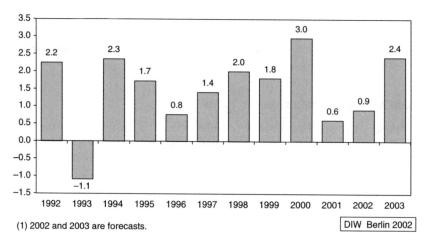

Figure 11.5 GDP for Germany (annual growth rates in per cent at 1995 prices).
Sources: Federal Statistical Office and own calculations.

high output growth and low unemployment rates, in Europe from 1993 onwards. The West German economy was bleeding from two wounds.

On the one hand, the attractive investment conditions in East Germany created by substantial direct subsidies, tax reductions, lower wages and longer working hours than in West Germany, redirected investment capital to this part of the united Germany. On the other hand, European integration, the integration of Eastern European countries and transcontinental globalisation of German multinational companies shifted capital from West Germany to other parts of Europe and the rest of the world. Managers and entrepreneurs of Germany put the blame for this behaviour on institutional failures in Germany to adjust to the new realities of the world economy and by this, creating a *Standortproblem* (location problem). Instead of rapidly upgrading the former West German economy to modern industries as in the US as the technologically leading economy to become a similar important player in an emerging information and network economy (see e.g. Erber *et al.* 1999), the profits of German companies were invested in significant parts outside the West German area.

The slowdown in economic growth in West Germany triggered a later labour shake-out and led to dramatic changes in the working conditions. Full-time employment was replaced by all kinds of part-time employment. High unemployment changed the bargaining position between the labour unions and the employers' organisations. Even at the end of the decade the future perspectives looked not too promising compared to the brilliant performance of the US economy since 1992, taking employment and output growth as criteria (Figures 11.6 and 11.7).

Estimating Okun's law for Germany gives the results shown in Table 11.2.

Compared to the US results the coefficient of determination is significantly lower and a high degree of autocorrelation is present in the residuals of the

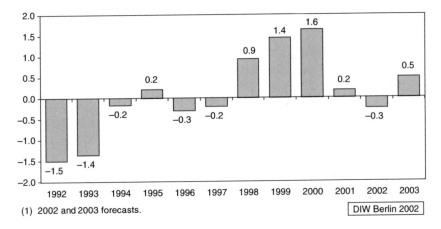

(1) 2002 and 2003 forecasts.

DIW Berlin 2002

Figure 11.6 Employees in Germany (annual growth rates in per cent).
Sources: Federal Statistical Office and own calculations.

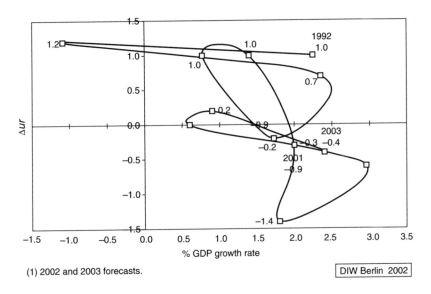

(1) 2002 and 2003 forecasts.

DIW Berlin 2002

Figure 11.7 Okun's law for Germany (1992–2003).
Sources: Federal Statistical Office and own calculations.

estimated equation. Even if the estimates of the Okun coefficient are a little bit higher for Germany compared to the previous estimation done in 1994 (Erber 1994), the coefficient is significantly lower compared to US values. Again, but much more pronounced, the Okun relation breaks down for the second half of the 1990s. The estimated coefficients are all insignificant. Looking at the graph of

Table 11.2 Estimating Okun's law for Germany

Estimation period	Constant term	g_{GDP}	Time	R^2 DW
1961–2001	1.5	−0.29	−0.02	0.61
	(6.5)	(−6.5)	(−3.4)	1.44
1961–1995	1.3	−0.28	−0.01	0.64
	(5.7)	(−7.4)	(−1.8)	1.41
1996–2001	7.8	−0.48	0.18	0.69
	(1.6)	(−1.7)	(−1.4)	2.54

Source: Own calculations.

the Okun relation for Germany this instability is not surprising. This raises great doubts whether a pure growth policy would be sufficient to tackle the unemployment problem for Germany. Higher macroeconomic growth might still contribute to reduce unemployment but it will not be the key driver to reduce unemployment significantly. The reason why growth might not be a satisfying remedy for Germany could be deduced to some extent from the Okun relation itself. The Okun relation could be used to estimate the neutral rate of growth with regard to a stable unemployment rate. Setting the right-hand side of the Okun equation equal to zero one could obtain an estimate for this long-term GDP growth rate that would keep the unemployment rate unchanged.

Taking estimates from Schnabel (2002) for the US and Germany as benchmarks for the long-term GDP growth rates, he found for the US rates from 3.2 to 3.8 per cent for the period 1995–2000. The latter resulted from estimates, which calibrated the changes in the unemployment rate around the long-term mean. The long-term growth rates estimated on the basis of the period from 1953 to 2000 gave a long-term rate of 3.3 per cent. For Germany the respective results are much lower. For the period 1992–2000 the GDP growth rates are about 2.1–1.5 per cent, while the estimates from 1964–2000 give values ranging from 3.1 to 2.6 per cent. In particular since German unification the long-term growth rate which leaves the unemployment rate unchanged is less than half as large as the one for the US economy. The weak growth performance of the German economy therefore seems not to have caused a significant underutilisation of its growth potential, but rests on deeply rooted structural rigidities in labour and product markets.

Decline in the unemployment rates in East and West Germany is therefore not primarily caused by improved labour-demand conditions but instead by changing market conditions on the supply side for demographic reasons. Demographic factors (fewer young people entering the labour market, increasing numbers of an ageing working population reaching retirement, premature retirements by special offers from companies and the government), a slowdown of labour migration from other countries, falling labour participation rates in particular for women, increasing numbers of voluntary or involuntary part-time workers are bringing the official unemployment rates somewhat down. Furthermore, active labour market policies especially in East Germany reduce the official unemployment numbers without creating new jobs in the first labour market.

However, major problems in East and West Germany remain to be solved for the German economy. The convergence of East Germany to the West German efficiency level has come to a halt at about 60–65 per cent since 1997. The premature rapid adjustment of East German wage levels to about 80 per cent leads to a persistent productivity wage-gap of about 20 per cent. To finance these high wages the government still has to subsidise East German companies or make significant transfer payments to all East Federal States (*Bundesländer*) and the social security and pension system.

All in all, Okun's law has lost much of the explanatory power it had in the previous decades for Germany. The mounting structural problems accumulating in the German economy are less and less tractable by simple Keynesian macroeconomic demand management policies. The lost credibility that simple Keynesian recipes of macroeconomic demand stimuli – be it by lowering interest rates or public deficits – would pull the German economy out of its current woes has been refuted in the political arena with the stepping down of Oskar Lafontaine as Minister of Finance after only a few months in office.

Looking now at the other side of the Atlantic we notice that the US economy managed to run high economic growth since 1992 for the rest of this decade. The performance during the 1990s is even better than during the 1980s when the US economy already outperformed West Germany and the other big West European countries with respect to output and employment growth. This development in the US is even more remarkable if one takes into account that the US economy runs a cumulative, significantly growing trade and current account deficit, i.e. it therefore supports employment elsewhere in the world. Okun's law as a stable macroeconomic relation for the US economy, however, lost its significance in the 1990s as well as in Germany and elsewhere in Europe. Looking at Figure 11.4 one notices the fuzziness of the relation compared to Figure 11.1.

Conclusions

Summing up the results of our analysis one might conclude that all in all significant structural changes in the OECD economies weakened the importance of such macroeconomic relations as Okun's law during the 1990s. In the US this new fuzziness of macroeconomic relations has triggered a debate on the New Economy. In Europe the focus is still on the persistence of labour and product market rigidities, which create a vicious circle of low growth and high unemployment. Studying the US experiences of the 1990s will therefore be an important exercise to understand how policies in Europe have to be redesigned to break the current deadlock.

Of course, one should not focus only on the positive aspects of the US experience but as well on the negative ones, especially the current risks that might come to the surface of the actual economy in the near future. The rapid growth in the US after 1995 is connected to a dramatic decrease in the saving rate of private households. Currently the private savings rate in the US is about zero, which has originated because of the positive wealth effect due to an asset price inflation of the stock market. Until now the deflating asset bubble, however, has not led to its recovery. Reflecting the economic consequences of the currently bursting bubble on the financial structure of the American economy, and taking the Japanese experiences of the 1990s after the financial bubble burst in the early 1990s, the current euphoria about the American miracle of the 1990s might be a little bit premature. Only the coming years will tell us whether the improved long-term growth and employment perspectives of the US were only a transitory phenomenon or are of a persistent nature.

Notes

1 If the slack capacity of the economy has become utilised, Okun's law therefore should break down, i.e. Okun's law is not valid when the economy is running above its long-term growth path.
2 This kind of expansion of the US economy in the first quarter of 2002 cannot, however, be solely attributed to the fiscal stimulus of the US government because the Fed reduced the short-term interest rates by more than 4 percentage points from the beginning of the recession which facilitated sufficient liquidity to soften the hard landing of the US economy. However, the implementation of an expansionary fiscal stimulus by a Republican President shows that the willingness to use Keynesian policy approaches under a threat of a major recession is a common policy issue for Republicans as well as Democrats accepted by all US governments.
3 One should keep in mind that this macroeconomic regularity observable to be empirically valid for most countries lacks a microeconomic foundation beside the fact that output expansion if it does not face slack labour capacities in the economy has to be complemented by additional labour demand assuming a production function approach. The proportional relation is an expression of a linear relation between output expansion and a single input factor, labour. If one tries to fit it into a production function approach, Okun's law would be an incomplete model with omitted variables (see e.g. Schnabel 2002).
4 This might result from the low frequency of observations used on an annual basis. Taking quarterly or even monthly data might lead to more conclusive results with regard to the direction of causality in Okun's law.

References

Erber, G. (1994) 'Okun's or Verdoorn's Law? Employment and Growth Experiences in OECD Countries, 1960–1993', DIW-Discussion Paper No. 98, Berlin.
——, Hagemann, H. and Seiter, S. (1999) *Wachstums- und beschäftigungspolitische Implikationen des Informations- und Kommunikationssek*tors, Gutachten im Auftrag der Hans-Böckler-Stiftung, Berlin-Stuttgart, March 1999.
Hagemann, H. and Seiter, S. (1999) 'Okun's Law', in P.A. O'Hara (ed.), *Encyclopedia of Political Economy*, Routledge: London-New York, 819–21.
Krugman, P. (1994) *Peddling Prosperity, Economic Sense and Nonsense in the Age of Diminished Expectations*, W.W. Norton & Company: New York-London.
Okun, A.M. (1962) 'Potential GNP: Its Measurement and Significance', *Proceedings of the Business and Economic Section, American Statistical Association*, Washington, DC: 98–104.
Perry, G.L. (1977) 'Potential Output and Productivity', *Brookings Papers on Economic Activity*, 1: 11–48.
Schnabel, G. (2002) 'Output trends and Okun's Law', BIS Working Paper No. 111, Bank for International Settlements, Basle, April 2002.

12 Health, labour productivity and growth

Joan Muysken, İ. Hakan Yetkiner and Thomas Ziesemer

Introduction

A key property of the neoclassical growth model is that an economy that starts out further below its own steady-state position tends to grow proportionately faster. The key word, however, is 'own', for empirical studies showed that this so-called absolute catch up proposition clearly failed in terms of the cross-country data. Many studies – for instance, Barro (1991), Barro and Sala-i-Martin (1992) and Mankiw, Romer and Weil (1992) – have shown that so-called *conditional* convergence is empirically more successful. In these studies country-specific characteristics are taken into account to control for differences in steady states. A typical example is human capital in the form of education (e.g., average years of schooling and literacy rate), which has consistently been used as a control variable in these studies.

Schultz (1961) and Mushkin (1962) have shown long time ago that human capital can also be accumulated through improvements in health.[1] In this context it is surprising that the second component of human capital, health, has been largely ignored in the growth literature. Indicators of health status like life expectancy at birth and the infant mortality rate have been used relatively rarely in convergence studies – see Barro and Sala-i-Martin (1995). Knowles and Owen (1995, 1997) introduced these indicators in the growth literature. For example, in their 1995 paper they augmented Mankiw, Romer and Weil's (1992) work by controlling for the health and education components of human capital separately. Knowles and Owen study takes the positive relation between output and health as given. The authors then estimate this relation in a Solovian growth framework. Contrary to our approach, Knowles and Owen did not consider optimal health expenditures.

The neglect of health as a relevant variable for economic growth is also generally encountered on the theoretical side. While the relationship between growth and education has been intensively investigated – see the many studies inspired by Lucas (1988) – the link between health and growth has hardly been researched in the theoretical literature. On the other hand, it has long been conceived that health by its very nature has important implications on labour supply – see Mushkin (1962). This notion is taken up by Cuddington *et al.* (1994) who analyse long-term growth in the presence of a communicable disease, namely AIDS, under the assumption of exogenous health expenditure. They show that an epidemic disease has important implications for size, structure, and productivity of labour and therefore for the growth performance of an economy – see Bloom and Mahal (1995) for an opposite view specific to AIDS on empirical grounds. Again, optimal health expenditure is not considered. Moreover, our model, unlike Cuddington *et al.* (1994), is not specific to a certain disease and, in that sense, is a general health-growth model.

Another theoretical study is van Zon and Muysken (2001). They include health into the Lucas's (1988) endogenous growth framework. In their model, healthy labour is not only used in the production of goods and knowledge, but it is also necessary to maintain health. As a consequence the characteristics of the health sector that have a clear impact on economic growth and optimal health expenditures are analysed. Our model differs from van Zon and Muysken's (2001) model because their model is very hard to characterise in the steady-state situation due to the fact that there does not exist a closed-form solution of the model and the transitional dynamics are not available.

We argue that there exists a positive association between health and economic development. On the one hand, economic growth provides more resources to sustained improvements in the health status of an economy. On the other hand, health itself is an important contributor to economic growth. Only those that have better health can be a source of economic development in terms of human capital accumulation, knowledge generation, etc. For example, creating new ideas requires healthy bodies, as much as well-educated researchers. Yet, while the two-way relationship between health and economic growth may be widely acknowledged, the theoretical link between them has not been fully developed. Many policy-makers, especially those of developing countries, do believe that economic growth precedes health status improvement of an economy. This is rather a biased view and perhaps arises partly due to lack of a solid theory, in which health 'supports' economic development as much as economic development fosters health improvement via increasing available resources for health expenditures.

The aim of this study is to show the (positive) association between the optimal health expenditure and status of an economy and all other variables. We thereby provide a theoretical background for using health variables in conditional convergence analyses, starting from the labour productivity implications of health. To this end we introduce health in a standard Ramsey-type growth model. In that context we develop an alternative measure of health status of an economy: the ratio of man-hours effectively supplied (and employed) to the total amount of man-hours available.

The basic model is presented in the section on 'The model'. This model shows a positive contribution of good health to steady-state output (and economic growth) for an exogenous health status. This exogeneity, however, can only be a first approximation. Therefore the model is extended in the section on 'Endogenous health and growth' to endogenise the health status, since assets have to be put aside to maintain and improve health. Consumers include this in their dynamic consumption-asset accumulation trade-off. Thus, the representative household's health optimisation problem is embodied in an optimal growth framework, which enables one to analyse the impact of changes in the expenditure of health care on steady-state growth and transition dynamics. An interesting finding of the study is that the optimal health expenditure and consumption in the transition to the steady-state are below (above) their steady-state values if the ratio of the stocks of capital and health is below (above) its steady-state value. In other words, if physical capital relative to health is relatively scarce (abundant) compared to the steady-state values, optimal expenditures for health and consumption are lower (higher) than in the steady-state but increase (decrease) towards their steady-state values. The last section concludes and summarises the study.

The model

This study builds on the standard Ramsey-type growth model – see Cass (1965) and Koopmans (1965). A typical assumption in standard neoclassical growth models is that each worker supplies a fixed amount of labour services per unit of time. By starting from labour supply implications of health, we will show how the performance of an economy is related to the health status of that economy.

The household [2]

Assume a representative household consisting of N members. It maximises overall utility, U, as given by

$$U = \int_0^\infty \frac{c^{1-\theta} - 1}{1 - \theta} e^{nt} e^{-\rho t} dt \quad \theta, \rho > 0 \tag{1}$$

In (1) c is the quantity of consumption per person, n is the (net) exogenous growth rate of the household members, and θ and ρ are the elasticity of marginal utility and subjective rate of time preference, respectively. Let us assume that each member's labour supply, l^i, is function of his/her health status in the form

$$l^i(h^i) = \begin{cases} 1 & h^i = 1 \\ 0 & h^i = 0 \end{cases} \quad i = 1, 2, \ldots, N \tag{2}$$

In (2) h^i denotes the health status of i. We assume that household members are either healthy or unfit to work, which corresponds to the values $h^i = 1$ and $h^i = 0$, respectively. Those who are unhealthy do not work and therefore they are not included in labour supply at any instant of time. So effective labour supply is the sum of labour supply of healthy workers. Suppose that there are N_1 healthy workers at a given time and $N_1 < N$. As each healthy worker supplies inelastically one unit of labour, total effective labour supply is also N_1.

The health status of the economy can be approximated by its average health status. In our model, the average health is the sum of 'healthy persons', N_1, divided by population N. Thus, the health index of the economy is

$$h = \frac{\sum_{i=1}^{N} h^i}{N} = \frac{N_1}{N} \tag{3}$$

Equation (3) can also be read as the ratio of healthy man-hours to total man-hours available in an economy at any instant of time. Hence, by using the intuition behind equation (2), we express the health status of the economy in a convenient way.[3] We conjecture that our health status measure does fit better in a growth framework than the usual measures of health owing to the fact that statistics like life expectancy at birth and infant mortality rate reflect nutrition and many other components of social development as much as health.[4]

Let us assume for the moment being that $h = N_1/N$ is constant, which implies that population and healthy workers grow at the same (exogenous) rate n. We will relax this assumption in the following section by endogenising h.

The flow budget constraint for the household is

$$\dot{A} = wN_1 + rA - cN_1 - c(N - N_1) \tag{4}$$

In (4) $N - N_1$ is the number of sick household members, A is the level of assets, and w and r are market-determined factor prices. According to equation (4), those who are sick are unable to work and, therefore, do not earn a wage income. Nevertheless, as is obvious from equation (4), sick members are supposed to keep on consuming (by spending savings and sharing current income at any combination). Therefore, the household's instantaneous utility function is independent of the health status of the household.

The flow budget constraint can be rewritten in per capita terms as follows:

$$\dot{a} = wh + (r - n)a - c \tag{5}$$

In (5) assets per person, a, is simply A/N. The household's optimisation problem is to maximise the overall utility U in equation (1), subject to the budget constraint in equation (5) given the stock of initial assets $a(0)$ and the transversality condition on the state variable a.

The present-value Hamiltonian is

$$J = \frac{c^{1-\theta} - 1}{1 - \theta} e^{-(\rho - n)t} + \lambda\{wh + (r - n)a - c\}. \tag{6}$$

The first-order conditions for a maximum of U and the standard transversality condition imposed on assets per capita define the household's optimum, yielding[5]

$$\frac{\dot{c}}{c} = \frac{1}{\theta}(r - \rho) \tag{7}$$

Equation (7) is the 'standard' expression for the optimum growth rate.

The firm

Suppose that there is perfect competition in the goods sector. A representative firm has the following production function

$$Y = K^{\alpha} N_1^{1-\alpha} \quad 0 < \alpha < 1 \tag{8}$$

In (8) K is the aggregate capital stock, and N_1 is the number of healthy workers.[6] The per capita production function becomes

$$y = k^{\alpha} h^{1-\alpha} \tag{9}$$

In (9) $h = N_1/N$ as previously. The representative firm's flow of profit π at any point is

$$\pi = N \left\{ k^{\alpha} h^{1-\alpha} - wh - (r + \delta)k \right\} \tag{10}$$

In (10) $r + \delta$ is the effective cost of capital, r the interest rate and δ is the rate of depreciation, and $k = K/N$. The first-order conditions for profit maximisation then yield:

$$r = \alpha k^{\alpha-1} h^{1-\alpha} - \delta \tag{11a}$$

$$w = (1 - \alpha)k^{\alpha} h^{-\alpha} \tag{11b}$$

The health status variable distinguishes equations (11a) and (11b) from the standard results.

Market equilibrium

We consider a closed economy model with no government. The assets accumulated by the households are used to finance the stock of capital, that is the interest rate mechanism will ensure $a = k$. Then using the household's flow budget constraint given in equation (5) and the conditions for r and w in equations (11a) and (11b) we get

$$\dot{k} = k^{\alpha} h^{1-\alpha} - (n + \delta)k - c \tag{12}$$

Moreover, substituting the interest rate in the solution of the household's optimisation problem – cf. equation (7) – yields

$$\frac{\dot{c}}{c} = \frac{1}{\theta}(\alpha k^{\alpha-1} h^{1-\alpha} - \rho - \delta) \tag{13}$$

Equations (12) and (13) construe the equations of motion in c and k.

The constant steady-state values for per capita consumption c and per capita capital stock k are determined by setting the expressions in equations (12) and (13) equal to zero:

$$\bar{k} = h \left(\frac{\alpha}{\rho + \delta} \right)^{1/(1-\alpha)} \tag{14a}$$

$$\bar{c} = h \left(\frac{\rho + \delta}{\alpha} - (n + \delta) \right) \left(\frac{\alpha}{\rho + \delta} \right)^{1/(1-\alpha)} \tag{14b}$$

In (14) a bar on top of a variable denotes steady-state. Note that the standard perfect-health Ramsey model's results are obtained when $h = 1$. With h smaller than unity, steady-state values of macroeconomic variables k, y, and c are lower than the respective standard perfect-health results. Figure 12.1 compares these two cases where 'ph' stands for 'perfect health' Ramsey results in the figure. The arrows of motion indicate the saddle-point stability of the steady state.

The steady-state analysis shows equilibrium values of c and k (and thus y) lower than in the perfect-health Ramsey model. In Figure 12.1 an exogenous increase in the health status of the economy – represented by an increase in h – shifts the $\dot{c} = 0$ line to the right and moves the $\dot{k} = 0$ curve up.[7] These shifts generate increases in $\bar{c}, \bar{k}$ and $\bar{y}$. This suggests that, in terms of its effects on growth, a change in the average health level of the population works in the same way as an exogenous change in the level of productivity in the Solow model. The crucial difference with productivity is that health has an upper limit, namely perfect health.

Our findings provide a theoretical background for using health status variables to characterise countries in conditional convergence analysis. A convergence analysis shows that h does not appear in the β-convergence coefficient – see Barro and Sala-i-Martin (1992, 1995) – for the reason that health status is assumed to be constant. Therefore h behaves in a similar way as an exogenous productivity parameter, which is not against the neoclassical conditional convergence argument.

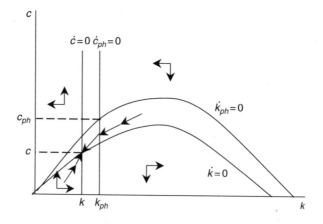

Figure 12.1 Market equilibria.

However, it is worth noting that h is neither constant nor exogenous in reality. In fact, health status and income affect each other.[8] Therefore, in the next section, we will endogenise the health measure to enrich our theoretical inquiry into the relationship between health status and per capita output and growth.

Endogenous health and growth

This section extends the previous analysis by assuming that the health status of the economy is endogenously determined within the model by allowing the representative household to optimise her health status in the consumption asset-accumulation trade-off. We first elaborate the specification of the production function of health status accumulation. Next, we discuss the representative household's trade-off when health status is endogenised and also elaborate the impact on market equilibrium. Finally, we analyse the implications for the relation between health and growth in the model at steady-state.

Endogenous health

As mentioned above we now assume that the health status is no longer exogenous, but health expenditures have to be made to maintain and improve health. These expenditures can be preventive (e.g. hindering dissemination of diseases) and/or curative (aiming to regain some sick labour). Both kinds of health expenditures are inevitable, because otherwise participation of labour in the production process is subject to a constant decay of the healthy labour stock. Actually we assume that in the absence of health expenditures, the number of healthy workers decreases at a rate v. However, this implies that workers who become sick fall only out of the labour market but they do not die. Therefore v is neither the mortality rate nor does it have any contribution to that rate.

Since we assume $v > n$, the number of healthy workers will decrease at a rate $v - n$. The impact of health expenditures X is to stop or slow down the constant decay of healthy labour and to bring the ratio of healthy labour to total labour, h, to some optimal level. We define the healthy workers' accumulation function as follows:

$$\dot{N}_1 = \zeta X^\beta N^{1-\beta} - (v - n)N_1 \quad 0 < \beta < 1 \tag{15}$$

where we assume that aggregate health expenditures X have decreasing returns, and ζ is a productivity parameter.[9] The generation of healthy labour N_1 depends on the existing stock of labour N as much as on preventive and curative health expenditures. This is so because health expenditures produce healthy labour from healthy labour (preventive effect) or from sick workers (curative effect).[10]

Since the Inada (1963) conditions hold for the production function (8), each factor of production is necessary for positive output. This implies that health expenditures are necessary and inevitable in this model. To see this, suppose for the moment that health expenditures are zero. Then, from equation (15), it is clear that the healthy labour stock would 'depreciate' at a constant rate. This would force (healthy) labour to zero at some point in time and thus output would be zero. Since the marginal return is very high as any factor of production approaches zero, the representative household would always prefer to incur some positive amount of health expenditures.

We can rewrite equation (15) by defining preventive and curative health expenditures per person $x = X/N$ and using the relationship $\dot{h}/h = \dot{N_1}/N_1 - \dot{N}/N$, which yields:

$$\frac{\dot{h}}{h} = \zeta x^{\beta} h^{-1} - v \tag{16}$$

This relation should be added as an additional constraint to the household optimisation process.

The household's trade-off

As a consequence of the necessity of health expenditures, households face a trade-off that endogenously determines the health status of an economy. On the one hand, by being healthier they participate more in the production process and therefore contribute positively to their welfare at any instant of time. On the other hand, they incur some health expenditures, which is foregone consumption, to maintain or improve their healthiness. This trade-off shows up in the intertemporal budget constraint, where health expenditures are at the detriment of asset accumulation:

$$\dot{a} = wh + (r - n)a - c - x \tag{17}$$

The constraints to maximisation of the utility function (1) are now not only the amended budget constraint (17), but also the healthy worker's accumulation function (16). This defines the dynamic optimisation process, in which households determine the optimal health status they would like to have.

The present-value Hamiltonian becomes

$$J = \frac{c^{1-\theta} - 1}{1 - \theta} e^{-(\rho - n)t} + \lambda\{wh + (r - n)a - c - x\} + \mu(\zeta x^{\beta} h^{-1} - v)h \tag{18}$$

In (18) c and x are the choice variables, a and h are the state variables, and λ and μ are the co-state variables.[11]

By solving equation (18) through the method of optimum control, one finds that the optimal path for consumption still is given by equation (7). This implies that as usual the interest rate determines consumption growth. The optimal path for health expenditures is given by

$$\dot{x} = \frac{v + r - n}{1 - \beta} x - \frac{\beta \zeta}{1 - \beta} w x^{\beta} \tag{19}$$

This should be considered simultaneous with the path for health creation (16) – we elaborate this in the next section.

Market equilibrium

Although firm behaviour is not directly affected by expenditures on health, one should realise that health also affects marginal productivity of both labour and capital and hence both the interest rate and the wage rate, as can be seen from equations (11a) and (11b), respectively. Moreover, since the accumulation of assets is influenced by health expenditures, the accumulation of capital will be too. We will return to that later on. First we discuss the dynamic process between health expenditures and health creation.

Note that substitution of (11a) and (11b) in the equation of motion for health expenditures, x, yields:

$$\dot{x} = \frac{v - n + \alpha(h/k)^{1-\alpha} - \delta}{1 - \beta} x - \frac{\beta\zeta(1-\alpha)}{1-\beta}\left(\frac{k}{h}\right)^{\alpha} x^{\beta} \qquad (20)$$

The dynamics between health expenditures and health creation then can be shown for any given value of the capital stock k, using equations (20) and (16), respectively. This is elaborated in Figure 12.2 where one sees that the $\dot{x} = 0$ line is decreasing in h and the $\dot{h} = 0$ line is increasing. Moreover, the equations of motion show that this part of the system is saddle-point stable. The equilibrium values, as functions of k, then are:

$$h^*(k) = \frac{\zeta}{\mu}\left[\frac{\beta\zeta(1-\alpha)}{(v-\delta-n)(h^*(k)/k)^{\alpha} + \alpha(h^*(k))/k}\right]^{\beta/(1-\beta)} \qquad (21a)$$

and

$$x^*(k) = \left[\frac{v}{\zeta}h^*(k)\right]^{1/\beta} \qquad (21b)$$

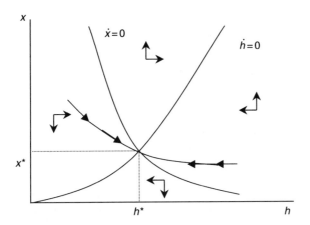

Figure 12.2 Stability of the health sector.

From Figure 12.2 one also sees that the saddle-path shows a negative relation between health expenditures and health. This is plausible since optimal health expenditures will be relatively high when health is relatively bad and vice versa, because health expenditures are an investment in the production factor labour.[12]

A problem with this partial analysis is that a simultaneous movement of k will shift the stationary line for x and the saddle-path of Figure 12.2. If, e.g., the movement goes from high to low x and from low to high h, the steady state is approached from the left. However, a simultaneous increase in k, moving up the curves, reinforces the increase in h but counteracts the decrease of x. This raises the question which of the two effects on x is stronger.

Analogous to equation (12), the accumulation function of capital is found from the budget constraint given in equation (17) to be:

$$\dot{k} = k^\alpha h^{1-\alpha} - (n + \delta)k - c - x \tag{22}$$

A second problem is that movements in h and x shift the stationary lines of Figure 12.2. Thus, we have to deal with the interaction of the variables c, k, h, x as captured in the equations (13), (16), (20) and (22). Although it is clear that our concave Hamiltonian function will result in a unique optimal growth path, it is far from clear what the dynamic process exactly looks like.

Theorems 5.3 and 5.4 in Feichtinger and Hartl (1986) provide conditions under which a linear approximation of a 4×4 system *in connection with dynamic optimisation* – i.e. of the so-called canonical system – will have two positive and two negative *real* roots (see appendix B in Muysken *et al.* (1999) for details).[13] In this case the constants of the two positive roots can be put equal to zero. Otherwise it would explode, which cannot be optimal. Consequently, the system for the analysis of local stability can be split up into two parts: First, the dynamics of h and k is considered *separately*; second, the dynamics of k and h is fed back into that of c and x, both in a very simple way. This separation avoids the feed back of c and x into the (k, h)-system and makes the whole problem tractable.

Unfortunately, we can prove some of the conditions critical to the application of the theorem only numerically (see appendix C in Muysken *et al.* 1999). Here we focus on the results. The parameter values used in the numerical approximation are the following: We put the rate of capital depreciation at $\delta = 0.03$ in accordance with national accounting results (see Mankiw *et al.* 1992). The share of capital is assumed to be $\alpha = 0.3$; the rate of time preference is set equal to $\rho = 0.06$ in order to make sure that $y/k = 0.3$ in accordance with equation (A.9). We use $n = 0.01$ as in Barro and Sala-i-Martin (1995). Next we fix $v = 0.02$ and $\beta = 0.5$ which make sure that health expenditure as a share of GDP is about 10 per cent in the steady-state[14] and consumption is between 70 and 80 per cent, 76.67 per cent for our values. Finally, we fix $\zeta = 0.045$ which makes sure that $h < 1$ in the steady state and allows us to avoid corner solutions for $h = 1$. Using these values we show in appendix C in Muysken *et al.* (1999) that the conditions of the theorem hold and derive the lines for the stationary loci for h and k (see Figure 12.3).

Both lines turn out to have positive slopes in (h, k)-space. The slope of the stationary line for k is 15 per cent and the slope of the line for h is about 7 per cent.

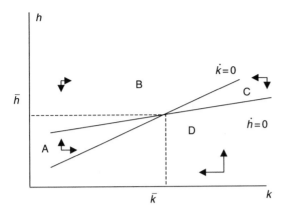

Figure 12.3 Steady-state solution.

Arrows in Figure 12.3 indicate that the system is stable for any given initial values of h and k. Hence k and h will always converge towards their steady-state values. When the initial values of k and h are in region B, k/h will increase whereas in region D it will decrease. In regions A and C the ratio k/h can both increase and decrease when moving towards the steady state.

For a better interpretation of Figure 12.3, we consider the case of low capital per capita, i.e. $k < \bar{k}$. Good examples of region D (with low health per capita and low capital per capita) and region B (with high health status and low capital per capita) are 'Africa' and 'Cuba', respectively. When health status increases due to positive health expenditures in region D (Africa), then k/h ratio will decrease due to rising health and falling capital. On the other hand, if capital accumulation is started to be given priority as in Cuba and the dynamics starts in region B, then the k/h ratio will increase due to the fact that more (less) resources will be reserved for capital accumulation (improving healthiness).

The implications for consumption of the movement of k/h towards the steady-state follow from equation (13). This is drawn in Figure 12.4, putting k/h on the horizontal and c on the vertical axis. If k/h starts below (above) its steady-state value and therefore increases (decreases), the change in c must be positive (negative). By implication, the initial value of c must be below (above) its steady-state value.

The implications for health expenditures, x, of the movement of k/h toward the steady-state follow from equation (20). Figure 12.5 shows the dynamics of health expenditure conditional on k/h. One sees that in the neighbourhood of the steady state $\dot{x}$ has the property $\partial \dot{x}/\partial x > 0$, which means that equation (20) is unstable for given values of k/h. As a consequence the process to a steady state requires that changes in health expenditures are accompanied by changes in k/h, and health expenditures can only adjust to their steady-state level by shifts of k/h. Since the *temporary stationary* value of x increases with the ratio k/h,[15] an increase

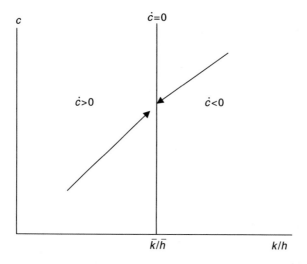

Figure 12.4 Implications for consumption of the movement of k/h towards the steady state.

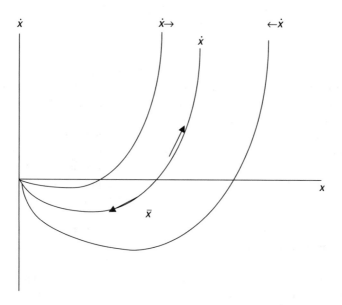

Figure 12.5 Dynamics of health expenditure.

Table 12.1 Gaps and dynamics of the capital–health ratio, consumption and health expenditure

Country/variable	$k/h - (\bar{k}/\bar{h})$	$c - \bar{c}$	$x - \bar{x}$	k/h	c	x
Cuba	–	–	–	↑	↑	↑
Africa	+	+	+	↓	↓	↓

(decrease) of k/h therefore shifts the stationary point to the right (left). If k/h increases (decreases) on its way to the steady state according to Figure 12.3 as in our example of 'Cuba' ('Africa'), x must be to the right (left) of the *temporary stationary* value of x but below the steady-state value of x, $\bar{x}$, and the change in x must therefore be positive (negative) until it comes to a halt through the shift in the $\dot{x}$ line and its stationary point at $\bar{x}$. In other words, if k/h is below (above) its steady-state value the value for optimal health expenditure x is below (above) its steady-state value and increasing (decreasing). Therefore, similar to optimal consumption, the health expenditures depend on the values of k/h in the transition, relative to those in the steady state. Optimal health and consumption expenditures are below their steady-state values in the transition to the steady state if the ratio of the stocks of capital and health is below (above) its steady-state value. Table 12.1 summarises the results. If physical capital relative to health is relatively scarce (abundant) as in our case of 'Cuba' ('Africa') compared to its steady-state value. Hence the gap $k/h - \bar{k}/\bar{h}$ is negative (positive), which requires negative (positive) gaps in consumption and health expenditures, $c - \bar{c}$, $x - \bar{x}$, respectively in order to reach the steady state. Therefore optimal expenditures for health and consumption are lower (higher) and increasing (decreasing) as is the ratio of k/h itself.

The impact of health parameters

It is interesting to analyse the impact of the characteristics of the health sector on the outcome of the model. The steady-state value of the health index is:

$$\bar{h} = \left(\frac{\beta(1-\alpha)}{v+\rho-n} \left(\frac{\alpha}{(\rho+\delta)} \right)^{\alpha/(1-\alpha)} \right)^{\beta/(1-\beta)} \frac{\zeta^{1/(1-\beta)}}{v} \qquad (23)$$

The steady-state health expenditures are:

$$\bar{x} = \left(\frac{\beta\zeta(1-\alpha)}{\rho-n+v} \left(\frac{\alpha}{(\rho+\delta)} \right)^{\alpha/(1-\alpha)} \right)^{1/(1-\beta)} \qquad (24)$$

The health sector is characterised mainly by its productivity ζ, the population growth rate n, and the rate of decay of health v. The impact of these parameters on the steady state of the model is summarised in Table 12.2.

From Table 12.2 one sees that an increase in productivity ζ affects all steady-state variables in a positive way. It seems rather obvious that an increase in productivity

Table 12.2 Impact of health parameters on the steady state

Steady-state value of parameters	y	c	k	h	x
ζ	+	+	+	+	+
n	+	?	+	+	+
v	−	−	−	−	−

in health care will lead to an improvement in health, *ceteris paribus*. This will enhance both capital accumulation and consumption. Hence output and the capital stock will increase too. Finally, the increase of health expenditures follows from a higher marginal return from these expenditures in the trade-off with consumption and investment in physical capital.

The negative impact of an increased rate of decay v on health is plausible because a higher rate directly means more sick workers. There also is an indirect effect through lower health expenditures, which result from a diminished marginal productivity of these expenditures. The negative effects on consumption, output and capital follow directly.

Finally, higher population growth n has a positive effect on health expenditures because it increases their productivity. The effects on capital and output then follow directly. The impact on consumption is ambiguous, however, because, on the one hand, consumption is affected negatively by population growth in the perfect health situation (as in Cass–Koopmans). However, the steady-state value of k also appears in the end of the expression for c. It depends on that of h because health is directly affected positively as can be seen from (15). This produces a positive incentive to increase health expenditure as can be seen from (24). In sum, as in Cass–Koopmans the c/k ratio is negatively related to population growth, but the optimal c not necessarily decreases with population growth.[16]

Concluding remarks

In this paper we have investigated optimal health expenditure and consumption by adding a health accumulation function to the Cass–Koopmans optimum-growth model.

The major finding was that optimal health expenditure and consumption in the transition to the steady state are below (above) their steady-state values if the ratio of the stocks of capital and health is below (above) its steady-state value. In other words, if physical capital relative to health is relatively scarce (abundant) compared to the steady-state values, optimal expenditures for health and consumption are lower (higher) than in the steady-state but increase (decrease) on their way towards it.

This result was found with the help of a theorem that allows separating the analysis of the dynamics of the state variables from that of the control variables. However, results could only be obtained for one set of parameter values for which the theorem could be applied. Other parameter values may lead to more complicated solutions. But so far we have no indication that such a set of parameter values can be found for reasonable orders of magnitude of the variables of the model. The search for other constellations is left for future research.

A second finding was that steady-state consumption is no longer necessarily negatively related to population growth (as it is in the standard model) because it enhances the steady-state percentage of healthy workers under the assumption of the health accumulation function used. An interesting alternative to this function is the epidemic health function used by Cuddington *et al.* (1994). However, none of the two functions is obviously better suited to modelling health processes then the other.

The main conclusion of this study is the observation that there exists a two-way relationship between health and economic development (growth). Causal observation shows that low-income (low capital-accumulation) countries are also those countries that have low health status, by and large. Our analysis shows that these countries need improvement in health in order to support a balanced growth of health and capital as in regions A and C in Figure 12.3, or, in region D, even at cost of an initial decrease in capital accumulation. We argue that this finding is a clear message to policy-makers that health must not be considered as a cost that must be avoided as much as possible but a factor supporting development and growth.

Finally, the limits that some readers may see for the Cass–Koopmans model are of course also limits of our analysis. One of these limits is the absence of endogenous growth. The transitional relation between health and technical change will be an interesting subject for future research.

Notes

1 This point has been brought to our attention by Knowles and Owen (1995, 1997).
2 We suppressed the time arguments for simplicity.
3 This approach is quite similar to that in van Zon and Muysken (2001) who also define productive labour as hN, where h represents the health status.
4 Our argument, nevertheless, does not mean that it is wrong to use these or other health status variables – see OECD (1999) for a rich set of health status variables.
5 Since the utility function (1) satisfies the Inada (1963) conditions we know that consumption will always be a positive finite number.
6 In Yetkiner (2000) it is argued that external effects in specification of production function becomes crucial when the public provision of health is considered, which falls out of the aims of this study.
7 For example, any exogenous development in curative or preventive medical technology may be the source of that shift.
8 As an example, look at Carrin and Politi (1995) to see the 'concave' relationship between life expectancy and real GDP per capita and the 'rectangular hyperbolic' relationship between infant mortality rate and real GDP per capita for 1990. Causality tests between

life expectancy and real GDP per capita for high, middle and low income countries show that the direction of causality changes from one to another as the income group changes, cf. Mazumdar (1996). Similar results are found for infant survival rate.

9 van Zon and Muysken (2001) use a similar function, except that they use productive labour to counter this decay.

10 Equation (15) is, in essence, a customary stock variable accumulation function frequently used in the growth literature. See, for example, Barro and Sala-i-Martin (1995).

11 See Appendix A for a complete solution of the optimum version of the model. Equations (11a) and (11b) are still applicable because the market solution and that of the central planner are the same.

12 Remember that h is not an argument in the utility function.

13 Readers not familiar with German may have a look at Turnovsky (1981).

14 The business press reports that health expenditures as a percentage of GDP are 6.7 per cent in the UK, 13.9 per cent in the US and slightly below 10 per cent in the Netherlands and Germany. Therefore fixing it at about 10 per cent is a reasonable order of magnitude.

15 The stationary value of x from equation (20) can be calculated as

$$x_{|\dot{x}=0} = \left[\frac{v - n - \delta + \alpha(k/h)^{\alpha-1}}{\beta\zeta(1-\alpha)(k/h)^{\alpha}} \right]^{1/(\beta-1)}$$

As the exponent is negative, the stationary value of x increases with k/h.

16 More technically, consumption is affected negatively by population growth in the perfect health situation (as in Cass–Koopmans) as can be seen also from the direct effects appearing in equation (A.16). However, the steady-state value of k also appears in the end of the expression for c. It depends on that of h (according to equation (A.12)) and that is positively affected by n as health expenditure was.

References

Barro, R.J. (1991) 'Economic Growth in a Cross-Section of Countries', *Quarterly Journal of Economics*, 106: 407–43.

Barro, R.J. and Sala-i-Martin, X. (1992) 'Convergence', *Journal of Political Economy*, 100: 223–51.

——(1995) *Economic Growth*, New York: McGraw-Hill.

Bloom, D.E. and Mahal, A.S. (1995) 'Does the AIDS Epidemic Really Threaten Economic Growth', NBER Working Paper No. 5148.

Carrin, G. and Politi, C. (1995) 'Exploring the Health Impact of Economic Growth, Poverty Reduction and Public Health Expenditure', *Tijdschrift Voor Economie en Management*, 40: 227–46.

Cass, D. (1965) 'Optimum Growth in an Aggregative Model of Capital Accumulation', *Review of Economic Studies*, 32: 233–40.

Cuddington, J.T., Hancock, J.D. and Rogers, C.A. (1994) 'A Dynamic Aggregative Model of the AIDS Epidemic with Possible Policy Interventions', *Journal of Policy Modelling*, 16: 473–96.

Feichtinger, G. and Hartl, R.F. (1986) *Optimale Kontrolle Ökonomischer Prozesse*, Berlin: de Gruyter.

Inada, K. (1963) 'On a Two-Sector Model of Economic Growth: Comments and a Generalisation', *Review of Economic Studies*, 30: 119–27.

Knowles, S. and Owen, D.P. (1995) 'Health Capital and Cross-Country Variation in Per Capita in the Mankiw–Romer–Weil Model', *Economics Letters*, 48: 99–106.

Knowles, S. and Owen, D.P. (1997) 'Education and Health in an Effective-Labour Empirical Growth Model', *Economic Record*, 73: 314–28.

Koopmans, T. (1965) 'On the Concept of Optimal Economic Growth', in *The Econometric Approach to Development Planning*, Amsterdam: North-Holland.

Lucas, R.E., Jr. (1988) 'On the Mechanics of Economic Development', *Journal of Monetary Economics*, 22: 3–42.

Mankiw, N.G., Romer D. and Weil, D.N. (1992) 'A Contribution to the Empirics of Economic Growth', *Quarterly Journal of Economics*, 107: 407–37.

Mazumdar, K. (1996) 'An Analysis of Causal Flow Between Social Development and Economic Growth: the Social Development Index', *American Journal of Economics and Sociology*, 55: 361–83.

Mushkin, S.J. (1962) 'Health as an Investment', *Journal of Political Economy*, 70: S129–57.

Muysken, J., Yetkiner, İ.H. and Ziesemer, T. (1999) 'Health, Labour Productivity and Growth', MERIT, Working Paper No: 2/99-030, Maastricht, The Netherlands. Available online at http://meritbbs.unimaas.nl/rmpdf/rmlist99.html (13 Dec. 2000).

OECD (1999) *OECD Health Data 1999: A Comparative Analysis of 29 Countries*, Paris.

Schultz, T.W. (1961) 'Investment in Human Capital', *American Economic Review*, 51: 1–17.

Turnovsky, S.J. (1981) 'The Optimal Intertemporal Choice of Inflation and Unemployment', *Journal of Economic Dynamics and Control*, 3: 357–84.

Yetkiner, İ.H. (2000) 'A Dynamic General Equilibrium Model of Health', mimeo, University of Groningen.

van Zon, A.H. and Muysken, J. (2001) 'Health, Education and Endogenous Growth', *Journal of Health Economics*, 20: 169–85.

Appendix A

The *current-value Hamiltonian* for the central planner's problem is

$$H = \frac{c^{1-\theta} - 1}{1 - \theta} e^{nt} + \lambda \{ K^\alpha N_1^{1-\alpha} - cN - X - \delta K \} + \mu \{ \zeta X^\beta N^{1-\beta} - (v-n)N_1 \}$$

(A.1)

λ and μ are the co-state variables. The *first-order conditions* are following:

$$\frac{\partial H}{\partial c} = c^{-\theta} - \lambda = 0$$

(A.2)

$$\frac{\partial H}{\partial X} = -\lambda + \mu \zeta \beta x^{\beta-1} = 0$$

(A.3)

$$-\frac{\partial H}{\partial K} = \dot{\lambda} - \rho\lambda = -\lambda(\alpha K^{\alpha-1} N_1^{1-\alpha} - \delta)$$

(A.4)

$$-\frac{\partial H}{\partial N_1} = \dot{\mu} - \rho\mu = -\lambda K^\alpha (1-\alpha) N_1^{-\alpha} + \mu(v-n)$$

$$= -\lambda(k/h)^\alpha (1-\alpha) + \mu(v-n)$$

(A.5)

$$\frac{\partial H}{\partial \lambda} = \dot{K} = K^\alpha N_1^{1-\alpha} - cN - X - \delta K \tag{A.6}$$

$$\frac{\partial H}{\partial \mu} = \dot{N}_1 = \zeta X^\beta N^{1-\beta} - (v - n)N_1 \tag{A.7}$$

Solving (A.2) for c and (A.3) for x and using the definitions for k and h yields the *canonical system*:

$$\dot{k} = k^\alpha h^{1-\alpha} - \lambda^{-1/\theta} - \left[\frac{\lambda}{\mu\beta\zeta}\right]^{1/(\beta-1)} - (n+\delta)k \tag{A.6'}$$

$$\dot{h} = \zeta \left[\frac{\lambda}{\mu\zeta\beta}\right]^{-\beta/(1-\beta)} - vh \tag{A.7'}$$

$$\dot{\lambda} = \lambda[\rho - \alpha(k/h)^{\alpha-1} + \delta] \tag{A.4'}$$

$$\dot{\mu} = \mu(v - n + \rho) - \lambda(1 - \alpha)(k/h)^\alpha \tag{A.5'}$$

Steady-state solutions

In a situation of steady-state growth k, h, λ and μ would have to be constant as would c and x.

$$\hat{y} = \hat{k} = \hat{h} = \hat{c} = \hat{x} = \hat{\lambda} = \hat{\mu} = 0 \tag{A.8}$$

From (A.4') we get

$$\frac{\bar{y}}{\bar{k}} = \frac{\rho + \delta}{\alpha} \tag{A.9}$$

Setting (A.7') equal to zero yields

$$\frac{\lambda}{\mu} = \left[\frac{vh}{\zeta}\right]^{(1-\beta)/-\beta} \zeta\beta \tag{A.10}$$

Setting (A.5') equal to zero yields (using (A.9) in the second equation below)

$$\left(\frac{\lambda}{\mu}\right) = \frac{v - n + \rho}{(1 - \alpha)(k/h)^\alpha} = \frac{v - n + \rho}{(1 - \alpha)((\rho + \delta)/\alpha)^{-\alpha/(1-\alpha)}} \tag{A.11}$$

In order to get positive shadow prices the numerator must be positive. Equating (A.10) and (A.11) and solving for h yields (where $\bar{h} \le 1$ by definition)

$$\bar{h} = \left[\frac{v - n + \rho}{\zeta\beta(1 - \alpha)((\rho + \delta)/\alpha)^{-\alpha/(1-\alpha)}}\right]^{-\beta/(1-\beta)} \frac{\zeta}{v} < 1 \tag{A.12}$$

Equations (A.3), (A.10) and (A.12) yield a solution for steady-state health expenditure:

$$\bar{x} = \left[\frac{\beta\zeta(1 - \alpha)}{\rho - n + v}\left(\frac{\alpha}{\rho + \delta}\right)^{\alpha/(1-\alpha)}\right]^{1/(1-\beta)} \tag{A.13}$$

Equations (A.9), (A.12) and the production function yield

$$\bar{k} = \left(\frac{\rho + \delta}{\alpha}\right)^{-1/(1-\alpha)} \bar{h} \tag{A.14}$$

From production function and equation (A.9), it follows that

$$\bar{y} = \left(\frac{\alpha}{\rho + \delta}\right)^{\alpha/(1-\alpha)} \bar{h} \tag{A.15}$$

We obtain the steady-state value of consumption and for λ from equations (A.2) and (A.6'):

$$\bar{c} = \left\{\frac{\rho + \delta}{\alpha} - (n + \delta) - \left(\frac{\rho + \delta}{\alpha} \frac{(1 - \alpha)v\beta}{\rho - n + v}\right)\right\} \bar{k} \tag{A.16}$$

$$\bar{\lambda} = \{\bar{k}^\alpha \bar{h}^{1-\alpha} - \bar{x} - (n + \delta)\bar{k}\}^{-\theta} \tag{A.17}$$

Finally, (A.5') or (A.11) yield

$$\bar{\mu} = \bar{\lambda} \frac{(1 - \alpha)((\rho + \delta)/\alpha)^{-\alpha/(1-\alpha)}}{v - n + \rho} \tag{A.18}$$

Part V

The empirics of growth

13 The importance of capital stock in unemployment and wage determination

An empirical investigation

Philip Arestis and Iris Biefang-Frisancho Mariscal

Introduction

The purpose of this chapter is to discuss and test empirically the relevance of capital stock in wage and unemployment determination. This is purely an empirical investigation where data from Germany and the UK are utilised. The theoretical underpinnings can be found in Rowthorn (1999). Arestis and Biefang-Frisancho Mariscal (1997, 1998) offer further theoretical developments and provide empirical evidence which is supportive of the notion that capital stock is a significant contributory factor to the determination of wages and unemployment.

The following section of the chapter summarises a theoretical wage model, the details of which can be found in Arestis and Biefang-Frisancho Mariscal (1997, 1998) where the capital shortage hypothesis is also accounted for. This model draws and extends the ideas in Rowthorn (1999), the essence of which is that demand elements are important in any form of NAIRU one might care to adopt. The main objective of this section is thus to show that capital shortage may cause persistent unemployment even when the initial adverse shock is reversed. The section on 'Empirical investigation' is concerned with estimation and testing of wages and unemployment in Germany and the UK using recently developed econometric techniques. The last section summarises and concludes.

Formalising the role of capital stock in wage and unemployment determination

A summary of the theoretical model

In this section we begin with a summary of the main ideas of a theoretical model that aims to explain the determination of wages and unemployment. This model has been put forward in Arestis and Biefang-Frisancho Mariscal (1997, 1998). The main concern of this section is to provide a full justification of the effect of capital shortage on wages and unemployment, thus extending our previous work.

The theoretical wage model presented in Arestis and Biefang-Frisancho Mariscal (1997, 1998), is based on the shirking model by Shapiro and Stiglitz (1984), where the equilibrium real wage is determined by labour productivity. For a given real wage, workers' productivity depends on the cost of job loss, which rises with an increase in the current real wage (W/P) and rising unemployment (U). It falls with higher expected real unemployment benefits (W_u^e/P^e) and higher outside wages (W^e/P^e). There are also other factors that affect effort and real wages. Workers are concerned about their relative position in the wage hierarchy and the expected real wage (W^e/P^e) is a benchmark below which it is impossible to set wages (Keynes 1936; Hicks 1975). Furthermore, high levels of unemployment do not insinuate high-wage pressure or workers' effort when the composition of unemployment has changed towards an increase in the long-term unemployed. This is so because the long-term unemployed effectively dropped out of the labour market (Nickell 1987).

Wages are negotiated on the basis of expected price inflation (P^e). Price inflation depends on the degree of conflict over income distribution between firms, workers, the government and the foreign sectors (Rowthorn 1977). The degree of conflict is measured by the aspiration gap (A) and worker militancy (X). Considering the model we have summarised above, we may write the negotiated nominal wage more formally as:

$$W_{t+1} = P^e k[(W^e/P^e), (W_u^e/P^e), LU, U, A] \qquad (1)$$
$$\quad\quad + \quad\quad\quad + \quad\quad + - + $$

where the sign under a variable denotes its first derivative. The aspiration gap is defined as the difference between firms' target and the negotiated profit shares (which is a residuum of the wage settlement process). Firms can raise their target profit share at a given level of taxes (T) and claims of the foreign sector (F), when demand conditions in the product market are favourable. Capacity utilization is used as an indicator for product demand and it is explained by the level of capital stock (K) and unemployment, where the latter serves as a proxy for economic activity (Rowthorn 1995). A fall in economic activity and/or a rise in capital stock reduce capacity utilisation and thus firms' ability to increase target profit shares. Consequently, the wage share rises *ceteris paribus*. Replacing A in equation (1) by the relevant variables that determine the aspiration gap, we may rewrite the negotiated wage as:

$$W_{t+1} = P^e k[(W^e/P^e), (W_u^e/P^e), LU, U, K, X, F, T] \qquad (2)$$
$$\quad\quad + \quad\quad\quad + \quad + - + + + + $$

If the aspiration gap is zero, which is the same as to say that price inflation is as expected, equilibrium unemployment can be derived from equation (1) as:

$$U = U[K, F, T, X, LU, (W_u/P)] \qquad (3)$$
$$\quad - + + + + \quad + $$

where the NAIRU is a declining function of capital stock.

The capital shortage hypothesis

The model we have just put forward may be utilised to elaborate the capital shortage hypothesis (see also Bean 1989; Carlin and Soskice 1990; and Rowthorn 1995, 1999). This is pursued with the help of Figure 13.1. On the vertical axis profit shares (Π^*, Π^n) are measured and on the horizontal axis unemployment at varying levels of capital stock [$U(K)$] and, implicitly varying levels of capacity utilization (Φ), are shown. The kinked curves describe firms' target profit shares (Π^*) in response to varying levels of capacity utilization. Firms increase profit shares (Π^*) when capacity utilization is above its desired level, which is shown in Figure 13.1 by the vertical and downward-sloping sections of the Π^*-curves. If the economy operates with maximum capacity (for a given capital stock), the corresponding lowest unemployment rate is denoted as $U^L(K)$. The vertical section of the Π^* curve shows pricing behaviour when maximum capacity is reached and the downward-sloping parts relate to the strategic spare capacity. When capacity is not fully utilised, firms' pricing is downward sticky, which we indicate by the rather flat part of the Π^*-curves. The upward-sloping curves describe negotiated profit shares (Π^n), as a result of wage negotiations, which rise in tandem with unemployment.

As our starting point, we may explain the conditions of the capital and labour markets at point A. Firms operate the given capital stock K_0 with desired capacity (Φ^*), indicating equilibrium in the capital market.[11] Since the negotiated and the target profit shares are equal, point A also describes a labour market equilibrium where unemployment is at its equilibrium level $U^*(K_0)$. The effect of a temporary demand shock on unemployment and capital accumulation may be gauged, using Figure 13.1. We will show that although the adverse shock may be temporary, the NAIRU rises and persists at a new, higher, level. We may use as a trigger for the demand shock, increased claims of the foreign sector. This would reduce income available for distribution between workers and employers which causes conflict in the labour market over who should bear the increased burden. As a result, inflation rises and in order to bring inflation down, governments introduce restrictive demand policies. Restrictive demand policies result in a fall in capacity utilisation and an increase in unemployment. In Figure 13.1, we move from point A to the right, say towards B. At point B, unemployment has risen and capacity utilisation has fallen. With the given capital stock K_0, firms' actual capacity is higher than desired. In response to excess capacity, investment declines and capital stock falls to K_1. With the fall in capital stock to K_1, the unemployment rate that is consistent with firms' desired capacity utilization is $U(K_1)$ – the labour market is not at equilibrium, of course.

If now it is assumed that restrictive demand policies are abandoned, capacity utilisation rises, unemployment falls and firms increase mark-ups. In Figure 13.1, there is a tendency to move back from point B towards A, and point A will only be reached if changes in demand for labour and changes in capital stock do not affect the labour market. Factor substitutability is low and previous employment levels cannot be achieved unless additional capital is installed.[2] This is the argument of the capital-shortage hypothesis. The installation of additional productive capital

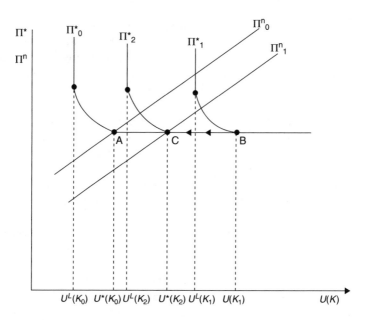

Figure 13.1 Profit share and unemployment.

is sluggish so that the composition of the unemployed changes in favour of a rise in the long-term unemployed.[3] This strengthens the position of the insiders and rising wage pressure shifts the Π^n-curve to the right. The rise in capacity utilisation stimulates investment and capital stock increases to K_2. At point C, firms operate with 'normal' capacity (Φ^*), which implies a level of unemployment of $U^*(K_2)$. Furthermore, at C, the Π_2^n-curve cuts the Π_2^*-curve so that $U^*(K_2)$ is the NAIRU corresponding to capital stock K_2. It is higher than the pre-recession NAIRU $U^*(K_0)$. Since capacity utilisation is at its desired level and since the labour market is in equilibrium, too, there is no market mechanism that would revert the NAIRU to its pre-shock level. It thus appears to be possible that an economy is locked into a situation of persistently high unemployment while operating with 'normal' capacity utilisation (Φ^*).

The most frequent argument of the opponents of the capital-shortage hypothesis is that capital-shortage unemployment is a short-run phenomenon and that it is downward inflexibility of wages that prevents a return to previous unemployment levels (Blanchard and Summers 1986; Lindbeck 1993). Furthermore, no policy measures discriminating in favour of investment are necessary, for there is no obvious market failure involved (Bean 1989). Turning to the first argument, the opponents of the capital-shortage hypothesis assume implicitly a high substitutability between labour and capital. A fall in real wages can only increase employment if firms substitute the cheaper factor labour against capital. However, numerous empirical studies show that substitutability is rather limited. In this case, a drastic fall in real wages increases mainly profit margins with only some effect on employment. We argued before that slow capital accumulation in the recovery does not only prevent unemployment from falling, but also reduces effective labour supply, thus enforcing the problem of persistently high unemployment. Policies that address the speed with which new capacity is installed may prevent, for example, insider effects in the labour market.

Empirical investigation

Estimable equations

We proceed to formulate the equations to be estimated, by assuming that expectations are formed as a random walk as in Nickell (1990). After some basic algebraic transformations, the equation for nominal wage acceleration ($\Delta \Delta w_t$) is derived (Arestis and Biefang-Frisancho Mariscal 1997, 1998):

$$\Delta \Delta w_t = \alpha_1 l p_t + \alpha_2 \Delta l p_t - \alpha_3 (w - p)_t - \alpha_4 \Delta (w - p)_t + \alpha_5 (w_u - p)_t$$
$$+ \alpha_6 \Delta (w_u - p)_t + \alpha_7 X_t + \alpha_8 t i_t + \alpha_9 \Delta t i_t + \alpha_{10} k_t$$
$$+ \alpha_{11} \Delta k_t + h(U) \tag{4}$$

where lower-case letters denote the logarithm of a variable and where $h(U)$ captures the unemployment rate (U), the ratio of the long-term unemployed (LU) and changes in the unemployment rate (ΔU). The long-run real wage equation can be obtained by setting $\Delta(w - p)$, $\Delta(w_u - p)$, $\Delta l p$, $\Delta t i$, Δu and Δk equal to zero to give:

$$(w - p - lp) = \beta_1 (w_u - p) + \beta_2 X - \beta_3 U + \beta_4 LU + \beta_5 t i + \beta_6 k \tag{5}$$

where the dependent variable is the real wage per unit of output, which implies that we assume productivity neutrality with respect to unemployment. Although the model itself does not impose this restriction this assumption is backed widely by empirical results (Manning1992; Elmskov 1993). We further assume that the NAIRU relationship is linear so that we may write:

$$U = \gamma_1 (w_u - p) + \gamma_2 x + \gamma_3 t i - \gamma_4 k + \gamma_5 LU \tag{6}$$

Data: nature, definitions and sources

The model is estimated using quarterly and seasonally adjusted data for the period 1966q1–1995q4 for the UK, which is dictated by data availability. For Germany, the model was estimated for the slightly shorter period, 1968q1–1994q4 and from 1991 onwards it includes unified Germany. We define and discuss briefly each variable that is used in the estimations, beginning with the UK. 'Real wages' ($w - p - lp$) is defined as real hourly average earnings per unit of output, where 'average earnings' is deflated by the consumer price index; labour productivity

(LP) is calculated as the ratio of output GDP to total employment; 'long-term unemployed' (LU) is calculated as the ratio of the unemployed who are so for more than 52 weeks over all unemployed; 'ti' accounts for claims by the foreign and government sectors and is defined as the gap between consumer and product wage, calculated as: $ti = ter + td + (p_c - p)$, where ter is the tax paid by employers, td is the tax rate on employee earnings, p_c is the consumer price deflator and p is GDP price deflator; finally the (non-residential) business sector capital stock variable is denoted as (k).

The definition of variables for Germany now follows. The variable 'real wage' refers to total wages and salaries, weighted by total employment, average hours worked and the consumer price deflator. The wedge variable 'ti' was calculated as a fourth quarter moving average: $ti = (w_{gr} - w_{net}) + (p_c - p)$ where w_{gr} are gross wages and salaries and w_{net} are net wages and salaries, respectively. The variables p and p_c are defined as for the UK. The capital stock variable is the (non-residential) capital stock of the business sector as defined by the OECD.

The data for the UK were collected from various issues of Economic Trends: UK Economic Accounts (A&B), Department of Employment Gazette, OECD Business Sector Database, and Annual Abstract of Statistics. The data for Germany come from Deutsche Bundesbank-Saisonbereinigte Wirtschaftszahlen, Amtliche Nachrichten der Bundesanstalt für Arbeit, Deutsches Institut für Wirtschaftsforschung, Lange Reihen der vierteljährlichen volkswirtschaftlichen Gesamtrechnung für die Bundesrepublik Deutschland, and OECD Business Sector Database.

Estimated equations

We apply the conventional Johansen (1988) estimation procedure and identify the cointegration relationships by imposing and testing restrictions on the cointegrating space spanned by the cointegrating vectors. We then proceed to the estimation and testing of error-correction models, which is followed by impulse response analysis.[4]

All variables were tested for their order of integration by applying conventional (augmented) Dickey–Fuller tests for the UK and compound (augmented) Dickey–Fuller tests for Germany (Harris 1995). The compound tests were necessary for Germany in order to account for the structural break due to unification. The tests suggest that all variables are integrated of order one.[5]

Cointegrating vector for real wages and unemployment: UK

We estimated an unrestricted VAR which included a constant, a deterministic trend and a dummy variable with the value 1 for the first quarter 1975 and zero elsewhere, accounting for exceptionally high wage growth (Clements and Mizon 1991). Likelihood ratio tests were used to test for the significance of the deterministic elements. The high wage dummy variable proved insignificant, while the likelihood ratio test for the remaining deterministic elements with a

Table 13.1 Results of the maximal eigenvalue and the
trace tests for the UK

H_0	Max. eigenvalue test	95%	Trace test	95%
$r = 0$	47.5	37.9	112.5	87.2
$r = 1$	27.7	31.8	65.0	63.0
$r = 2$	18.7	25.4	37.3	42.3
$r = 3$	11.5	19.2	18.6	25.8
$r = 4$	7.2	12.4	7.2	12.4

$\chi^2(10) = 22.5$ suggests the inclusion of trend and constant. The usual information criteria[6] were inconclusive and we decided the lag length on the absence of
serial correlation.[7]

The cointegrating VAR was estimated with unrestricted intercepts and restricted
trends in the VAR, since data are trended and since we wished to avoid the possibility of quadratic trends in some of the variables (Pesaran *et al.* 1997). The results
of the maximal eigenvalue and the trace tests are presented in Table 13.1.

The results of the cointegration tests are inconclusive in that the trace test clearly
suggested two cointegrating vectors while the maximal eigenvalue tests only suggested one cointegrating vector at the 5 per cent significance level. There is also
some indicative support from the Hannan–Quinn and the Akaike information criteria for two cointegrating vectors so that we will proceed on this basis. The two cointegrating vectors may not be economically sensible. They span a space in which any
linear combination is another cointegrating relationship. Consequently, general
restrictions according to the theoretical model, were imposed and tested for significance (Pesaran and Shin 1994). We began with testing the co-trending restriction
(Pesaran *et al.* 1997). Since the test results of the VAR indicated the inclusion of
a deterministic trend, its significance was also tested in the cointegrating vectors,
although the theoretical model does not include a trend variable. The likelihood
ratio test indicates at the 13 per cent level (with a $\chi^2(2) = 4.1$) the absence of a
deterministic trend in the long-run relationship. Further overidentifying restrictions
were imposed and the results arrived at are reported in (7) and (8):

$$(w - p - lp) = -0.25U + 0.0001LU - 0.7241ti + 0.96k + 0.0T \qquad (7)$$
$$(NA) \qquad (NA) \qquad (0.311) \qquad (0.177) \; (NA)$$

where T is the deterministic trend variable and the values in brackets are the
estimated standard errors. *NA* denotes that the coefficient was restricted in the
identifying procedure. The restrictions imposed on the system are just accepted at
the 9 per cent level with a $\chi^2(5) = 9.51$.

The first equation describes the average hourly real wage per unit of output
$(w - p - lp)$, determined by unemployment (U), long-term unemployment (LU),
tax- and import costs (ti) and capital stock (k). The second equation explains unemployment by long-term unemployment and capital stock. Investment in productive
capacity affects both wages and the NAIRU. At a given level of economic activity,

a higher capital stock implies lower-capacity utilisation, thereby reducing firms' ability to increase prices and allowing real wages to rise. Furthermore, investment in new capacity reduces unemployment. Tax and import costs are significant in the wage equation. Increases in the wedge are borne to a high degree by labour. The coefficient is, however, less than unity, indicating that firms also bear some of the burden. This is a 'new' result for the UK in that studies that cover a period until the 1980s usually find high-wage resistance (Bean *et al.* 1986; Layard and Nickell 1986). The change in the coefficient may very well be explained by the 'flexibility' of the labour market experienced since the early 1980s (Barrell 1994). It should, however, be noted that, although wages respond to changes in import and tax costs, unemployment is not affected. The coefficient of the variable capturing tax- and import costs in the unemployment equation was close to zero and insignificant, so that we restricted it to zero. Although long-term unemployment does not affect real wages, it increases the NAIRU nonetheless. It appears to be that downward pressure on wage setting is entirely determined by the short-term unemployed. The effect of long-term unemployment on the NAIRU may be the result of the inability of the long-term unemployed to price themselves into the market, or, of fewer job matches at given vacancies.

Other variables, such as benefits and militancy, were either not significant or not economically sensible in the cointegrating relationship. In any case, there are some doubts about the econometric properties of these two variables (Hall and Henry 1987). These doubts concern the appropriate choice of the proxy for worker militancy and unemployment benefits as well as its unstable econometric performance.

Cointegrating vector for real wages and unemployment: Germany

In a preliminary analysis of an unrestricted VAR model we tested for the significance of deterministic variables. The VAR model contained a constant and a deterministic trend, a dummy for unification with the value 1 since 1991q1 and zero elsewhere, a dummy which takes the value one for 1984 and zero elsewhere, accounting for the miners' strike, and an impulse dummy for 1992q1, which was necessary because of an outlier in the equation for capital stock. We tested for the significance of the deterministic components in the unrestricted VAR. The likelihood ratio test denotes significance with a $\chi^2(25) = 757.5$. The lag length of the vector autoregressive model (VAR) is 4, where the same decision criteria applied as for the UK.

In parallel to the UK estimations, a cointegrating VAR model was estimated with unrestricted intercepts and restricted trends. The results of the cointegration test are given in Table 13.2.

The results of both cointegration tests indicated clearly the presence of two cointegrating vectors at the 5 per cent significance level. As in the UK case, we turn to the identification of the cointegrating vectors by imposing overidentifying restrictions. The likelihood ratio test for the co-trending restriction indicates with

Table 13.2 Results of the maximal eigenvalue and the
trace tests for Germany

H_0	Max. eigenvalue test	95%	Trace test	95%
$r = 0$	123.2	37.9	202.5	87.2
$r = 1$	35.9	31.8	79.3	63.0
$r = 2$	20.6	25.4	43.5	42.3
$r = 3$	17.4	19.2	22.9	25.8
$r = 4$	5.5	12.4	5.5	12.4

a $\chi^2(2) = 1.05$ and an empirical significance level of 60 per cent that this restriction is valid. The identification of economically interpretable vectors demanded further overidentifying restrictions on the system of cointegrating vectors. The results are:

$$(w - p - lp) = -0.01U + 0.0001LU + 0.7ti + 0.16072k + 0.0T \tag{9}$$
$$ (NA) \quad\quad (NA) \quad\quad (NA) \quad\quad (NA) \ \ (NA)$$

$$U = 0.23815LU + 0.17612ti - 0.02k + 0.0T \tag{10}$$
$$ (0.015) \quad\quad (0.037) \quad\ (NA) \quad (NA)$$

The likelihood ratio test accepts the validity of the overidentifying restrictions of the cointegrating vectors with a $\chi^2(6) = 9.70$ and a probability level of 14 per cent. The first equation describes the average hourly real wage per unit of output $(w - p - lp)$, determined by unemployment (U), long-term unemployment (LU), tax- and import costs (ti) and capital stock (k). The second equation explains unemployment by long-term unemployment and capital stock. All variables are correctly signed in both equations. The greatest effects in the wage equation come from the capital and wedge variables, while the unemployment equation is dominated by long-term unemployment and the import and tax variable.

The high *positive* coefficient of the tax and import effect (ti) in the wage vector is rather striking. We argued before that a rise in the wedge generates the potential for real wage resistance by threatening a reduction in living standards. In the German case, it appears that real wage resistance is very high. This is in contrast with the study by Bean *et al.* (1986) which found a negative coefficient for the wedge in the wage equation for West Germany from the 1960s until the 1980s. This result indicates that during that period German workers absorbed at least some of the tax and import burden. It is argued in the same study that in corporatist economies that exhibit a high degree of consensus, as for example (West) Germany, resistance with respect to increases in taxes and import prices is less pronounced and it is thus expected that (in contrast to the UK) the coefficient for the wedge should be negative. However, unification has changed the German labour market dramatically. Wage behaviour in West Germany changed after unification as workers shifted forward a higher proportion of tax increases. In response to a range of tax increases that was implemented in 1991 to help finance the cost of unification, with further rises in 1992 and 1993 that were already announced in 1991, unions demanded and achieved substantial wage increases after 1990 which amounted to 5 per cent per year on average. Tullio *et al.* (1996) conclude that high-wage growth in West Germany marks at least a temporary breakdown of the social consensus.

In order to see whether there was a marked difference in wage setting in response to the wedge after unification, we re-estimated the relationships (9) and (10) for West Germany over the period 1968q1–1990q4. We fixed all coefficients at their values obtained for the period 1968q1–1994q4, except for the wedge which was left free to be re-estimated. The coefficient for the wedge turned out to be negative and insignificant with a value of -0.097276 and a standard error of 0.518. The likelihood ratio test of the overidentifying restrictions is $\chi^2(7) = 11.9$, which indicates that the imposed restrictions are valid at the 10 per cent level.

The effect of the other variables on wage and unemployment determination is as expected, although the effect of the capital stock on unemployment is rather low. After the oil price shocks, investment fell dramatically during the 1980s and was not made up in the 1990s (Burda 1988). Furthermore, Germany inherited an economically obsolete capital stock from East Germany. There seems to be evidence of capital shortage unemployment in East Germany (Hagemann 1997). This, however, may not be evident in our analysis of unified Germany.[8]

The cointegrating VAR included a proxy capturing unemployment benefits. It was calculated as direct government expenditure per unemployed (Arbeit-slosengeld and expenditures by the Bundesanstalt für Arbeit; interpolated from annual data using the number of unemployed as the reference series). The proxy proved to be insignificant, which may be due to the problem of proxying a rather complex benefit system. There are three relevant types of benefit payments in Germany, depending on the duration of unemployment (OECD 1996). They are unemployment benefit, unemployment assistance and social assistance. The first two are related to previous net earnings. Unemployment benefits are between 60 and 67 per cent of previous net earnings and can be paid for up to 32 months while once this entitlement lapses, unemployment assistance is at a rate of 53 and 57 per cent. Social assistance is related to the level of the local 'low wage and salary group'. The proxy we use is just an average of unemployment payments.

Dynamic structural models

In the second step of the cointegrating analysis we estimate and discuss dynamic structural models that incorporate the results of the long-run analysis. The estimation period is shortened by the last four quarters for the UK and Germany in order to allow for the testing of the out-of-sample performance of the models. We proceed by discussing error-correction models for the two countries separately. At the end of this subsection, we compare the dynamic results.

Error-correction models: UK

Equations (11) and (12) are parsimonious representations of a more general dynamic model. Nominal hourly wage acceleration is determined by:

$$\Delta\Delta w = -0.055 - 0.053 \; ecmw_{t-1} - 0.245 \; ecmu_{t-3} - 0.645\Delta(w - p)_{t-1}$$
$$(0.6) \qquad\qquad (3.5) \qquad\qquad (4.5) \qquad\qquad\qquad (10.3)$$
$$- 0.016\Delta\Delta U_{t-5} - 0.194\Delta ti_{t-1} - 0.574\Delta\Delta lp_{t-1}$$
$$(1.8) \qquad\qquad (2.1) \qquad\qquad (5.3)$$
$$- 0.669\Delta\Delta lp_{t-2} - 0.748\Delta\Delta lp_{t-3}$$
$$(5.31) \qquad\qquad\qquad (7.1) \tag{11}$$

$$R^2 = 0.664 \quad AR = 1.06 \quad RESET = 1.67 \quad NORM = 2.6 \quad HET = 10.5$$
$$ARCH(12) = 1.34 \quad PRED.F = 0.53$$

and changes in unemployment are explained as:

$$\Delta U_t = -0.013 - 0.007 \; ecmw_{t-2} - 0.031 \; ecmu_{t-3} + 1.080\Delta U_{t-1}$$
$$(1.4) \qquad\quad (4.9) \qquad\qquad (5.9) \qquad\qquad\quad (23.3)$$
$$- 0.251\Delta\Delta U_{t-4}$$
$$(2.6) \tag{12}$$

$$R^2 = 0.870 \quad AR = 1.58 \quad RESET = 0.89 \quad NORM = 1.9 \quad HET = 6.76$$
$$ARCH(12) = 0.59 \quad PRED.F = 1.4$$

where the meaning of the variables is as before, with the exception of *ecmw* and *ecmu*, which stand for the error-correction terms from the long-run wage and unemployment relationships, respectively. The values in brackets under the coefficients denote the t-statistic. R^2 is the adjusted coefficient of determination and the meaning of the diagnostic tests is as follows: AR is the Lagrange multiplier test of serial correlation up to fourth order, RESET is Ramsey's RESET test for functional form misspecification, NORM is the Jarque–Bera test for normality in the residuals, HET is a test for heteroscedasticity based on the squared residuals on fitted values, ARCH is a Lagrange Multiplier test for autocorrelated squared residuals and PRED.F is an out-of-sample forecasting test (see Pesaran and Pesaran 1997, for more details). All diagnostics are reported in their F-version, except for the normality test, which is in its χ-square version.

Estimations are conducted with ordinary least squares and it appears that all included variables, particularly the error-correction terms, are significant at the 5 per cent level.[9] Nominal wage acceleration is explained by the error-correction terms of both cointegrating vectors, real hourly wage growth, the growth in the wedge, acceleration in productivity and unemployment. The dynamic unemployment equation depends on the error-correction terms, changes and acceleration in unemployment. In both equations, growth of capital stock was insignificant.

All diagnostic tests, except the test for heteroscedasticity, do not show any problem of misspecification. Although heteroscedasticity does not affect the unbiasedness of the coefficients, OLS estimators are inefficient. We applied two different estimators for the determination of covariance-consistent parameter estimates. For the wage equation we applied Newey–West adjusted estimates, using Parzen weights.[10] The re-estimated standard errors did not change inference with respect to the OLS results, except for unemployment acceleration which now clearly showed to be significant at the 5 per cent level. The correlation coefficients of the residuals of the dynamic unemployment equation were low and the Lagrange multiplier test did not show any sign of autocorrelation at any of the lags up to lag length 12. We used for the unemployment equation White's heteroscedasticity-consistent variance–covariance estimation. Again, the results of the adjusted standard errors and the recalculated t-statistics did not change inference.[11]

Error-correction models: Germany

We turn to the results of the dynamic relationships for Germany, where nominal wage acceleration per unit output is presented in equation (13) as:

$$\Delta\Delta(w - lp) = 0.194 - 0.051\ ecmw_{t-4} - 1.352\Delta(w - p - lp)_{t-1}$$
$$(3.0) \qquad (2.8) \qquad\qquad (15.4)$$
$$+ 0.280\Delta(w - p - lp)_{t-4} - 0.022\Delta U_{t-5}$$
$$(3.1) \qquad\qquad (3.4)$$
$$- 0.961\Delta ti_{t-3} + 1.008\Delta ti_{t-4} - 0.463\Delta k_{t-4}$$
$$(2.0) \qquad\qquad (2.0) \qquad\qquad (2.6) \qquad\qquad (13)$$

$$R^2 = 0.722 \quad AR = 1.96 \quad RESET = 0.23 \quad NORM = 4.193$$
$$HET = 0.661 \quad ARCH(12) = 2.4 \quad PRED.F = 0.611$$

and the parsimonious dynamic unemployment equation (14) as:

$$\Delta U_t = 0.005 - 0.034\ ecmu_{t-6} + 0.736\Delta U_{t-1} + 0.175\Delta ti_{t-2}$$
$$(2.8) \qquad (2.2) \qquad\qquad (11.0) \qquad\qquad (4.3)$$
$$- 0.185\Delta ti_{t-3} + 0.110\Delta ti_{t-4} + 0.167\Delta k_{t-4} - 0.122\Delta k_{t-5}$$
$$(3.6) \qquad\qquad (2.8) \qquad\qquad (10.3) \qquad\qquad (6.7)$$
$$- 0.002D$$
$$(10.9) \qquad\qquad\qquad\qquad\qquad\qquad\qquad (14)$$

$$R^2 = 0.745 \quad AR = 0.20 \quad RESET = 1.9 \quad NORM = 0.70 \quad HET = 0.16$$

$$ARCH(12) = 0.549 \quad PRED.F = 0.76$$

where the variables and diagnostics are as before. In both equations all variables are correctly signed and significant. The diagnostics do not indicate any problems of misspecification. Wage acceleration is explained by the error-correction term (*ecm*) from the cointegrating relationship, by real wage growth, growth in the wedge and capital stock and changes in unemployment. The error-correction term of the long-run unemployment relationship is insignificant in dynamic wage determination. This is an important result in that it implies that disequilibrium errors from the unemployment relationship are not corrected in the dynamic wage equation. Similarly, the dynamic unemployment equation is only determined by the error correction of the long-run unemployment relationship so that unemployment does not respond to errors in wage setting. The growth of tax and import costs increases both wages and unemployment. There is a significant effect from capital stock growth on wages and unemployment.

Impulse response analysis

The focus of this chapter is the effect of capital stock on wage and unemployment determination in both the short and the long-run. Cointegration is concerned with the relationship between variables over the long-run. We may also study the effect of capital stock on wages and unemployment in the short-run by utilising impulse response analysis. It may help with the interpretation of cointegrating vectors and may give interesting insights into the short-run as well as the long-run relations of the variables under consideration in response to a shock. Any shock to one of the variables in the system will generate a time-path that will eventually settle down in a *new* equilibrium provided no further shocks occurred (Lütkepohl and Reimers 1992; Mellander *et al.* 1992).

We apply the 'generalised' impulse response analysis since it circumvents the problem of dependence of the orthogonalised impulse responses on the ordering of the variables in the VAR (Koop *et al.* 1996; Pesaran and Shin 1997). The effect of a shock of the size of one standard error in the equation for capital stock on the estimated wage (CV1) and the unemployment (CV2) relationships can be seen in Figure 13.2 for the UK. The impulse causes a permanent increase in wages and a permanent, although rather small, fall in unemployment.[12] After about 26 periods, the two variables have reached their long-term position.

For Germany, the results of the generalised impulse analysis for a shock in the equation of capital stock is depicted in Figure 13.3. In contrast to the UK, there is a transitory effect on wages and unemployment. After about six years, the system converges to its previous equilibrium. The effect of the shock on wages is positive in the short and medium run, as was also indicated by the cointegrating vector in equation (21). The effect of a shock in capital stock on unemployment is rather low (perhaps even insignificant).

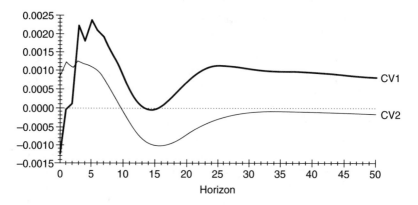

Figure 13.2 Generalised impulse response(s) to an SE shock in *k*; UK.

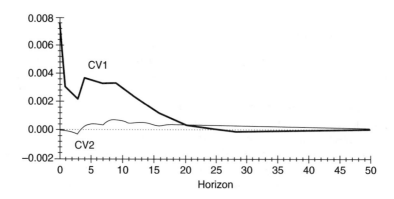

Figure 13.3 Generalised impulse response(s) to an SE shock in *k*; Germany.

Summary and conclusions

A general theoretical model in which wages and unemployment were determined, is postulated. Its main ingredients are conflict in the wage determination, ideas about efficiency wage and wage relativities, and insider-outsider propositions. In this model, capital stock plays an important role in that it affects capacity utilisation and firms' ability to increase their target profit share and thus the negotiated wage. Furthermore, due to the limited substitutability between capital and labour, a fall of investment may increase unemployment in the long-run.

The main proposition of this chapter, that capital stock is an important variable in wage and unemployment relationships, is empirically validated in the cases of the UK and Germany. We argue that this is an important result in that it demonstrates that on the basis of theory and the empirical evidence produced in this chapter,

NAIRU is not merely affected by supply-side factors only. Demand variables are also important, and should not be ignored, as they have been hitherto, in relevant studies.

Notes

1 Capital stock is defined as the accumulation of investment over time minus depreciation (δ):

$$K = \sum_{0}^{t} I - \delta \tag{i}$$

Investment is related to capacity utilization and real interest rates. Firms are interested in keeping strategic spare capacity because they try to keep their share of the market and deter market entrance to competitors (Dixit 1980). We assume that firms invest when actual capacity utilization is higher than desired (Φ^*), and they will reduce investment when actual capacity utilization is lower than desired, so that we may write:

$$I = I((\Phi^* - \Phi), \underline{R}) \quad \text{for } \Phi^* - \Phi > 0 \quad \frac{\delta I}{\delta t} > 0$$

$$\text{for } \Phi^* - \Phi < 0 \quad \frac{\delta I}{\delta t} < 0 \tag{ii}$$

Equilibrium in the capital goods market is achieved when desired capacity utilization is equal to the actual:

$$\Phi^* = \Phi \tag{iii}$$

2 Rowthorn (1999) reports that half of more than 30 studies estimate an elasticity of substitution between capital and labour of less than 0.58. Only in five studies was the elasticity of substitution greater or equal to one.

3 Conventionally, the long-term unemployed are those who are so for more than a year, which may give some idea on the time-horizon with respect to *sluggish* adjustment.

4 All estimations reported in this section were undertaken on the computer package MICROFIT4.0. The test procedures applied are those suggested by Pesaran and Shin (1994), which are also implemented in MICROFIT4.0.

5 The results of these tests for both countries are not reported here, but can be obtained from the authors upon request.

6 These are the Akaike, Bayesian and Hannan–Quinn criteria; see Lütkepohl (1991) for a helpful explanation and discussion of these criteria.

7 This criterion is also used to determine the lag length of the VAR in Johansen and Juselius (1992).

8 A separate analysis of East and West Germany may be more informative in this respect. However, the analysis is restricted to data after 1990, because it is generally considered that data for East Germany are unreliable prior to this date.

9 An exception is unemployment acceleration in the wage equation, which is significant at the 8% level.

10 A major problem is in the determination of the lag lengths for the weights (Andrews 1991). Varying lag lengths affect the results of the estimated standard errors. We are not aware of any 'exact' procedure to determine the lag length (L), but that the lag length should be so large that autocorrelations greater than L are small enough to be ignored. The autocorrelation function for the residuals of the wage equation showed a significant

fall of the coefficients after the eleventh lag. Furthermore, the Lagrange multiplier test for serial correlation revealed that there was significant correlation at lag lengths 10 and 11. On this basis, we used the Newey–West method with a truncation lag length of $L = 11$.

11 The results of these tests for both countries are not reported here, but can be obtained from the authors upon request.

12 A permanent effect of a one-time shock means that the system converges to a new equilibrium. Cointegrated systems may display permanent effects. This is in contrast to the time path in a stationary VAR (Lütkepohl and Reimers 1992).

References

Allen, C. and Nixon, J. (1997) 'Two Concepts of the NAIRU', in C. Allen and S. Hall (eds), *Macroeconomic Modelling in a Changing World*, Wiley.

Andrews, D.W.K. (1991) 'Heteroskedasticity and Autocorrelation Consistent Covariance Matrix Estimation', *Econometrica*, 59: 817–58.

Arestis, P. and Biefang-Frisancho Mariscal, I. (1997) 'Conflict, Effort and Capital Stock in UK Wage Determination', *Empirica*, 24: 179–93.

—— (1998) 'Capital Shortages and Asymmetric Reactions as Factors in UK Long-term Unemployment', *Economic Dynamics and Structural Change*, 9: 189–204.

Barrell, R. (1994) *The UK Labour Market*, Cambridge: Cambridge University Press.

Bean, C.R. (1989) 'Capital Shortage and Persistent Unemployment', *Economic Policy*, 14: 12–53.

——, Layard, R.G. and Nickell, S.J. (1986) 'The Rise in Unemployment: A Multi-country Study', *Economica*, Supplement, 53: S1–22.

Blanchard, O.J. and Summers, L.H. (1986) 'Hysteresis and the European Unemployment Problem', in S. Fischer (ed.), *NBER Macroeconomics Annual 1986*. Cambridge Mass.: MIT Press.

Bruno, M. and Sachs, J. (1985) *Economics of Worldwide Stagflation*, Oxford: Blackwell.

Burda, M.C. (1988) 'Is there a Capital Shortage in Europe?', *Weltwirtschaftliches Archiv*, 124: 38–57.

Carlin, W. and Soskice, D. (1990) *Macroeconomics and the Wage Bargain*, Oxford: Oxford University Press.

Clements, M.P. and Mizon, G.E. (1991) 'Empirical Analysis of Macroeconomic Time Series', *European Economic Review*, 35: 887–932.

Dixit, A. (1980) 'The Pole of Investment in Entry Deterrence', *Economic Journal*, 90: 95–106.

The Economist (1996) 'Germany: Is the Model Broken?', 4–6 May.

Elmskov, J. (1993) 'High and Persistent Unemployment: Assessment of the Problem and its Causes', Economics Department Working Paper No. 132, Paris: OECD.

Hagemann, H. (1997) 'Die gesamtwirtschaftlichen Beschäftigungswirkungen von Lohnsenkungen', in D. Sadowski and M. Schneider (eds), *Vorschläge zu einer neuen Lohnpolitik*, Frankfurt/Main: Campus.

Hall, S.G. and Henry, S.G.B. (1987) 'Wage Models', *National Institute Economic Review*, 70–75.

Harris, R.I.D. (1995) *Using Cointegration Analysis in Econometric Modelling*, London: Prentice-Hall.

Hicks, J. (1975) *The Crisis in Keynesian Economics*, Oxford: Basil.

Johansen, S. (1988) 'Statistical Analysis of Cointegrating Vectors', *Journal of Economic Dynamics and Control*, 12: 231–54.

Johansen, S. and Juselius, K. (1992) 'Testing Structural Hypotheses in a Multivariate Cointegration Analysis of the PPP and the UIP for UK', *Journal of Econometrics*, 53: 211–44.

Keynes, J.M. (1936) *The General Theory of Employment, Interest and Money*, London: Macmillan.

Koop, G., Pesaran, H.M. and Potter, S.M. (1996) 'Impulse Response Analysis in Nonlinear Multivariate Models', *Journal of Econometrics*, 74: 119–47.

Layard, R. and Nickell, S. (1986) 'Unemployment in Britain', *Economica*, 53: S121–69.

—— and Jackman, R. (1991) *Unemployment*, Oxford: Oxford University Press.

Lindbeck, A. (1993) *Unemployment and Macroeconomics*, Cambridge, Mass.: MIT Press.

—— and Snower, D.J. (1986) 'Wage Setting, Unemployment and Insider-Outsider Relations', *American Economic Review*, 76: 235–9.

Lütkepohl, H. (1991) *Introduction to Multiple Time Series Analysis*, Berlin-Heidelberg: Springer-Verlag.

—— and Reimers, H.E. (1992) 'Impulse Response Analysis in Cointegrated Systems', *Journal of Economic Dynamics and Control*, 16: 53–78.

Manning, A. (1992) 'Productivity Growth, Wage Setting and the Equilibrium Rate of Unemployment', Discussion Paper No 63, London: Centre for Economic Performance, London School of Economics.

Mellander, E., Vredin, A. and Warne, A. (1992) 'Stochastic Trends and Economic Fluctuations in a Small Open Economy', *Journal of Applied Econometrics*, 7: 369–94.

Nickell, S. (1987) 'Why is Wage Inflation in Britain So High?', *Oxford Bulletin of Economics and Statistics*, 49: 103–29.

—— (1990) 'Unemployment; A Survey', *Economic Journal*, 106: 391–439.

OECD (1994) *The OECD Jobs Study*, Part 1, Paris: OECD.

—— (1996) *Economic Surveys. Germany 1996*, Paris: OECD.

Pesaran, M.H. and Pesaran, B. (1997) *Microfit4.0*, Oxford: Oxford University Press.

—— and Shin, Y. (1994) *Identification of and Testing for Cointegrating Relations with General Non-homogeneous Restrictions*, mimeo, Department of Applied Economics, Cambridge.

—— (1997) *Generalized Impulse Response Analysis in Linear Multivariate Models*, Unpublished manuscript, Cambridge University.

—— and Smith, R.J. (1997) 'Structural Analysis of Vector Error Correction Models With Exogenous I (1) Variables', Department of Applied Economics Working Papers, No. 9706, University of Cambridge.

Phelps, E.S. (1994) *Structural Slumps*, Cambridge, Mass.: Harvard University Press.

Rowthorn, R.E. (1977) 'Conflict, Inflation and Money', *Cambridge Journal of Economics*, 1: 215–39.

—— (1995) 'Capital Formation and Unemployment', *Oxford Review of Economic Policy*, 11: 26–39.

—— (1999) 'Unemployment, Wage Bargaining and Capital-Labour Substitution', *Cambridge Journal of Economics*, 23: 413–25.

Shapiro, C. and Stiglitz, E. (1984) 'Equilibrium Unemployment as a Worker Discipline Device', *American Economic Review*, 74: 433–44.

Tullio, G., Steinherr, A. and Buscher, H. (1996) 'German Wage and Price Inflation before and after Unification', in P. de Grauwe, S. Micossi and G. Tullio (eds), *Inflation and Wage Behaviour in Europe*, Oxford: Clarendon Press.

14 Job growth and social harmony

A Dutch miracle?

Joan Muysken

Introduction

It is interesting to note that until recently the stickiness of the Dutch institutional structure was stressed and ridiculed, both internationally and within the Netherlands. However, now it is hailed as a fruitful model to combine social harmony with job growth. It is the newest fashion in the long row of first the US model, then the Japanese model and till the early 1990s the Swedish model (Freeman 1998).

Nonetheless it is interesting to look at the Dutch experience. This experience is in contrast with most other European countries, where a rather painful process of economic reform is taking place in order to curb rising unemployment. The pain of this process also often caused social unrest. Then how did the Netherlands succeed in combining job growth and social harmony during the last 15 years? The answer to this question usually is sought in the unique institutional features of the Dutch society, in particular those of the labour market, summarised in the phrase 'polder model'. This polder model is deeply rooted in the Dutch culture that is consensus-oriented, and in which consultation plays an important role. Typical elements are also the importance of solidarity and equality.[1]

The aim of this chapter is to analyse the nature of the polder model and to investigate to what extent this model indeed has contributed to the job growth in the Netherlands. To put the polder model in a European perspective, I start out by briefly reviewing the features of European labour markets in general. A useful way to look at these characteristics is to compare the European to the US labour market, which I do in the next section. The European labour market then has many welfare-state characteristics, amongst others a high-income equality, which are in contrast to the free-market orientation of the US labour market, which shows a much higher job growth. It is interesting to observe that the countries with the best performance on job growth within Europe show similar differences: the UK mimics the free market system rather closely, whereas the Netherlands typically represents the European welfare state. Nonetheless, the Dutch economy shows a much higher job growth than its larger neighbour and trading partner, Germany – which also typically represents the European welfare state.

In the section on 'The Dutch polder model', I therefore further analyse the nature of the Dutch polder model. Its central features are the process of wage formation and its elaborate social security system. Wage negotiations are based on consensus-seeking behaviour by employers and employees, in which the government plays an important role too. Moreover, solidarity considerations prevent too high wage increases because of the danger of unemployment. The result is a moderate development of wages since the early 1980s. Together with a very strict monetary policy, attaching the Dutch guilder strictly to the Deutschmark (DM), this resulted in a strong decline in wage costs relative to for instance Germany. The resulting enhancement of our competitive position explains our good economic performance. The important ingredient of the polder model of social harmony was ensured by our system of social security.

However, both wage moderation and the development of the social security system have also created tensions in the Netherlands, which might undermine both job growth and social harmony. This is elaborated in the section on 'A Dutch miracle'. Finally, I present some concluding remarks in the last section.

A comparison between the European and the US labour market

A useful background to assess the features of the Dutch polder model is to look at the features of European labour markets more in general. These features can be presented best by contrasting them with the features of the US labour market. There is a host of literature comparing both types of labour markets, which follows from the increased awareness in economics of the impact of institutions on the labour market – and more in general – on the economic performance of a country, including of course unemployment.[2] And since both the unemployment situation and institutions are radically different in the US and Europe, the two are compared frequently to analyse the relation between institutions on the labour market and economic performance, in particular unemployment.[3] Actually, the comparison of the performance across the Atlantic is often used to argue that there is kind of a trade-off between income inequality and unemployment: 'The rise in joblessness in Europe is thus the flip side of the rise in earnings inequality in the US' (Freeman 1995: 19). Europe then represents the welfare state with a lot of labour market rigidities, while the US represents the free market economy with flexible labour markets.

The employment performance of the US and Europe is presented in Figures 14.1 and 14.2, respectively. From the figures one sees how employment recovered relatively fast after both oil crises in the US whereas in Europe after the second oil crisis employment stagnated. Consequently, in Europe unemployment rose to an unprecedented level according to post-war standards, and has not succeeded in decreasing significantly. About half of the unemployed persons have been unemployed for longer than one year.

The performance in the US and Europe

In a recent issue of the *Journal of Economic Perspectives*, the behaviour of European labour markets was compared to the US labour market by Nickell (1997) and

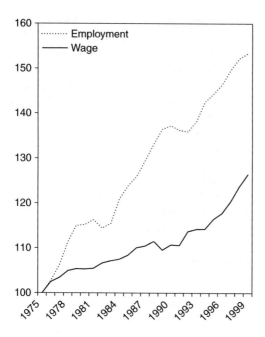

Figure 14.1 Moneyless US (1975–99) (1975 = 100).

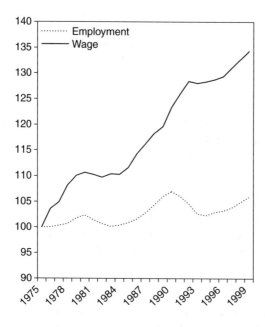

Figure 14.2 Jobless Europe (1975–99) (1975 = 100).

Siebert (1997). Siebert points out that both the US and Europe have been exposed to the same exogenous shocks as the oil crisis and the productivity slow-down. Hence the explanation for the relatively poor employment growth and the high rate of unemployment in Europe should be ascribed to institutional differences.[4] Actually, one can observe in Europe in the 1960s and 1970s a strong development to the welfare state in which equity considerations play an important role. As is also emphasised by Nickell, in the 1980s developments start to diverge somewhat and one can distinguish between various institutional responses in Europe to the oil shocks and productivity slow-down.

While Siebert presents the more or less standard view, Nickell points out that many of the factors which are assumed to cause rigidity, do not contribute significantly to unemployment in Europe. The standard view is that high unemployment is generated by a combination of generous unemployment benefits with a long duration, which causes high taxes which in turn lead to high-wage demands. Because of high unionisation and collective bargaining, these high demands are translated in too high wages. Since we find many of these features in European economies but much less in the US, these institutional differences are thought to explain the phenomenon so aptly described by Krugman as 'Money-less America, Jobless Europe'. Figures 14.1 and 14.2 provide a striking illustration of this statement.[5]

However, Nickell rectifies this picture in some important respects.[6] He stresses that no impact can be observed of rigidities like employment protection and labour standards – Siebert does not agree with this.[7] Also generous benefits are not a problem *per se*, provided they are combined with a limited duration of these benefits and complemented with active labour market policy. Finally, Nickell argues that a high rate of unionisation and coverage of wage contracts does not necessarily lead to high wages, as long as this is offset by high levels of coordination between unions on the one hand and between employers on the other.

In this respect, it is important to notice that Nickell bases his points on cross-section estimations for many OECD-countries using average data for 1983–88 and for 1989–94. He correlates both unemployment and the participation rate with many institutional features and assesses the size of their impact. The estimation results then lead to his conclusions mentioned above. This inductive procedure is typical of a lot of research on institutional differences and their impact and has generated a lot of insights that have further stimulated theoretical analysis. I will return to that analysis in the next section.

With respect to the earnings inequality, Siebert observes 'It is striking that in the 1980s and 1990s relative wages have become more differentiated in the US and the UK, while differentiation has remained largely unchanged in some European countries' (Siebert 1997: 45). Thus, the US typically have a much larger income inequality than Europe.[8] However, Siebert and Nickell differ in opinion on the implications for two important issues.

First the impact of unemployment on wages: According to Siebert the long-term response of wages to unemployment tends to be higher in Europe, and occurs at a slower pace: 'the institutional characteristics of the labour market do require a larger correction of the real wage' (Siebert 1997: 44). However, Nickell finds from his estimation results that in this respect 'there is no dramatic contrast between Europe and North America' (Nickell 1997: 59). His findings are supported by Teulings and Hartog (1998) who find that nominal rigidities are much higher in the US than in Europe, which they attribute to the dominance of insider behaviour – I will return to that issue in the next section.

Second the truncation of the earnings distribution from below typically can be seen as an important cause of low-skilled unemployment. To substantiate this, Siebert cites another study by Nickell. However, in his article Nickell (1997) stresses that it is not true 'that labor market flexibility per se is associated in any simple way with such effects' and points out that 'there has been a substantial rise in unskilled unemployment in the US since the early 1970s (over 100 per cent) despite (because of?) the fall in unskilled real wages' (Nickell 1997: 71).

The fall in real unskilled wages in the US is a point that is quite often ignored in the discussion. However, this has enormous implications for the American society as Phelps (1997) points out forcefully. He stresses that the resulting wage now is too low to live a decent life, i.e. one cannot earn 'more than family, charity and the welfare system can provide' (Phelps 1997: 4). And one should realise that the inability to earn a sufficient wage has created an enormous feeling of powerlessness and despair. The group of 'second-class workers' that has thus emerged comprises according to Phelps's calculations one-third of the labour force in the US. Moreover, in his view this low-wage trap is the cause and not the consequence of the much-decried decline in morality, drugs abuse and social breakdown and unrest.

The performance within Europe

As I mentioned above the performance of European countries shows a lot of variety, and the countries also have large institutional differences. In this context it is interesting to observe that according to Siebert the UK and the Netherlands are the best-performing European countries. Both have a new approach to the labour market, and succeed in reducing unemployment – in particular in the Netherlands. One should realise, however, that the models used in both countries are quite different. Nonetheless, while job growth stagnated in both the UK and the Netherlands till the mid-1980s, afterwards job growth was steady in the Netherlands, but slackened again in the UK from 1990 onward. The question then is why the Netherlands, with all its labour market rigidities of a typical European country, in a sense outperforms the UK who did most to imitate the US situation.

The 'Dutch Miracle' also can be illustrated by comparing the development of Dutch unemployment to that in Germany[9] – the latter being also more or less representative for the development in Europe. This is done in Figure 14.3. For comparison the US unemployment is also included in the figure. As I have already discussed in Figure 14.2, unemployment rose in Europe to unprecedented standards in the early 1980s. However, whereas the Netherlands recovered gradually, also after the recession in the early 1990s, Germany was hit severely by that recession and unemployment rose again. In this context the attention for the polder model should be understood.

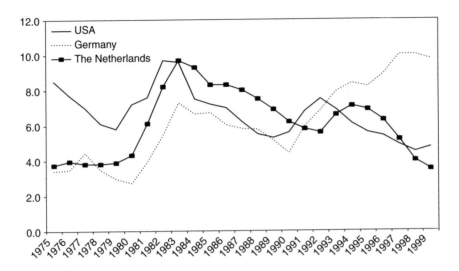

Figure 14.3 Unemployment in the US, Germany and the Netherlands (1975–99) (percentage of the labour force).

The Dutch polder model

The nature of the polder model

When one speaks about the polder model, it first of all is important to realise that it is not a constructed model. It is not consciously and diligently created according to some specific design, but it is the result of an evolutionary process with trial and error.

This evolutionary view is consistent with the view of Hayek (1978) and North (1990). According to this view, institutions are formed in such a way that all participants benefit from them. If the interests of one group cannot be accommodated by the rules of the institution, those rules will be changed in the course of time. Therefore institutions are only sustainable when they are useful for society. And as long as they are useful, they are also self-enforcing since everybody has an interest in maintaining them.

In this context it is a typical fallacy to consider institutions as forms of agreements which can be enforced by laws only, and which are independent of the culture of society. For such rules have to be always consistent with the culture of the society, since this culture defines its beliefs and norms – and hence defines the rules which are necessary for any social activity.

A related fallacy is to consider institutions as those forces, which are not consistent with the free market system.[10] Actually the free market system shows one direction according to which institutions can be formed – and one should realise that it requires many strict rules to let this system function – and corporatism shows another. The differences in institutions between various countries then reflect to a large extent cultural differences.[11]

When institutional differences are reduced to cultural differences, which are further left unexplained, one might wonder what insights have been gained. One important implication follows directly: a country cannot simply copy any institutional form it wishes, for this might not be consistent with the culture of that country.[12] Thus one cannot simply select those features of the polder model one likes, and implement them straightforwardly – most probably this won't work.

Another insight which follows from pursuing the above line of thought is that one should try to explain how, given a certain culture, the current institution implies rules from which everybody benefits – provided that institution is considered to be sustainable.[13] That is, it is always important that one can show the rationality of a certain institution. This also enables one to think about adaptations of the existing system to changing circumstances.

Following the above line of thought, the polder model is deeply rooted in Dutch culture and in that light its rationality should be further investigated. This culture is consensus-oriented, and consultation plays an important role. Typical elements are also the importance of solidarity and social security, and equality and fairness notions.[14]

To discuss the consequences of these cultural features for the institutions, I will concentrate on two important features of the polder model: the wage-formation process and the social security system. This will enable me on the one hand to elaborate on some differences between the US and Europe, as discussed in the previous section. On the other hand, it will also be possible to highlight some typical Dutch features within the European setting. However, before discussing these two features, it is useful to give some further information on the economic performance of the Netherlands. This should especially be compared to the performance of Germany, which after all is the economic motor of the European Union.

Intermezzo: the economic performance of the Netherlands

When looking at the economic performance of the Netherlands, one should realise that the Dutch economy is a very open economy. About 50 per cent of its GDP is exported and the Netherlands traditionally has a surplus on its trade balance of about 3 per cent of GDP. The main trading partner for the Netherlands is Germany and since the early 1980s Dutch monetary policy has been to link the Dutch guilder (Fl) firmly to the German DM. This can be seen in Figure 14.4, where the stability of the Fl/DM after 1983 is remarkable. As a consequence Dutch monetary policy has been essentially dictated in Frankfurt, where the German Central Bank is located. Amongst others, this enabled the Dutch economy to mimic the German low-inflation record – and after the German unification, Dutch inflation even dropped below German inflation.

However, whereas German wage costs increased steadily, the Netherlands succeeded in showing a remarkable wage moderation from the early 1980s. As a consequence unit labour costs in the Netherlands fell dramatically relative to the

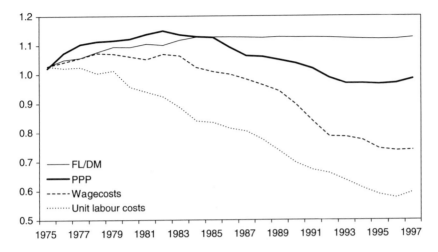

Figure 14.4 The guilder (Fl) relative to the Deutschmark (DM) (1975–97) (1975 = 1).

German unit labour costs, as can also be seen from Figure 14.4. This was enhanced by the strong increase in Dutch labour productivity, which at times also outperformed the German productivity increase – as can be seen from comparing wage costs per employee and unit labour costs. Hence it is not surprising that in terms of Purchasing Power Parity (PPP) the Dutch guilder depreciated strongly relative to the German Deutschmark and the competitive position of the Netherlands increased strongly.[15] This might be considered as a typical beggar-thy-neighbour policy.[16] Salverda (1999) does not agree with this interpretation because of the unimpressive Dutch export performance in his view. However, Dutch exports increased yearly by 6.2 per cent on average in the period 1970–98, whereas the relevant world trade increased by 5.6 per cent on average. There is not a typical break in the difference between both series in the mid-1980s, when the guilder was coupled to the DM. On the other hand, when one looks at the effective exchange rate of the Dutch guilder, compared to its competitors, this increased only by 1 per cent on average each year in the period 1970–85. Whereas from 1986 onwards it started to increase by 2.5 per cent on average each year – cf. CPB (1999), Annex B1.

Another aspect of the wage moderation is that it also enabled firms to restructure their financial positions. These positions eroded dramatically in the 1970s, since the deterioration in terms of trade as a consequence of both oil crises was initially passed on to profits instead of wages.[17]

As mentioned already, the German economy has a very strong position in the European Union. Since Figure 14.4 shows the good performance of the Netherlands relative to Germany, it also explains an important part of the Dutch success more in general. Next to the monetary policy, the key to this success lies in particular in wage moderation. The question then is how this wage moderation has been achieved, without creating a lot of social unrest – as typically is observed in France, but also in Germany. The answer to this question lies in the nature of the Dutch polder model, and in particular its impact on wage formation.

The process of wage formation

When discussing wage formation one should realise first that when starting an employment relation both firms and workers have a hold-up problem due to sunk costs.[18] The employers have a hold-up problem because when they invest in for instance training of workers, the employees may demand higher wages after being trained. On the other hand, when the workers invest in firm-specific training, this might not result in the wage increase from the firm, which they will probably expect. If no solution to this problem is found, no investment in training will take place although both parties would benefit from it – this is the hold-up problem.

The US solution to this problem is a contract of long duration with a fixed nominal wage, then both parties know exactly what to expect and can base their investment decisions on that information. This type of solution leads to nominal wage rigidity, albeit within boundaries: when too large shocks occur, renegotiations will take place. Since American unions need an enormous amount of information on firm-specific characteristics to negotiate wages and to monitor the contracts, this is an important reason why these unions are firm-based.

The European solution to the hold-up problem is to allow wages to be settled outside the firms. When the contract is made independent of employers and employees, neither party can use the contract to exploit the rents generated after sunk costs have been made. Wage negotiations therefore take place at a sectoral or even central level, and unions are much broader and do not have strong interests in specific firms. As a consequence agreement about wages is not based on enforcement, because the information to monitor this appropriately is lacking. It is based on agreement and social control. Moreover, macroeconomic circumstances play an important role in these contracts – this aspect has to do with the solidarity discussed below. As a consequence of these different approaches, wages in the US are less sensitive to macroeconomic shocks, but more sensitive to firm-specific shocks, when compared to Europe. Teulings (1997) presents this insight to explain that it is a fallacy to think that corporatism is opposite to a flexible functioning of markets.[19]

Thus far I have only discussed the corporatist model in general, in a European context. However, the Dutch situation has some specific features which are characteristic of the polder model. First of all, wage negotiations take place both at the central and the sectoral level. Although the contracts (Collective Agreements) are formulated at the sectoral level, rough guidelines have often been negotiated at the central level. This implies that macroeconomic circumstances have a strong feed-back on wage formation.[20] A typical example is the so-called 'Akkoord van Wassenaar' in 1982 where the central organisations of employers and employees agreed to wage moderation, and which started the long period of low wage

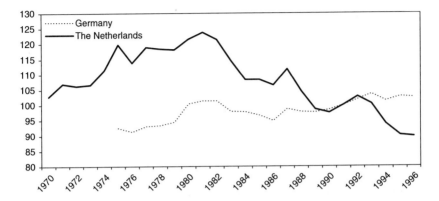

Figure 14.5 Share of labour income in GDP (1970–96) (1991 = 100).

growth.[21] The impact of low wage growth appears in Figure 14.5, where the development of the share of labour income in national income is depicted. The decrease in this share from 1982 onwards shows that in general wage increases did not exceed increases in productivity. The development of the German share is included for comparison and shows a rather persistent upward trend. This is also consistent with the decrease in relative unit labour costs of the Netherlands, depicted in Figure 14.4.

A second feature which is very important for the Dutch model is that government is heavily involved in wage negotiations, although at the central level only.[22] At that level they closely monitor wage negotiations, and at the sectoral level they have to sanction the Collective Agreements. The contribution of government in wage negotiations at the central level is partly that of moderator, but also an important role is that changes in taxes and the social security system can be an element of the negotiations. This latter role is rather implicit, however, since these changes of course have to be implemented through the political process and have to be approved by the parliament. An example is that government may point out forcefully that unemployment benefits cannot be maintained at the current level when too high wage increases are agreed upon, because a further rise in unemployment then can be foreseen.[23] This also relates to the solidarity aspect of the Dutch culture.

Another example is that the government has been lowering the wedge between wage costs and net wages in order to enhance wage moderation. As can be seen from Figure 14.6, the wedge has increased consistently until it reached about 55 per cent of wage costs by the early 1980s. However, then in order to enhance wage moderation the wedge was decreased and now is stabilised at a level around 52 per cent of wage costs – which still is 67 per cent of gross wages.[24]

A final example is that government has moderated wages of civil servants and related employees strongly. This point is also emphasised by Salverda (1999) who

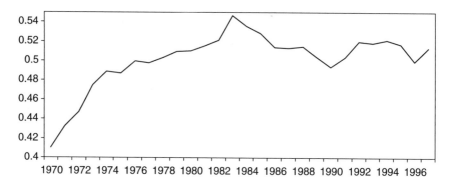

Figure 14.6 The wedge between wage costs and net wages (per cent of wage costs).

shows that wages in that sector fell by 20 per cent relative to wages in the private sector in the period 1980–5. Afterwards relative wages stabilised again.

The direct involvement of government follows from the fact that it has to sanction Collective Agreements at the sectoral level. Then these agreements become binding for all persons employed in this sector. This is in particularly interesting since only a low number of workers, about 25 per cent, are members of a trade union. Nonetheless these unions are negotiating on behalf of all workers (and unemployed persons too). Actually as Teulings (1997) argues, the relatively low union density makes the union a credible negotiations partner. On the one hand, this makes the union not too dangerous because it is not able to enforce monopolistic rent-sharing; on the other hand, union members cannot force unions to strong insider behaviour, since there are many outsiders.

Finally, one should realise that since the government has to sanction the Collective Agreements, this gives it a powerful position in the central negotiations. A recent example occurred when employers complained that minimum wages were too high. However, it was then discovered that the lowest wage level in Collective Agreements was far above the legal minimum wage. Subsequently the government decided not to lower the legal minimum wage but to sanction only those Collective Agreements that decreased the lowest wage level towards the legal minimum wage.

In line with our earlier discussion on the role and viability of institutions, it is important to point out that the system of Collective Agreements which are sanctioned by the government, as well as the participation of government in negotiations and consultations at the central level, is supported explicitly by both employers and employees. One of the results of this system is that strikes hardly ever occur in the Netherlands and, as mentioned earlier, labour productivity is high. Moreover, as I explained above, the hold-up problem is solved through the system of Collective Agreements. Another result is that the rather implicit role of the government ensures that agreements are based on consensus. As a consequence wage drift – i.e. wage increases above the agreed increase – is relatively low in the Netherlands, whereas it is typically high in a country like Sweden, where wage increases are decided upon at the central level – cf. Van Veen (1997, ch. 2).

The system of social security

When comparing the US and Europe in the previous section, I pointed out that Europe puts a larger emphasis on the welfare state. This can partly be understood from the differences in culture between Europe and the US. The US then is a highly individualistic and competitive society, whereas Europe is much more 'social' - oriented. However, as can be seen from Hofstede's comparison of cultures between countries, this picture is far too simple: within Europe the differences are quite large. For the purpose of this analysis I will concentrate on some features of the Dutch situation.

Above I have stressed the importance of solidarity and equality notions in the Dutch culture. The solidarity implies that a typical aim of the Dutch social security system, as it was implemented after the Second World War, was to give persons without employment – for whatever reason – a benefit which is very much related to at least the minimum wage, since this is indicative of the means one should have for a decent living. The implicit notion then was that persons without employment are either not able to work, for reasons for which they cannot be held responsible, or they are entitled to stop working, either temporally since they have to look after their children, or permanently because of old age. The equality notion implied amongst others that wage differences should not be too large. I have discussed this already in the comparison above between Europe and the US.

The rationale of the welfare state can be discussed in many ways.[25] On the one hand, we have a theoretical and philosophical discussion along the lines of Sen (1987) who argues that rights of co-determination and access to education and health care is an important instrument to transform inefficient, conflicting behaviour into efficient cooperative activities. On the other hand, we have a more pragmatic discussion based on the European experience of the overshooting of the welfare state – see for instance Lindbeck (1994) and Snower (1994) – and the American experience of the absence of the welfare state – see the discussion of Phelps (1997) mentioned above.

Here I will confine myself to the observation that in the Netherlands the system of social security has ensured a remarkable social harmony. One important function of the system of social security is to accommodate structural changes in the economy. Examples are the closing of the coal mines in the 1960s – which has been a very painful process in the UK and is still a problem in Germany. In the Netherlands this occurred relatively smoothly, partly because the system of social security compensated relatively well for involuntary job losses. A similar story can be told for the demise in the textile industry, and in some other industries.

Another important function lies in its interaction with the wage-formation process. Wage moderation in a situation of rising social security premiums is accepted when it is realised that social security is important. This is another impact of the notion of solidarity in the Dutch culture.

Table 14.1 Expenditures on social security in 1980, 1993 and 1995 (% GDP)

	Belgium	Denmark	Germany	France	The Netherlands	UK	Sweden
1980	28.0	28.7	28.8	25.4	30.1	21.5	32.0
1993	29.0	—	29.1	31.0	33.5	28.4	38.8
1995	29.7	34.3	—	30.6	31.4	27.7	35.6

Source: Social Affairs (1999), annex 1.O.

Amongst others, the relative extensive system of the Dutch system of social security shows up from Table 14.1, where the social security expenditures are presented as a share of GDP for several European countries. One sees that Dutch expenditures consistently are the largest, except for Sweden, till the most recent year of recession 1993. After 1993 this share falls although it remains distinctly above the EU average. It is obvious that the extensive character of the social security system also is responsible for the relative high wedge, as depicted in Figure 14.6 above.

A Dutch miracle?

As I have mentioned above in several places, the characteristics of consensus and solidarity are elements of the Dutch culture which are reflected in the polder model. As a consequence the process of wage formation is based on consensus-seeking behaviour by employers and employees, in which government plays an important role too. Moreover, solidarity considerations prevent too high-wage increases because of the danger of unemployment. The result is a moderate development of wages since the early 1980s. Together with a very strict monetary policy, attaching the Dutch guilder strictly to the DM, this resulted in a strong decline in wage costs relative to Germany. Since Germany is the main trading partner of the Netherlands and also one of the strongest economies in Europe, this explains the Dutch job growth to a large extent.

Social harmony is ensured by the Dutch system of social security, which also reflects the culture of solidarity. This system has accommodated structural reforms of the Dutch economy. It has also played an important role in the acceptance of wage moderation. However, both wage moderation and the development of the social security system have also created tensions in the Netherlands, which might undermine both job growth and social harmony. I will elaborate this below.

Wage moderation, job growth and income growth

The debate on a possible drawback in wage moderation was instigated by Kleinknecht in his inaugural lecture and provoked a heated debate in the Netherlands. Essentially Kleinknecht's position is that wage moderation is retarding the process of creative destruction and hence to the detriment of technical progress.[26] Therefore the spread of process and product innovations declined, in particular in the small and medium enterprises. This might hamper the competitive position of the Dutch economy in the long run and make adjustment to new developments more difficult.

It is debatable, however, to what extent Kleinknecht's claims are correct. Van Ark and de Haan (1997) do observe a deceleration in multi-factor productivity growth in the Netherlands in the late 1980s and early 1990s. However, this is concentrated in the services group. Further analysis leads them to the conclusion that it is not a problem of insufficient technology creation but more of technological diffusion and organisational innovations. Apart from that, a productivity slowdown was observed world wide, and not only in the Netherlands. Therefore our productivity growth is more or less in line with that of other European countries nowadays – although the level of productivity is markedly higher, as I have also discussed in connection with Figure 14.4.[27] This is also consistent with the observation made earlier that the competitive position of the Netherlands is quite strong and there is no structural tendency to a weakening position in this respect. Hence, at least at this moment, after 15 years of wage moderation, the effects indicated by Kleinknecht cannot be observed.

Another element which might be considered is the extent to which wage moderation did lead to job growth. In this respect it is often pointed out that it is in particular part-time jobs that have constituted job growth. This is illustrated by the fact that the number of jobs increased by 27 per cent in the period 1985–97, whereas the number of hours worked increased by 16 per cent only.[28] To put it in a different perspective: in 1997 part-time work in the Netherlands was 29.1 per cent of total employment (and 54.6 per cent of female employment), whereas it was 15.9 per cent in the European Union and 13.2 per cent in the USA. Since full-time employment has remained more or less stable since the early 1980s, job growth in the Netherlands is less of a miracle than it might appear at first sight.[29]

Finally it is useful to look at the relation between the growth of real wages and income growth. This is illustrated in Figure 14.7, where I present the development of GDP per capita for the Netherlands, since this is frequently used as an indicator of the welfare of a country. As one can see from the figure, GDP per capita did increase steadily. However, because of the growing rate of inactivity in the 1970s and 1980s – see Figure 14.8 below – it declined relative to that of other rich European countries, and started increasing again in the 1990s.[30] Against this background it is interesting to note, as can also be seen from the figure, that net income has hardly increased for the modal wage-earner since the early 1970s. There are three reasons for this.

The first reason is that a large part of income growth has been used to finance the growing inactivity – see Figure 14.8 below. As a consequence, the discrepancy between gross and net wages increased over time. This is also reflected in the development of the wedge between labour costs and net income, cf. Figure 14.6 above. Hence moderation in gross wages resulted in a very moderate development of net wages.

The second reason is that income inequality in the Netherlands is starting to increase again, although it is quite low when compared to other countries. Salverda

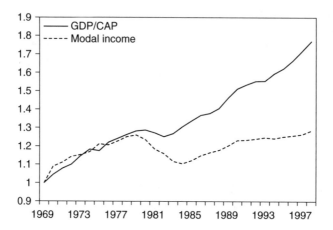

Figure 14.7 GDP/capita and net modal income per worker (1969–98) (1969 = 1).
Source: Based on CPB (1999; Annex A3).

(1999) emphasises that wage moderation can be found in particular in minimum wages – cf. Figure 14.9 below – and wages for young workers, next to the relative decrease in wages for government employees and related workers mentioned above. This has reversed the trend towards growing income equality.

Last but not least, the third reason lies in the increase of the share of capital income in GDP, which is the counterpart of the decrease in the share of labour income shown in Figure 14.5 above. The wage moderation has improved the profitability and solvability of firms in the Netherlands. Partly the improved profitability has been used to restore the financial positions of firms which were eroded in the 1970s – this was also recognised as an explicit element in the discussion on wage moderation. Later the retained profits have been used to a considerable extent for direct investments abroad, which did not generate income that shows up in net modal income. However, I do not want to conclude that for that reason wage moderation also led to a decrease in consumption as has been suggested by both Kleinknecht (1998) and Salverda (1999). The remarkable long boom period in the Netherlands in the second half of the 1990s is due to a persistently high level of consumption expenditures, which are ascribed to the development of stock prices and housing prices.[31] As such is in spite of the decline in the share of labour income in national income.

Turning back to Figure 14.7, it is obvious that there is a strong discrepancy between the development of average welfare, represented by GDP per capita, and net modal income. Hence many wage-earners experience that their net income hardly increases, while firms are doing quite well and GDP grows consistently. It might be expected that in the long run this will lead to tensions because people will no longer understand why this discrepancy persists. The increased wage inequality and the unclear reasons why wage growth is consistently below GDP growth will undermine the necessary solidarity.[32,33] That these tensions have not yet occurred is typically the Dutch miracle.

Social security and solidarity

A problem in the Dutch situation in my view is that the social security system should not exploit solidarity too much. In that context I would like to point to two elements in the Dutch experience that are not always recognised in the appraisal of the polder model.

The first element in the Dutch experience is the high level of inactivity which has evolved over time in the Netherlands. This point has been put forward in various OECD publications and has received some attention in the discussion of the polder model. However, my impression is that it is not sufficiently recognised. The OECD (1998) states that a lot of unemployment in the Netherlands is hidden in the social security system: when unemployment is defined in a broad sense (including that hidden unemployment) the unemployment rate should be 27 per cent instead of the official rate of about 5 per cent.

This is confirmed by the data presented in Figure 14.8. From that figure one sees that the share of persons entitled to social security is almost 40 per cent of the working population. On the one hand, far more persons are entitled to unemployment benefits than there are officially unemployed.[34] On the other hand, the enormous amount of persons entitled to disability benefits – almost 15 per cent of the working population – is a typical Dutch phenomenon. This phenomenon is also illustrated in Figure 14.8. Since disability benefits were more generous than unemployment benefits, the deterioration of the employment situation in the early 1980s induced the employers and employees to accept more persons into

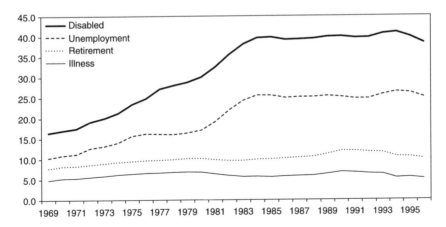

Figure 14.8 Persons entitled to social security in the Netherlands (1969–98) (per cent labour force, cumulated).

Source: Based on CPB (1999; Annex A7).

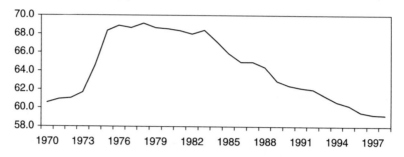

Figure 14.9 Net benefits/net average wage (1970–98) (percentage).

the disability system than was actually warranted. Hence there was a large spill-over from unemployment to disability, which essentially reduced the workforce considerably.

This process has been recognised explicitly in the political discussions in the last six years. Therefore, measures are being discussed and implemented to restructure the social security system such that the rate of inactivity is reduced. This is a difficult process which requires a lot of trial and error.[35] As Figure 14.8 shows, the size of the problem is enormous. But also the nature is problematic. For instance, about 50 per cent of the unemployed workers have been unemployed for at least one year, and hence it is quite difficult for them to find a job again. Another problem is that once one has been labelled as a disabled person, one effectively remains forever outside the labour force.

The measures undertaken are on the one hand those mentioned by Nickell – cf. the previous section. That is a limitation of the duration of benefits, combined with a more active labour policy. On the other hand, access to social security benefits has been made more difficult and also benefits have been lowered. The impact from the latter can be seen from the development of the so-called replace-ment rate, as is shown in Figure 14.9. One sees that in reaction to the depression after the first oil crisis in 1973, net benefits increased from just above 60 per cent to almost 70 per cent of the average net wage. They remained at that level for almost a decade. However, from the early 1980s onwards, the replacement rate started to decrease gradually but consistently to a level below 60 per cent at present.[36] A consequence of these developments is that the problem of poverty has become an item in public debate. About 900,000 persons (15 per cent of the working population) have been living on the social minimum level for at least five years during the past ten years. Also the incidence of loss of work amongst immigrant workers is about four times as high compared to domestic workers.

The second element in the Dutch experience is related to this first element. It concerns the large share of income that is taxed to finance the benefits (and other government expenditures).[37] Next to the persons mentioned in Figure 14.8, these benefits also accrue to persons outside the working population – for instance, everybody above the age of 65 receives a benefit. As a consequence, the total amount of persons entitled to benefits is 86 per cent of the workforce.

Moreover, as can be seen from Figures 14.6 and 14.7, a large part of the income growth has been used to finance the growing inactivity.[38] The recognition of this wedge between labour costs and net income is another reason why the restructuring of the social security system has gained political attention. However, solidarity notions are still strong in the current system of social security.[39]

Although several reforms in social security provoked heated debates, this never resulted in general unrest – compare the recent autumn strikes in France. Moreover, solidarity notions are still strong in the current system of social security. This explains to a large extent how job growth can be combined with social harmony.

Concluding remarks

The dangers of the developments mentioned in the last section should be recognised explicitly. The growing inactivity is demotivating by itself. As Phelps (1997) also stresses, most persons feel entitled to have access to a reasonable job, which pays enough for at least a decent living. When those jobs are not available, or access to such jobs is denied to persons with a minor deficiency, the danger is that people start to feel themselves outcasts and in society a dichotomy starts to emerge. The disadvantaged group may then start political actions that are threatening to the welfare state, which they feel has abandoned them.[40]

On the other hand, the higher the level of inactivity is, the larger the wedge will be between wage costs and net wages, provided that benefits remain at a reasonable level. This will put a strong demand to solidarity, as Figure 14.7 illustrates. The risk becomes larger then that such a solidarity cannot be maintained. Figure 14.9 illustrates how this leads to a relative decline in net benefits. Such a decline may then strengthen the process of dichotomy mentioned above. Also political tensions will increase when solidarity declines. In short, there is a limit to the pressures that the polder model can survive.

Finally, one should realise that such a high level of inactivity implies a lot of idle productive capacity. This is also one of the reasons for the relatively low level of GDP per capita in the Netherlands, when compared to the past. But this level is increasing again relatively, consistent with the continuous job growth. I hope that this job growth will be strong enough not only to employ new entrants to the labour market, but also to reduce the overall level of inactivity. In that case, job growth and social harmony can continue to go hand in hand.

Notes

1 Sometimes the consensus and solidarity orientation are explained as being consistent with the ever-existing struggle against the sea and the water in the Netherlands, which can only be won by cooperation. In the late Middle Ages the Netherlands already had

the tradition of solving conflicts by deliberation and consensus seeking, instead of by command and brute force. This probably also explains the term 'polder model', since a 'polder' is a part of land which lies below sea-level, but has been claimed from the sea by building dykes around it and removing the water.

2 Seminal studies in this respect are Bruno and Sachs (1985) and Calmfors and Drifill (1988). It has gained wide attention in the literature with the introduction in the influential textbook by Layard, Nickell and Jackman (1991).

3 Krugman (1994) is a famous example; more recently see Cohen *et al.* (1997), Nickell (1997), Siebert (1997) and Teulings and Hartog (1998).

4 Siebert and Nickell stress the differences within Europe – in particular Nickell – so the picture clearly reflects an average tendency.

5 Figures 1–4 are based on CPB (1999, Annex B3). The data for Europe are the weighted average for the 15 countries of the European Union.

6 For a critical discussion see also Modigliani (1996) who argues that the current European problem is mainly caused by demand factors (high real rate of interest) and emphasises that wage differences between US and Europe reflect differences in productivity.

7 'Job protection rules can be considered to be at the core of continental Europe's policy toward the unemployment problem: protecting those who have a job is reducing the incentives to create new jobs' (Siebert 1997: 49). A similar view is expressed in Cohen *et al.* (1977). However, referring to OECD data, Nickell (1997: 59) claims that 'there is no evidence that jobs are created and destroyed at a more rapid rate in North America than in Europe'.

8 See also Blau and Kahn (1996). Moreover, Machin (1997) points out that the decline in labour market institutions, like minimum wages and trade unions, led to a rise in wage inequality in Britain.

9 A further comparison of the Dutch economy with that of Germany is found in Hollanders and Ziesemer (1999).

10 Teulings (1997), who discusses this fallacy and the previous one, cites in this context Lazear (1994):'I define institutions as those constraints, either formal or informal, that operate outside the price system' (Teulings 1997: 73).

11 A question remains of course where these cultural differences stem from and how the culture of a country changes over time.

12 This point is stressed by for instance Freeman (1998) and Theeuwes (1997).

13 In Keizer and Muysken (1997) we have argued, for instance, that the economic reforms in New Zealand are not consistent with the culture in that country. Therefore, we predict that these reforms will lead to social and economic problems. For a critical survey and comparison of the apparent successes of both the 'Polder model' and the 'Kiwi model' see Gorter and Poot (1998).

14 For a description of the Dutch culture and its relation to other cultures see Hofstede (1980).

15 This is also argued in OECD (1998), cf. their figure 6.

16 One should realise that Germany has about five times as many inhabitants as the Netherlands. Economically the Netherlands sometimes is considered as the thirteenth Bundesland.

17 The share of labour income in GDP was extremely high, about 95 per cent, in the early 1980s after the oil crises, but has dropped to about 82 per cent nowadays. See Figure 14.5.

18 This problem is elaborated in Teulings and Hartog (1998) who refer to MacLeod and Malcomson (1993). The argument here is based on Teulings (1997).

19 Another fallacy he mentions is that wage negotiations are about the wage level instead of wage increases. It is obvious that at the sectoral or central level only changes of wages in line with changes in macroeconomic circumstances can be negotiated.

20 For an overview see Van Veen (1997, ch. 2).

21 In Muysken, Van Veen and De Regt (1999) we find no specific impact of the 'Akkoord van Wassenaar' on wage formation, however. The deterioration of unemployment at that time – cf. Figure 14.3 – provides a sufficient explanation.

22 This point is stressed by CPB (1997b) to explain the difference in wage development with Germany, where employers and employees, without government intervention, determine wages.

23 See also Alesina and Perotti (1996).

24 By definition gross wages are net wages plus employees, taxes and social security contributions, while wage costs are gross wages plus employers, taxes and social security contributions.

25 An overview is given in Barr (1993). Here I use the arguments presented in Keizer and Muysken (1997).

26 This is elaborated in the English version of his inaugural lecture, Kleinknecht (1998). Kleinknecht also mentions adverse demand–pull effects of wage moderation on technical progress.

27 A similar observation is found in Hollanders and Ziesemer (1999).

28 This difference also is due to a general labour-time shortening over the relevant period. In terms of man-years, the increase was 19 per cent – hence 3 per cent-points of the difference is due to reduction in normal working time. The growth of population of age 15–64 in that period was 7 per cent.

29 The discrepancies in employment growth are elaborated in Salverda (1999), who also is very critical in this respect.

30 Compare figure 3 in OECD (1998). Van Ark and de Haan show that this relative increase is not due to increased productivity but due to a catching-up effect in the rate of participation. This is consistent with the observed job growth discussed above.

31 CPB (1999).

32 In an interesting publication CPB (1995) concludes that of the cumulated GDP growth of 8.9 per cent in the period 1994–6, only 2.4 per cent points went to households, while 4.2 per cent points went to firms and 1.2 per cent points went to the collective sector. The remaining 1.2 per cent points went to pension funds.

33 A typical example is the threat by employees' organisations in summer 1999 to withdraw from wage negotiations when employers do not stop the practice of exorbitant bonus payments in the form of options for managers. In reaction, spokesmen of the employers' organisation have already criticised this practice and expressed their fear that this will lead to higher wage demands.

34 This reflects that the official definition for unemployment is quite narrow. For instance, when one is employed for 12 hours a week, but still looking for an additional job of 26 hours, one is not counted as unemployed according to the official definition. However, one is entitled to a benefit for 26 hours.

35 The OECD (1998: 78) sketches how in the 1980s measures mainly were directed towards a reduction of social security benefits for employees, whereas in the 1990s the emphasis shifted towards influencing the behaviour of employers and the administrative bodies.

36 A similar development can be observed for the net minimum wage, which is closely linked to the net benefits.

37 Actually, the share of non-benefit government expenditures in GDP has hardly increased over time. The increase in the share of total government expenditures is mainly due to social security expenditures.

38 In addition, the remaining part has been invested abroad, but that is another story.

39 For instance, as mentioned above, the level of net benefits is still almost equal to the net minimum wage.

40 A typical example is the emergence of extremist right-wing groups and parties in several EU countries.

References

Alesina, A. and Perotti, R. (1996) 'Income Distribution, Political Instability, and Investment', *European Economic Review*, 6: 1203–28.

Ark, B. van and de Haan, J. (1997) *The Delta-Model Revisited: Recent Trends in the Structural Performance of the Dutch Economy*, Research Memorandum GD-38, University of Groningen, the Netherlands.

Barr, N. (1993) *The Economics of the Welfare State*, Stanford: Stanford University Press.

Blau, F.D. and Kahn, L.M. (1996) 'International Differences in Male Wage Inequality: Institutions versus Market Forces', *Journal of Political Economy*, 4: 791–836.

Bruno, M. and Sachs, J.D. (1985) *Economics of Worldwide Stagflation* Oxford: Blackwell.

Calmfors, L. and Drifill, J. (1988) 'Bargaining Structure, Corporatism and Macroeconomic Performance', *Economic Policy*, 1: 13–47.

Cohen, D., Lefranc, A. *et al.* (1997) 'French Unemployment: A Transatlantic Perspective', *Economic Policy*, 2: 265–91.

CPB (1995) *Waar blijft de groei van het nationaal inkomen?* Working Paper No. 76, Central Planbureau: Den Haag, the Netherlands.

—— (1997a) *Centraal Economisch Plan 1997*, Den Haag, the Netherlands: Sdu Uitgevers.

—— (1997b) *Challenging Neighbours, Rethinking German and Dutch Economic Institutions*. Heidelberg: Springer.

—— (1999) *Centraal Economisch Plan 1999*, Den Haag, the Netherlands: Sdu Uitgevers.

Freeman, R.B. (1995) 'Are Your Wages Set in Beijing?', *Journal of Economic Perspectives*, 3: 15–32.

—— (1998) 'War of the Models: Which Labour Market Institutions for the 21st Century?', *Labour Economics*, 3: 1–24.

Gorter, C. and Poot, J. (1998) *The Impact of Labour Market Deregulation: Lessons from the 'Kiwi' and 'Polder' Models*, Tinbergen Institute, Free University of Amsterdam.

Hayek, F.A. v. (1978) *New Studies in Philosophy, Politics, Economics and the History of Ideas*, London: Routledge and Kegan Paul.

Hofstede, G. (1980) *Culture's Consequences*, Thousands Oaks: Sage.

Hollanders, H. and Ziesemer, Th. (1999) 'Some Aspects of Growth in the Netherlands 1970–1998: An International Comparison', *Maandschrift Economie*, 63: 283–94.

Keizer, P. and Muysken, J. (1997) *The Future of the Welfare State*, Research Memorandum 97-009, METEOR, Maastricht University.

Kleinknecht, A. (1998) 'Is Labour Flexibility Harmful to Innovation?', *Cambridge Journal of Economics*, 22: 387–96.

Krugman, P. (1994) *Past and Prospective Causes of High Unemployment. Reducing unemployment: Current Issues and Policy Options: A Symposium Sponsored by the Federal Reserve Bank of Kansas City, Jackson Hole, Wyoming, August 25–7, 1994*, C. Federal Reserve Bank of Kansas: Kansas City, 49–80.

Layard, R., Nickell, S. and Jackmann, R. (1991) *Unemployment: Macroeconomic Performance and the Labour Market*, Oxford: Oxford University Press.

Lazear, E. (1994) *Personnel Economics*, Stockholm: Wicksell Lecture.

Lindbeck, A. (1994) 'Overshooting, Reform and Retreat of the Welfare State', *De Economist* 142: 1–19.

Machin, S. (1997) 'The Decline of Labour Market Institutions and the Rise in Wage Inequality in Britain', *European Economic Review*, 41: 647–57.

MacLeod, W.B. and Malcomson, J.M. (1993) 'Investments, Holdup, and the Form of Market Contracts', *American Economic Review*, 83: 811–37.

Modigliani, F. (1996) 'The Shameful Rate of Unemployment in the EMS: Causes and Cures', *De Economist*, 144: 363–96.

Muysken, J. (1998) 'Job Growth and Social Harmony: Reflections on the Dutch Polder Model', in Qiu Yuanlun and Lou Hongbo (eds), *A Comparative Study of Employment Policies in European Union and China*, China Economics Publishing House: Beijing.

——, van Veen, T. and de Regt, E. (1999) 'Does a Shift in the Tax Burden Create Unemployment?', *Applied Economics*, 31: 1195–205.

Nickell, S. (1997) 'Unemployment and Labor Market Rigidities: Europe versus North America', *Journal of Economic Perspectives*, 11: 55–74.

North, D.C. (1990) *Institutions, Industrial Change and Economic Performance*, Cambridge: Cambridge University Press.

OECD (1998) *OECD Economic Surveys, Netherlands*, Paris, France: OECD.

Phelps, E.S. (1997) *Rewarding Work: How to Restore Participation and Self-support to Free Enterprise*, Cambridge, Mass.: Harvard University Press.

Salverda, W. (1999) 'Polderblijheid, polderblindheid', *Economische Statistische Berichten (ESB)* (84), No. 4196: 224–9.

Sen, A. (1987) *On Ethics and Economics*, Royer Lectures series, New York and Oxford: Blackwell.

Siebert, H. (1997) 'Labor Market Rigidities: At the Root of Unemployment in Europe', *Journal of Economic Perspectives*, 11: 37–54.

Snower, D.J. (1994) *What is the Domain of the Welfare State?* London: Birkbeck College.

Teulings, C.N. (1997) *Een onderhandelaar als marktmeester*, Inaugural Lecture, Universiteit van Amsterdam.

—— and Hartog, J. (1998) *Corporation or Competition. An International Comparison of Labour Market Structures and the Impact on Wage Formation*, Cambridge: Cambridge University Press.

Theeuwes, J. (1997) *At Least Two Sides of the Labour Market*, EALE Meetings, Aarhus.

Van Veen, A.P. (1997) *Studies in Wage Bargaining, The Influence of Taxes and Social Security Contributions on Wages*, Dissertation, Maastricht University.

15 Some aspects of growth in the Netherlands 1970–98

An international comparison

Hugo Hollanders and Thomas Ziesemer

Introduction

This chapter presents some information on issues that have some importance for those who try to learn from the economic policy of the Netherlands. In particular we discuss the following questions:

(i) Does growth in the Netherlands differ from that of other Western European countries?
(ii) In which branches and sectors is the Gross Domestic Product (GDP) of the Netherlands and Germany produced (share of metal, services, etc.)?
(iii) What was the impact of wage policy on the innovative capabilities in the Dutch industry?
(iv) What is the impact of wage moderation on productivity?

Each of these questions is treated in one of the following sections. In the final section a policy view is presented.

GDP growth in the Netherlands compared to other Western European countries

As some Germans want to learn from the Dutch experience we start with a comparison of German and Dutch GDP growth rates for the years 1970–98 as plotted in Figure 15.1. The whole period is divided into subperiods by vertical lines drawn in Figure 15.1. In the subperiod 1970–5 in some years Dutch growth rates are larger than the German growth rates and in other years it is the other way around. In the period 1976–83 Dutch growth rates are lower throughout. Between the wage agreement of 'Wassenaar' (1982) and the German Unification, the Netherlands have higher or equal growth rates with the exception of the year 1988. However, an alternative way of reading the data is to say Dutch growth rates were higher for three years after 1983 and from 1987 to 1990 there is a changing pattern again. From 1993 until 1998 Dutch growth rates are higher. This is the period after Prime Minister Lubbers had shifted more emphasis of Dutch policy towards the reduction of the wage wedge, the difference between gross and net wages. The employers' part of the wedge has been decreased more strongly than that of the employees.[1] In contrast, they had gone up in Germany after the Unification.

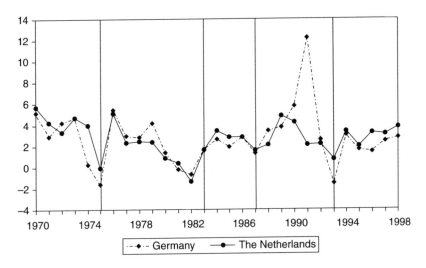

Figure 15.1 Dutch and German GDP growth (%) (1970–98).

For the period after 1983 the question arises whether the higher growth is due to wage moderation or just to the fact that these are the years after the world recession which affected small countries more than large countries. In more drastic words, one could hypothesise that the relatively weak Dutch growth performance before 1983 was due to the weak world economic situation, which affected the small Netherlands more than the large Germany. Similarly, the relatively strong growth after 1983 could stem from the upswing – after the 1982 low of the world economy – affecting the small Netherlands more favourably than the large Germany. If these hypotheses are correct, a comparison of the Netherlands with smaller countries should be less favourable than with the large Germany. This comparison is made in Table 15.1. Table 15.1 considers the GDP growth rate of the country mentioned in the pre-column minus the GDP growth rate of the Netherlands. The bold entries in the table are those where the result is negative, which means that the Netherlands had higher growth. To repeat, the comparison with Germany (denoted GER in the table) yields a negative value for 1984–7 indicating higher Dutch growth after the 1982 recession. The comparison with Belgium and Austria, the country that invented its own form of wage moderation after the Second World War, is only slightly different. The comparison with Denmark, Sweden and Norway is much less favourable. The reason for the latter result, however, is the strong development of the UK, which is well known to have its own business cycle and a strong impact on Denmark. Norway is strongly dependent on oil prices and the value of the US dollar. The comparison with Belgium and Austria therefore seems to be more to the point. It seems impossible to argue that the relative Dutch performance around 1983 was *merely* due to country-size effects. It is also clear that Dutch growth performance after 1983 was less strong

Table 15.1 Relative GDP growth in the Netherlands compared to other Western European countries

	AUT	BEL	GER	DNK	FRA	GBR	NOR	SWE
1970	1.43	0.65	**−0.55**	**−3.67**	0.04	**−3.38**	**−2.16**	0.78
1971	0.89	**−0.47**	**−1.33**	**−1.56**	1.19	**−1.52**	0.64	**−3.28**
1972	2.90	2.04	0.90	1.97	2.59	**−1.02**	**−0.17**	**−1.02**
1973	0.20	1.28	0.00	**−1.06**	0.68	2.93	0.56	**−0.72**
1974	**−0.02**	0.21	**−3.69**	**−4.90**	**−0.73**	**−4.96**	0.59	**−0.77**
1975	**−0.27**	**−1.35**	**−1.50**	**−0.57**	0.57	**−0.48**	2.57	2.64
1976	**−0.54**	0.55	0.29	1.35	**−0.88**	**−1.34**	**−1.32**	**−4.06**
1977	2.04	**−1.74**	0.63	**−0.70**	0.90	**−1.25**	**−0.05**	**−3.91**
1978	**−1.94**	0.41	0.42	**−0.98**	0.89	1.12	1.15	**−0.71**
1979	2.34	**−0.21**	1.78	1.17	0.87	**−0.26**	5.08	1.47
1980	2.15	3.28	0.50	**−1.31**	0.76	**−2.96**	7.82	0.81
1981	**−1.04**	**−2.75**	**−0.57**	**−2.36**	0.80	**−1.13**	12.09	0.94
1982	3.25	2.66	0.65	4.06	3.79	2.70	1.08	1.73
1983	1.07	**−1.35**	**−0.05**	1.11	**−1.26**	2.22	1.27	0.69
1984	**−3.25**	**−1.15**	**−0.82**	1.11	**−1.81**	**−0.89**	4.23	0.37
1985	**−0.22**	**−2.02**	**−0.97**	1.01	**−1.28**	0.80	0.66	**−0.60**
1986	**−0.86**	**−1.25**	**−0.02**	1.31	**−0.19**	1.18	**−6.91**	**−0.64**
1987	0.07	0.70	**−0.25**	**−1.28**	0.45	3.15	**−1.42**	1.28
1988	1.30	2.45	1.31	**−0.88**	2.04	2.90	**−3.53**	0.31
1989	**−0.83**	**−1.17**	**−1.05**	**−4.33**	**−0.85**	**−2.51**	**−1.96**	**−2.58**
1990	0.53	**−0.96**	1.51	**−2.99**	**−1.77**	**−3.80**	**−2.34**	**−2.78**
1991	1.19	**−0.50**	10.06	**−0.66**	**−1.21**	**−4.31**	0.38	**−3.40**
1992	**−0.63**	**−0.73**	0.35	**−1.89**	**−1.49**	**−2.34**	**−2.15**	**−3.59**
1993	**−0.23**	**−2.15**	**−2.27**	0.62	**−1.74**	1.11	2.15	**−3.04**
1994	**−1.17**	**−1.04**	**−0.30**	0.74	**−0.79**	0.78	0.14	0.33
1995	**−0.01**	0.28	**−0.33**	0.63	0.12	0.54	2.14	1.45
1996	**−1.83**	**−1.85**	**−1.79**	**−0.62**	**−1.75**	**−0.74**	3.94	**−2.02**
1997	**−1.11**	**−0.61**	**−0.66**	**−0.10**	**−0.55**	0.04	0.68	**−1.11**
1998	**−0.72**	**−1.03**	**−0.99**	**−1.54**	**−0.65**	**−1.55**	**−0.74**	**−1.06**
Average								
1970–82	0.88	0.35	**−0.19**	**−0.66**	0.88	**−0.89**	2.14	**−0.47**
1983–98	**−0.42**	**−0.77**	**−0.42**	**−0.48**	**−0.80**	**−0.21**	**−0.22**	**−1.03**

Note
Calculated as the growth rate of each country minus the growth rate of the Netherlands.

for some years when a comparison is made with respect to smaller countries. The average of the growth rate difference from 1983 to 1998, however, is exactly the same for Austria as it is for Germany, and for Belgium the result is even more favourable for the Netherlands. This is clear enough to *reject the idea* that the Netherlands might have grown faster because it is a small country affected more strongly by world developments.

What is more impressive though when looking at Table 15.1 is the great difference in relative Dutch growth performance before 1989 and after 1989. After 1989 Dutch growth outperforms that of other countries with only few interesting exceptions. One is the German Unification in 1991. Denmark starts its own policy of wage moderation in 1993 and has some relatively good years 1993–5. These years, however, are also relatively good years in the UK, which may have pulled the Scandinavian countries. The strongest exception, however, is Norway with five years of stronger growth. Four of these years are years of increasing oil prices.

Kleinknecht (1998, figure 3) presents data showing that from 1984 to 1993 the Netherlands had higher growth rates of GNP than the average of the EU-15 except for two years. Our interpretation of these data is that growth was relatively strongest after 'Wassenaar' (1983) and after the policy against the wedge in the early 1990s. It seems hard to deny that these events have been causal although the differential impact of country size is present after 1983 when the resumption of world economic growth did contribute to small countries' growth more than that of large countries. In the 1990s this aspect of world economic growth seems to be less relevant. After the German Unification the wage wedge is decreased in the Netherlands and increased by the German government.

In which sectors and branches is the GDP of the Netherlands and Germany produced?

It can be seen from Figure 15.2 that the Netherlands does have a higher share of services as a percentage of GDP than Germany, but a lower one than the US. In agriculture[2] the ranking is US, Netherlands and Germany. Industry's share is about equal in the US and the Netherlands, but Germany has a higher one than these countries.

The shares concerning employment[3] are slightly different as can be seen from Figure 15.3. The Dutch share of agriculture in GDP is higher than that of employment. For services and industry the result is the same as it was concerning output.

Overall, the greatest remarkable difference is the share German industry has in GDP and employment compared to these countries. However, we will come back to the development of services later.

When looking at the share of the metal industry in Figure 15.4 it is obvious that it is higher in Germany than in the other two countries. For Germany this share is about twice as large as that of the Netherlands and about 50 per cent larger than that of the US. It is decreasing in Germany only after the Unification. Together with the high export share in production of the metal industry this partly explains the strong position of the metal unions in Germany as far as this is based on market forces. In the Netherlands there are no unions of similar strength. The relative strength of the unions may be an important aspect in explaining the difference in the inclination to agree to a policy of wage moderation when trying to understand the Dutch model. The policy of checks and balances has given relatively little power to unions in the Netherlands – a fact that cannot be ignored when trying to learn from the 'Polder model'. The plots do not show any obvious structural beggar-thy-neighbour impact of Dutch policy on German sectors. The phenomenon seems to be limited to the border regions.

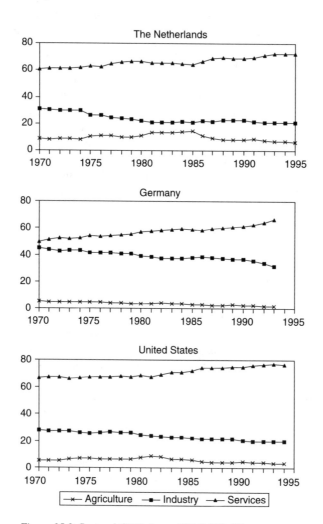

Figure 15.2 Sectoral GDP shares (%) (1970–95).

What was the impact of wage policy on the innovation capabilities in the Dutch industry?

Figure 15.5 shows R&D of some sectors as a share of the value-added of that sector. In all four cases shown this share is developing fairly smooth in German industries and until 1983 parallel to the Dutch number with the exception of ISIC 37, the smaller part of the metal industry. But it is getting a strong boost in the Netherlands from 1984 to 1987. Afterwards it is getting back almost to the level of the 1970s for industry as a whole and for ISIC 38.[4] In both of these cases it is going below the German shares whereas in ISIC 37 it is diverging from the German shares in

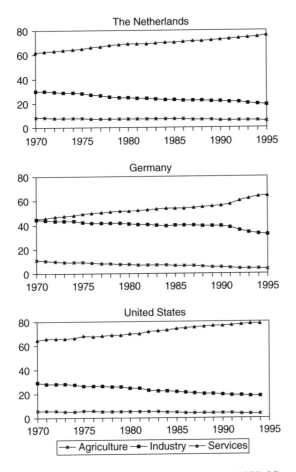

Figure 15.3 Sectoral employment shares (%) (1970–95).

the upward direction. Whereas it cannot be excluded that the early boost is due to 'Wassenaar', it is hard to see how the later long-run *differences between the sectors* can be explained by the early *macro* policy.

What is the impact of wage moderation on productivity?

The major attack on the 'Polder' model has come from productivity analysis. Kleinknecht (1998, table 1) presents data pointing out that

(i) since 1986 annual percentage growth of value-added per employee is almost half of what it was from 1981–5;

(ii) it is only 50 per cent of productivity growth of the EU-15 since 1986.

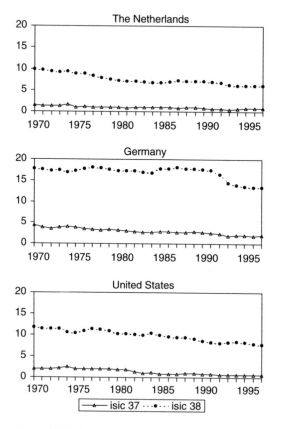

Figure 15.4 Metal industries: GDP shares (%) (1970–97).

Productivity analysis deserves special attention therefore. The major aspect is whether productivity should be measured per employee or per hour. Figure 15.6 presents data on productivity *per employee* (in full-time-equivalents (FTEs)) and Figure 15.7 *per hour*. The upper part of both figures looks at the large countries, the lower part at the small countries.

Productivity per employee is highest in the US in the whole period. All other countries seem to catch up with the US, maybe with the exception of the UK. Among the small countries the Netherlands is the leader in the 1970s, about equal with Belgium from 1980 to 1986 and falls behind Belgium afterwards but remains more productive than the other small countries. Figure 15.6 for productivity *per employee* indeed reflects a slow-down in productivity growth.

When looking at productivity *per hour* one can see from Figure 15.7 that the Netherlands leapfrogs the US in 1983, France does so in 1987 and West Germany catches up around 1991 but Germany as a whole falls behind due to the Unification. Moreover, looking at the slope of the Dutch time-series we see here that the

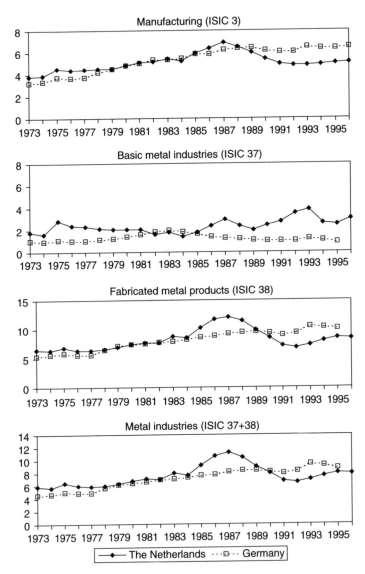

Figure 15.5 R&D intensities (%): Dutch and German manufacturing industries (1973–96).

productivity slow-down is much less, if any, in terms of per hour productivity (see Table 15.2) – in particular the jump from 1993–4. Again with the exception of 1994, Dutch productivity per hour is larger than that of Belgium, which it was not when measuring productivity per employee. The remaining slow-down of productivity per hour is quite natural in the sense that fewer productive people

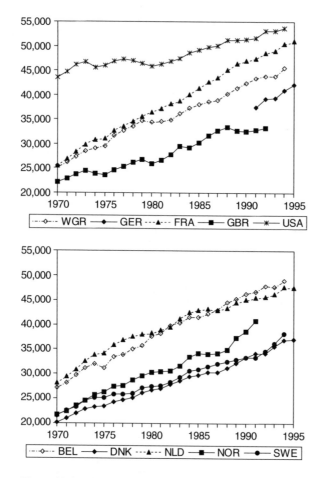

Figure 15.6 Labour productivity (output per employee in 1990 purchasing power parity dollars) (1970–95).

have been reintegrated into the production process after they had been taken out before.[5]

Interesting aspects are revealed when looking at productivity at the sector level. Figure 15.8 shows that productivity per employee in Germany is higher in services and lower in industry when compared to the total. In the Netherlands and the US this was also the case during the early or middle of the 1980s but then industry and services reverse their positions, which they do not do in Germany. Probably this is an effect supported by wage moderation but clearly setting in much before 'Wassenaar' in 1983. The service sectors of the Netherlands and the US have added more and more low-productivity jobs. This is an important aspect because German employers tend to believe that wage moderation would increase the number of jobs in industry. However, general equilibrium effects may induce structural change

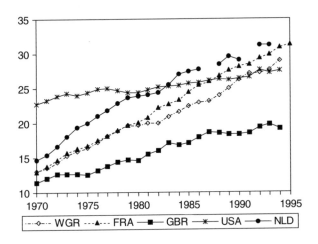

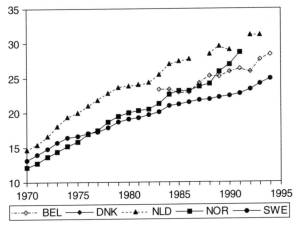

Figure 15.7 Labour productivity (output per man-hour in 1990 purchasing power parity dollars) (1970–95).

Table 15.2 The Netherlands, labour productivity, average growth

	Per employee	*Per man-hour*
1981–85	2.28	2.91
1986–90	1.01	1.12
1991–95	1.03	2.47[a]

Note
a 1991–3.

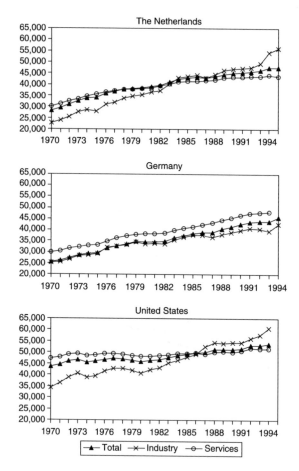

Figure 15.8 Labour productivity (output per employee in 1990 purchasing power parity dollars): industry versus services (1970–95).

creating jobs in services. The reason is that services are relatively labour-intensive and more labour-intensive sectors can be expected to benefit more from wage moderation than less labour-intensive sectors. Clearly, it reduces the incentive for industry unions to agree with wage-moderation policies if new jobs are created in services rather than their own industry.

In particular, all curves are fairly smooth. No kinks are generated by Dutch policies. Beggar-thy-neighbour effects are clearly limited to the border regions. Given the size of the countries this may be different if Germany changes its policy.

A policy view

There are several aspects, which make it difficult to transfer the Dutch model to Germany. When trying to judge about the feasibility of the Dutch policy for

Germany it seems to be important to be aware of the fact how costly this is. Unit wage costs relative to those of Germany have been decreasing by 35 per cent but net wages show a difference of only about 10 per cent. In more detail, relative unit labour costs fell from 1.05 to 0.7, which is a 35 per cent reduction.[6] The change in the difference of the unemployment rate is 5.7 per cent: the Dutch rate of unemployment has gone from 9.7 per cent in 1983 to 6.3 per cent in 1996, a reduction by 3.4 per cent. For Germany the corresponding numbers are 7.7 and 9.0 per cent, an increase by 2.3 per cent.[7] This boils down to requiring a 6 per cent (35 per cent: 5.7) decrease in relative unit labour costs in order to get a 1 per cent decrease in the difference of unemployment rates. This is a fairly expensive policy. It is even more expensive to the extent that the gains in employment rates possibly have to be attributed to other developments such as world economic growth or labour time reduction.[8] In short, increasing employment through wage cost reduction is very expensive. On the other hand German industries are in markets of high quality. The skills of workers are higher than in other countries.[9] This may justify higher wages. In this sense relative unit labour costs of Germany compared to the Netherlands, which have a value larger than unity, do not necessarily reflect too high wages but rather may reflect skill differences.

The standard argument in favour of employment policy is that an increase in employment can be considered to be a Pareto improvement, saying that everybody *can* be made better off. The crucial question in negotiations is whether everybody *is actually* made better off. Going to Dutch net wages would imply a reduction of wages in spite of the fact that a large part of the reduction in Dutch wage costs has been achieved by a reduction of the wedge rather than net wages. This actually means that going to Dutch net wage levels German workers would not benefit from the policy (although they could if a Pareto improvement could be achieved). Instead of participating they would pay the bill. It seems fairly clear that there will be no employment gains in Germany if the negotiators are not able to make sure that everybody gains. This requires a reduction of the wedge that is large enough to decrease wage costs and increase employment without a reduction in net wages.

In Germany from the 1960s to the 1980s there were wage increases for low-skilled workers, which were often higher than productivity increases. In all likelihood this policy is responsible for a lot of low-productivity jobs that have been lost or not created. Dutch policy has created a similar problem during the wage moderation policy. Wage increases have been moderated partly irrespective of the skills and the Dutch have a pertinent shortage of high skills and are unwilling to solve this by wage policy.[10] The most recent variant of this policy was to ask wage-earners in industry for solidarity with those in the government sector. The reason was that the latter should not get higher wages according to the plans of the Dutch government in spite of the fact that the Netherlands have come close to very low unemployment and, of course, workers have now to participate in the gains from productivity enhancement. This shortage of high skills may be part of the explanation of the slow-down of productivity growth. It is also clear that if there will be any wage moderation in Germany it will not take place in the segments of scarce skills. Germany may prefer going to a differentiated labour market policy above a policy that tries to reduce wages in labour-market segments where there is actually scarcity – however unpopular this may be at the moment.

What might the compromise look like? Employers get lower gross wage costs and offer more employment. The government gets more employment and decreases the taxes for the low-skill, low-wage workers. Employees get higher net wages and more safe jobs but lower wage increases to the extent that their labour-market segment has higher unemployment. As most of the jobs can be created in the low productivity, low-skills sectors, wage moderation policy will probably be concentrated in the services sector.

The role of the service sector seems to be somewhat under-emphasised in the *Bündnis für Arbeit* (Employment Pact) until now. This implies that *before* wage moderation is used, other parts of the economic system like taxes and maybe barriers to entry for firms have to be adjusted because they slow down the level or growth of vacancies if they are unchanged. If these adjustments are not implemented, the necessary wage decreases (or slow-down of increases) to get a certain amount of additional employment are unnecessarily high. This may be the reason why unions have kept wage agreements out of the *Bündnis für Arbeit*. This is another example where sequencing of policy measures matters.

Labour markets could be differentiated according to the unions' and employers' federation responsible, skills offered and required, scales of salaries, regions and other things. Differentiation according to firms, however, seems to be a non-viable concept. It creates problems of asymmetric information about costs and revenues of the firm. Even accountants working for the unions will have the same problems and are no way out. This is well known from the profit-sharing debate. All types of unanimity problems have to be expected under asymmetric information. Statistics from the labour office do not suffer from this disadvantage and seem to be a better basis for the differentiation.

The major change in the responsibilities will be that the government takes over responsibility for issues of equality and justice from the Labour unions, which they were not willing to leave to the previous government. Another implication of the concept is that in labour markets with unemployment gross wages decrease, and net wages do not increase, whereas in labour markets without unemployment gross and net wages are increased in accordance with productivity enhancement, inflation correction and some necessary modifications.

It is obvious that government financing of this concept leaves little room for other expansive measures like expansive family policies, reduction of high-tax brackets and shorter working hours. The government will have to postpone other expenditures until the policy creates more jobs and more taxpayers, which will partly compensate for the tax reductions. Moreover, labour time shortages could be conflicting with financing old-age insurance. It should be kept in mind that in the Netherlands the highest tax rate of 60 per cent[11] is applied at a taxable income of about fl. 130,000. This means that the rate is higher than in Germany. It is applied to lower incomes than the top taxes in Germany are. And it is simply not true that Germany has the highest income taxes in Europe. High tax rates are essential in financing employment policies.

Finally, ideas in Germany to stimulate employment by more innovation[12] and in the Netherlands on stimulating innovation at the cost of employment[13] provoke the following comments. It is clear that innovation should not be pushed by high wages at the cost of creating unemployment. Moreover, R&D policy should not be expected to create many jobs. R&D expenditures are no more than 2 or 3 per cent of GDP. *Changes* in them cannot be expected to reduce the unemployment problem, which has an order of magnitude of about 2 or 3 per cent of GDP itself.[14] Returns of innovation policy could be stretched over decades of years. A solution of the unemployment problem in Germany should not take that long.

Acknowledgement

This Chapter is the extended version of a presentation given at the Max Planck Institute for the Study of Societies, Cologne, November 1998. We have benefited from comments received by participants at a seminar at Maastricht University and the conference 'New Developments in Growth Theory and Growth Policy'. We are also grateful to Huub Meijers for a useful discussion. Responsibility is entirely ours.

Notes

1 See van Veen (1997), ch. 6.
2 Defined as ISIC 1 (agriculture, hunting, forestry and fishing) and ISIC 2 (mining and quarrying).
3 Defined in full-time-equivalents (FTEs).
4 ISIC 38 is 'Manufacture of fabricated metal products, machinery and equipment'. ISIC 37 is 'Basic metal industries'.
5 See de Neubourg and Slabbers (1992) for the effect of taking out less-productive employees. Pomp (1998) argues that reintegration in the second half of the 1980s has reduced productivity.
6 See Muysken (1999).
7 See Hassel (1998).
8 CPB (1991) provides calculations saying that 400,000 jobs have been created by wage moderation and between 30,000 and 40,000 by labour time reduction.
9 See Cörvers (1999, ch. 6).
10 See Gelauff (1998). He argues that labour time reduction has reinforced the scarcity of highly skilled labour.
11 From 2001 onwards this will be 52 per cent because the value-added tax goes up by 2 points and tax-deduction allowances get more limited.
12 For example, by Chancellor Schröder.
13 For example, in the debate on suggestions made by Professor Kleinknecht.
14 Assume that unemployment goes from 10 per cent to 5 per cent. With a labour elasticity of production of 0.7 this would create an increase in GDP of 3.5 per cent. Taking into account that the newly employed have a lower productivity, one gets an order of magnitude of 2 per cent or 3 per cent. However, if low-skilled labour has an elasticity of production of only 1/3 as in Mankiw *et al.* (1992) the effect is only 1.7 per cent.

Data sources

OECD, Analytical Business Enterprise Research and Development (ANBERD).
OECD, International Sectoral Database (ISDB).
OECD, Main Science and Technology Indicators (MSTI).
OECD, Structural Analysis Database (STAN).
The labour productivity data in Figure 15.7 are updated for Belgium (1983–94), the Netherlands (1988–90, 1992–4) and the UK (1993–4) using de Neubourg (1998).

References

Cörvers, F. (1999) *The Impact of Human Capital on International Competitiveness and Trade Performance of Manufacturing Sectors*, Maastricht: Research Centre for Education and the Labour Market (ROA).

CPB (1991) De werkgelegenheid in de jaren tachtig, Working Paper No. 41.

Gelauff, G.M.M. (1998) *Löhne, Arbeitszeit und Institutionen, Der niederländische Arbeitsmarkt in den vergangenen Jahrzehnten*, Den Haag: CPB.

Hassel, A. (1998) *Das niederländische Modell*, Cologne: Max Planck Institute for the Study of Societies.

Kleinknecht, A. (1998) 'Is Labour Market Flexibility Harmful to Innovation?', *Cambridge Journal of Economics*, 22: 387–96.

Mankiw, G.N., Romer, D. and Weil, D. (1992) 'A Contribution to the Empirics of Economic Growth', *Quarterly Journal of Economics*, 107: 407–37.

Muysken, J. (1999) *Job Growth and Social Harmony: A Dutch Miracle?*, METEOR Research Memorandum 99/015, Maastricht University.

Neubourg, de C. (1998) *Productivity Below Sea-Level: Economic Leadership and Market Distortions-led Productivity Growth 1973–1994*, mimeo.

—— and Slabbers, M. (1992) *The Rise of Small Powers: Explaining Productivity Growth Since 1973*, Maastricht: Maastricht University.

Pomp, M. (1998) 'Labour Productivity Growth and Low Paid Work', *CPB Report 98/1*: 34–7.

Veen, van T. (1997) *Studies in Wage Bargaining*, Maastricht: Universitaire Pers.

Index